Union & States' Rights

Legal Thought
Across Disciplines
Published in Cooperation with
The University of Akron School of Law

Elizabeth Reilly, editor, *Infinite Hope and Finite Disappointment: The Story of the First Interpreters of the Fourteenth Amendment*

Kalyani Robbins, editor, *The Laws of Nature: Reflections on the Evolution of Ecosystem Management Law & Policy*

Neil H. Cogan, editor, *Union & States' Rights: A History and Interpretation of Interposition, Nullification, and Secession 150 Years After Sumter*

Union & States' Rights

★ ★ ★ ★ ★

A History and Interpretation of Interposition, Nullification, and Secession 150 Years After Sumter

Edited by Neil H. Cogan

University of Akron Press
Akron, Ohio

 • First Edition 2014 • Manufactured in the United States of America. All inquiries and permission requests should be addressed to the Publisher, the University of Akron Press, Akron, Ohio 44325–1703.

18 17 16 15 14 5 4 3 2 1

ISBN: 978-1-937378-13-4 (paper)
ISBN: 978-1-937378-38-7 (ePDF)
ISBN: 978-1-937378-39-4 (ePub)

LIBRARY OF CONGRESS CATALOGING-IN-PUBLICATION DATA
Union & states' rights : a history and interpretation of interposition, nullification, and secession 150 years after Sumter / edited by Neil H. Cogan. — First edition.
pages cm. — (& law : legal thought across disciplines)
Includes index.
ISBN 978-1-937378-13-4 (pbk. : alk. paper)
1. Federal government—United States—History—19th century. 2. States' rights (American politics)—History—19th century. 3. Nullification (States' rights)—History—19th century. 4. Secession—United States—History—19th century. I. Cogan, Neil H. (Neil Howard), 1944– editor of compilation. II. Title: Union and states' rights.
KF4612.U55 2013
342.73'042—dc23

2013014442

∞ The paper used in this publication meets the minimum requirements of ANSI / NISO Z39.48–1992 (Permanence of Paper).

Union & States' Rights was designed and typeset by Amy Freels, with assistance from Lauren McAndrews. The typeface, Stone Print, was designed by Sumner Stone in 1991. *Union & States' Rights* was printed on sixty-pound natural and bound by Bookmasters of Ashland, Ohio.

The following originally appeared in the *Akron Law Review*, volume 45, issue 2 and have been reproduced with permission: Neil H. Cogan, "Introduction," in a slightly different form, as "Symposium: Union and States' Rights: Secession, 150 Years After Sumter;" Daniel A. Farber, "The Fourteenth Amendment and the Unconstitutionality of Secession;" Paul Finkelman, "States' Rights and Nullification in the North: Opposition to the Fugitive Slave Laws," as "States' Rights, Southern Hypocrisy, and the Crisis of the Union;" Daniel W. Hamilton, "Still Too Close to Call? Rethinking Stampp's 'The Concept of a Perpetual Union;'" Robert G. Natelson, "James Madison and the Constitution's 'Convention for Proposing Amendments;'" and Stephen C. Neff, "Secession and Breach of Compact: The Law of Nature Meets the United States Constitution."

For my children, Eliya, Aviel, Saraleah, Chava, Hillel, Adina, and Jacob, and my grandchildren, Jonah, Jack, Eli, Sam, Caleb, and Anabella, with love and respect.

[A] new nation, conceived in liberty and dedicated to the proposition that all men are created equal.
—Abraham Lincoln

Contents

Contributors

Neil H. Cogan, Professor of Law, Whittier (College) Law School. B.A. University of Pennsylvania College; LL.B. University of Pennsylvania Law School; and Ph.D. candidate University of California, Irvine.

Daniel A. Farber, Sho Sato Professor of Law and Codirector of the Center for Law, Energy, and the Environment, University of California, Berkeley. B.A., M.A., and J.D. University of Illinois.

Paul Finkelman, President William McKinley Distinguished Professor of Law and Public Policy and Senior Fellow, Government Law Center, Albany Law School. B.A. Syracuse University; M.A. University of Chicago; and Ph.D. University of Chicago.

Christian G. Fritz, Henry Weihofen Chair of Law and Professor of Law, University of New Mexico. B.A. and Ph.D. University of California, Berkeley; and J.D. University of California, Hastings College of Law.

Daniel W. Hamilton, Professor of Law and History, Associate Dean for Faculty Development, and Codirector of the Illinois Legal History Program, University of Illinois College of Law. B.A. Oberlin College; Ph.D. Harvard University; and J.D. George Washington University.

Sanford V. Levinson, Professor of Government and W. St. John Garwood and W. St. John Garwood, Jr. Centennial Chair in Law, University of Texas Law School. A.B. Duke University; Ph.D. Harvard University; and J.D. Stanford Law School.

Robert G. Natelson, retired Professor of Law, University of Montana; Senior Fellow in constitutional jurisprudence, Independence Institute; Senior Fellow, Montana Policy Institute. A.B. Lafayette College and J.D. Cornell University.

Stephen C. Neff, Reader in Public International Law, University of Edinburgh School of Law. A.B. Harvard College; J.D., LL.M., and S.J.D. University of Virginia School of Law.

H. Jefferson Powell, Professor of Law, Duke Law School. B.A. St. David's University College University of Wales; A.M. Duke University; M.Div. Yale Divinity School; J.D. Yale Law School; and Ph.D. Duke University.

Jack N. Rakove, W. R. Coe Professor of History and American Studies and Professor of Political Science at Stanford University. A.B. Haverford College and Ph.D. Harvard University.

Norman W. Spaulding, Sweitzer Professor of Law, Stanford Law School. B.A. Williams College and J.D. Stanford Law School.

Lee J. Strang, Professor of Law, University of Toledo College of Law. B.A. Loras College, J.D. University of Iowa College of Law, and LL.M. Harvard Law School.

Acknowledgements

I am sincerely grateful to Paul Finkelman, who urged me to select the topic that ultimately produced this collection and gave me valuable advice along the way. Dan Farber also provided valuable advice along the way. I am much appreciative.

I was fortunate that Farber, Finkelman, Hamilton, and Neff, all eminent scholars, graciously agreed to participate in the Section on Legal History at the Annual Meeting of the Association of American Law Schools on January 7, 2011, and subsequently agreed to expand their papers for inclusion in a published law review symposium. I was also fortunate that seven other eminent scholars agreed to contribute papers to this collection. I thank each of them.

I was indeed fortunate that Elizabeth Reilly, Interim Dean and C. Blake McDowell Professor at the University of Akron Law School, agreed to comment on the papers at the annual meeting and supported the initiation and completion of this project.

As always, I am indebted to Curtis Jones, reader services librarian at Whittier Law School for his always superb, tireless, and gracious assistance, and to everyone at the University of Akron Press for their superb editing, professional judgment, and constant courtesy.

Introduction

Neil H. Cogan, Whittier (College) Law School

This collection addresses questions fundamental to the American Union, from historical, legal, political, and social/moral perspectives. When deep substantive disagreements between the federal and state governments long persist without foreseeable resolution, what extraordinary options do the governments and the people have? That is, what options are available beyond discussion and compromise in the federal legislative and executive branches and political forums?

Do the states, on behalf of themselves and their citizens, have rights that authorize extraordinary options? May states interpose themselves between the federal government and the people? May states enact legislation nullifying federal law? May the states secede from the Union? May states call for regular constitutional conventions?

These are questions about the structure of our Union and the relationships of the Union, states, and people—about their 'rights' under the Constitution. This collection addresses the arguments and the history and memory of arguments made at the founding of our Union, during the antebellum and Civil War period, and today. The papers collected here assess those arguments, those interpretations of the Constitution.

At the beginning of national formation in the 1770s, when the states first met in Congress, they disagreed about the structure of their association and their relationships with one another. Disagreements about structure and relationships continued through and following the Revolution and War of Independence, into the Continental Congress, and under the Articles of Confederation and Perpetual Union. And notwithstanding the historic agreement in 1787 at the Philadelphia convention, the ratification of the Constitution, and the foundational 1st Congress, the disagreements continued without abatement, as the United States of America became a nation and Americans a people.

Did the states remain sovereigns? If not, did they retain some attributes of sovereignty? If so, what attributes did they retain?

For seventy-six years, from the ratification of the Constitution through the end of the Civil War—or longer, in President Abraham Lincoln's viewpoint, from the Articles of Association in 1774 and the Declaration of Independence in 1776—the issues of federal and state power tore the fabric of nationhood until more than six hundred thousand combatants and the President himself lay dead. Now, 150 years after South Carolina's secession from the Union—and the *Charleston Mercury*'s declaration that "The Union is Dissolved"—and 150 years since mortar rounds were launched against federal troops holding Fort Sumter, the contributors to this collection and I think that it is important to remember and reassess the arguments used to justify those actions. The arguments were not stilled with the last gunshots at Appomattox and the surrender by the Confederacy.

In brief, the antebellum arguments fall largely within the popular political term 'states' rights,' a term that remains resonant.[1] Within decisional constitutional law, by contrast, the courts identify various and conflicting theories of federalism (sometimes capitalized as 'Federalism' or 'Our Federalism') as defining or underlying the structure and relationships of the United States and the states and as limiting federal power to burden the 'rights' of the states.[2] However styled, the arguments are being made once again in support of state nullification of federal law and even in support of secession.

In addressing the issues of Union and states' rights, the contributors parse the 'original meaning' and 'original understanding' of the Constitution and other founding documents, the principles at stake in the antebellum debates, and the legal effect of both the Union's victory in the Civil War and the states' ratification thereafter of the 14th Amendment. The chapters discuss whether the people, in ratifying the Constitution, relinquished the states' and their option of revolution. They address contemporary arguments for interposition and nullification. The collection concludes with a chapter on revisionism in the memories of slavery, secession, and war.

As editor of this collection, I am honored by and respectful of the learned papers of each of the contributors, whether they support or oppose states' rights and federalism arguments for interposition, nullification, and secession, as well as constitutional convention. As editor, I am compelled to add that constitutional interpretation must reflect morality, as well as original meaning and understanding and attributes of sovereignty. The truth is that in seceding from the Union and instigating the Civil War, the states of the Confederacy were defending their dubious 'right' to subjugate and terrorize in chattel slavery more than four million descendants of Africans who survived kidnap and transportation to the United States. Moral blindness, racism, and economic self-interest, in my respectful opinion, underlay and enabled much of the legal, political, and social argument. Unconscionably, they promoted the enslavement of millions and the murder and rape of countless; and triggered the bloodiest and most senseless of our wars, what is politely termed the Civil War. Notwithstanding these tragedies and notwithstanding the postwar Reconstruction Amendments and civil rights laws, we as a nation failed to reflect adequately on the moral failures of slavery and its justifications, and the legal, political, and social restructuring that the war itself and the amendments had wrought.

I. ANTEBELLUM STATES' RIGHTS DISPUTES, IN BRIEF

In the decades before the Civil War, disputes—about slavery's abolition and its territorial limitation or expansion, federal enforcement and opposition to the return of fugitive slaves, the availability of money and credit and imposition of tariffs, and the acquisition of territory and initiation of war—divided the states by region as well as the states and federal government. When the federal government pursued policies that antagonized deeply held state positions on these issues, states frequently responded with claims that they held rights under or beyond the Constitution to oppose federal authority and, ultimately, to secede from the Union, or the Compact as they frequently termed the relationship.

One form of the claim was interposition—that the states had authority to interpose in some manner on behalf of their citizens against the federal government in order to prevent the unlawful exercise of federal authority. The Virginia Resolution of 1798, written by James Madison, made this state' rights claim but did not specify how interposition would be carried out.

Another form of the claim was nullification—that the states had authority to nullify federal law through the enactment of state law. The Kentucky Resolution of 1798, written by Thomas Jefferson, made this claim. The resolution was considered and rejected by several states at the time, but it gained traction in subsequent years. Antislavery advocates also argued for nullification of federal fugitive slave laws. In 1832, South Carolina adopted an Ordinance of Nullification, which declared two federal tariffs unconstitutional, and the state prepared to resist the tariffs by military force. John Calhoun resigned from the vice-presidency over the issue, and the Congress passed the Force Bill to authorize military action against South Carolina.

The third form of the claim was secession—the idea that states had a reserved or inherent right to secede from the Union because of the federal government's breach of the Constitution or Compact. Whether the Union is perpetual and whether grounds exist for separation were issues raised during several crises, including at the Hartford Convention convened in 1814 to oppose the War of 1812 and at William Lloyd Garrison's New England Anti-Slavery Society Convention convened in 1844 to accelerate the abolition movement. The ultimate tragedy of the claim came in 1860, when South Carolina seceded from the Union, followed by ten other states, and then in 1861 when its troops launched a bombardment of the federal military installation at Fort Sumter.

II. POSTBELLUM JUDICIAL DEVELOPMENTS, IN BRIEF

The Civil War and the Reconstruction Amendments, it is often contended, ended once and for all the states' sights arguments supporting interposition, nullification, and secession. While prior to the war some might have argued that the United States of America 'are,' after the war it could only be said that the United States of America 'is.' That is, prior to the war, states might plausibly have argued that as sovereigns they were not ultimately bound by the actions of the Congress and President; after the war they could no longer make that argument. After the war, states were limited to pressing their interests in the Congress—indeed, until the ratification of the 17th Amendment in 1913, state legislatures appointed the members of the Senate—and federal law ultimately reflected those interests as negotiated and compromised among Representatives and Senators. Once federal law was enacted, it was supreme, and states qua states could not assert that the law did not bind them. That contention was not unanimously shared.

However states' rights fared in the popular arena, moreover, within the courts the 'rights' of states and principles and theories of federalism remained, sometimes prominent and sometimes quiescent. In the nineteenth century, particularly postbellum, and well into the twentieth century, the Supreme Court held that federal law could be challenged as overreaching the federal government's domain when the federal government sought to regulate activity that was within the exclusive jurisdiction of the states. Thus, notwithstanding negotiations and compromises by and between Representatives and Senators elected by the people of the states, the Court interpreted the Congress's power to regulate commerce and its power to tax and spend in a manner that placed 'local matters' well beyond the competence of the United States.[3] Then, from about 1937 until the mid-1990s, the Court reversed track.[4] But, then again, for the last twenty years, the Court has reverted to its earlier interpretation that there are matters that traditionally belong to the states to regulate and not the United States. The mantra is that principles of federalism (not states' rights) justify the decisions.[5]

Moreover, for forty years, the Court has identified areas in which the Congress may not regulate the states and state officials. The Court has created doctrines, assertedly founded in principles and theories of federalism and supported by the 10th Amendment, that preclude suits against the states unless the suits come within 'exceptions' such as voluntary and knowing state consent to suit[6] or 14th Amendment remedial legislation.[7] In my view, Court doctrines that now protect the states from federal coercion or 'commandeering' would have surprised those who prevailed in the Civil War and enacted the transformative Reconstruction Amendments.[8]

III. RECENT ASSERTIONS OF NULLIFICATION AND SECESSION

Calls for states to nullify federal actions, particularly legislative actions, or to interpose the states between the federal government and the people have been frequent in recent years. Groups affiliated with the Tea Party movement are vigorously urging states to nullify federal legislation, with a special fervency against the Patient Protection and Affordable Care Act, President Barack Obama's health reform initiative. As one example, the Tenth Amendment Center lists on its website several nullification initiatives and proposals, including those against federal regulation of firearms, healthcare, and marijuana. The center urges its readers to attend national tours of prominent Tea Party activists with the slogan "Nullify Now."

Organizations that support nullification and interposition hold rallies, sponsor tours, distribute literature, and maintain websites.[9] Wyoming passed the Firearms Freedom Act, and the governor signed it on March 12, 2010.[10] The act calls for disobedience to federal firearms laws and regulations. In the 2011 session of the Texas House, H.B. 1937 was introduced to criminalize all searches, including airport screenings by the Transportation Security Administration, conducted without probable cause.[11] In 2010–11, bills were filed in thirteen legislatures to nullify 'Obamacare.'[12] In the election of 2012, voters in Colorado and Washington approved the use of recreational marijuana, ostensibly in conflict with federal law, and a recent survey found that 51 percent of persons favor an exemption from federal law for persons who follow state law in using marijuana.[13]

In 2009, Governor Rick Perry of Texas twice adverted to whether Texas might lawfully secede from the Union.[14] His comments were noteworthy because they came from the governor of a large and influential state and because Governor Perry was a well-regarded candidate for the Republican presidential nomination. But his comments are not unique. Following the election of 2012, it is reported that 60,000 Texans and citizens of fifteen other states filed petitions to secede from the Union.[15] At the state and local level, there have been both recent and past calls for secession from states and the formation of new states.[16]

Arguing that "our Republic does not work as our Framers intended," on September 24–25, 2011, Harvard Professor Lawrence Lessig joined with Mr. Mark Meckler, a Tea Party Patriots national coordinator, to convene the Conference on the Constitutional Convention at Harvard Law School to discuss the advisability and feasibility of organizing a constitutional convention.[17] One of our authors, Sanford V. Levinson, is a nationally prominent critic of the defects in the Constitution's structure and an advocate for substantial amendment.[18]

IV. THE COLLECTION

This collection grew out of the symposium on Legal History I organized at the annual meeting of the American Association of Law Schools on January 7, 2011. Five eminent scholars gave four excellent papers and commentary on the legal history of secession and the related claims of interposition and nullification. Because of the excitement generated by the symposium, I asked the panel members whether they would be willing to expand their papers for publication and other scholars agreed to join the project. The expanded scope is intended to offer a comprehensive discussion of issues arising when disagreements between the states and the federal government cannot be resolved by ordinary political arrangements.

Part I of this collection discusses James Madison, of significance in parsing the views of a principal Framer. Part II discusses antebellum arguments for and against secession and nullification. Part III examines the antebellum debate and the impact of the 14th Amendment. In part IV, contemporary arguments for interposition and nullification are examined. And in part V, one chapter looks critically at arguments for federalism, and one chapter looks critically at collective memory of secession.

In part I, Jack N. Rakove and Robert G. Natelson examine Madison's views. Rakove notes that James Madison was interested in including a power of coercion over the states in both the Articles of Confederation and the Constitution, which could be used to force the states to perform their obligations. Madison did not pursue the interest at the Constitutional Convention beyond an initial proposal. The reason, Rakove argues, is that although he was dubious about its effectiveness, Madison relied upon judicial review for the resolution of disputes between the United States and the states. Rakove argues, too, that upon reflection Madison did not endorse the power of states to interpose themselves or nullify federal law. The United States was not a league or partnership, but a new creation, which did not envision such action by the states.

Robert G. Natelson argues that after concluding that nullification was not an effective means to check federal government 'excesses,' Madison supported frequent constitutional conventions as an appropriate remedy for deep Union-state disagreements. Natelson examines materials previously not found and discussed in the constitutional scholarship.

In part II, Paul Finkelman, Daniel W. Hamilton, Stephen C. Neff, and H. Jefferson Powell critique antebellum arguments for and against secession and nullification. Finkelman argues that most people think of states' rights, nullification, and secessionist arguments as coming from Southern supporters of slavery and segregation. But from the 1820s to 1861, Northern opponents of slavery and some Northern state governments adopted states' rights arguments in the face of a proslavery national government and the implementation of a proslavery constitution. The most radical abolitionist, William Lloyd Garrison, argued for the secession of the free states under the slogan "No Union with Slaveholders." This chapter explores the application of states' rights theory by opponents of slavery.

Daniel W. Hamilton notes that in a classic article in the *Journal of American History*, Kenneth Stampp made the claim that the arguments in favor of the constitutionality of secession made by the Southern states were as strong, if not stronger, than the constitutional arguments made, then and now, in opposition to secession. In light of the 150th anniversary of secession, Hamilton says that it is useful to reconsider Stampp's famous thesis in light of the questions it raises about our current understanding of the meaning of the Civil War. Did Stampp, in his emphasis on constitutional thought standing alone, shed light on secession or mischaracterize the centrality of slavery in the secession crisis? Is it possible to answer the question: was secession legal? If so, and the answer is, as Stampp suggests, likely yes, then does this change our assessment of Lincoln's drive to war? If there is no definitive answer to the question, then are there other essential issues revolving around the Civil War that are equally indeterminate?

Stephen C. Neff argues that in Southern political theory, the American federal union was regarded as a compact between sovereign states—and consequently as governed by general natural-law rules on pacts or agreements. Under natural law, a breach of the pact by some of the parties (the Northern states) entitled the nonbreaching parties (the Southern states) to terminate the compact—or, in popular parlance, to secede from the Union.

H. Jefferson Powell describes William Rawle as a prominent antebellum constitutionalist. He was, Powell notes, neither an adherent of the Jeffersonian compact theory of the Constitution nor a Southern defender of slavery. In his widely read 1825 book on constitutional law, however, Rawle was seen as endorsing the right of states to secede. As a result, his book attracted wide attention. But as Powell argues, readers did not fully appreciate his argument. Read as Rawle evidently intended, however, his discussion of secession was intended to cordon the option off as a moral, political, and religious wrong.

In part III, Daniel A. Farber reviews the impact of the 14th Amendment on arguments for secession. Farber argues that the constitutional status of secession was deeply intertwined with conflicting antebellum views about the relationship between state and national citizenship. The citizenship clause of the 14th Amendment made national citizenship paramount, thereby establishing the principle that Americans owed their primary allegiance to the federal government rather than their states.

In part IV, Christian G. Fritz and Lee J. Strang review and critique contemporary arguments for interposition, nullification, and secession. Fritz argues that interposition has been misunderstood because of its historic connection with nullification and secession. He argues in part that it is a mistake to associate interposition solely with federalism and that it is important to understand the people's role in constitutionalism, in checking governmental abuse of power.

Lee J. Strang argues that originalism, as a theory of constitutional interpretation, cannot answer—and does not have the resources internal to the theory to answer—some or all of the questions presented by the concepts of interposition, nullification, and secession.

In part V, Sanford V. Levinson looks critically at arguments for federalism, and Norman W. Spaulding looks critically at collective memory of secession. Levinson critically examines the federal structure of the United States and asks what boundaries the Constitution gives to that structure and what benefits, protections, and guarantees it provides to the United States and the states. Analogizing the federal structure to a marriage, he asks why the United States would oppose the secession of a state unhappy with its place in the Union.

Norman W. Spaulding reviews the Fort Sumter National Monument and critiques its embedding of secessionist memory with *no* mention of slavery. He argues that there remains a failure—not only by historians but also by political leaders and courts—to resolve the endurance of African chattel slavery and the nation's inability to end slavery except by secession and war. And Spaulding challenges us to recognize the implications for our democracy.

NOTES

1. K. Johnson, *States' Rights Is Rallying Cry for Lawmakers*, N.Y. Times, March 16, 2010.

2. Recently, a Supreme Court justice made a most remarkable argument in support of such rights. Dissenting from a decision that recognized the federal sovereign's exclusive power to control and regulate the admission of persons entering the United States, the justice said: "The United States is an indivisible 'Union of sovereign States.' . . . Today's opinion . . . deprives States of what most would consider the defining characteristic of sovereignty: the power to exclude from the sovereign's territory people who have no right to be there. Neither the Constitution itself nor even any law passed by Congress supports this result. Arizona v. United States, 132 S. Ct. 2492, 2511 (2012) (Scalia, J., quoting from a decision about the rights of states to dispute where their territorial boundaries are drawn).

3. Hammer v. Dagenhart, 247 U.S. 251 (1918).

4. Heart of Atlanta Motel Inc. v. United States, 379 U.S. 241 (1964).

5. United States v. Morrison, 529 U.S. 598 (2000) (the United States may not prohibit rape, notwithstanding extensive congressional findings that sexual assaults against women substantially interfere with their travel across state lines).

6. Pennhurst State School and Hospital v. Halderman, 451 U.S. 1 (1981).

7. United States v. Georgia, 546 U.S. 151 (2006).

8. National Federation of Independent Business v. Sebelius, 132 S. Ct. 2566 (2012).

9. *Nullify Now!*, www.nullifynow.com (last visited Nov. 16, 2011); the Tenth Amendment Center, www.tenthamendmentcenter.com (last visited Nov. 16, 2011).

10. "A personal firearm, a firearm action or receiver, a firearm accessory, or ammunition that is manufactured commercially or privately in the state to be used or sold within the state is not subject to federal law or federal regulation, including registration, under the authority of congress to regulate interstate commerce." Wy. Stat. 1977 § 6-8-404 (2011). See Jeremy Pelzer, *Firearms Freedom Act: Symbolic Declaration of Rights or State-Federal Standoff?*, Trib.com (Mar. 12, 2010), http://trib.com/news/state-and-regional/govt-and-politics/article_06b41f54-b4cb-566b-8ac2-c61ecf272d04.html. See also O. Shane Balloun, *The Disarming Nature of the Wyoming Firearms Freedom Act: A Constitutional Analysis of Wyoming's Interposition between its Citizens and the Federal Government*, 11 Wyo. L. Rev. 201 (2011).

11. Connor Boyack, Brian Roberts, & Michael Boldin, *Feds Issue Threat: No Fly Zone for Texas?,* Tenth Amendment Center (May 24, 2011), http://www.tenthamendmentcenter.com/2011/05/24/feds-issue-threat-no-fly-zone-for-texas/.

12. Matt Spalding, *Rejecting Nullification: Idaho Draws the Line,* Heritage Foundation (Mar. 2, 2011), http://blog.heritage.org/2011/03/02/rejecting-nullification-idaho-draws-the-constitutional-line/print/.

13. Micah Cohen, *Marijuana Legalization and States Rights,* N.Y. Times, December 8, 2012.

14. "When we came into the nation in 1845, we were a republic, we were a stand-alone nation," the governor can be heard saying. "And one of the deals was, we can leave anytime we want. So we're kind of thinking about that again." Maggie Haberman, *Rick Perry Critics Unearth Another Secession Comment,* Politico (Aug. 10, 2011), http://www.politico.com/news/stories/0811/61030.html.

> I think there's a lot of different scenarios. Texas is a unique place. When we came in the union in 1845, one of the issues was that we would be able to leave if we decided to do that. You know, my hope is that America and Washington in particular pays attention. We've got a great nation. There is absolutely no reason to dissolve it. But if Washington continues to thumb their nose at the American people, you know, who knows what may come out of that? But Texas is a very unique place and we're a pretty independent lot to boot.

Interview with Kelley Shannon, Associated Press, April 2009. R. G. Ratcliffe, *Perry Says Texas Can Leave the Union if It Wants To,* Chron.com (Apr. 15, 2009), http://blogs.chron.com/texaspolitics/archives/2009/04/perry_says_texa.html.

15. *Texas proves everything's bigger there, including the will to secede,* MSN (11/13/2012), http://now.msn.com/texas-secession-petition-gets-enough-signatures-to-earn-white-house-response; *Anarchy in the USA? Folks in 15 states file petitions to secede,* MSN (11/11/2012), http://now.msn.com/15-states-start-petitons-to-leave-the-usa; *Texas judge says Obama re-election might trigger civil war,* MSN (8/23/2012), http://now.msn.com/tom-head-texas-judge-says-obama-re-election-could-lead-to-civil-war; City of Austin files counter-petition to secede from Texas, MSN (11/15/2012), http://now.msn.com/austin-files-petition-to-secede-from-texas.

16. See generally James Erwin, Declarations of Independence (2006).

17. Conference on the Constitutional Convention, Harvard Law School, www.conconcon.org (last visited Nov. 16, 2011). Lawrence Lessig and Mark Meckler cochaired the conference. Lessig is the director of the Edmond J. Safra Center for Ethics at Harvard University and the Roy L. Furman Professor of Law at Harvard Law School. He cofounded Change Congress, which aims to reduce the influence of private money in American politics. Meckler is the cofounder and a national coordinator for Tea Party Patriots (along with his cofounder and fellow national coordinator, Jenny Beth Martin), the largest grassroots Tea Party organization in the nation with over 3,500 chapters spanning every state.

18. Sanford Levinson, Our Undemocratic Constitution (2008).

I

James Madison's Views

1 "A Real Nondescript"

James Madison's Thoughts on States' Rights and Federalism

Jack N. Rakove, Stanford University

On March 12, 1833, four days before his eighty-second birthday, James Madison wrote Senator William Cabell Rives to commend the speech that his Virginia protégé had just given denouncing the dangerous constitutional theory of nullification emanating from South Carolina. "It seems strange that it should be necessary to disprove this novel and nullifying doctrine," Madison observed, "and stranger still that those who deny it should be denounced as Innovators, heretics & Apostates." That was a comment for the crisis of the moment, but Madison used it, as he often did in his writings, to introduce a more sustained analysis of the question at hand. "Our political system is admitted to be a new Creation—a real nondescript," he observed. "Its character must therefore be sought within itself; not in precedents, because there are none; not in writers whose comments are guided by precedents." Who could possibly know how writers like "Vattel and others of that class" could make sense of the "Compound & peculiar system" that was the American federal republic?[1]

"Nondescript" to Madison meant something very different from its colloquial use in American English today. Here it indicated that the object to be examined—the American form of federalism—had never been previously known, much less adequately described. Or as Madison wrote John Tyler, Virginia's other senator, about the same time as he wrote Rives, "[T]he system was to be a new & compound one—a nondescript without a technical appellation for it."[2] Tyler had taken a position very different from that of Rives in the Senate debates, and Madison's intention was to correct Tyler's charge that the purpose of the Virginia Plan of May 1787 "was to render the states nothing more than the provinces of a great Government, to rear upon the ruins of the old Confederacy a Consolidated Government, one and indivisible."[3] Reasoning like this drove Madison to a borderland of intellectual dejection. To analyze the nature of a constitution, he insisted, "let candor decide whether it be not more reasonable & just to interpret the name or title by facts on the face of it, than to torture the facts by a bed of Procrustes into a fitness to the title."[4]

This was not a new motif in Madison's political thinking. In *Federalist* No. 37, his remarkable meditation on the difficulty of constitution-making, Madison had laid out an epistemological model for the rational discussion of political phenomena. There he emphasized the difficulty of tidily dividing and distinguishing the powers of government either between state and nation or among its departmental institutions. The first application of this approach came only two essays later, in the discussion of the national and federal (that is, state-based) aspects of the proposed Constitution in *Federalist* No. 39. Some commentators find Madison's fivefold analysis of this problem frustrating in its detail or perhaps even disingenuous in slighting the decisive advantages that the national government might finally obtain over the states. Yet Madison's scheme for classifying the different modes in which the system would operate was fully consistent with the principles he had set out in *Federalist* No. 37. Equally important, it remained the basis upon which Madison continued to reason about federalism for the next four decades and thus a source of his annoyance and concern with the dangerous tendencies he saw in American politics during the final years of his life. Madison understood that the truth of American federalism—that "nondescript," unprecedented form of government—could be grasped only in its details. Instead, he lived long enough to worry that the discourse of federalism was degenerating into a contraposition of two absolute and simplistic formulas, one based on an appeal to the irreducible primordial sovereignty of the states and the other on the invocation of a national "We the people" that could be read to threaten the residual source of state autonomy he thought needed to be preserved. Nullification was the immediate object of his concern in the early 1830s, but the threat of secession trailed not very far behind. Madison's intellectual despair for the Union was thus a function of the risks that political leaders were taking by substituting simplistic formulae for the civic duty to understand, and thus work with, the "nondescript" federal system his generation had created.

A conventional piece of American constitutional wisdom holds that the question of secession was definitively settled on the battlefield. *Inter arma leges silent,* and why cannot that adage apply just as readily to questions of constitutional import as it does to the ordinary violence of war? In July 1863, Gettysburg and Vicksburg rendered the key initial verdicts on the controversy, opening prospects for an ultimate Union victory, and Appomattox ended any possibility for a final appeal. On the other side of the question, one can easily imagine the counterfactual alternative, that a Southern victory at arms could have established a conclusive precedent validating the right of secession. Just as the Northern victory made the idea of secession permanently unconstitutional, so a Southern victory would have confirmed the ultimate conclusion that long lay latent in states' rights thinking.

Against these suppositions, however, there stands a different premise grounded in the original statement of the promise of American constitutionalism set by Alexander Hamilton in the opening paragraph of *The Federalist.* "It has been frequently remarked," Hamilton observed, "that it seems to have been reserved to the people of this country, by their conduct and example, to decide the important question, whether societies of men are really capable or not of establishing good government from reflection and choice, or whether they are forever destined to depend for their political constitutions on accident and force." A constitutional doctrine either established or disproven by military success would fall closer to the "accident and force" pole of Hamilton's contrast than to "the reflection and choice" model that *The Federalist* was written to support. To reduce or equate the validity of secession with the course of war would convert a basic problem of constitutional governance into a matter of military fate.

Equally important, in the absence of an explicit warrant in the text of the Constitution, the idea of either secession or nullification as legitimate constitutional options seems just as problematic. In both cases, the appeal to force is a likely, indeed necessary element in a new equation of governance. Nullification supposes that the physical intervention of state authorities will prevent the execution of national law, and secession is credible only when one can imagine the people of a state or region mobilizing to sustain such a decision. Why would a national government wielding legislative authority under the Supremacy Clause relent in enforcing its law, if the population it would govern had not already expressed its capacity to resort to force against the federal union?

Secession itself was not an issue that came under discussion during the constitutional debates of the late 1780s. If it had, modern scholars would be familiar with an array of relevant quotations, and would not need to speculate so much. Yet the question of the use of force against recalcitrant states had been part of prior discussions of the federal system. Among those most interested in this question was James Madison. As a young member of the Continental Congress, Madison was part of a committee of three appointed just as the Articles of Confederation took effect on March 1, 1781. The committee's task was to "prepare a plan to invest the United States in Congress assembled with full and explicit powers for carrying into execution in the several states all acts or resolutions passed agreeably to the Articles of Confederation."[5] Its report, written in Madison's hand, took the radical step of suggesting that Congress should propose a new amendment to the Confederation to deal with states that "shall refuse or neglect" to perform their federal duties under Article 13. Congress would be "fully authorized to employ the force of the United States as well by sea as by land to compel such State or States to fulfill their federal engagements," particularly by closing off their commerce with other states or foreign nations.[6]

This proposal did not long survive in the two succeeding committees that took over the original committee's work.[7] Still, the idea of using coercion as the mechanism of federal enforcement retained some appeal in Madison's thinking. Writing to Governor Thomas Jefferson on April 16, 1781, Madison suggested that the use of coercion would not be such a difficult matter. One method of enforcement might be to dispatch small contingents of Continental troops, "acting under Civil authority," into the delinquent state. "But there is a still more easy and efficacious mode," Madison continued. Virtually every state would be subject to naval coercion; park a frigate or two outside its principal port or ports, and it would soon be willing to comply. Over the long run, Madison mused, a navy formed under proper national authority would have further benefits. It "would not only be a guard against aggression & insults from abroad; but without it what is to protect the Southern States for many years to come against the insults & aggressions of their N[orthern] Brethren?"[8]

The shelling of Fort Sumter began exactly fourscore years (minus four days) after Madison wrote this letter. It was a grim, if perverse, echo of Madison's 1781 observation. Fort Sumter was built to defend Charleston, not to isolate it, but in 1861 it threatened to become a simple variation of Madison's notion of naval enforcement. (By contrast, the role of the federal navy in the blockade of the Confederacy is the obverse of what Madison had envisioned in 1781.) Beyond this irony, however, what remains more striking is the constitutional question with which Madison was already wrestling. Was coercion the only or final mechanism for enforcing federal measures, or could there be some other basis for coordinating national governance with the states?

For nearly six years after Madison wrote to Jefferson, that question lay moot. The American victory at Yorktown in October 1781 made the absence of direct congressional authority over the states less urgent. The attention of nationally minded leaders shifted instead to the task of ratifying the various amendments to the Confederation that Congress sent to the states: the impost of 1781; the revenue measures, including a revised impost, proposed in April 1783; and then two amendments relating to foreign commerce recommended a year after that. So long as those amendments set the agenda for reform, the underlying premise was that the essential structure of the Confederation would remain intact, with moderate changes in the authority of Congress.

That agenda shifted, of course, after September 1786, when the rump conference at Annapolis led to the general convention that assembled at Philadelphia in May 1787. Madison played a critical role in these developments, both by attending the Annapolis Convention and then by taking on the task of framing a broad agenda for Philadelphia. As it became clear that this agenda would not be limited to enumerating incremental powers to be vested in the Continental Congress but would instead involve a fundamental reconsideration of the entire federal union, the nature of the ties between an emerging national government and the existing governments of the states again became essential.

Madison's initial thoughts about the future structure of the Union were first expressed in two sets of documents that have become quite familiar to scholars: the memorandum known as *Vices of the Political System of the U. States* and the three corresponding letters to Jefferson, Edmund Randolph, and Washington. Together, these documents show Madison moving away from, yet not wholly abandoning, the idea of coercion of the states to which he had appeared far more partial in 1781.

Item seven of the Vices is titled "want of sanction to the laws, and of coercion in the Government of the Confederacy." Assuming, as contemporary political scientists now do, that there are many "federalisms," Madison defined the underlying premise of the Articles of Confederation, as first drafted in 1776–77, in these terms: that the states would voluntarily comply with the decisions of Congress, legally implementing them in the means most convenient and productive within their territorial limits. Under such a condition, this form of federalism was, in reality, he now concluded, "nothing more than a treaty of amity of commerce and of alliance, between so many independent and Sovereign States." How had this condition arisen, Madison asked? Initially because the "compilers" of the Articles acted under "a mistaken confidence" that the states would simply do the right thing—a confidence that accurately reflected the prevailing republican assumptions of the mid-1770s. Experience since then had only confirmed the error of this supposition. Indeed, Madison continued—in what was effectively a game theoretical analysis of this form of federalism—there were structural reasons why any system relying on the voluntary compliance of the states with national decisions "will never fail to render federal measures abortive."[9]

Thus far, Madison's analysis was consistent with the idea that the states might indeed need to be coerced. Compare congressional resolutions to state legislation, Madison observed: "[W]hat probability would exist, that they would be carried into execution," if state laws were merely "recommendatory to their citizens" or left to the discretion of "County authorities" to enforce, as congressional resolutions could be said to be to the states?

Madison also mentioned the idea of a coercive power over the states in his letter to Washington of April 16, 1787, the third and most expansive of the three personal letters converting the analysis of the *Vices* into a rough agenda of reform. That idea had not appeared in the earlier letters to Jefferson and Randolph, but now Madison explicitly stated that "the right of coercion should be expressly declared." Echoing his thoughts of 1781, Madison added, "With the resources of Commerce in hand, the national administration might always find means of exerting it by sea or land." Yet Madison also indicated a measure of uneasiness with the idea of coercion. "The difficulty & awkwardness of operating by force on the collective will of a State, render it particularly desirable that the necessity of it might be precluded." Perhaps his favored measure of a negative on state laws—to be used to protect both the Union from interfering laws of the states and minorities within the individual states against unjust laws—could accomplish the task, obviating the need for coercion by preventing improper legislation from acquiring legal effect ex ante.[10]

Madison often expressed key insights with a concision that later commentators often wish he had not indulged. Another sentence or two of elaboration here would be much appreciated. Still, "difficulty & awkwardness" can embrace an array of problems. Not least among them is a recognition that American federalism might become a story of repeated overt quarrels between national and state authority. The logic of Madison's negative on state laws, as well as his gloomy views of state legislatures and legislators, presupposed that the states would remain a recurring source of difficulty in a federal system dependent on their direct role in the administration of national measures. Any system of federalism based on the voluntary compliance of autonomous state governments with national measures would remain perpetually vulnerable to inefficiency, inconsistency, or outright conflict.

The alternative to this model was a federalism that would work not on the states but on their citizens. The states would survive as independent jurisdictions, legally regulating most of the ordinary activities of their residents and conducting federal elections (subject to various review powers vested in the national government). But the national government would deal directly with citizens in the same way, enacting, executing, and adjudicating its own laws. State governments would not be dragooned or 'commandeered' (a verb that appears in modern jurisprudence about states' rights but that did not yet exist) into executing the ordinary work of national government. Coercion would apply not against the states as entities but against individuals.

This idea did not emerge in full form at the outset of the Federal Convention. Indeed, as the debate began, the Virginia Plan did include a power of coercion of the states among the prospective powers of "the National Legislature," which the final provision of Article 6 authorized "to call forth the force of the Union agst. any member of the Union failing to fulfill its duty under the articles thereof."[11] But when the convention first discussed this provision on May 31, Madison immediately abandoned this proposal, and in decided terms. In his notes of debates, Madison

> observed that the more he reflected on the use of force, the more he doubted the practicability, the justice and the efficacy of it when applied to people collectively and not individually. A union of the States containing such an ingredient seemed to provide for its own destruction. The use of force agst. a State, would look more like a declaration of war, than an infliction of punishment, and would probably be considered by the party attacked as a dissolution of all previous compacts by which it might be bound. He hoped that such a system would be framed as might render this recourse unnecessary, and moved that the clause be postponed.

The convention endorsed this suggestion without dissent.[12]

The provision was not revived in the further discussion of the Virginia Plan, but a version of it appeared in the New Jersey Plan that William Paterson presented on June 15. Its sixth resolution ended with this clause:

> [I]f any State, or any body of men in any State shall oppose or prevent ye carrying into execution such acts or treaties, the federal Executive shall be autho-

> rized to call forth ye. power of the Confederated States, or so much thereof as may be necessary to enforce and compel an obedience to such Acts, or an observance of such Treaties.[13]

When Madison briefly alluded to this proposal in his lengthy speech of June 19, he pointedly noted that it would never apply equally against all the states. "The coercion, on which the efficacy of the [New Jersey] plan depends, can never be exerted but on themselves," he argued. "The larger States will be impregnable, the smaller only can feel the vengeance of it."[14] Perhaps there was an element of bluffing in this claim, overlooking the danger that the militias of New England and Pennsylvania would execute a pincer attack on the fleshly delights of Albany. Even so, this observation illustrated the direction in which the thinking of many delegates was moving. Whatever the underlying federal structure of the Union, its governance would be national, pivoting on a division between the tasks that the national government and the states would separately discharge. It would not be a federalism in which the implementation of national measures would depend on the compliance—voluntary or coerced—of its member states.

Of course, Madison's vision of how this federal system should function was severely damaged by two decisions that the convention took four weeks later: one granting each state an equal vote in the Senate, the misnamed "Great" or "Connecticut Compromise" of July 16, and the other taken the next day, with the rejection of the negative on state laws. In Madison's view, a national government without this negative would remain vulnerable to a host of interfering—one could say *interposing*—acts from the states. Instead, the maintenance of the boundaries of federalism would rely primarily on enforcement by the courts, acting under the general authority of the Supremacy Clause. That provision began its life as part of the New Jersey Plan, as the clause antecedent to the provision authorizing the use of coercion against delinquent states. As first stated by Paterson, it bound the state judiciaries to obey federal acts and treaties, "any thing in the respective laws of the Individual States to the contrary notwithstanding."[15] Whether the omission of any reference to state *constitutions* in this formula was inadvertent or deliberate is left uncertain. But over time, and without debate or controversy, the Supremacy Clause evolved into its final form, precluding a state constitution from barring state judicial compliance with national acts.

Madison left the convention doubting that reliance on the judiciary would work. As he explained in his lengthy letter to Jefferson of October 24, 1787, he still expected states to seek to interfere with national authority. The states, to his way of thinking, would not have much to fear from "dangerous encroachments" from the national government. But the states, which would be "continually sensible of the abridgment of their power" by the Constitution, would remain "stimulated by ambition to resume the surrendered part of it." Madison doubted that the judiciary would be able to "keep the States within their proper limits, and supply the place of a negative on their laws." Not only would it be better to prevent the enactment of a harmful law than to have to deal with it reactively, Madison reasoned, but it was also the case that

> a State which would violate the Legislative rights of the Union, would not be very ready to support a Judicial decree in support of them, and that a recurrence to force, which in the event of disobedience would be necessary, is an evil which the new Constitution was meant to exclude as far as possible.

Here again, Madison returned to the concerns he first considered in 1781.[16]

Still, this private skepticism soon yielded to a more tempered view as Madison placed his reservations behind him and moved ahead with the ratification campaign. On the question of judicial authority, he used another concise passage in *Federalist* No. 39 to endorse the idea that the Supreme Court would be the arbiter of disputes over federalism. In "the *extent* of its powers"—the fourth of his five categories for analyzing federalism—the new government would not be wholly national, Madison held, because the states retained "a residual and inviolable sovereignty over all other objects" not classed among those entrusted to the national government. "It is true that in controversies relating to the boundary between the two jurisdictions, the tribunal which is ultimately to decide, is to be established under the general government," he conceded. But again, "the most effectual precautions are taken to secure this impartiality." Equally important, it had to be agreed that "[s]ome such tribunal is clearly essential to prevent an appeal to the sword, and a dissolution of the compact." The only way that such a system would work, he concluded, was for that tribunal to be established under the authority of the national government, not that of the states.[17]

Madison's comment in *Federalist* No. 39 matters for all those scholars who still agonize over whether judicial review was part of the original constitutional understanding. In terms of Madison's own thinking, however, judicial power remained a relatively minor concern.[18] It did not figure notably in his political writings during the 1790s, nor did it seem important as matters of war and peace preoccupied his attention as secretary of state and president after 1801. As is well known, he and President Jefferson ignored the purportedly landmark case of *Marbury v. Madison*, in which Chief Justice John Marshall and his *Federalist* brethren ostensibly established the principle of judicial review. After Madison's retirement from the presidency in 1817, however, and the development of controversies over both the Marshall Court and the rise of strong states'-rightist sentiment in both Virginia and South Carolina, the retired president and statesman had to reconsider questions that had first troubled him as a budding constitutionalist in the 1780s.

The source of concern after 1817 arose from the challenge mounted by Marshall's leading critic, Spencer Roane, a member of the Virginia Court of Appeals and fittingly the son-in-law of Madison's old political foe, Patrick Henry.[19] Since at least 1814, Roane had concluded that the Supreme Court could not review state court decisions on matters of constitutional law. That controversy grew more intense with the subsequent decisions in *McCulloch v. Maryland* and *Cohens v. Virginia*. Roane made a concerted effort to recruit Madison and Jefferson to his cause, only to discover that his views were far more popular at Monticello than they proved to be at Montpelier. In a series of three letters written between 1819 and 1821, Madison dealt politely with Roane, but the longer they wrote, the more Madison felt compelled to develop and clarify the basic position of *Federalist* No. 39.

Madison sympathized with Roane on the character of Marshall's jurisprudence. In *McCulloch*, of course, the chief justice relied on the same appeal to the Necessary and Proper Clause that Hamilton had first invoked in 1791. Madison had made his peace with the logic of a national bank as a disputed issue finally settled through a process of political contestation and acquiescence. But the broad reading of the Necessary and Proper Clause remained objectionable on terms consistent with Madison's longstanding concern with what he sometimes called the plasticity of legislative power. To accept that argument in full, Madison held, would erode any sense of restraint in Congress and thereby risk bringing the Union and the states into more active conflict over the boundaries of national power.

Yet on the key jurisdictional claims that formed the core of Roane's attack, Madison ultimately sided with Marshall—or at least with the Court that Marshall embodied and symbolized. Roane's notion that state and federal judiciaries should be coequal in their authority was unacceptable. Given the choice between them, there remained no question that legal supremacy belonged to the federal courts. To put the point more simply, the brief reference that Madison had made to the Court in *Federalist* No. 39 had now become a main plank in his mature constitutional orthodoxy. Rather than treat national and state judiciaries as rivals jealously monitoring each other's decisions, Madison instead hoped that the increasing legal competence of state courts would enable state and federal judges to collaborate more effectively "and thereby mutually contribute to the clearer & firmer establishment of the true boundaries of power, on which must depend the success & permanency of the federal republic."[20]

In this evolving judicial federalism, Madison hoped, broad-gauged assertions of the kind he critically associated with the pronouncements of the Marshall Court should give way to more pointed, narrowly drawn judgments. The interpretive meaning of either a law or the Constitution, Madison observed, should "result from a course of particular decisions, and not these from a particular and abstract comment on the subject."[21] Such a mode of reasoning would also correspond to Madison's epistemology of federalism. That is, courts would puzzle their way through an array of questions, clarifying the issues and producing over time a doctrine that would mark an intellectual convergence between national and state judges. As Madison had remarked back in *Federalist* No. 37, "All new laws, though penned with the greatest technical skill, and passed on the fullest and most mature deliberation, are considered as more or less obscure and equivocal, until their meaning be liquidated and ascertained by a series of particular discussions and adjudications."[22] Liquidation, in this formula, became one answer to the problem of "nondescript" federalism. It would help provide the description that the absence of prior examples left open.

Beneath this hopeful prospect of judicial federalism, however, lay a more sobering political assessment. Madison's correspondence with Roane coincided with the Missouri Crisis of 1819–21. One lesson that crisis taught, beyond its public expression of antislavery sentiments, was that the political arithmetic of the 1780s was badly miscalculated. Then it had been assumed that population movements would bring the South closer to demographic parity with the North, reinforced by the Three-Fifths Clause. Now it was apparent that even with the coefficient of reapportionment, the South would remain a permanent minority within the nation. In that situation, Madison must have understood, reliance on a Supreme Court respectful of the original understandings of American constitutionalism might provide greater security to the South than Roane, driven by his animus against Marshall, appreciated. More grimly, Madison also understood that the danger of sectional confrontation pivoting on the presence or absence of slavery remained the great exception to the advantages of a multiplicity of factions that had been the basis for his political theory since 1787. "Should a State of parties arise, founded on geographical boundaries and other permanent and Physical distinctions which happen to coincide with them," he asked in 1819, "what is to control those great repulsive Masses from awful shocks agst. each other?"[23]

In the judicial realm, then, *Federalist* No. 39 remained Madison's mature solution to the problem of resolving conflicts over federalism. He reminded Jefferson of that in 1823, when Jefferson's continued enthusiasm for Roane's position led to one of those exchanges between the two friends that again illuminated the distinct ways in which they often reasoned. Should the national and state governments reach some constitutional impasse, Jefferson had suggested, let the people call a new convention to resolve the difference. This, of course, was an echo of the state-based proposal for resolving constitutional conflicts that Madison had gone out of his way to refute, rather decisively, in *Federalist* Nos. 49 and 50, and he echoed those criticisms in explaining his objections to Jefferson's proposal. It was true, Madison conceded, that "the Court, by some of its decisions, and still more by extrajudicial reasonings & dicta," had gone too far in enlarging national authority. "But the abuse of a trust does not disprove its existence."[24] Over the long run, Southern regional interests might benefit more from the Court than they would from a legislature in which Northern majorities would dominate.

Yet within a few years, the apparent dominance of Northern economic interests in securing the enactment of the protectionist Tariff of 1828 pushed radical Southern thinking in a different direction. Nullification, not judicial review, became South Carolina's preferred answer to the so-called Tariff of Abominations. Here again, the development of the South Carolina argument, spearheaded by its great constitutional theorist, John C. Calhoun, may have carried Madison back to his earlier thoughts. Back in 1798, and perhaps with Jefferson's flirtation with nullification in the Kentucky Resolutions in mind, Madison had reminded Jefferson that it was important to ask *how* a state could act as "the ultimate Judge of infractions" on the Constitution. The *legislature* of the state could not go that far, Madison reasoned, but a *convention* might, because "a Convention was the organ by which the Compact was made."[25]

The thought, as enunciated in 1798, was left incomplete—a personal query meant for Jefferson and another one of those occasional interjections by which Madison tried to pull his neighbor at Monticello, who was more prone to impulsive statements, back to a more prudent position. But thirty years later, the thought that Madison had left dangling in 1798 became a fundamental element of South Carolina's nullification campaign. It was not the legislature that would take the decisive act of nullification, but a special convention—that distinctively innovative American legal fiction that gave a people an expression of popular sovereignty higher than the ordinary processes of legislative ratification.

Madison's correspondence and papers after 1828 contain numerous references to the heresies emanating from South Carolina. To examine even the limited number of documents reprinted in the Library of America edition of Madison's

Writings is to realize how profoundly troubled he was by nullification, not only for its flawed premises and conclusions but also, by implication, for the ominous light it shed on the character of American political reasoning. Madison's efforts to counteract the Calhounian discourse remained consistent with the epistemology that both guided and was reinforced by his role as constitutional lawgiver in the 1780s. He drafted these documents mindful not only of the need to explain a "nondescript" Constitution in its details but also of the fundamental ends of republican government. As Drew McCoy has aptly observed, Madison consistently understood that the logic of the South Carolina position was an attack on the fundamental principle of majority rule. Madison had long worried, of course, about the problem of factious majorities and majority misrule. But his concerns on these subjects were designed not to reject majority rule in principle, as South Carolina was surely doing, but to improve the basis on which majorities would properly form.[26]

Thus, in the course of a lengthy letter to Joseph Cabell on the legitimacy of a protectionist tariff, Madison used the multiple sources of power he found in the Constitution to reflect on the presence in the text of "Pleonasms, tautologies & the promiscuous use of terms & phrases differing in their shades of meaning" as evidence of the framers' overlapping concerns, "the imperfections of language," and even "the imperfection of man himself."[27] These were all variants on points registered in *Federalist* No. 37, where Madison had concisely distilled the linguistic analysis of John Locke's *Essay Concerning Human Understanding* into a sober lesson of the limitations and snares of political language. After then elaborating eight specific reasons why a protectionist tariff was constitutional, Madison then turned to precedent and stability as guiding values. The objections emanating from South Carolina violated four decades of settled practice—an "unbroken current... prolonged & universal." Any "novel construction" challenging this understanding could plausibly require only "the intervention of the same authority which made the Constitution," that is, an appeal to a superlegislative popular convention. But if that precedent of 1787–88 was now invoked, Madison warned, "there would be an end to that stability in Govt. and in Laws which is essential to good Govt. & good Laws; a stability, the want of which is the imputation which has at all times been levelled agst. Republicanism with most effect by its most dexterous adversaries." To allow so grave a challenge and cavalier a rejection of settled practice to go unanswered would ultimately lead to a situation in which "every new Legislative opinion might make a new Constitution."[28]

The constitutional validity of the 1828 tariff soon became a secondary concern for Madison, not least because the answer to the question seemed so obvious. The real danger lay in the concept of nullification itself. Here the first challenge that Madison faced was to correct the pernicious misperception that the "doctrine of 1798" provided a legitimate and powerful foundation for the heresies of South Carolina, which supposed that an individual state should be entitled to resist an act of Congress until and unless its position was corrected by a common resolution or action of three quarters of the states. Madison was reluctant to speak at length about the *Kentucky Resolutions*, of which Jefferson was the original author. In his old age, as in the 1790s, Jefferson's enthusiasm for states' rights had a radical edge that Madison resisted.[29] Madison had much greater confidence in his recollection of the purposes and limitations of the *Virginia Resolutions*. These had never been conceived to interpose the legal authority of the state to prevent the enforcement of the Alien and Sedition Acts. The resolutions were designed instead to rally a larger set of states, acting concurrently, as agencies of political protest. Madison's views of the capacity of the state governments had obviously shifted significantly in the decade since the adoption of the Constitution. Having to deal with the effective consolidation of *Federalist* political power in all three branches of the national government, the states now appeared to be the last political forum that the Republican opposition could immediately hope to mobilize. But that mobilization would not take the path of legal interposition. Instead, it would operate as a medium for rallying public opinion. Indeed, as Colleen Sheehan has recently explained, Madison's plans for the *Virginia Resolutions* reflected the more sophisticated understanding of public opinion that he had formed since the 1780s. This was a strategy for political opposition, not legal or constitutional confrontation, and it was properly tied, not to the development of heretical doctrines, but to the political judgment that the election of 1800 soon vindicated.[30]

Correcting historical misperceptions about 1798, however, was only a partial step. Once it was realized that the doctrine of 1798 did not lay a foundation for the heresies of 1832, Madison still had to explain what its significance was. In Madison's view, the Federal Constitution was formed on the basis of a compact among the people of the states, and that compact created a national government possessing substantial manifestations of sovereignty that the states no longer retained. It was the collective nature of this compact as binding all states, rather than a compact between each individual state and the Union, that exposed a decisive flaw in the South Carolina position. The latter notion again carried Madison back to a position with which he had flirted in 1787: that if the Articles of Confederation were conceived as a league or treaty among sovereign states, then the failure of a state to abide by any of its provisions might release all the states from their collective obligations.[31] However plausible that claim might have seemed in 1787—and it did not receive a favorable hearing when Madison mentioned it at the convention—it could not describe the situation of 1832. The implication that "the Constitutional band which holds [the states] together, is a mere league or partnership, without any of the characteristics of sovereignty or nationality" was both an absurdity and the basis for Madison's response that the American "political system" was "a new Creation—a real nondescript."[32]

Madison's position left open the theoretical possibility that the Union could dissolve if a mutual consensus existed among the states that its continuation was no longer compelling. But that would require a collective act akin to 1787–88, when such a consensus had formed, first within the convention at Philadelphia and then among the people of the states. South Carolina's stand-alone action could not pass that high threshold. But its lack of constitutional authority did not provide a sovereign cure to the political passions that had been released.

> The natural feelings which laudably attach the people composing a State, to its authority and importance, are at present too much excited by the unnatural feelings, with which they have been inspired agst. their brethren of other States, not to expose them, to the danger of being misled into erroneous views of the nature of the Union and the interest they have in it.[33]

Here, as in *The Federalist,* Madison still reflected on the ways in which opinions and passions, rather than moderated reasoning, could become the determinants of political commitment. Should "an actual secession" occur "without the consent of the Co-States," Madison concluded, "the course to be pursued by these involves questions painful in the discussion of them." To put the point more directly, the coercion he had first contemplated in the Continental Congress half a century earlier and then abandoned as a viable mode of federal governance might yet again become the final source of national authority.

Madison understood that secession, as a revolutionary act, could not itself be nullified by constitutional means. Yet his preferred alternative throughout was that Americans should strive to understand both the origins of the federal constitutional union and the complexities of its governance. The passage of time and the inflammation of rhetoric made both tasks ever more difficult. In effect, what Madison wanted was for his countrymen to be more Madisonian, not only in their devotion to the Union but in their ability to grapple, as he repeatedly did, with the details of federalism, in the expectation that their first commitment was to the Union itself. That was why his final public text, which he called *Advice to My Country*, took the form of a posthumous appeal to Union. A quarter century after his death in 1836, that hope asked more of his countrymen than they were capable of providing.

NOTES

1. Letter from James Madison to William Cabell Rives (Mar. 12, 1833), *in* James Madison: Writings 864 (Jack N. Rakove ed., 1999).

2. Letter from James Madison to John Tyler (n.d., 1833), *in* 9 The Writings of James Madison, 508 (Gaillard Hunt ed., 1910). Hunt notes that the letter was evidently not sent; *id.* at 502n.

3. *Id.* at 502.

4. *Id.* at 509.

5. 9 Journals of the Continental Congress, 1774–1789 236 (Worthington C. Ford ed., 1904–37).

6. *Id.* at 20: 469–71.

7. For further discussion, *see* Jack N. Rakove, The Beginnings of National Politics 289–91 (1979).

8. Letter from James Madison to Thomas Jefferson (Apr. 16, 1781), *in* 3 The Papers of James Madison 71–72 (William Hutchinson, William Rachal, et al. eds., 1962).

9. 9 Papers of Madison, *supra* note 8, at 351–52. For further discussion of this point, which offers a revealing insight into Madison's active mode of political thinking, *see* Jack Rakove, Revolutionaries 363–65 (2010).

10. Letter from James Madison to George Washington (Apr. 16, 1787), *in* 9 Papers of Madison, *supra* note 8, at 385.

11. 1 Records of the Federal Convention of 1787 21 (Max Farrand ed., 1911).

12. *Id.* at 54.

13. *Id.* at 245.

14. *Id.* at 320.

15. *Id.* at 245.

16. Letter from James Madison to Thomas Jefferson (Oct. 24, 1787), *in* 10 Papers of Madison, *supra* note 8, at 215.

17. Federalist 39, *in* 10 Papers of Madison, *supra* note 8, at 381.

18. Nor can one overlook the brief yet skeptical comment on judicial power included in his review of Jefferson's ideas for a revised Virginia constitution: *Observations on the "Draught of a Constitution for Virginia"* (Oct. 1788), *in* 11 Papers of Madison, supra note 8, at 293.

19. In this and the following paragraphs, I rely on my earlier essay, *Judicial Power in the Constitutional Theory of James Madison*, 43 William & Mary L. Rev. esp. 1533–47 (2002).

20. Letter from James Madison to Spencer Roane (June 29, 1821), *in* James Madison: Writings, *supra* note 1, at 779.

21. Letter from James Madison to Spencer Roane (Sept. 2, 1819), *id.* at 733.

22. *Federalist* 37, in 10 Papers of Madison, *supra* note 8, at 362.

23. Letter from James Madison to Robert Walsh (Nov. 27, 1819), *in* James Madison: Writings, *supra* note 1, at 744.

24. Letter from James Madison to Thomas Jefferson (June 27, 1823), *id.* at 801–2.

25. Letter from James Madison to Thomas Jefferson (Dec. 29, 1798), *id.* at 592.

26. Drew McCoy, The Last of the Fathers 136–39 (1989).

27. Letter from James Madison to Joseph Cabell (Sept. 18, 1828), *in* James Madison: Writings, *supra* note 1, at 814.

28. *Id.* at 819.

29. As McCoy and others have noted, defending Jefferson and the *Kentucky Resolutions* was a real problem that Madison's best reasoning could not wholly resolve. McCoy, *supra* note 26, at 143–51.

30. Colleen Sheehan, James Madison and the Spirit of Republican Self-Government 130–34 (2009).

31. *Cf.* the second point in the eighth item of Madison's *Vices of the Political System of the United States*, in James Madison: Writings, *supra* note 1, at 74.

32. Madison to Rives (Mar. 12, 1833), *id.* at 864.

33. *Id.* at 865.

2 James Madison and the Constitution's "Convention for Proposing Amendments"

Robert G. Natelson, The Independence Institute

I. THE FOUNDERS' HISTORY: PRIOR EXPERIENCES WITH CONVENTIONS

Article V of the Constitution provides in relevant part:

> The Congress, whenever two thirds of both Houses shall deem it necessary, shall propose Amendments to this Constitution, or, on the Application of the Legislatures of two thirds of the several States, shall call a Convention for proposing Amendments, which, in either Case, shall be valid to all Intents and Purposes, as Part of this Constitution, when ratified by the Legislatures of three fourths of the several States, or by Conventions in three fourths thereof, as the one or the other Mode of Ratification may be proposed by the Congress.[1]

This language requires all amendments to be *ratified* by three-fourths of the states (through legislatures or conventions). It also provides for two distinct ways of *proposal*: by two-thirds of each chamber of Congress or by a "Convention for proposing Amendments," called by Congress on application by two-thirds of the state legislatures.

James Madison was a principal drafter of Article V.[2] That he and the other Framers should turn to conventions, particularly interstate conventions, as tools for amendment was not at all surprising: Conventions were well-precedented ways of accomplishing specific political tasks of the kind best not left to legislatures. Moreover, as Madison grew in age and experience, he came to view the "Convention for proposing Amendments" as an instrument by which states could resist an abusive or overreaching federal government. This chapter traces that development in Madison's thought.

The founding generation employed the word *convention* in the political context to denote an assembly that, unlike a legislature, was assembled for a particular project, to be dissolved once its work was complete.[3] It was, in other words, a sort of ad hoc committee. In the seventeenth century, the English-speaking peoples had made much use of this device: "Convention Parliaments" reorganized the government in England in 1660 and 1689,[4] and in the latter year, the American colonists held at least four conventions of their own.[5] During the eighteenth century, American colonists continued to resort to conventions,[6] particularly during the Founding Era.[7]

Founding Era conventions differed widely in the scope of their powers. Some, referred to as "plenipotentiary" conventions, enjoyed very wide authority.[8] A plenipotentiary constitutional convention might both draft a new state constitution and adopt it.[9] The authority of other conventions was more restricted, and some were limited to a single discrete task. For example, the 1777 Georgia Constitution authorized conventions whose only purpose was to draft and promulgate any constitutional amendment whose subject matter was specified in petitions from a majority of counties.[10] Similarly, the U.S. Constitution authorized state conventions that were limited either to ratifying or rejecting the Constitution[11] or to ratifying or rejecting proposed amendments.[12] The distinction between plenipotentiary and limited-purpose conventions often is forgotten today, particularly by people who confuse conventions held under the Constitution with plenipotentiary constitutional conventions.[13] But the distinction is crucial to understanding the role of and the rules governing gatherings held under Article V.

Although many Founding Era conventions served only a single colony or state, some were intercolonial or interstate gatherings.[14] From 1774 until 1787, there were at least a dozen intercolonial or interstate conventions.[15] Most of these meetings were called by one or more colonial or state legislatures or by governing state conventions; a few were called by Congress or by prior interstate conventions.[16] The principal intercolonial assembly was the 1st Continental Congress (also referred to as a convention);[17] the interstate conventions included the 1787 Philadelphia gathering and at least ten others: two in Providence, Rhode Island (1776–77 and 1781); one in Springfield, Massachusetts (1777); one in York Town, Pennsylvania (1777);[18] one in New Haven, Connecticut (1778); two in Hartford,

Connecticut (1779 and 1780); one in Philadelphia (1780); one in Boston (1780); and one in Annapolis (1786).[19] Attendance at these gatherings ranged from three states to twelve.

Interstate conventions, like their intrastate counterparts, varied in the scope of their authority. The scope of the 1st Continental Congress (1774) was nearly plenipotentiary: "[T]o consult and advise [i.e., deliberate][20] with the Commissioners or Committees of the several English Colonies in America, on proper measures for advancing the best good of the Colonies."[21] The Springfield Convention of 1777 probably enjoyed the second-broadest scope. It was entrusted with issues of currency, monopoly and economic oppression, and interstate trade restrictions—although its authority was limited explicitly to matters outside the competence of Congress.[22] The three-state Boston Convention of 1780 was charged with all aspects of the ongoing Revolutionary War. The convention interpreted this charge liberally to include recommendations on trade and currency.[23]

The first Providence Convention (1776–77) was restricted to price-stabilization and defense measures.[24] Shortly thereafter, Congress recommended that states attend interstate conventions in York Town, Pennsylvania, and Charleston, South Carolina, to consider the single subject of price-stabilization.[25] Because the meeting at Providence had recommended measures on that subject for New England,[26] Congress recommended that New York, New Jersey, Pennsylvania, Maryland, Delaware, and Virginia meet at York Town, and that the Carolinas and Georgia convene at Charleston. That the Charleston convention ever took place has not been verified;[27] the York Town convention did meet, but adjourned without issuing a recommendation because of a tie vote among the states present.[28]

Interstate meetings at New Haven (1778) and Philadelphia (1780) also focused exclusively on price regulation.[29] The first Hartford Convention (1779) was empowered to address currency and trade,[30] and the second (1780) met "for the purpose of advising and consulting upon measures for furnishing the necessary supplies of men and provision for the army."[31] The second Providence Convention (1781) was entrusted only with recommending how to provide supplies to the army for a single year.[32] The 1780 Philadelphia gathering was empowered to commit the participating states to the solutions it devised.[33] Most interstate conventions, however, were authorized only to issue proposals for state ratification.[34]

The last of the limited-subject interstate gatherings is today the most famous. The Annapolis Convention of 1786 was to focus on "the trade and Commerce of the United States."[35] Its limited scope induced Madison, who served as a delegate, explicitly to distinguish it from a plenipotentiary convention.[36]

For the most part, all of these conventions—today we might call them 'task forces'—remained within the scope of their calls.[37] If there was an exception, it was the abortive assembly at Annapolis, and that exception was solely to express the "wish" and "opinion" that another convention be held to consider defects in the political system.[38]

As a result of all this experience, federal convention customs, practices, and protocols were fairly well standardized when Article V was written.[39] As explained below,[40] those customs, practices, and protocols formed the basis for how the Constitution's convention for proposing amendments was expected to operate.

II. MADISON AND THE ADAPTATION OF THE CONVENTION TO THE AMENDMENT PROCESS

The famous Virginia Plan was presented on May 29, 1787, to the Constitutional Convention by Virginia Governor Edmund Randolph but probably was penned largely by Madison. The Virginia Plan stated that "provision ought to be made for the amendment of the Articles of Union whensoever it shall seem necessary, and that the assent of the National Legislature ought not to be required thereto."[41] Cutting the national legislature out of the process would require an alternative procedure, which the Virginia Plan did not specify.

On August 6, the committee of detail—five delegates charged with preparing the first draft of the Constitution—reported a plan that utilized an amendments convention. It provided that "[o]n the application of the Legislatures of two thirds of the States in the Union, for an amendment of this Constitution, the Legislature of the United States shall call a Convention for that purpose."[42] This proposal looked much like that in the Georgia Constitution mentioned earlier.[43] Two-thirds of the states (instead of voters in a majority of counties, as in Georgia) would decide what kind of amendments they wanted, whereupon Congress would be required to call a convention to draft and impose them. The committee of detail's plan did not provide for a further ratification procedure.

Delegates raised three sorts of objections to the committee's formulation. Alexander Hamilton of New York suggested that Congress as well as the states ought to have power to propose amendments because its position would enable it readily to perceive defects in the system.[44] Elbridge Gerry of Massachusetts objected to amendment without final approval by the states.[45] Madison wondered why, if states applied for one or more amendments, a convention was necessary: He "did not see why Congress would not be as much bound to propose amendments applied for by two thirds of the States as to call a Convention on the like application."[46] The delegates accommodated Hamilton's objection by granting Congress coequal power to propose. They met Gerry's objection by adding a requirement that three-fourths of states approve amendments.[47] Madison's objection was not met, probably because the delegates did not believe that Congress should be entrusted with drafting state-promoted amendments designed to limit congressional power. Madison then wondered whether the issue should be reconsidered because it was unclear to him how an amendments convention would be formed and what its rules or the force of its acts would be.[48] Nonetheless he eventually became reconciled to the convention procedure.[49]

Madison may have been persuaded because it was readily understandable what sort of assembly the "Convention for proposing Amendments" would be, as well as the nature of its incidents and procedures.[50] The obvious model was an institution resorted to repeatedly during the preceding thirteen years: the interstate convention assigned to propose to the states a solution to one or more assigned problems. Indeed, established legal doctrine would have incorporated their customs and protocols into the law of the Constitution.[51]

What were those customs and protocols? Interstate convention procedures were based on gatherings of international diplomats.[52] Like international conventions, interstate conventions were called to deliberate on one or more problems and recommend one or more solutions. The charge could be a broad one, but more often it was rather specific.[53]

An interstate convention consisted of delegations (committees) from each state, made up of delegates (commissioners). The gathering as a whole sometimes was referred to a convention of "the states"[54] or a convention of "committees."[55] The delegates were empowered, and the scope of their authority defined, by documents called 'commissions' or 'credentials.' Like other agents, delegates were bound by the scope of their authority.[56] They were subject to additional legislative instructions.[57] The rule of suffrage was one vote per state.[58]

Interstate conventions enjoyed uncontested authority to set their own rules and elect their own officers.[59] Within the scope of their authority, interstate conventions were deliberative bodies, not mere rubber stamps: They were, after all, commissioned to solve problems.[60]

Madison recognized the role of the amendments convention as a diplomatic meeting of the states; this is evidenced by his observation in *The Federalist* that, because of the state-application-and-convention procedure, the Constitution "equally enables the general and the State governments to originate the amendment of errors."[61] For the state governments to enjoy such equality, they had to possess the same power to propose amendments that Congress had. The convention was their vehicle for doing so.

III. MADISON AND THE AMENDMENTS CONVENTION AS A CHECK ON THE FEDERAL GOVERNMENT

The two central issues during the ratification debates were whether the Constitution granted undue power to the federal government and whether the Constitution's language was indefinite enough to enable federal officials to exceed or abuse the intended scope of their authority. Madison acknowledged the potential danger. He saw the state governments as a principal remedy:

> [S]hould an unwarrantable measure of the federal government be unpopular in particular States, which would seldom fail to be the case, or even a warrantable measure be so, which may sometimes be the case, the means of opposition to it are powerful and at hand. The disquietude of the people; their repugnance and, perhaps, refusal to co-operate with the officers of the Union; the frowns of the executive magistracy of the State; the embarrassments [i.e., obstacles] created by legislative devices, which would often be added on such occasions, would oppose, in any State, difficulties not to be despised; would form, in a large State, very serious impediments; and where the sentiments of several adjoining States happened to be in unison, would present obstructions which the federal government would hardly be willing to encounter.
>
> But ambitious encroachments of the federal government, on the authority of the State governments, would not excite the opposition of a single State, or of a few States only. They would be signals of general alarm. Every government would espouse the common cause. A correspondence would be opened. Plans of resistance would be concerted. One spirit would animate and conduct the whole. The same combinations, in short, would result from an apprehension of the federal, as was produced by the dread of a foreign, yoke; and unless the projected innovations should be voluntarily renounced, the same appeal to a trial of force would be made in the one case as was made in the other.[62]

Several options set forth in this passage presage state actions in later years—most recently, in state resistance to the 2010 federal health care law.[63] But in this passage Madison, unlike some other Founders,[64] did not refer explicitly to the state-application-and-convention process as a potential tool to counter federal overreaching. The process was encompassed, perhaps, by the general expression "[p]lans of resistance would be concerted," but there was no specific mention of it. For this, there was good reason: at that point, Madison wished to discourage a second convention.

In the summer of 1788, when it was apparent that Anti-Federalists could not prevent ratification of the Constitution, they turned their efforts toward obtaining a new federal convention with nearly plenipotentiary authority to rewrite the document. Anti-Federalist sentiment was particularly strong in Virginia and in New York. The New York ratifying convention issued a circular letter both recommending a new conclave and proposing over thirty amendments.[65] Both New York and Virginia soon applied to Congress under Article V. The New York application asked for a convention with an unlimited charge. The Virginia application can be read as either limited or unlimited; but even if limited, the convention requested still would have been able to consider all of the dozens of amendments proposed by the state ratifying conventions.[66]

In late 1789 and early 1790, Madison wrote a series of letters to private correspondents counseling against such efforts. Madison now acknowledged (as he had not earlier) that a bill of rights was desirable, but he insisted that proposal by Congress would be the "most expeditious mode."[67] Congress, he said, should be granted the opportunity to act, and would likely do so.[68] Regardless, recent electoral results had shown that a sufficient number of other states would not apply, leaving the campaign short of the necessary two-thirds.[69] This was fortunate, because Federalists, he said, would never agree to a complete revision of the Constitution—a "mutil[ation of] the system"[70]—and some might oppose even useful amendments if proposed by a convention.[71] A revision such as that proposed by New York was unnecessary and certainly would be upsetting to American foreign policy and foreign creditors[72] but might be the unfortunate result of a convention dominated by Anti-Federalists[73] elected "in the present temper of America."[74] Further, it was unclear to Madison that New York was restricting itself to an Article V convention; it might really want a plenipotentiary body.[75]

A passage from a letter written by Madison around this time has been touted as evidence that he opposed Article V conventions in general.[76] His correspondence as a whole, however, shows that his opposition was limited to the unrestricted sort of convention advocated by New York[77] and only during that period: Madison repeatedly asserted that he would not object to such a gathering in a year or two, after political passions had cooled, Congress had had a chance to adopt a bill of rights, and the government was in operation.[78]

At this time, however, Madison remained silent on whether amendments conventions could be used to resist federal overreaching. In 1798, he drafted the *Virginia Resolution*,[79] which objected to the federal Alien and Sedition Acts as unconstitutional. The resolution did not call for nullification of federal laws, as sometimes is claimed, but neither did it specifically suggest a convention. Rather, it urged that "necessary and proper measures . . . be taken by [other states] for co-operating with this State, in maintaining unimpaired the authorities, rights, and liberties reserved to the States respectively, or to the people."[80]

Although the *Virginia Resolution* and its Kentucky counterpart (which did call for nullification)[81] are widely remembered today, it is less known that none of the other thirteen states then in the Union responded favorably to them: No state issued a resolution in support, and at least seven issued resolutions of condemnation.[82]

However, while rejecting the Virginia and Kentucky resolutions, the Massachusetts legislature suggested as an alternative the use of Article V:

> [T]he people in that solemn compact, which is declared to be the supreme law of the land, have not constituted the state legislatures the judges of the acts or measures of the Federal Government, *but have confided to them the power of proposing such amendments of the Constitution, as shall appear to them necessary to the interests, or conformable to the wishes of the people whom they represent.*[83]

Madison seems to have been intrigued. When drafting resolutions for the Virginia legislature the following year, he relied on Article V to demonstrate that it was proper for the states to communicate with each other on constitutional issues: "The Legislatures of the States have a right also to originate amendments to the Constitution, by a concurrence of two-thirds of the whole number, in applications to Congress for the purpose."[84] Against the claim that Virginia was acting extraconstitutionally, he added:

> It is no less certain, that other means might have been employed which are strictly within the limits of the Constitution. The Legislatures of the States might have made a direct representation to Congress with a view to obtain a rescinding of the two offensive acts; or they might have represented to their respective Senators in Congress their wish that two-thirds thereof would propose an explanatory amendment to the Constitution; *or two-thirds of themselves, if such had been their option, might, by an application to Congress, have obtained a Convention for the same object.*[85]

Thus, the Article V convention had become an appropriate weapon in Madison's arsenal for resisting federal power. The Article V convention was a tool of potential state "interposition"[86] against congressional abuse.

Madison pressed this point further during the nullification crisis of the late 1820s and early 1830s. South Carolina officials claimed power to nullify within state borders any federal legislation they believed violated the constitutional compact. To his chagrin, Madison witnessed the nullifiers relying, in part, on his 1798 *Virginia Resolution*.

Accordingly, Madison penned a public letter to Edward Everett, a member of Congress and newspaper editor. In the letter, Madison argued that the nullifiers were misinterpreting the *Virginia Resolution*.[87] The Constitution's checks and balances, not nullification, comprised the proper tools for state resistance to federal overreaching:

> On the other hand, as a security of the rights & powers of the States in their individual capacities, agst. an undue preponderance of the powers granted to the Government over them in their united capacity, the Constitution has relied on, 1. The responsibility of the Senators and Representatives in the Legislature of the U. S. to the Legislatures & people of the States. 2. The responsibility of the President to the people of the U. States; & 3. The liability of the Ex. and Judiciary functionaries of the U. S. to impeachment by the Representatives of the people of the States, in one branch of the Legislature of the U. S. and trial by the Representatives of the States, in the other branch; the State functionaries, Legislative, Executive, & judiciary, being at the same time in their appointment & responsibility, altogether independent of the agency or authority of the U. States.[88]

The independence of "State functionaries" presumably would give them the flexibility they needed to employ the tools of resistance Madison had suggested in *Federalist* No. 46.[89] And what if those tools were to prove insufficient? Madison's answer was one that Jefferson also had finally accepted:[90] the next recourse was not nullification, but the state-application-and-convention procedure.

> Should the provisions of the Constitution as here reviewed be found not to secure the Govt. & rights of the States agst. usurpations & abuses on the part of the U. S. the final resort within the purview of the Constn. lies in an amendment of the Constn. according to a process applicable by the States.[91]

That, however, was the final constitutional route to resolution. Beyond the Article V convention, Madison wrote, remained only the *ultima ratio*: resort to arms.[92]

IV. CONCLUSION

The Constitutional Convention of 1787 was far from the only meeting of its kind. During the Founding Era, the interstate, or federal, convention was a common problem-solving device, employed by the states at least a dozen times from 1774 to

1787. The interstate convention process was governed by well-recognized rules and protocols. The frequency and familiarity of the device explain why the delegates drafting the Constitution resorted to it as a method of permitting the states to amend the document without the substantive participation of Congress.

During the drafting process, Madison raised some questions about using the interstate convention for amendment purposes. Those questions apparently were answered to his satisfaction, for he seems to have dropped his objections. The best way to explain his acquiescence was the familiarity of interstate conventions and of the rules and customs governing them.

During the ratification process, Madison suggested several tools the states could employ in the event the federal government exceeded or abused its power. Except perhaps indirectly, Madison did not mention the state-application-and-convention process. Indeed, at that point Madison feared another interstate convention, because those promoting one planned to use it to substantially rewrite the Constitution. However, Madison never opposed the state-application-and-convention process in general.

After most of the other states rejected his 1798 *Virginia Resolution*, Madison came to view the Article V convention as a way to guard against federal governmental excesses. By 1830, he was strongly promoting state-application-and-convention process as an alternative to nullification, and—in the event of otherwise incorrigible federal abuse—as the last constitutional step states should pursue prior to revolution.

NOTES

1. U.S. Const. art. V (emphasis added).

2. The Records of the Federal Convention of 1787, at 559 (Max Farrand ed., 1937) (reproducing Madison's offer to the convention of nearly final language).

3. Robert G. Natelson, *Proposing Constitutional Amendments by Convention: Rules Governing the Process*, 78 Tenn. L. Rev. 693, 706 (2011).

4. Russell L. Caplan, Constitutional Brinksmanship 5–6 (1988).

5. *Id.* at 6 (discussing two conventions in Massachusetts, one in New York, and one in Maryland).

6. *Id.* at 7–9. *See also* Richard D. Brown, Revolutionary Politics in Massachusetts 29–31 (2006) (describing the 1768 Massachusetts Convention of Towns, which met in lieu of the colonial assembly, which the royal governor had dissolved); Robert C. Newbold, The Albany Congress and Plan of Union of 1754, at 28 (1955) (mentioning numerous intercolonial conventions on Indian affairs).

7. In this chapter, the term "Founding Era" refers to the period from 1774, when the 1st Continental Congress met, through 1791, when the Bill of Rights was ratified.

8. Caplan, *supra* note 4, at 23. On this usage, *see also id.* at xx–xxi (explaining usage) and 20 (quoting Hamilton).

9. An example was the Delaware Constitution of 1776. *See The Avalon Project at the Yale Law School*, http://www.yale.edu/lawweb/avalon/states/de02.htm (editors' note).

10. Ga. Const. of 1777, art. LXIII: "No alteration shall be made in this constitution without petitions from a majority of the counties, and the petitions from each county to be signed by a majority of voters in each county within this State; at which time the assembly shall order a convention to be called for that purpose, specifying the alterations to be made, according to the petitions preferred to the assembly by the majority of the counties as aforesaid."

11. U.S. Const. art. VII.

12. *Id.* art. V.

13. While there has long been some confusion along these lines, it did not become widespread until the twentieth century. *See generally* Robert G. Natelson, *Amending The Constitution by Convention: Lessons for Today from the Constitution's First Century*, available at http://liberty.i2i.org/files/2012/03/IP_5_2011_c.pdf (2011). Thus, the distinction was still understood when George Bancroft wrote his celebrated history of the United States. 6 George Bancroft, A History of the United States 197 (1882, 1884) (referring to the need in the 1780s for a plenipotentiary interstate convention, as opposed to a convention of more limited scope).

Particularly since the 1960s, activists seeking to discourage use of the state-application-and-convention procedure have argued that a convention for proposing amendments would be a "constitutional convention," or "con-con," and thus a body inherently plenipotentiary and uncontrollable. Caplan, *supra* note 4, at vii–viii (quoting various public figures) and 146–47 (quoting Theodore Sorensen). Groups such as the John Birch Society have devoted considerable resources promoting this claim. *See, e.g., Constitution Threatened by New Constitutional Convention Initiative*, http://www.jbs.org/freedom-campaign/4941. However, it is difficult to find historical or legal justification for this position.

14. The initial impulse was to call them "Congresses," adapting a term then commonly used for an assembly of sovereignties. This had been done for the Albany Congress of 1754, and the term was applied to the 1st and 2nd Continental Congresses. Perhaps because "Congress" came to be used for the assembly that provided regular central government (however weak)—*see generally* Articles of Confederation of 1781 after the 1st Continental Congress all ad hoc interstate gatherings were referred to as conventions.

15. For a survey and discussion of all these conventions, see Robert G. Natelson, *Founding-Era Conventions and the Meaning of the Constitution's "Convention for Proposing Amendments,"* Fla. L. Rev. (forthcoming 2013). Excluded from this count are the 2nd Continental Congress, which served as a (weak) central government for more than six years; the 1785 meeting at Mt. Vernon between Maryland and Virginia to discuss rights to the Potomac River and other bodies of water; and the Confederation Congress (1781–89), which was a regularly established government, albeit with very limited powers.

16. *See, e.g.*, Simeon E. Baldwin, *The New Haven Convention of 1778, in* Three Historical Papers Read Before the New Haven Historical Society 3, at 37–38 (1882) (listing and discuss-

ing those interstate conventions commissioned to deal with issues of public credit). For example, Massachusetts called the Springfield Convention, State of Connecticut, the Public Records of the State of Connecticut—From October, 1776, to February, 1778, Inclusive 599 (Charles J. Hoadly ed., 1894) [hereinafter 1 Hoadly]; Congress called the York Town Convention, 7 J. Cont. Cong. 124–24 (Feb. 15, 1777); and the Hartford Convention of 1779 called the Philadelphia Convention of 1780, State of Connecticut, the Public Records of the State of Connecticut—From May, 1778, to April, 1780, Inclusive 568 (Charles J. Hoadly Ed., 1895) [Hereinafter 2 Hoadly] (reproducing the call); *id.* at 574 (reproducing the Rhode Island and Connecticut credentials to the Philadelphia convention, referring to the call at Hartford); *id.* at 575 (reproducing the New Jersey credentials to the Philadelphia convention, referring to the call at Hartford).

17. 1 J. Cont. Cong. 17–18 (Sept. 5, 1774) (quoting the credentials of the Connecticut delegates, empowering them to attend the "congress, or convention of commissioners, or committees of the several Colonies in British America").

18. On the York Town Convention, *see infra* note 28 and accompanying text.

19. For a summary of special purpose conventions, *see* Natelson, *Founding Era, supra* note 15; Caplan, *supra* note 4, at 17–21, 96. Caplan does not mention the Boston Convention, which is referenced at 17 J. Cont. Cong. 790 (Aug. 29, 1780) and 18 J. Cont. Cong. 790, at 932 (Oct. 16, 1780). The journals of the Providence, Springfield, New Haven, Hartford, Boston, and Philadelphia (1780) conventions are reproduced in 1 Hoadly, *supra* note 16, at 585–620; 2 Hoadly, *supra* note 16, at 562–79; and State of Connecticut, the Public Records of the State of Connecticut—From May, 1780, to October, 1781, Inclusive 559–76 (Charles J. Hoadly ed., 1922) [hereinafter 3 Hoadly]. The journal ("minutes") of the York Town convention are in State of New Jersey, Selections from the Correspondence of the Executive of New Jersey From 1776 to 1786, at 34–45 (1848) [hereinafter Selections].

The roster and recommendations of the Annapolis Convention are at http://avalon.law.yale.edu/18th_century/annapoli.asp.

20. On the meaning of "to advise" in this context as "to deliberate," *see* Robert G. Natelson, The Original Constitution 72–74 (2d ed. 2011).

21. 1 J. Cont. Cong. 17–18 (Sept. 5, 1774) (reproducing commission of Connecticut delegates). However, state credentials differed on whether delegates had the power to determine questions, *e.g., id.* at 15 (reproducing New Hampshire credentials empowering delegates "to devise, consult, and adopt"), or merely to propose solutions to the states, *e.g., id.* at 23 (reproducing Virginia credential empowering delegates only "to assemble . . . to consider").

22. 1 Hoadly, *supra* note 16, at 599.

23. 3 Hoadly, *supra* note 19, at 559–64.

24. 1 Hoadly, *supra* note 16, at 585–86.

25. Caplan, *supra* note 4, at 17; 7 J. Cont. Cong. 124–25 (Feb. 15, 1777) (reproducing the congressional recommendations).

26. Massachusetts, Connecticut, New Hampshire, and Rhode Island attended. Maine was then part of Massachusetts, and Vermont had not yet been admitted to the union.

27. *Cf.* Caplan, *supra* note 4, at 17 (asserting that it did not). Similarly, when Congress called the New Haven Convention for the eight northernmost states, it also recommended that Maryland, Virginia, and North Carolina convene in Fredericksburg and that South Caro-

lina and Georgia meet in Charleston, 9 J. Cont. Cong. 956–57 (Nov. 22, 1777), but I have found no evidence that the latter two gatherings ever occurred.

28. Selections, *supra* note 19, at 43–45. *See also* Byron W. Holt, *Continental Currency, in* 5 Sound Currency 81, 106–7 (Apr. 1, 1898) (discussing the York Town convention and other "price conventions"). The claim in 3 Richard Hildreth, A History of the United States of America 182 (1880) that the York Town convention arrived at a price-fixing agreement is inaccurate.

29. 1 Hoadly, *supra* note 16, at 607 (New Haven); 2 Hoadly, *supra* note 16, at 572 (Philadelphia).

30. 2 Hoadly, *supra* note 16, at 562.

31. 3 Hoadly, *supra* note 19, at 565 (commission of New Hampshire delegate).

32. *Id.* at 575–76.

33. This is reflected in the call to Philadelphia by the 1779 Hartford Convention, 2 Hoadly, *supra* note 16, at 568, and in all but one of the state commissions. *Id.* at 572–77 (reproducing commissions).

34. *E.g.*, 7 J. Cont. Cong. 124 (Feb. 15, 1777) (reproducing congressional call for York Town convention "to consider of, and form a system of regulation adapted to those States, to be laid before the respective legislatures of each State, for their approbation").

35. *Proceedings of Commissioners to Remedy Defects of the Federal Government* (Annapolis, Sept. 11, 1786), *available at* http://avalon.law.yale.edu/18th_century/annapoli.asp. Because only five states were present, the delegates voted not to proceed with their charge and suggested to Congress that it call a convention with a broader charge. *Cf.* John M. Harmon, Constitutional Convention: Limitation of Power to Propose Amendments to the Constitution, 3 Op. O. L. C. 390, 398 (1979) (pointing out that the Annapolis Convention was limited in nature).

36. Caplan, *supra* note 4, at 23. On this usage, *see also id.* at xx–xxi (explaining usage) and 20 (quoting Hamilton).

37. *See generally* Natelson, *Founding Era, supra* note 15. The recommendation of a day of prayer by the first Providence Convention, 1 Hoadly, *supra* note 16, at 598–99, would have been seen by the founding generation as within the call.

38. *See supra* note 35.

39. Natelson, *Proposing Constitutional Amendments, supra* note 3, at 718.

40. *Infra* notes 51–60.

41. 1 Farrand, *supra* note 2, at 22 (May 29, 1787). *See also id.* at 202–3 (June 11, 1787), paraphrasing George Mason in discussing a resolution "for amending the national Constitution hereafter without consent of Natl. Legislature":

> Amendments therefore will be necessary, and it will be better to provide for them, in an easy, regular and Constitutional way than to trust to chance and violence. It would be improper to require the consent of the Natl. Legislature, because they may abuse their power, and refuse their consent on that very account. The opportunity for such an abuse, may be the fault of the Constitution calling for amendment.

Mason was supported on this point by Edmund Randolph. *Id.*

42. 2 Farrand, *supra* note 2, at 188 (Aug. 6, 1787).

43. *Supra* note 10.

44. 2 Farrand, *supra* note 2, at 558 (Sept. 10, 1787) (paraphrasing Alexander Hamilton as stating, "The National Legislature will be the first to perceive and will be most sensible to the necessity of amendments.").

45. *Id.* at 557–58:

> Mr Gerry moved to reconsider art XIX. viz, "On the application of the Legislatures of two thirds of the States in the Union, for an amendment of this Constitution, the Legislature of the U. S. shall call a Convention for that purpose."
>
> This Constitution he said is to be paramount to the State Constitutions. It follows, hence, from this article that two thirds of the States may obtain a Convention, a majority of which can bind the Union to innovations that may subvert the State-Constitutions altogether. He asked whether this was a situation proper to be run into–.

46. 2 Farrand, *supra* note 2, at 629–30. *See also* Harmon, *supra* note 35, at 390, 398–401 (discussing this remark in wider context).

47. 2 Farrand, *supra note* 2, at 558–59:

> On the motion of Mr. Gerry to reconsider
>
> N. H. divd. Mas. ay– Ct. ay. N. J– no. Pa ay. Del. ay. Md. ay. Va. ay. N– C. ay. S. C. ay. Geo. ay. [Ayes– 9; noes– 1; divided– 1.]
>
> ****
>
> Mr. Sherman moved to add to the article "or the Legislature may propose amendments to the several States for their approbation, but no amendments shall be binding until consented to by the several States"
>
> Mr. Gerry 2ded. the motion
>
> Mr. Wilson moved to insert "two thirds of" before the words "several States"—on which amendment to the motion of Mr. Sherman
>
> N. H. ay. Mas. <no> Ct. no. N. J. <no> Pa. ay– Del– ay Md. ay. Va. ay. N. C. no. S. C. no. Geo. no. [Ayes– 5; noes– 6.]
>
> Mr. Wilson then moved to insert "three fourths of" before "the several Sts" which was agreed to nem: con:

48. *Id.* at 558 (Sept. 10, 1787) ("Mr Madison remarked on the vagueness of the terms, 'call a Convention for the purpose.' as sufficient reason for reconsidering the article. How was a Convention to be formed? by what rule decide? what the force of its acts?").

49. To my knowledge, Madison never raised even private objections to it after the convention, as he did to the Constitution's failure to, for example, include a federal veto of state laws. Madison's initial amendment proposal is recorded *id.* at 559:

> Mr. Madison moved to postpone the consideration of the amended proposition in order to take up the following,
>
> 'The Legislature of the U— S— whenever two thirds of both Houses shall deem necessary, or on the application of two thirds of the Legislatures of the several States, shall propose amendments to this Constitution, which shall be valid to all intents and purposes as part thereof, when the same shall have been ratified by three fourths at least of the Legislatures of the several States, or by Conventions in three fourths thereof, as one or the other mode of ratification may be proposed by the Legislature of the U. S.:'

50. *See* Natelson, *Proposing Constitutional Amendments, supra* note 3, at 706–8 (summarizing the historical record pertaining to Founding Era conventions).

51. *Id.* at 703–6 (explaining the application of then-prevailing rules fiduciary responsibility and incidental power).

52. Caplan, *supra* note 4, at 95–96 (citing Emer Vattel's then-popular work on international law).

53. *Supra* notes 20–32 and accompanying text.

54. *E.g.*, 2 Hoadly, *supra* note 16, at 578 (reproducing a resolution of the 1780 Philadelphia convention, referring to it as a "meeting of the several states"). After the Constitution was ratified, early state applications applied similar nomenclature to a convention for proposing amendments. *See* source cited *infra* note 66.

55. *E.g.*, 17 J. Cont. Cong. 790 (Aug. 29, 1780) (referring to the 1780 Boston Convention as a "convention of committees").

56. Caplan, *supra* note 4, at 95–96. *See also* The Federalist No. 40, at 199 (James Madison) (George W. Carey & James McClellan eds., 2001) ("The powers of the convention ought, in strictness, to be determined by an inspection of the commissions given to the members by their respective constituents.").

57. *E.g.*, 2 Hoadly, *supra* note 16, at 574 (reproducing Rhode Island's instructions to its delegates at the 1780 Philadelphia Convention, which dealt with price inflation).

58. Natelson, *Proposing Constitutional Amendments, supra* note 3, at 741. *See also* Selections, *supra* note 19, at 43–44 (recording votes by states at the York Town Convention).

59. Natelson, *Proposing Constitutional Amendments, supra* note 3, at 740. *See also* Selections, *supra* note 19, at 36 (recording that Lewis Burwell of Virginia served as chairman at the York Town Convention, and the convention's selection of a ways and means committee).

60. Natelson, *Proposing Constitutional Amendments, supra* note 3, at 744.

61. The Federalist No. 43, *supra* note 56, at 238–39 (James Madison).

62. The Federalist No. 46, *supra* note 56, at 253 (James Madison).

63. The Patient Protection and Affordable Health Care Act, Pub. L. 111-148, 124 Stat. 119 (2010).

64. *E.g.*, Natelson, *Proposing Constitutional Amendments, supra* note 3, at 699–700 n.21 (mentioning George Mason and Edmund Randolph); 23 The Documentary History of the Ratification of the Constitution 2522 (Merrill Jensen et al. eds., 1976), quoting Samuel Jones in the New York legislature as stating:

> The reason why there are two modes of obtaining amendments prescribed by the constitution I suppose to be this—it could not be known to the framers of the constitution, whether there was too much power given by it or too little; they therefore prescribed a mode by which Congress might procure more, if in the operation of the government it was found necessary; and they prescribed for the states a mode of restraining the powers of the government, if upon trial it should be found they had given too much.

65. Ratification of the Constitution by the State of New York (July 26, 1788), *available at* http://avalon.law.yale.edu/18th_century/ratny.asp (listing amendments and calling for a new convention).

66. *See* Caplan, *supra* note 4, at 165–68 (reproducing Virginia and New York applications).

67. Letter from Madison to George Eve (Jan. 2, 1789), *in* The Founders' Constitution (Philip B. Kurland & Ralph Lerner eds., 1987), *available at* http://press-pubs.uchicago.edu/founders/documents/v1ch14s48.html; letter from Madison to Thomas Mann Randolph (Jan. 27, 1789), *in* 2 Documentary History of the First Federal Elections 338, 340 (Gordon DenBoer ed., 1989).

68. James Madison, Letter from Madison to Edmund Pendleton (Oct. 20, 1788), *in* 5 The Writings Of James Madison 277 (Galliard Hunt ed., 1900) [hereinafter, Madison, Writings] ("In the mean time the other mode of amendments may safely be employed to quiet the fears of many by supplying those further guards for private rights which can do no harm to the system in the judgment even of its most partial friends, and will even be approved by others who have steadily supported it."); letter from Madison to George Eve (Jan. 2, 1789), *in* Founders' Constitution, *supra* note 67 ("Under this change of circumstances, it is my sincere opinion that the Constitution ought to be revised, and that the first Congress meeting under it, ought to prepare and recommend to the States for ratification, the most satisfactory provisions for all essential rights.").

69. *E.g.*, letter from Madison to Philip Mazzei (Dec. 10, 1788), *in* 5 Madison, Writings, *supra* note 68, at 316 ("All the States except North Carolina and Rhode Island have ratified the proposed Constitution. Seven of them have appointed their Senators, of whom those of Virginia, R. H. Lee and Col. Grayson, alone are among the opponents of the system."); letter from Madison to Jefferson (Dec. 8, 1788), *in* 5 Madison, Writings, *supra* note 68, at 310 ("Here is already a majority of the ratifying States on the side of the Constitution.").

70. Letter from Madison to Thomas Jefferson (Aug. 23, 1788), *in* 5 Madison, Writings, *supra* note 68, at 254 ("The object with them now will be to effect an early Convention composed of men who will essentially mutilate the system."); letter from Madison to Jefferson (Dec. 8, 1788), *in* 5 Madison, Writings, *supra* note 68, at 195, 196 ("Those who have opposed the Constitution, are on the other hand, zealous for a second Convention, and for a revisal which may either not be restrained at all, or extend at least as far as alterations have been proposed by any State.").

71. Letter from Madison to George Lee Turberville (Nov. 2, 1788), *in* 5 Madison, Writings, *supra* note 68, at 298–300; letter from Madison to George Eve (Jan. 2, 1789), *in* Founders' Constitution, *supra* note 67; letter from Madison to Thomas Mann Randolph (Jan. 27, 1789), *in* 2 Documentary History of the First Federal Elections 338, 339 (Gordon DenBoer ed., 1989).

72. Letter from Madison to George Lee Turberville (Nov. 2, 1788), *in* 5 Madison, Writings, *supra* note 68, at 300–301.

73. Letter from Madison to Edmund Pendleton (Oct. 20, 1788), *in* 5 Madison, Writings, *supra* note 68, at 278 ("An early Convention . . . will comprehend men having insidious designs agst the Union."); letter from Madison to Philip Mazzei (Dec. 10, 1788), *in* 5 Madison, Writings, *supra* note 68, at 316 ("The object of the Anti-Federalists is to bring about another general Convention, which would either agree on nothing, as would be agreeable to some, and throw everything into confusion, or expunge from the Constitution parts which are held by its friends to be essential to it.").

74. Letter from Madison to Thomas Jefferson (Aug. 23, 1788), *in* 5 Madison, Writings, *supra* note 68, at 254 ("in the present temper of America"); letter from Madison to Thomas Jefferson (Aug. 10, 1788), *in* 5 Madison, Writings, *supra* note 68, at 244 ("The great danger in

the present crisis is that if another Convention should be soon assembled it would terminate in discord, or in alterations of the federal system which would throw back *essential* powers into the State Legislatures.). *See also* letter from Madison to George Lee Turberville (Nov. 2, 1788), *in* 5 Madison, Writings, *supra* note 68, at 298; letter from Madison to George Eve (Jan. 2, 1789), *in* Founders' Constitution, *supra* note 67 ("in the present ferment of parties, and containing perhaps insidious characters from different parts of America"); letter from Madison to Thomas Mann Randolph (Jan. 27, 1789), *in* 2 Documentary History of the First Federal Elections 338, 340 (Gordon DenBoer ed., 1989) ("in the present foment of parties").

75. Letter from Madison to George Lee Turberville (Nov. 2, 1788), *in* 5 Madison, Writings, *supra* note 68, at 299 ("A Convention cannot be called without the unanimous consent of the parties who are to be bound by it, if first principles are to be recurred to; or without the previous application of... the State legislatures, if the forms of the Constitution are to be pursued."). *Cf.* letter from Madison to Philip Mazzei (Dec. 10, 1788), *in* 5 Madison, Writings, *supra* note 68, at 316 ("The [Federalists] are willing to gratify their opponents with every supplemental provision for general rights, but insist that this can be better done in the mode provided for amendments.").

76. *See, e.g.*, Larry Greenley, *States Should Enforce, Not Revise, the Constitution!*, New American (Nov. 29, 2010), http://www.thenewamerican.com/index.php/usnews/constitution/5299-states-should-enforce-not-revise-the-constitution (John Birch Society webpage) (referring to a letter from Madison to George Lee Turberville (Nov. 2, 1788), *in* 5 Madison, Writings, *supra* note 68, at 297).

77. Letter from Madison to George Lee Turberville (Nov. 2, 1788), *in* 5 Madison, Writings, *supra* note 68, at 298 ("You wish to know my sentiments on the project of another general Convention as suggested by New York.").

78. *E.g.*, Letter from Madison to Thomas Jefferson (Aug. 23, 1788), *in* 5 Madison, Writings, *supra* note 68, at 254 (suggesting a delay of a year); letter from Madison to Thomas Jefferson (Aug. 10, 1788), *in* 5 Madison, Writings, *supra* note 68, at 244 ("The delay of a few years will assuage the jealousies which have been artificially created by designing men and will at the same time point out the faults which really call for amendment."); letter from Madison to Edmund Pendleton (Oct. 20, 1788), *in* 5 Madison, Writings, *supra* note 68, at 278 (opposing a "premature Convention").

79. 6 Madison, Writings, *supra* note 68, at 178–79, *available at* http://www.constitution.org/cons/virg1798.htm.

80. *Id.* at 179.

81. *The Kentucky Resolutions of 1798, available at* http://www.constitution.org/cons/kent1798.htm ("[W]here powers are assumed which have not been delegated, a nullification of the act is the rightful remedy.").

82. The counterresolutions are available at http://www.constitution.org/rf/vr_04.htm.

83. *Id.* (emphasis added).

84. 6 Madison, Writings, *supra* note 68, at 403.

85. *Id.* at 404.

86. *Virginia Resolution, in* 6 Madison, Writings, *supra* note 68, at 326 ("[T]he states... have the right, and are in duty bound, to interpose for arresting the progress of the evil, and for

maintaining within their respective limits, the authorities, rights and liberties appertaining to them.").

87. 9 Madison, Writings, *supra* note 68, at 383–403 (Aug. 28, 1830).

88. *Id.* at 395–96.

89. *Supra* note 62 and accompanying text.

90. Letter from Thomas Jefferson to Spencer Roane (June 27, 1821), *in* 10 The Writings of Thomas Jefferson 190 (Paul Leister Ford ed., 1904–5); *see also* 12 The Writings of Thomas Jefferson 314 (Paul Leister Ford ed., 1905) ("But, finally, the peculiar happiness of our blessed system is, that in differences of opinion between these different [state and federal] sets of servants, the appeal is to neither, but to their employers peaceably assembled by their representatives in Convention.").

91. 9 Madison, Writings, *supra* note 68, at 398.

92. *Id.*:

> And in the event of a failure of every constitutional resort, and an accumulation of usurpations & abuses, rendering passive obedience & non-resistence a greater evil, than resistence & revolution, there can remain but one resort, the last of all, an appeal from the cancelled obligations of the constitutional compact, to original rights & the law of self-preservation. This is the ultima ratio under all Govt. whether consolidated, confederated, or a compound of both....

Cf. James Madison, *Notes on Nullification, in* 9 Madison, Writings, *supra* note 68, at 597 (1835):

> The plain answer is that the remedy is the same under the government of the United States as under all other Govts. established & organized on free principles. The first remedy is in the checks provided among the constituted authorities; that failing the next is in the influence of the Ballot-boxes & Hustings; that again failing, the appeal lies to the power that made the Constitution, and can explain, amend, or remake it. Should this resort also fail, and the power usurped be sustained in its oppressive exercise on a minority by a majority, the final course to be pursued by the minority, must be a subject of calculation, in which the degree of oppression, the means of resistance, the consequences of its failure, and consequences of its success must be the elements.

II

Antebellum Arguments

3 States' Rights, Southern Hypocrisy, and the Crisis of the Union

Paul Finkelman, Albany Law School

December 20, 2010, marked—one cannot say celebrated—the sesquicentennial of South Carolina's secession. By the end of February 1861, six other states had followed South Carolina into the Confederacy. Most scholars fully understand that slavery was at the root of secession and the war that followed. As Abraham Lincoln noted in his second inaugural in 1865, "One-eighth of the whole population were colored slaves, not distributed generally over the Union, but localized in the southern part of it. These slaves constituted a peculiar and powerful interest. All knew that this interest was somehow the cause of the war."[1]

What Lincoln admitted in 1865, Confederate leaders had asserted much earlier. After secession but before the Civil War broke out, Alexander H. Stephens, the Confederate vice president and one of the two most perceptive and brightest men in the Confederate government,[2] forcefully set out the reasons for secession in his famous "Cornerstone Speech." Here, Stephens tied slavery to race, making clear that the cornerstone of the Confederacy was not merely chattel slavery, but the total subordination of black people for the benefit of white people. In this sense, the Confederacy was the political grandparent of Nazi Germany and apartheid-era South Africa—regimes founded on the assumption of the racial and ethnic superiority of the ruling class and the utter inferiority and subordination of other races and groups. Thus Stephens declared, "Our new government is founded upon . . . its foundations are laid, its corner-stone rests, upon the great truth that the negro is not equal to the white man; that slavery—subordination to the superior race—is his natural and normal condition."[3]

Stephens denounced the Northern claims (which he incorrectly attributed to Thomas Jefferson) that the "enslavement of the African was in violation of the laws of nature; that it was wrong in *principle*, socially, morally, and politically."[4] He unabashedly asserted: "Our new government is founded upon exactly the opposite idea."[5] Stephens argued that it was "insanity" to believe "that the negro is equal" or that slavery was wrong.[6] He proudly predicted that the Confederate Constitution "has put at rest, *forever*, all the agitating questions relating to our peculiar institution—African slavery as it exists amongst us—the proper *status* of the negro in our form of civilization."[7]

Stephens echoed South Carolina's declaration, explaining that it was leaving the Union because

> A geographical line has been drawn across the Union, and all the States north of that line have united in the election of a man to the high office of President of the United States, whose opinions and purposes are hostile to slavery. He is to be entrusted with the administration of the common Government, because he has declared that that "Government cannot endure permanently half slave, half free," and that the public mind must rest in the belief that slavery is in the course of ultimate extinction.[8]

In other words, South Carolina was leaving the Union because Lincoln believed slavery was wrong and should one day—in the far distant future—be ended.

Shortly after South Carolina left the Union, Georgia did the same. Beginning with the second sentence of its Declaration of Secession, Georgia made it clear that slavery was the force behind secession:

> For the last ten years we have had numerous and serious causes of complaint against our non-slave-holding confederate States with reference to the subject of African slavery. They have endeavored to weaken our security, to disturb our domestic peace and tranquility, and persistently refused to comply with their express constitutional obligations to us in reference to that property, and by the use of their power in the Federal Government have striven to deprive us of an equal enjoyment of the common Territories of the Republic. This hostile policy of our confederates has been pursued with every circumstance of aggravation which could arouse the passions and excite the hatred of our people, and has placed the two sections of the Union for many years past in the condition of virtual civil war.[9]

Mississippi emphatically made the same point, starting with the second sentence of its own declaration: "Our position is thoroughly identified with the institution of slavery—the greatest material interest of the world."[10]

Despite the almost universal understanding of serious scholars that slavery and racial subordination were at the root of secession and the Civil War—and the almost endless statements of Confederate leaders supporting this analysis—a considerable number of Americans cling to the belief that secession was about 'states' rights' and that Southerners left the Union to escape a tyrannical national government that was trampling on their rights. Advocates of this old-fashioned, and simultaneously modern, neo-Confederate ideology rarely discuss the substance of Southern states' rights claims, because they will either lead to an intellectual dead end or lead back to slavery.

The relationship of secession to states' rights is often misunderstood, especially by those who argue that the slave states left the Union to protect their states' rights. The Southern states did not leave the Union because the national government was trampling on their rights. The states that left the Union never asserted that they were being denied their states' rights—that the national government had obliterated the lines between national power and state power. Nor did the Southern states complain that the national government was too powerful and that it threatened the sovereignty of the state governments. On the contrary, the Southern states mostly complained that the Northern states were asserting *their* states' rights and that the national government was not powerful enough to counter these Northern claims. Similarly, the secessionists did not complain that an oppressive national government was infringing on the civil liberties of Southern citizens; rather the complaint was that the national government refused to suppress the civil liberties of Northern citizens.

Under federal law and policy in 1860, the Southern states should have had few complaints. Since 1850, they had won almost every debate in Congress, and almost every federal law dealing with slavery had benefited the South. A series of Supreme Court decisions on slave transit,[11] black citizenship,[12] the right of masters to take slaves into the territories,[13] and the constitutionality of the Fugitive Slave Law of 1850[14] had all favored the South. Significantly, two of these decisions were unanimous, even though throughout the period four of the nine justices were Northerners. Two of the Northerners dissented in *Dred Scott v. Sandford*, the Court's most proslavery decision of the decade.[15] But, by 1860, one of these dissenters, Benjamin R. Curtis, had left the Court and been replaced by an adamantly proslavery Northern Democrat, Nathan Clifford.

I. THE 1850S: THE HIGH POINT OF PROSLAVERY NATIONALISM

The 1850s was a remarkable decade for supporters of slavery. In three areas of law—involving the territories, the recovery of fugitive slaves, and the right to travel with slaves—all three branches of the national government expanded the rights of slave owners. At the same time, in two other areas of law, the national government dramatically restricted the rights of free blacks.

By the end of the decade, slavery was legal in all the federal territories, the federal government was vigorously enforcing a draconian fugitive slave law that enabled hundreds of masters to recover their runaways, and the Supreme Court had expanded the right of masters to travel in the free states with their slaves. Furthermore, the Court hinted that it would guarantee masters even greater rights of transit, when given the opportunity to do so.[16] Congress prohibited blacks from testifying on their own behalf at a fugitive slave hearing, suspended the writ of habeas corpus for alleged fugitives throughout the nation to remand them to slave catchers, and provided harsh punishments for anyone interfering with the return of a fugitive slave. Meanwhile, the Supreme Court ruled that blacks, even if free, and even if accorded equal rights of citizenship in their own states, would never be considered citizens of the United States and in effect had no rights under the Constitution. At the same that it denied any constitutional rights to free blacks, the Court held that slavery was a specially protected institution under the Constitution. Under the Court's reasoning, Congress could and should protect slavery property in the territories but could never restrict it.

A. *Restrictions and Limitations on Slavery in 1850*

In 1850, Southerners could not have imagined they would be so successful in securing federal support for slavery over the next ten years. At the beginning of the decade, slave owners were closed out of virtually all the existing federal territories. The United States had acquired vast amounts of land from Mexico, but the area was closed to slavery. During the Mexican War, the House of Representatives had passed the Wilmot Proviso, banning slavery from the new territories. The proviso never made it through the Senate, where the South had a majority from early 1845 until mid-1848.[17] But even after the North gained parity in the Senate, it was impossible to pass any law organizing the new territories. Thus, the new territories remained unorganized with no functioning government. Meanwhile, thousands of people were pouring into California after gold was discovered there. With no territorial government, there were no laws allowing slavery, and the only existing law was that of Mexico, which prohibited slavery. Thus, slave owners felt cut out of the gold rush and unable to move into what would later become Arizona, New Mexico, Utah, Nevada, and much of Colorado.

Slavery was also officially excluded in all of the land left over from the Louisiana Purchase except the Indian Territory, but white slave owners had little opportunity to move there. Nor was slavery allowed in the Oregon country—the present-day states of Oregon, Washington, and part of Idaho. Southerners believed they should be entitled to settle the new lands acquired from Mexico, especially because a disproportionate number of Southerners had fought in the Mexican War. Indeed, the two heroes of the Mexican War were Zachary Taylor, a Kentuckian by birth who owned sugar plantations and many slaves in Louisiana,[18] and Winfield Scott, who was a slave owner from Virginia.[19] Many Southerners also believed that the Compromise of 1820, which banned slavery north of the southern boundary of Missouri, unconstitutionally deprived them of a right to settle land owned by all Americans.[20]

In 1850, masters had a constitutional right to recover slaves wherever they could find them. The Fugitive Slave Law of 1793 authorized federal judges and state and local magistrates at any level to hear fugitive slave cases and remand runaways to those who claimed them.[21] In *Prigg v. Pennsylvania*,[22] the Supreme Court gave masters a right of recaption to seize fugitive slaves wherever they found them and peacefully take them South without any judicial superintendence.[23] However, this right was mostly impossible to assert in the taking of slaves that had traveled far into the North. To recover slaves who were more than a day's ride from the South, masters needed the help of law enforcement officers. But after *Prigg*, most Northern states passed laws closing their jails and courtrooms to slave catchers and prohibiting states officials from helping recover runaway slaves.[24] Illustrative of this state activity was the 'Latimer Law' of Massachusetts, which prohibited any state judge from hearing a case under the Fugitive Slave Law of 1793 or any sheriff or other official from arresting a fugitive slave.[25] Any state or local official violating this law could be fined and imprisoned.[26] Thus, while Southerners had a *right* to recover runaway slaves anywhere in the nation, they lacked the ability to easily do so. Without federal enforcement, Southerners seeking runaways would be frustrated by Northern states' rights.

By 1850, most of the free states had adopted the principle that no one could be held as a slave without positive law.[27] This principle was first articulated by Chief Justice Lord Mansfield in *Somerset v. Stewart*,[28] a case decided in Britain before the American Revolution and thus part of the common law at the time of independence. Under the *Somerset* principle, masters could not travel with their slaves through most of the North without the risk of losing them. During and after the Revolution, some of the Northern states had made accommodations for visiting masters. Pennsylvania granted them a right of transit of up to six months,[29] and New York gave them nine months.[30] But in 1841, New York repealed its law,[31] and Pennsylvania did the same in 1847.[32] Thus, by 1850, Southern masters felt deprived of their right to travel throughout the nation with their slaves. Similarly, under the Missouri Compromise, they were prohibited from taking their slaves into most of the western territories, even for a visit.[33]

Thus, as the 1850s began, slave owners had reason to complain about the legal structure of the nation. In their own states, slave owners were secure. Despite annoying denunciations of slavery by abolitionists and antislavery senators and congressmen, the national government had no constitutional power to interfere with slavery in the existing states. The states' rights of the Southern states were secure. But Southerners felt their federal constitutional rights were at risk when they entered the free states because those states emancipated any slaves voluntarily brought within their jurisdiction.[34] Thus, Southerners felt that the Northern states were denying them the right to travel with their constitutionally sanctioned property. Similarly, if their slaves ran away to the free states, those states were refusing to fulfill their constitutional obligations by cooperating in the return of fugitive slaves.

B. *The Great Proslavery Shift of the 1850s*

In the 1850s, supporters of slavery won huge victories in Congress, which legalized slavery throughout the West. Congress further protected the rights of masters to recover fugitive slaves with a new and powerfully nationalistic fugitive slave law. Added to this were Supreme Court decisions that made slavery a specially protected institution under the Constitution, allowed slavery in all the federal territories, concluded that free blacks had virtually no rights under the Constitution and could never be considered citizens of the United States, and undermined the right of free states to emancipate visiting slaves.

1. *THE COMPROMISE OF 1850*

In January 1850, Senator Henry Clay of Kentucky introduced a series of resolutions to settle the issues pending before the nation.[35] Clay's resolutions, and his Omnibus Bill that followed, overwhelmingly favored the South. Clay's Omnibus Bill ultimately collapsed but was revived in a series of separate laws known as the Compromise of 1850.[36] The compromise organized the new territories without any ban on slavery, thus opening more than 400,000 square miles to masters and their bondsmen and bondswomen. This eviscerated the Missouri Compromise, which Clay himself had crafted in 1820, by allowing slavery north of the 36° 30' parallel.[37] Much of the Mexican Cession—what became Utah and Nevada and parts of Colorado and Wyoming—was north of the Missouri Compromise line. In addition, the compromise gave Texas tens of thousands of acres of land and ten million dollars so that the government in Austin could pay off its prestatehood debts.[38]

In return for these sweeping concessions to slavery in the West, the compromise brought California into the Union as a free state. This was hardly a concession to the free states, however, because by the time Congress passed the California bill there were nearly 100,000 free people there and, at most, a few hundred slaves.[39] California was destined to be a free state, and even Southern nationalists knew it. This gave the free states a two-vote majority in the Senate, but there was no reason to believe that this would be permanent. The rest of the Mexican Cession was large enough to accommodate five or six or even more new slave states.[40]

The compromise also dealt with two nonterritorial issues involving slavery. The new Fugitive Slave Law of 1850 was one of the most repressive and unfair federal laws in our history.[41] The law provided for the appointment of federal commissioners in every county who, along with federal judges, were to "hear and determine the case" in "a summary manner" without a jury.[42] Under this law, the slave owner or his agent had only to present "satisfactory proof" that the person claimed was a fugitive slave.[43] This could be done by "deposition or affidavit" certified "in writing" before any judge or magistrate in the home state of the slave owner.[44] The potential for fraud, or even mistaken identity, was huge. The claimant could bring any black who fit the description in the "deposition or affidavit" before a judge and demand the right to remove the person as a fugitive slave.[45]

Alleged fugitives were prohibited from testifying at their own hearings, even to explain that the wrong person had been seized.[46] The law also prohibited any judge—state or federal—from issuing a writ of habeas corpus for an alleged slave. This was the first time Congress had ever suspended the writ of habeas corpus—and it was done in clear violation of the procedures set out in the U.S. Constitution.[47] The habeas provision of the Constitution envisioned a suspension for an immediate emergency caused by an invasion or rebellion. But in 1850, Congress indefinitely suspended the Great Writ throughout the whole country even though there was no immediate crisis.

Under the law, anyone aiding a fugitive slave or interfering with the rendition process was subject to a $1,000 fine plus court costs, six months in jail, and civil damages of $1,000 to be paid to the slave owner for each slave who was not recovered.[48] If the law was literally enforced, a Northerner could be fined, jailed, or sued merely for giving a black person walking down the road a piece of bread or a cup of water or for allowing the black traveler to sleep in his barn, because such an act of charity could be construed as helping a fugitive escape. Hiring a black who turned out to be a fugitive came with enormous potential costs. In an age when there were no meaningful forms of identification, and thus no way to know if a black was free or a fugitive, the law effectively encouraged Northerners—even free black Northerners—to refuse to hire blacks because they might turn out to be fugitive slaves. The harsh penalties and the minimal standards of proof could force Northern whites to assume that all blacks they saw were fugitives, even though in 1850 there were more than 150,000 free blacks living in the North.[49] From the perspective of blacks and many white Northerners, the act of 1850 had brought the law of slavery into the free states and required Northerners to do the bidding of Southerners.

The statute created, for the first time, a national system of law enforcement through the appointment of one or more federal commissioners in every county in the nation. The act of 1850 authorized the commissioners to hear fugitive slave cases and summon sufficient force to secure the return of runaways. Federal marshals and commissioners were empowered to call on the militia or the army or to create a posse to enforce the law. The statute gratuitously declared that "all good citizens are hereby commanded to aid and assist in the prompt and efficient execution of this law," although there was no clear remedy if citizens refused.[50] If these measures failed, however, and marshals were unable to prevent a rescue, they could be held personally liable for the value of any slave who escaped their custody. No other federal law had ever provided such penalties for officers who were unable to implement a law.

Someone could be dragged South as a slave without even being permitted to offer his or her own voice as evidence that he or she was free. The outrageousness of the prohibition on testimony was matched by the provision for paying the commissioners and judges who heard these cases. If a judge ruled in favor of the alleged slave, thus setting him or her free, the judge was entitled to a five-dollar fee.[51] If the judge ruled for the master, he got a ten-dollar fee.[52] Most Northerners viewed this as a blatant attempt to bribe the courts.[53]

The Fugitive Slave Law was an utterly one-sided statute that threatened the liberty of every black in the North, while also jeopardizing their white friends, neighbors, and employers. The 'compromise' offered in return for passage of this law was a ban on the public sale of slaves in the District of Columbia. This ban would not harm slave owners or the system of slavery but merely would end the embarrassment of having slaves marched through the national capital in chains or publicly auctioned off in the shadow of the White House and the Capitol.[54] Northerners (and even a few Southerners) were deeply offended by this. But Southerners understood that the ban was merely symbolic because slave owners in the district could easily take their slaves to Virginia for sale.[55] They could also privately sell their slaves. Southern opposition to ending the trade in the district was not based on the fear that it would actually harm the system of slavery—because it clearly would not—but as a matter of proslavery principle. Ending the slave trade in the district would be an admission that buying and selling slaves was morally wrong—which extreme Southern nationalists would not admit and did not believe.

At the same time, shrewd Southerners may have understood the ban on the trade in the national capital would actually benefit them. The ban virtually ended the demands of Northern Congressmen for the abolition of slavery in the District of Columbia. Thus, what was sold to the Northerners as a victory was strategically valuable to the South.

In sum, the Compromise of 1850 was a boon to the South. It opened up vast amounts of land to slavery, much of it north of the Missouri Compromise line. This territory would eventually accommodate four full states and parts of three others, but it might easily have been used to create six or seven new slave states. It transferred ten million dollars from the national government to the state of Texas, the largest transfer of money from the national government to a state since the nation had begun. The new fugitive slave law committed the national government to spending huge sums of money, created a new level of court officers, and vastly expanded the reach and power of the national government, just to accommodate slave owners. The law also trampled on states' rights, reaffirming the Supreme Court's holding in *Prigg* that the Northern states had no right to protect the liberty of their black residents and citizens, even those who were born free. The law provided no penalties for Southerners who purposefully kidnapped or mistakenly seized free blacks but provided harsh penalties for Northerners who tried to prevent the removal of their neighbors, friends, and relatives, even if they believed they were free. The law trampled on the rights of the free states by sending federal commissioners, marshals, and troops into Northern communities to round up blacks.

In return for these huge concessions, Congress banned the public slave trade in the District of Columbia, and the North gained California as a free state. But this result was hardly a concession to the North, because everyone understood that Californians wanted their home to enter the Union as a free state. Even Robert Toombs of Georgia did "not consider the admission of California an aggression on the South" because he acknowledged that the new state's residents were overwhelmingly opposed to slavery.[56] More significantly, Congress and President Millard Fillmore refused to consider a proposed constitution from citizens of New Mexico, which would also have led to that territory's entry as a free state.[57]

2. *THE KANSAS-NEBRASKA ACT*

Four years after the Compromise of 1850—which from a Northern perspective might better be called the Appeasement of 1850[58]—the South made new and spectacular gains in the Kansas-Nebraska Act.[59] This law provided for the organization of territorial governments in most of the remaining western lands, which included all or part of the present-day states of Nebraska, Kansas, South Dakota, North Dakota, Montana, Wyoming, Colorado, and Idaho. In 1820, Congress had banned slavery in all of this territory as part of the Missouri Compromise. Extreme proslavery Southerners had long argued that the Missouri Compromise was unconstitutional because Congress could not deprive them of the right to enter a federal territory with their property. This argument had little resonance in the North or among moderate Southerners, who accepted the power of Congress to regulate the territories. Furthermore, if Congress could prohibit slavery in some territories, it could specifically allow slavery and protect it in other territories. In the Florida Territory, for example, federal and territorial authorities prosecuted the ship captain Jonathan Walker when he tried to help a boatload of slaves escape to the British West Indies, where they would have been free.[60] After his conviction, Walker was branded on his hand with the letters S.S., for "slave stealer."[61] Such support for slavery in some of the territories was seen, at least by moderate Southerners, as a reasonable trade-off for banning slavery in other territories.

After the Mexican War, a number of moderate Southerners seemed willing to simply extend the Missouri Compromise line through the new territories; Southern extremists opposed this, however, and they were joined by two Northern doughface leaders. After Henry Clay's Omnibus Bill collapsed, Senator Stephen A. Douglas of Illinois picked up the pieces of Clay's proposal and guided them through Congress one bill at a time.[62] Thus, Douglas willingly opened all the new territories to slavery, pleasing his Southern friends and allies in the

Democratic Party and positioning himself to run for president in 1856. Millard Fillmore, the Whig accidental president, eagerly signed the compromise bills while refusing to submit to Congress a constitution for the territory of New Mexico—written by a democratically elected convention in the territory—because it would have created a free state of New Mexico.[63] Both men assumed their relentless support of slavery in the compromise package would strengthen their presidential ambitions. Fillmore was unable to win the Whig nomination in 1852, but Douglas, who was only thirty-nine years old, was still building his career with the presidency as his ultimate goal.

Douglas furthered his presidential ambitions in 1854 by sponsoring the Kansas-Nebraska Act. This law provided for the creation of territorial governments in what would become most of the Great Plains states. The Missouri Compromise of 1820 had banned slavery in all of this area, but Douglas's bill would allow slavery in all of the area. Douglas said that the issue of slavery would be determined by "popular sovereignty," inviting proslavery and antislavery settlers to move there.[64] The result was not a peaceful referendum on slavery, but a mini-Civil War known as Bleeding Kansas.[65] Aggressive supporters of slavery, aided by the administrations of Franklin Pierce and James Buchanan, created a proslavery government in the territory, even though a clear majority of the settlers were Northerners who opposed slavery.[66] Eventually, Buchanan pushed for the admission of Kansas as a slave state based on the Lecompton Constitution, which was written by a fraudulently elected convention and ratified in an equally suspect referendum.[67]

In 1858, Douglas broke with Buchanan over Lecompton, but not because it would lead to a slave state in Kansas. Douglas famously declared that he did not care whether slavery was voted "up or down."[68] Douglas objected to the Lecompton Constitution because it was written and ratified by a patently fraudulent process, and everyone in the United States knew it. But on the main principle—popular sovereignty—Douglas, Buchanan, and almost every other Democratic leader agreed that slavery was an issue for the settlers of the territories, not the Congress or the president. It should be remembered that throughout this period, Democrats controlled the Senate, and had there been no secession, the Democrats would have been able to block Lincoln at every turn. Furthermore, the three-state majority[69] that Northerners held in the Senate in 1860—the votes of six senators—was fragile and hardly dominant. A solid South could always find a few Northern senators—the four they would need—to outvote the North on significant sectional issues.

Whatever the outcome of Kansas settlement, it is hard to see how Southerners could complain about the process. Fillmore and Douglas in 1850 and Pierce and Douglas in 1854 had opened up almost all the territories to slavery. That Southerners were unable to win the vote in Kansas was simply a result of more Northerners than Southerners settling in a territory that was fairly far north. But that did not mean they might not win the settlement race in other territories. Most important, opening all the territories to slavery in 1850 and 1854, along with the Fugitive Slave Law of 1850, reflected a Congress more than willing to support the South. Whatever else Southerners had to grumble about, they could not legitimately complain that Congress had harmed their states' rights, or slavery, in the previous decade.

3. The Supreme Court and Slavery in the 1850s

The Supreme Court heard a number of cases involving slavery in the late 1840s and 1850s. With one minor exception,[70] slave owners won every one of these cases, and the Court overwhelmingly supported the power of Congress to assist them in recovering fugitive slaves. In *Jones v. Van Zandt*,[71] a unanimous Court held that Northerners could be held liable for the fugitive slaves they aided, even if they did not have any notice that the person they helped was a fugitive. In this case, Van Zandt, an Ohio farmer, had given a ride to a group of blacks walking along a road outside of Cincinnati.[72] He was subsequently sued by the owner, Jones, for the cost of recovering them and the value of one who was never recovered.[73] Van Zandt argued there was a presumption of freedom for everyone in Ohio, and thus he could not know that the people he gave the ride to were fugitive slaves.[74] The Court rejected this argument, essentially applying the law of the South—that all blacks were presumptively slaves—to the free states.[75] The opinion was written by Justice Levi Woodbury of New Hampshire, and even the antislavery Justice John McLean of Ohio accepted the result.

In *Strader* v. *Graham*,[76] the Court considered for the first time the thorny problem of slave transit into free states. The Constitution allowed for the recovery of fugitive slaves but said nothing about the right to voluntarily take a slave to a free state. *Strader* involved three slave musicians who, with the permission of their master (Graham), had traveled on a number of occasions from Kentucky to Ohio and Indiana to perform.[77] After a number of such trips, they boarded Strader's steamboat without Graham's permission and escaped.[78] Graham won a judgment in the Kentucky courts because Strader had allowed the slaves on his ship without their master's written permission, in violation of Kentucky law.[79] On appeal, Strader argued that the slaves had become free under the Northwest Ordinance and the laws of Ohio and Indiana when Graham had previously allowed them to go to those free jurisdictions.[80] This argument was based on a legal theory, first developed in *Somerset v. Stewart*[81] by Lord Chief Justice Mansfield, that a slave became free when taken to a free jurisdiction because there was no positive law creating slavery—and once free, the former slave was always free. By 1850, almost every Northern state had adopted this rule, as had a many Southern states.[82] But by this time, a number of slave state jurists and politicians had begun to question the propriety of following this rule when slaves returned from visits to free states.

In *Strader*, the Court faced the problem indirectly. The Kentucky courts had ruled that the status of Graham's slaves was not at issue, and whether they were entitled to their freedom by previous trips to the North could be determined only if they appeared before the state courts.[83] But until they appeared in a Kentucky court, they were presumptively slaves. Therefore, Strader had violated Kentucky law by allowing Graham's slaves on his ship, and he was liable to Graham for their value.[84] The U.S. Supreme Court ruled that it must defer to the state of Kentucky on this matter and upheld the judgment against Graham.[85] Under this rule, the slave states were free to decide for themselves who was a slave and who was not. In other words, the Court gave the slave states sanction to ignore free state law, and perhaps federal law, in determining who was a slave and who was not. The decision implied that the slave states could ignore the Full Faith and Credit provision of Article 4 of the Constitution, just as Kentucky had ignored the constitutions of Indiana and Ohio. The true proslavery implications of this case would become apparent in *Dred Scott v. Sandford*, six years later.

A year after *Strader*, the Court clarified an aspect of the jurisprudence of fugitive slaves in *Moore v. Illinois*.[86] In *Prigg*,[87] the Court had struck down all state personal liberty laws. In that case, Justice Joseph Story had declared that no state could add to the requirements for the return of fugitive slaves and that all personal liberty laws providing due process for alleged fugitives were therefore unconstitutional.[88] Despite this huge victory for slavery, in a concurring opinion Chief Justice Roger B. Taney complained that the decision would also prevent the free states from helping in the return of fugitive slaves.[89] But in *Moore*, the Court upheld an Illinois statute that punished Illinois citizens for harboring fugitive slaves.[90] This was one more victory for slavery.

Five years later, the Court decided *Dred Scott v. Sandford*,[91] the most notoriously proslavery decision in the nation's jurisprudence. The outcome of the case—that Scott remained a slave—was plausibly correct on the basis of *Strader v. Graham*, if nothing else.[92] Scott claimed his freedom because he had lived in the free state of Illinois and in the Wisconsin Territory, where slavery was banned by the Compromise of 1820 and various other federal laws.[93] The Court initially planned to decide the case on the basis of *Strader*, and had it done so, the case would probably be long forgotten. But the Southerners on the Court insisted on a more comprehensive result, which led to Taney's massive and extraordinarily proslavery opinion.[94] Writing for the Court, Taney held that (1) slavery was a specially protected property under the Constitution; (2) free blacks could never be considered citizens of the United States and essentially had "no rights" under the Constitution; (3) that Congress had no power to ban slavery in the federal territories; (4) no law in the territories could free slaves because that would be an unconstitutional taking under the 5th Amendment; and (5) the Missouri Compromise unconstitutionally banned slavery in the federal territories, and by implication the ban on slavery in the Act creating the Oregon Territory was also unconstitutional. This sweeping opinion settled the issue by allowing slavery in all existing federal territories.

A concurring opinion by Justice Samuel Nelson of New York also directly telegraphed how the Court would rule on the issue of slave transit. Nelson noted at the very end of his opinion:

> A question has been alluded to, on the argument, namely: the right of the master with his slave of transit into or through a free State, on Business or commercial pursuits, or in the exercise of a Federal right, or the discharge of a Federal duty, being a citizen of the United States, which is not before us. This question depends upon different considerations and principles from the one in hand, and turns upon the rights and privileges secured to a common citizen of the republic under the Constitution of the United States. When that question arises, we shall be prepared to decide it.[95]

The implication was clear: as soon as the Court had an opportunity, it would guarantee that masters could travel anywhere in the United States with their slaves. In his "House Divided Speech,"[96] Abraham Lincoln predicted that the logic of *Dred Scott* would lead to legalizing slavery in the North through the "next Dred Scott decision."[97] Nelson's opinion certainly made this seem likely.

The final presecession decision on slavery was *Ableman v. Booth*,[98] arguably the most anti–states' rights decision since *Martin v. Hunter's Lessee*,[99] *McCulloch v. Maryland*,[100] and *Cohens v. Virginia*.[101] But the difference between the cases is striking. *Martin*, *McCulloch*, and *Cohens* were seen as attacks on the sovereignty of Southern states, leading to complaints by some Virginians that the Court had eviscerated the rights of the states. *Ableman* was directed at Northern states and supported the Fugitive Slave Law of 1850. The case began when Sherman Booth, an antislavery editor in Milwaukee, helped lead a mob that rescued a fugitive slave named Joshua Glover, who had been in federal custody.[102] U.S. Marshal Stephen Ableman then arrested Booth. At this point, the Wisconsin Supreme Court intervened, freeing Booth with a writ of habeas corpus.[103] In its decision the Wisconsin Court declared that the Fugitive Slave Law of 1850 was unconstitutional.[104] The Wisconsin Supreme Court subsequently refused to send a record of the case to the U.S. Supreme Court. Thus, the U.S. Supreme Court did not decide the case until 1859, when Chief Justice Taney emphatically asserted:

> No State judge or court, after they are judicially informed that the party is imprisoned under the authority of the United States, has any right to interfere with him, or to require him to be brought before them. And if the authority of a State, in the form of judicial process or otherwise, should attempt to control the marshal or other authorized officer or agent of the United States, in any respect, in the custody of his prisoner, it would be his duty to resist it, and to call to his aid any force that might be necessary to maintain the authority of law against illegal interference. No judicial process, whatever form it may assume, can have any lawful authority outside of the limits of the jurisdiction of the court or judge by whom it is issued; and an attempt to enforce it beyond these boundaries is nothing less than lawless violence.[105]

Northern states' rights claims would gain no support from the Supreme Court, nor was the Court troubled by the Fugitive Slave Law of 1850. Speaking for a unanimous Court, Taney unambiguously proclaimed: "the act of Congress commonly called the fugitive slave law is, in all of its provisions, fully authorized by the Constitution of the United States."[106] Taney noted that the Wisconsin Supreme Court had asserted its supremacy over the federal courts. This astounded the Chief Justice, as he noted:

> These propositions are new in the jurisprudence of the United States, as well as of the States; and the supremacy of the State courts over the courts of the United States, in cases arising under the Constitution and laws of the United States, is now for the first time asserted and acted upon in the Supreme Court of a State.[107]

Ableman was a strongly nationalist opinion—as strong as anything Justice Story or Chief Justice John Marshall might have written. But it was proslavery nationalism. It upheld the Fugitive Slave Law of 1850 and emphatically rejected the antislavery jurisprudence of a Northern state. It was a decision slave owners loved.

4. *THE PROSLAVERY 1850S*

The 1850s was a decade of enormous political success for the South and slavery. In 1849, slavery was illegal in almost all of the federal territories. After 1857, for the first time since the Constitution was adopted, slavery was legal in every federal territory. In 1849, there was a weak federal fugitive slave law with few viable enforcement mechanisms. After 1850, the nation developed, for the first time in American history, a national law enforcement bureaucracy, solely for the purpose of returning fugitive slaves. In 1849, almost all the free states emancipated visiting slaves with no constitutional restrictions. By 1857, the Supreme Court had made it clear that it would strike down such behavior at the first opportunity. In the 1840s, blacks were gaining rights in the North, as Rhode Island enfranchised them and Ohio repealed its black laws.[108] Black lawyers were beginning to appear in Northern courts, and it seemed to be only a matter of time before some black attorney would seek admission to the bar of the U.S. Supreme Court.[109] By 1860, Congress and the president had teamed up to deny every black in the nation the right to fundamental due process when seized as a fugitive slave, and the Supreme Court had expanded this deprivation of their status by holding that blacks could never be citizens of the United States and that under the Constitution, blacks "had no rights which the white man was bound to respect; and that the negro might justly and lawfully be reduced to slavery for his benefit."[110] Finally, in the 1850s, Congress and the Courts worked in tandem to undermine the rights of residents of the free states to protect their black neighbors or resist the encroachments of slavery into their communities.

II. SECESSION AND STATES' RIGHTS

After a decade of spectacular success at the national level, in 1860–61 the most aggressive proslavery politicians led their states out of the Union. Were they concerned about states' rights? Was the right of the states to control their own domestic institutions at the heart of secession? The answer is clearly no.

There was not a single example of deprivation of states' rights that Southerners could complain about. The national government did not threaten to end slavery in the states or even interfere with it. In his first inaugural address, Lincoln reaffirmed this position while quoting his own party's platform:

> Apprehension seems to exist among the people of the Southern States that by the accession of a Republican Administration their property and their peace and personal security are to be endangered. There has never been any reasonable cause for such apprehension. Indeed, the most ample evidence to the

> contrary has all the while existed and been open to their inspection. It is found in nearly all the published speeches of him who now addresses you. I do but quote from one of those speeches when I declare that—
>
> I have no purpose, directly or indirectly, to interfere with the institution of slavery in the States where it exists. I believe I have no lawful right to do so, and I have no inclination to do so.
>
> Those who nominated and elected me did so with full knowledge that I had made this and many similar declarations and had never recanted them; and more than this, they placed in the platform for my acceptance, and as a law to themselves and to me, the clear and emphatic resolution which I now read:
>
> "*Resolved*, That the maintenance inviolate of the rights of the States, and especially the right of each State to order and control its own domestic institutions according to its own judgment exclusively, is essential to that balance of power on which the perfection and endurance of our political fabric depend; and we denounce the lawless invasion by armed force of the soil of any State or Territory, no matter what pretext, as among the gravest of crimes."[111]

Lincoln certainly hated slavery and always had. But he understood the Constitution precisely as did John C. Calhoun or Jefferson Davis: that the national government had no power to regulate slavery in the states. Lincoln had "no inclination" to interfere with slavery in the states because he had no power to do so; nor did any other politician in the Lincoln administration or in Congress. Southern states' rights had not been threatened in the 1850s, and there was no threat to them from the incoming administration. Whatever Lincoln's policies were toward the territories, there was no threat to states' rights in the South. The secession documents underscore this. Most of the complaints of the seceding states were about national policies outside the Southern states or about actions of the North.

The only significant state right that any of the Southern states claimed was the right to secede. The secessionists claimed that this right was rooted in the inherent sovereignty of the states. South Carolina noted that the federal government's "encroachments upon the reserved rights of the States, fully justified" the state in "withdrawing from the Federal Union" and that "now the State of South Carolina" had "resumed her separate and equal place among nations."[112] Thus, the right to secession was rooted in a particular view of states' rights that most of the states of the Union had never accepted. However, the substantive reasons for secession were not the rights of the states. While South Carolina and other seceding states claimed that the national government had "encroached" on their "reserved rights," none of them offered any examples of this wrong, because in fact there were none. Instead, all of their examples—the reasons they offered to justify secession—were about national policy involving slavery in the territories, the admission of new slave states, John Brown's raid at Harpers Ferry, Northern opposition to slavery, the refusal of Northern states to aggressively help in the return of fugitives slaves, and other actions by Northern state governments that were hostile to slavery. Most of these complaints were not, in fact, about the national government impinging on Southern states' rights; rather they were complaints that the national government had not impinged on Northern states' rights. There are, therefore, four significant ironies to the states' rights issue and secession.

First, because the Constitution of 1787 was deeply protective of slavery and the Supreme Court enhanced this protection, there was a direct tie to nationalism and slavery. This meant that before 1861, the slave states did not need to have a states' rights ideology to protect their most important social and economic institution. A nationalist position did that for them. Most of the complaints about the national government and slavery in the secessionist documents were not about the national government impinging on Southern states' rights. For example, South Carolina complained that the Northern states were not helping to enforce the Fugitive Slave Law of 1850, and thus "laws of the General Government have ceased to effect the objects of the Constitution."[113]

Second, because the Constitution was proslavery and supporters of slavery controlled the national government almost continuously from 1801 until 1861, the most important proponents of states' rights in the antebellum period were Northern opponents of slavery. Northerners needed to assert states' rights in order to protect free blacks in their community from kidnapping and protect their fugitive slave neighbors from being returned to bondage. Thus, starting in the 1820s, most free states passed personal liberty laws that frustrated the implementation of the Fugitive Slave Law of 1793. In the 1830s, courts in Pennsylvania, New York, and New Jersey upheld state personal liberty laws that undermined the 1793 law and effectively held that the 1793 law was unconstitutional, in part on states' rights grounds.[114] In the early 1840s, Governor William H. Seward of New York and three successive governors of Maine refused to surrender Northern free blacks wanted in the South for helping slaves escape. Just before the Civil War, Governors Salmon P. Chase and William Dennison, Jr. of Ohio also refused to surrender a free black who had helped a slave escape.[115] These Northern governors rested their actions on states' rights arguments.[116] Finally, after the Supreme Court struck down the first wave of Northern personal liberty laws in *Prigg*,[117] many Northern states responded with new laws, which simply withdrew Northern cooperation in the return of fugitive slaves.[118] This was a variant of states' rights philosophy. In these laws, passed in the 1840s and in the decade after the adoption of the fugitive slave law of 1850, the Northern states took the position that they did not have to cooperate with the federal government. In doing so, they made enforcement of the 1850 law difficult or, in some places, nearly impossible.

Third, the most aggressive states' rights arguments of the antebellum decade came from Northerners, particularly judges in Ohio,[119] New York,[120] and most of all Wisconsin.[121] In response to the Oberlin-Wellington rescue in Ohio, that state's supreme court came within one vote of causing a confrontation with the federal government by issuing a writ of habeas corpus directed at the U.S. marshal in Cleveland.[122] The Wisconsin Supreme Court was not so circumspect and, in fact, issued a writ of habeas corpus that forced U.S. Marshal Stephen Ableman to surrender the abolitionist Sherman Booth after he had been arrested for helping rescue a fugitive slave. In New York, in *Lemmon v. The People*, the state's highest court rejected any measure of comity toward visiting slaveowners.[123] In that case, the state courts emancipated eight Virginia slaves who had been brought into New York City for just long enough to take the next steamboat to New Orleans.[124] They were in the city only because New York was the only East Coast port that had direct transit to New Orleans. The decision in *Lemmon* was legitimate within the context of American constitutional law and state police powers. But Southerners believed this decision, and similar ones in other states, violated the spirit of the Union and the comity that should be given to citizens of other states. In addition, some Southerners believed the decision in *Lemmon* actually violated the Commerce Clause or the Privileges and Immunities Clause of the Constitution because it denied Southerners the right to travel throughout the United States with their constitutionally protected property *and* it interfered with interstate commerce.

Finally, while Southerners proclaimed their support for states' rights, they insisted that the road to states' rights ran in only one direction. They denied that Northerners could assert *their* states' rights when it came to slavery. Thus, for example, South Carolina complained that the Northern states

> assume the right of deciding upon the propriety of our domestic institutions; and have denied the rights of property established in fifteen of the States and recognized by the Constitution; they have denounced as sinful the institution of slavery; they have permitted open establishment among them of societies, whose avowed object is to disturb the peace and to eloign the property of the citizens of other States.[125]

In other words, South Carolina opposed the idea that the free states could have their states' rights to allow antislavery organizations to operate. Similarly, South Carolina denounced the *Lemmon* decision as a violation of comity, without any sense of the irony that it was actually opposing states' rights. Since the 1820s, South Carolina had successfully refused to allow Northern free black sailors to enter its ports, and almost every other Southern state with an ocean port passed a similar black seamen's law. Under these laws, free black sailors were jailed while their ships were in Southern ports and were only released when the ship was about to sail, *if* the ship captain paid the jailer for feeding and housing these sailors. Although believing such laws violated the Commerce Clause, the Supremacy Clause, and the treaty power, Justice William Johnson, while riding circuit, refused to interfere with their enforcement.[126] The Southern states insisted that states' rights empowered them to arrest free black sailors (or any other free blacks) entering their jurisdiction. In the 1840s, Massachusetts sent commissioners to South Carolina and Louisiana to negotiate some accommodation for free black sailors from the North, but both states refused to meet with the commissioners and basically expelled them.[127]

Ironically then, the Southern states argued that states' rights allowed them to decide whom they would let into their states. But when Northerners applied the same logic to visiting Southerners with slaves, South Carolina suddenly rejected its support for states' rights and argued this was grounds for secession.

Thus, in the end, secession was not based on the need of the Southern states to protect their states' rights from an aggressive national government. On the contrary, the Southern states argued that they were leaving because the Northern states insisted on asserting their own states' rights to oppose slavery. Nor was it about the "encroachments" of the national government, because there were none. Nor was it about the failure of the national government to protect slavery. Federal troops had been used to suppress John Brown's invasion of Harpers Ferry, Virginia. Federal troops had been used to bring the fugitive slave Anthony Burns out of Boston. The national government had expended enormous resources to prosecute people who rescued or tried to rescue fugitive slaves in New York,[128] Massachusetts,[129] Pennsylvania,[130] Ohio, [131] Wisconsin,[132] Illinois,[133] and elsewhere. While many of those prosecutions were unsuccessful, there were convictions in Ohio after the Oberlin rescue, in Wisconsin after the Joshua Glover rescue, and in other places. While Wisconsin may have resisted the fugitive slave law in Sherman Booth's case, the federal government won in the end; Booth's printing press was seized and sold for the benefit of the slave owner,[134] and after the Supreme Court decision, Booth went to jail and the Wisconsin Supreme Court declined to intervene.[135] Despite intense opposition to the Fugitive Slave Law in Northern Ohio, the Buchanan administration managed to cobble together two juries made up of supporters of the law and to convict two of the Oberlin rescuers.[136] The Ohio Supreme Court refused to assert its states' rights to release the Oberlin rescuers from federal custody.[137]

Thus, history showed a growing Northern states' rights opposition to slavery but also a firm federal support of slavery that, if anything, trampled on the states' rights of the North. For the seceding states, however, these Northern developments were intolerable. So, too, were Northern demands for political action against the spread of slavery. Georgia could not complain that slavery was excluded from the federal territories, because it was allowed in *all* the federal territories in 1860. Georgia could complain only that "Northern anti-slavery men of all parties asserted the right to exclude slavery from the territory by Congressional legislation and demanded the prompt and efficient exercise of this power to that end" and that these demands were "insulting and unconstitutional."[138] Georgia complained that the incoming Lincoln administration was opposed to allowing slavery in the territories and that this opposition justified secession. In other words, without any legislation on the table, Georgia claimed it could leave the Union because it objected to the platform of the new president. Secession was not about 'states' rights,' but about political power. Southerners did not like the outcome of the presidential election, so they claimed the right to leave the Union.

Mississippi was equally appalled at Northern states' rights actions and beliefs. Mississippi complained that Northerners had "broken the compact which our fathers pledged their faith to maintain."[139] This was because in the North, "hostility" to slavery "advocates negro equality, socially and politically, and promotes insurrection and incendiarism in our midst."[140] This hostility had "enlisted" the North's "press, its pulpit and its schools against us, until the whole popular mind of the North is excited and inflamed with prejudice."[141] Northerners had "made combinations and formed associations to carry out" their "schemes of emancipation in the States and wherever else slavery exists."[142] In other words, Northerners exercised their rights of free speech, freedom of religion, and state political autonomy to support policies the South did not like. The issues were not based on constitutionalism or states' rights, but on political power and the power of ideas. Southerners left the Union because they disagreed with Northerners. Mississippi complained that Northerners believed in "negro equality"[143] and that this belief was enough to justify secession.

Texas also asserted that it was leaving the Union because of Northern states' rights, not the denial of Southern states' rights. The Texans complained:

> The States of Maine, Vermont, New Hampshire, Connecticut, Rhode Island, Massachusetts, New York, Pennsylvania, Ohio, Wisconsin, Michigan and Iowa, by solemn legislative enactments, have deliberately, directly or indirectly violated the 3rd clause of the 2nd section of the 4th article [the fugitive slave clause] of the federal constitution, and laws passed in pursuance thereof; thereby annulling a material provision of the compact, designed by its framers to perpetuate the amity between the members of the confederacy and to secure the rights of the slave-holding States in their domestic institutions—a provision founded in justice and wisdom, and without the enforcement of which the compact fails to accomplish the object of its creation.[144]

Like the secessionists in Mississippi, Texans complained that Northerners refused to agree with them on the fundamental inequality of blacks. Texans declared they had to leave the Union because Northerners were "proclaiming the debasing doctrine of equality of all men, irrespective of race or color—a doctrine at war with nature, in opposition to the experience of mankind, and in violation of the plainest revelations of Divine Law."[145]

In the end, the root of secession was just as Alexander Stephens said: racism and slavery. For the first time in its history, the United States had elected a president who was prepared to stand up against the demands of slavery and to fight its spread. He had no power—and thus no inclination—to interfere with slavery in the states. He would not trample on the states' rights of the South. But he would fight slavery on the political level. Northerners agreed with him. Having legitimately lost the election, Southerners had two choices. They could accept the outcome of the election and participate in politics, or, they could turn against their own country.

In 1860–61, Southerners could not legitimately claim, as their ancestors had in the Declaration of Independence, that they were being denied a place at the political table or a voice in the political process. Americans in 1776 had no political voice in Britain, no seats in Parliament, and no vote. Southerners held almost half the seats in the Senate and with their Northern Democratic allies they could control that body; they were a majority of the Supreme Court, and of the four Northerners on the Court only the aging John McLean—the longest-serving Justice—was even moderately opposed to slavery, and he had voted in favor of the fugitive slave laws on a number of occasions.[146] While a minority in the House of Representatives, Southerners had still been able to pass enormously significant legislation supporting slavery in the previous decade.

Thus, the decision to leave the Union was not about access to politics; it was about whether Southerners could win every election or control any Northerner who won, thus maintaining their version of racial hegemony and protecting slavery. Having lost the election, they feared they would lose more in the future. While most Northerners rejected full racial equality, blacks voted in some Northern states and had some rights in all the free states. This, along with hostility to slavery, was reason enough to leave the Union. The decision was, of course, a disaster. Southern leaders believed their own ideology and followed their prejudices down a horrible road that led to war and destruction. Slavery was safe within the Union, where the Constitution protected it at every turn[147] and where the South had a perpetual veto over all Constitutional amendments.[148]

But once the South rejected the Constitution and Southerners who had taken an oath to defend the Constitution made war on their own country, these protections were gone. In the end, secession led to exactly what the Southern disunionists—some might call them the Southern traitors—feared most: an end to slavery and at least formal constitutional equality for all Americans, no matter what their race. It led to what Lincoln memorably called a New Birth of Freedom.

NOTES

1. Abraham Lincoln, *Second Inaugural Address, in* 8 The Collected Works of Abraham Lincoln 332 (Roy P. Basler ed., 1953).

2. The other one was Judah P. Benjamin, who held a number of positions in the Confederate cabinet and then enjoyed a second career as one of the leading barristers in England.

3. Alexander H. Stephens, *The Corner Stone Speech* (Mar. 21, 1861), *reprinted in* Henry Cleveland, Alexander H. Stephens, in Public and Private. With Letters and Speeches, Before, During, and Since the War 717, 721 (1886).

4. *Id.* (emphasis in original).

5. *Id.*

6. *Id.*

7. *Id.*

8. *Declaration of the Immediate Causes Which Induce and Justify the Secession of South Carolina from the Federal Union* (1861), *reprinted in* J. A. May & J. R. Faunt, South Carolina Secedes 76–81 (1960), *available at* http://avalon.law.yale.edu/19th_century/csa_scarsec.asp (last visited Sept. 24, 2011). This was adopted four days after the state officially seceded. The *Declarations of Secession* for Georgia, Mississippi, South Carolina, and Texas are conveniently found at http://avalon.law.yale.edu/subject_menus/csapage.asp.

9. *Georgia Secession* (1861), *reprinted in* 1 Fred C. Ainsworth & Joseph W. Kirkley, The War of the Rebellion: A Compilation of the Official Records of the Union and Confederate Armies

81–85 (Ser. 4, 1900), *available at* http://ebooks.library.cornell.edu/cgi/t/text/pageviewer-idx?c=moawar;cc=moawar;q1=Georgia;rgn=full%20text;idno=war00127;didno=war00127;view=image;seq=0093.

10. *A Declaration of the Immediate Causes Which Induce and Justify the Secession of the State of Mississippi from the Federal Union, reprinted in* Journal of the State Convention 86–88 (1861), *available at* http://docsouth.unc.edu/imls/msconven/menu.html.

11. Strader v. Graham, 51 U.S. (10 How.) 82 (1851).

12. Dred Scott v. Sandford, 60 U.S. (19 How.) 393 (1857).

13. *Id.*

14. Ableman v. Booth, 62 U.S. (21 How.) 506 (1859).

15. Arguably, *Prigg v. Pennsylvania*, 41 U.S. (16 Pet.) 539 (1842), was equally as proslavery. For a discussion of this point, *see* Paul Finkelman, *Story Telling on the Supreme Court:* Prigg v. Pennsylvania *and Justice Joseph Story's Judicial Nationalism*, 1994 Sup. Ct. Rev. 247 (1994).

16. *Dred Scott*, 60 U.S. at 468 (Nelson, J., concurring).

17. The admission of Florida on March 3, 1845, gave the South a one-state majority in the Senate. The admission of Texas on December 29, 1845, gave the South a two-state majority. The South maintained this two-state majority until December 28, 1846, when Iowa entered the Union, and parity was not reached until Wisconsin became a state on May 26, 1848. This history undermines the notion, perpetuated by many scholars, that the admission of California ended a history of parity in the Senate. With the opening of the Mexican Cession to slavery, it was perfectly possible to imagine new slaves states entering the Union in the southwest.

18. *See* John S. D. Eisenhower, Zachary Taylor (2008).

19. *See* John S. D. Eisenhower, Agent of Destiny: The Life and Times of General Winfield Scott (1999).

20. James A. Dorr, Justice to the South! An Address 10 (1856).

21. Fugitive Slave Act of 1793, ch. 7, 1 Stat. 302 (1793).

22. Prigg v. Pennsylvania, 41 U.S. (16 Pet.) 539 (1842).

23. For a full discussion of the proslavery implications of *Prigg*, *see* Finkelman, *supra* note 15. *See also* Paul Finkelman, *Sorting Out* Prigg v. Pennsylvania, 24 Rutgers L.J. 24 (1993).

24. Paul Finkelman, Prigg v. Pennsylvania *and Northern State Courts: Anti-Slavery Use of a Pro-Slavery Decision*, 25 Civ. War His. 5 (1979).

25. An Act Further to Protect Personal Liberty, 1843 Mass. Acts, ch. 69, at 33.

26. *Id.* For a full history of these laws, *see* Thomas D. Morris, Free Men All: The Personal Liberty Laws of the North, 1780–1861 (1974).

27. For detailed discussions of these laws and the common-law evolution of this principle in the North, *see* Paul Finkelman, An Imperfect Union: Slavery, Federalism, and Comity (1981).

28. Somerset v. Stewart, (1772) 98 Eng. Rep. 499 (K.B.). For a discussion of this case, *see* William M. Wiecek, The Sources of Antislavery Constitutionalism in America, 1760–1848 (1977).

29. 1 Laws of the Commonwealth of Pennsylvania 492–96 (1810).

30. 1799 N.Y. Laws, ch. 62, reenacted in 1817 N.Y. Laws, ch. 137.

31. 1841 N.Y. Laws, ch. 247.

32. Act of March 3, 1847, 1847 Pa. Laws 206. For detailed discussions of these laws and the common law evolution of this principle in the North, *see* Finkelman, *supra* note 27.

33. As the facts of *Dred Scott* show, some masters did take their slaves into the area, especially those like Captain John Emerson, who were posted at military bases. Most masters, however, did not venture into the area with their property. For example, in an unreported case a court in Muscatine, Iowa, emancipated the slave Jim White whose master brought him there before statehood. *The Negro Case*, Bloomington Herald, Nov. 18, 1848. *See also* J. P. Walton, *Unwritten History of Bloomington (Now Muscatine), in Early Days*, 1 Annals of Iowa 40–44 (1882).

34. Finkelman, *supra* note 27.

35. Paul Finkelman, *The Appeasement of 1850, in* Congress and the Crisis of the 1850s 36 (Paul Finkelman & Donald R. Kennon eds., 2012).

36. David M. Potter, The Impending Crisis, 1848–1861 98–101 (Don E. Fehrenbacher ed., 1976).

37. Finkelman, *Appeasement of 1850*, *supra* note 35, at 54; Paul Finkelman, *The Cost of Compromise and the Covenant with Death*, 38 Pepp. L. Rev. 845 (2011).

38. Act of Sept. 9, 1850, ch. 49, 9 Stat. 446.

39. Finkelman, *The Cost of Compromise and the Covenant with Death*, *supra* note 37, at 862.

40. For a more detailed discussion of the 1850 debate, *see id.*, and Paul Finkelman, Millard Fillmore (2011).

41. Fugitive Slave Act of 1850, ch. 60, 9 Stat. 462.

42. *Id.*

43. *Id.*

44. *Id.*

45. *Id.*

46. *Id.* ("In no trial or hearing under this act shall the testimony of such alleged fugitive be admitted in evidence.").

47. U.S. Const. Art. 1, § 9 ("The Writ of Habeas Corpus shall not be suspended, unless in Cases of Rebellion or Invasion the public Safety may require it."). *See* Paul Finkelman, *Limiting Rights in Times of Crisis: Our Civil War Experience—A History Lesson for a Post–9-11 America*, 2 Cardozo Public L. Policy & Ethics J. 25 (2003).

48. Fugitive Slave Act of 1850 § 7.

49. The Court had essentially held this in *Jones v. Van Zandt*, 46 U.S. (5 How.) 215 (1847).

50. *See* Fugitive Slave Act of 1850 § 5.

51. *Id.* § 8.

52. *Id.*

53. The differential payment was based on the fact that it took commissioners much more time to fill out the paperwork necessary to return a fugitive slave than to set a black free. While the different fees made economic sense, they created the appearance that justice was for sale in the North. The payment scale was a public relations disaster for the national government and the Fillmore administration.

54. *See generally* the essays in In the Shadow of Freedom: The Politics of Slavery in the National Capital (Paul Finkelman & Donald R. Kennon eds., 2011).

55. A. Glenn Crothers, *The 1846 Retrocession of Alexandria: Protecting Slavery and the Slave Trade in the District of Columbia*, *in* Finkelman & Kennon, In the Shadow of Freedom, *supra* note 54, at 141.

56. Finkelman, Millard Fillmore, *supra* note 40, at 114.

57. *Id.* at 83–85, 89.

58. Finkelman, *Appeasement of 1850*, *supra* note 35.

59. Kansas-Nebraska Act, ch. 59, 10 Stat. 277 (1854).

60. Alvin F. Oickle, Jonathan Walker: The Man with the Branded Hand 1–13 (1998).

61. *Id.*

62. Potter, *supra* note 36, at 109–11.

63. Finkelman, Millard Fillmore, *supra* note 40, at 84; Potter, *supra* note 36, at 110–11.

64. Potter, *supra* note 36, at 172–74.

65. Nicole Etcheson, Bleeding Kansas: Contested Liberty in the Civil War Era (2004).

66. Michael F. Holt, Franklin Pierce (2010).

67. Potter, *supra* note 36, at 297–328.

68. *Id.* at 349.

69. By this time Minnesota and Oregon had become free states, along with California.

70. Norris v. Crocker, 54 U.S. (13 How.) 429 (1851).

71. Jones v. Van Zandt, 46 U.S. (5 How.) 215 (1847).

72. *Id.* at 219.

73. *Id.* at 220.

74. *Id.* at 221.

75. *Id.*

76. Strader v. Graham, 51 U.S. (10 How.) 82 (1851).

77. *Id.* at 93.

78. *Id.*

79. *Id.* at 92–93.

80. *Id.* at 85–86.

81. Somerset v. Stewart, (1772) 98 Eng. Rep. 499 (K.B.).

82. The history of this rule is set out in Finkelman, *supra* note 27.

83. *Strader*, 51 U.S. at 89.

84. *Id.*

85. *Id.* at 96–97.

86. Moore v. Illinois, 55 U.S. (14 How.) 13 (1852).

87. Prigg v. Pennsylvania, 41 U.S. (16 Pet.) 539 (1842).

88. *Id.* at 625–26.

89. *Id.* at 627–28 (Taney, J., concurring).

90. *Moore*, 55 U.S. at 22.

91. Dred Scott v. Sandford, 60 U.S. (19 How.) 393 (1857).

92. Paul Finkelman, *Was Dred Scott Correctly Decided? An "Expert Report" For the Defendant*, 12 Lewis & Clark L. Rev. 1219 (2008); Paul Finkelman, *Coming to Terms with Dred Scott: A Response to Daniel A. Farber*, 39 Pepperdine L. Rev. 495 (2012).

93. These statutes are set out in Paul Finkelman, Dred Scott v. Sandford: A Brief History with Documents 8–10 (1997).

94. The best discussion of the internal politics of the Court on this point is Don E. Fehrenbacher, The Dred Scott Case: Its Significance in American Law and Politics (1978).

95. *Dred Scott*, 60 U.S. at 468 (Nelson, J., concurring).

96. Abraham Lincoln, *A House Divided: Speech at Springfield, Illinois*, *in* 2 The Collected Works of Abraham Lincoln, *supra* note 1, at 461.

97. For a discussion of this, *see* Finkelman, *supra* note 27.

98. Ableman v. Booth, 62 U.S. (21 How.) 506 (1859).

99. Martin v. Hunter's Lessee, 14 U.S. (1 Wheat.) 304 (1816).

100. McCulloch v. Maryland, 17 U.S. (4 Wheat.) 316 (1819).

101. Cohens v. Virginia, 19 U.S. (6 Wheat.) 264 (1821).

102. For a full history of the case, *see* H. Robert Baker, The Rescue of Joshua Glover: A Fugitive Slave, The Constitution, and the Coming of the Civil War (2006).

103. In re Booth & Rycraft, 3 Wis. 157 (1854).

104. *Id.* at 212.

105. Ableman v. Booth, 62 U.S. (21 How.) 506, 524 (1859).

106. *Id.* at 526.

107. *Id.* at 514.

108. Paul Finkelman, *Prelude to the Fourteenth Amendment: Black Legal Rights in the Antebellum North*, 17 Rutgers L.J. 415 (1986).

109. Paul Finkelman, *Not Only the Judges' Robes Were Black: African-American Lawyers as Social Engineers*, 47 Stan. L. Rev. 161 (1994).

110. *Dred Scott*, 60 U.S. at 407 (1857).

111. Abraham Lincoln, *First Inaugural Address—Final Text*, Mar. 4, 1861, *in* 4 The Collected Works of Abraham Lincoln 262–63 (1953).

112. *Declaration of the Immediate Causes Which Induce and Justify the Secession of South Carolina from the Federal Union*, *supra* note 8.

113. *Id.*

114. *See* State v. Sheriff of Burlington, No. 36286 (N.J. 1836) (also known as Nathan, Alias Alex. Helmsley v. State); Jack v. Martin, 14 Wend. 507 (N.Y. 1835). *State v. Sheriff of Burlington*, which is unreported, is discussed in Paul Finkelman, *State Constitutional Protections of Liberty and the Antebellum New Jersey Supreme Court: Chief Justice Hornblower and the Fugitive Slave Law of 1793*, 23 Rutgers L.J. 753 (1992). The Pennsylvania Supreme Court upheld its state personal liberty law in an unreported opinion in *Prigg v. Pennsylvania*.

115. *See* Kentucky v. Dennison, 65 U.S. (24 How.) 66 (1861).

116. Paul Finkelman, *States Rights North and South in Antebellum America*, *in* An Uncertain Tradition: Constitutionalism and the History of the South 125–58 (Kermit L. Hall & James W. Ely, Jr., eds., 1989); Paul Finkelman, *The Protection of Black Rights in Seward's New York*, 34 Civ. War His. 211–34 (1988); Paul Finkelman, *States' Rights, Federalism, and Criminal Extradition in Antebellum America: The New York-Virginia Controversy, 1839–1846*, *in* German and American Constitutional Thought: Contexts, Interaction, and Historical Realities 293–327 (Hermann Wellenreuther ed., 1990).

117. Prigg v. Pennsylvania, 41 U.S. (16 Pet.) 539 (1842).

118. *See generally* Morris, *supra* note 26.

119. Ex parte Bushnell, Ex parte Langston, 9 Ohio St. 77 (1859).

120. Lemmon v. The People, 20 N.Y. 562 (1860).

121. In re Booth & Rycraft, 3 Wis. 157 (1854), *rev'd*, Ableman v. Booth, 62 U.S. (21 How.) 506 (1859).

122. *Bushnell*, 9 Ohio St. at 77.

123. *Lemmon*, 20 N.Y. at 565.

124. *Id.*

125. *Declaration of the Immediate Causes Which Induce and Justify the Secession of South Carolina from the Federal Union*, *supra* note 8.

126. Elkison v. Deliesseline, 8 F. Cas. 493, 496–98 (C.C.D.S.C. 1823).

127. Finkelman, *States' Rights North and South in Antebellum America*, *supra* note 116.

128. United States v. Cobb, 25 F. Cas. 481 (C.C.N.D.N.Y. 1857); United States v. Reed, 27 F. Cas. 727 (C.C.N.D.N.Y. 1852).

129. United States v. Stowell, 27 F. Cas. 1350 (C.C.D. Mass. 1854); United States v. Scott, 27 F. Cas. 990 (D. Mass. 1851); United States v. Morris, 26 F. Cas. 1323 (C.C.D. Mass. 1851).

130. United States v. Hanway, 26 F. Cas. 105 (C.C.E.D. Pa. 1851).

131. Jacob R. Shipherd, History of the Oberlin-Wellington Rescue (1859).

132. Ableman v. Booth, 62 U.S. (21 How.) 506 (1859); United States v. Rycraft, 27 F. Cas. 918 (D. Wis. 1854).

133. United States v. Hossack, 26 F. Cas. 378 (N.D. Ill. 1860) (unreported). For a full discussion of this case, *see* Paul Finkelman, Slavery in the Courtroom 128–34 (1985).

134. In June 1861, after the Civil War had begun, the Wisconsin Supreme Court affirmed the validity of this sale in *Arnold v. Booth*, 14 Wis. 180 (1861).

135. Ableman v. Booth, 11 Wis. 498 (1859).

136. Paul Finkelman, *A Political Show Trial in the Northern District: The Oberlin-Wellington Fugitive Slave Rescue Case*, *in* Justice and Legal Change on the Shores of Lake Erie 15–36 (Paul Finkelman & Roberta Sue Alexander, eds., 2012).

137. Ex parte Bushnell, Ex parte Langston, 9 Ohio St. 77 (1859). See also Finkelman, *A Political Show, supra* note 136.

138. *Georgia Secession, supra* note 9.

139. *A Declaration of the Immediate Causes which Induce and Justify the Secession of the State of Mississippi from the Federal Union, supra* note 10.

140. *Id.*

141. *Id.*

142. *Id.*

143. Most Northern whites, of course, did not believe in racial equality.

144. *A Declaration of the Causes which Impel the State of Texas to Secede from the Federal Union, reprinted in* Yale Law School, *Confederate States of America: Documents*, Journal of the Secession Convention of Texas 61–66 (E. W. Winkler), *available at* http://sunsite.utk.edu/civil-war/reasons.html.

145. *Id.*

146. *See* Ableman v. Booth, 62 U.S. (21 How.) 506 (1859); Jones v. Van Zandt, 46 U.S. (5 How.) 215 (1847). On McLean and antislavery, *see* Paul Finkelman, *John McLean: Moderate Abolitionist and Supreme Court Politician*, 62 Vanderbilt L. Rev. 519 (2009).

147. For a discussion of the proslavery nature of the Constitution, *see* Paul Finkelman, Slavery and the Founders: Race and Liberty in the Age of Jefferson (2d ed. 2001).

148. It takes three-fourths of the states to ratify a constitutional amendment. In 1860, there were fifteen slave states. If all of these states had remained in the Union, to this day, in 2012, it would be impossible to end slavery by amendment, since it would take forty-five free states to outvote the fifteen slave states.

4 Still Too Close to Call?

Rethinking Stampp's "The Concept of a Perpetual Union"

Daniel W. Hamilton, University of Illinois College of Law

In a classic article in the *Journal of American History,* which was based on his presidential address to the Organization of American Historians in 1978, the great Civil War historian Kenneth Stampp made the claim that the arguments in favor of the constitutionality of secession made by the Southern states were as strong, if not stronger than the constitutional arguments made, then and now, in opposition to secession.[1] Stampp is probably the greatest Civil War historian of the twentieth century, and his views on secession remain required reading and are cited routinely today.

This is not to say Stampp was correct but only to use his classic article on the 150th anniversary of secession as a jumping off point for reconsidering the legality and constitutionality of secession and also, I think, to go to first principles to consider whether it is possible or useful to definitively try and answer the question: was secession legal?

This is a thought piece, a historiographical meditation, or more accurately something of a polemic, with very little of archival heavy lifting but still asking questions that bedevil Civil War historians about the perhaps irresistible presentism in the field of Civil War legal history.[2]

Stampp presented secession as "the fundamental issue of the [Civil W]ar" and framed secession as a constitutional crisis that turned on questions surrounding "the locus of sovereignty in the political structure that the Constitution of 1787 had formed."[3] In particular, Stampp asked, did the Constitution "create a union of sovereign states, each of which retained the right to secede at its own discretion? Or did it create a union from which no state, once having joined, could escape except by an extra-constitutional act of revolution?"[4] The Constitution, Stampp concluded, was "silen[t] on this crucial question."[5] Indeed, he argues that "the unionist case was sufficiently flawed to make it uncertain whether in 1865 reason and logic were on the side of the victors."[6] This is not to say the union was wrong, and Stampp is quick to add that "in the tangled web of claim[] and counterclaim[]," it was unclear whether reason and logic were "indisputably on either side."[7]

In this way, Stampp lays the groundwork for the proposition that the Confederate constitutional argument for secession was as reasonable and logical as the Union's, and in particular, Lincoln's constitutional argument for a perpetual union. This was novel both then and now—even heretical, in so far as it challenges Lincoln's arguments in the First Inaugural and elsewhere that secession was manifestly unconstitutional and illegal, a position later adopted by the Supreme Court in 1869 in *Texas v. White.*[8]

To do this, Stampp deploys a kind of historically nuanced originalism, not in the service of answering a modern constitutional question, but in the service of demonstrating an essential ambiguity in Philadelphia in 1787 on the question of whether the Constitution created a perpetual union, concluding, "In truth, the wording of the Constitution gives neither the believers in the right of secession nor the advocates of a perpetual union a case so decisive that all reasonable persons are bound to accept it."[9]

Turning from the text to the debates in Philadelphia, Stampp found similar "baffling inconsistencies and obscurities."[10] Moreover, the ratification debates did not provide greater clarity, so that "in 1789, when the present Union came into existence, the question of whether a member state could secede at will remained unresolved."[11] The question of the legality of secession was, of course, continually debated in the antebellum era, over the Kentucky and Virginia resolutions, over the admission of slave and free states to the Union, and most dramatically in the Nullification Crisis in the 1830s. It was then that for Stampp an American President offered, in Andrew Jackson's Proclamation on Nullification in 1832[12] that "the concept of a perpetual union had achieved its full development, and a President of the United States had pledged himself to use all the power of the federal government to uphold it."[13] Lincoln and the Supreme Court relied on Jackson's proclamation in making their arguments for a perpetual union decades later.

Even then, though, Stampp argues that by the time of the Nullification Crisis, "the case for state sovereignty and the constitutional right of secession had flourished for forty years before a comparable case for perpetual union had been devised."[14] Thus, "because that case came so late, because the logic behind it was far from perfect, because the Constitution and the debates over ratification were fraught with ambiguity," it remained the case that the question could ultimately be settled only by war.[15] And there Stampp ends the article.

This is a radical endpoint, one that embraces historical uncertainty on a crucial constitutional question, perhaps the central constitutional question of the Civil War. Stampp poses the question: "Was secession unconstitutional?" And he answers with a salutary and even correct answer: "We don't know." Both sides had compelling arguments made over decades, both sides could draw on history in making their claims, and each claim was as logical and reasonable as the other.

This is a radical endpoint for two reasons. First, because it refuses to answer the question: "Was secession constitutional?" Stampp refuses to answer this question because it is, he shows, essentially unanswerable, or at least too close to call and unresolved as a legal and constitutional matter at the time of secession. If Stampp is correct, this raises the question whether the nation, 150 years later, can stand uncertainty on such a fundamental constitutional question of the Civil War. What if one cannot definitively answer the question: "Did Lincoln have the legal authority to wage war to suppress secession?" Second, Stampp's argument is radical for the simple reason that it suggests that the Confederacy's legal claim for secession was as valid as the Union's claim for perpetual union. It is here that Stampp may have mischaracterized secession by making the claim that act can be considered as a legal question standing alone.

Each point deserves to be taken in turn. More than sixty years ago, David Donald wrote his landmark essay *Getting Right with Lincoln.*[16] Donald wrote mostly about politicians' use of Abraham Lincoln after his assassination and in particular, how Lincoln was transformed from a deeply divisive symbol into, by the end of World War II, "everybody's grandfather" or a "nonpartisan, nonsectional hero." It thus became increasingly necessary to seek Lincoln's imagined blessing for a given political position or candidate or party, and by the middle of the twentieth century, "no reputable political organization could omit a reference to the Great Emancipator, nor could the disreputable ones." What Donald brought to light most vividly was the blatantly opportunistic use of Lincoln in political discourse. Yet in the end, he is careful not to mock or condemn outright this practice, which remains a staple of our politics. The symbolism of Lincoln remains potent and has a history of its own.[17] Donald is also careful not to try and get right, or get wrong, with Lincoln; if anything, his treatment is admiring but wary—concluding that "perhaps the secret of Lincoln's continuing vogue is his essential ambiguity."[18]

What Donald brought to light most vividly was the drive to get right with Lincoln in American politics. Yet the drive to get right with Lincoln is also at the heart of most of the legal and constitutional history of the Civil War. The academic manifestation of this drive is twofold. First, Lincoln is most often at the center of the story, making the Congress and the courts and other legal actors bit players, relevant only in so far as they interact with Lincoln. Second, Lincoln is forced, in varying degrees, into the present. This presentism takes the form of different versions of the same basic question: Was Lincoln right, was he justified in doing what he did during the Civil War?[19] Was he right to meet secession with military force? To suspend the writ of habeas corpus? Or to declare a blockade or to call up the army or to exile political prisoners to the Confederacy? Was he right to issue the Emancipation Proclamation? These questions are central to much of the academic writing on the Civil War, and it is here that the popular and academic drives to get right with Lincoln merge. The popular and cultural force of Lincoln remains so strong, he remains such a talisman for our time, that even historians cannot consign him to the past. Not only do they need him to make rulings on our actions in the present—what would Lincoln think of Guantanamo—but also to make rulings on his actions as President as part of our ongoing debates on presidential power and the Constitution in wartime.[20]

This is not to say that legal historians of the Civil War are predominantly presentist, or that they are interested only in whether Lincoln was right. But there is in much Civil War history a central presentist preoccupation that does not loom as large in any other era: namely, whether particular legal and constitutional actions were justified in some absolute sense. Historians do not generally ask whether Lord Grenville was right to issue the Stamp Act or whether Jackson was right to crush the Bank of the United States or whether Wilson was right to sign the Treaty of Versailles. They do not, in other words, usually ask whether a historical actor was right or wrong by their own lights. Yet few can resist asking this about legal actors during the Civil War, particularly Lincoln. I simply do not know whether Lincoln was right to suspend the writ of habeas corpus, and I maintain we cannot answer this question historically. We might be able to explain why he suspended the writ, or the effects of its suspension then and afterwards. We can also bring to light the competing legal arguments made at the time, and explain why some won and others lost. But we cannot survey the sources and come to a definitive ruling on the merits on these central legal questions any more than we can come to a definitive understanding of the original meaning of the Due Process Clause. Whether Lincoln was right or justified in his legal actions is no more ascertainable than whether Cromwell and his supporters were right to execute Charles I.

This is also not to say that historians need to put on a white coat and make scientific judgments about the weight of the facts. Of course, our values infuse our writing of history; we only care about history, in large part, because of its meaning in the present. We always and at all times bring our values into our work, yet these values are best left at the service of the history we tell. We may present the Declaration of Independence as radical and egalitarian or as conservative and hierarchical or somewhere in between. The sources are open to either interpretation. We do not, however, ask historians of the era to come to a definitive conclusion as to whether Jefferson was right to assert the Revolution was justified by international and natural law at the time and so justifies revolution today.

The question that comes to mind in considering the legality of secession, as Stampp did thirty years ago, is whether we are willing to accept Stampp's answer of indeterminacy. That is, whether we might have a legal history of the Civil War that does not ultimately attempt to answer these kinds of questions. Can we have a legal history of the Civil War that does not evaluate constitutional and legal actions on the merits, treating them as resolvable if only we get the law right? More important perhaps, do we want one? If we lose Lincoln as the centerpiece, do we lose a galvanizing figure that has given the field coherence over decades? If we resist making rulings on legal actions and not providing answers to questions that people want answered by historians, do we risk obscurity and familiar charges of relativism? If there are no definitive answers to the question, then are there other essential issues revolving around the Civil War that are equally indeterminate?

It is almost customary that in books on the legal and constitutional history of the Civil War there is an explicit move to seek out lessons that we might draw on in the present. This concern for lessons is a red flag for Lincoln and Civil War presentism and is a part of many rich and important histories. Lincoln's actions and those of the Congress and the courts are parsed and declared either legally and constitutionally sound or unsound. To be sure, this makes the work more timely and immediate and allows historians to take part in a decades-long conversation assessing Lincoln's wartime actions. Yet to go into the Civil War looking to answer modern questions is, to my mind, to distort the inquiry and is in the end too high a price to pay. Legal arguments invite counterarguments, but this temptation itself reveals the mostly fruitless nature of this kind of historical debate. Legal arguments are made back and forth with no winner because there can be no winner in a ruling on the past. What if we walk away with a much richer understanding of the relationship of President and Supreme Court in the Civil War and nothing else? This is enough for almost any other era, but it seems that on the great constitutional questions of the Civil War, we are largely unwilling to leave them indeterminate.

This is not to say that legal actors in the Union and the Confederacy did not themselves reach legal and constitutional conclusions. But we in the present remain open to arguments from all sides and remain rooted in uncertainty and argumentation. Was secession legal? Was the confiscation of enemy property constitutional? Was the blockade within presidential power? All of these questions rest on the status of the Union and the Confederacy during the Civil War, which was contested during the Civil War and for decades afterward.

It is, of course, the case that there were winners and losers in the Civil War and that this outcome colors the way we understand the legal questions we pose about the war. It is not enough to say that these questions about the nature of the Civil War cannot be definitively answered. Even as we reconstruct the arguments made on both sides on secession, we must recall at all times this was not a debating society but a contest over power during war. If today we cannot make a definitive ruling on the ultimate legality of secession, it is folly to reconstruct the legal arguments made during the War without attention to who won and who lost the argument and why. At points, it is surely a case of might making right or a legal argument settled at the point of a gun. Whatever the legality of secession, it was surely settled as a practical matter at Appomattox. But that is only the ending.

It is the contingent and uncertain path to that point that is historically compelling. If our task is to definitively determine the legality of secession, then once that is done we know who is right and who is wrong and how the Civil War ought to have turned out. If, by contrast, we do not ourselves settle the question, then we see this argument played out over years of warfare, and we see the relative power of these ideas inside Northern and Southern society. It surely matters that the legality of secession was ultimately rejected, and this is in no small part a story of the relative power of competing ideologies inside societies at war.

The Stampp piece, to my mind, has stood the test of time and remains essential reading—indeed it remains the model for how the legal inquiry on secession ought to be pursued. It remains the model not because Stampp arrives at the right answer, but instead for his embrace of historical uncertainty.

Any who write on the Civil War are asked the questions Stampp raises, and others: Was secession justified? Who was right in the debate over habeas corpus, Taney or Lincoln? Who was right and who was wrong across a number of great constitutional questions? The answer I am calling for—"I do not know"—distances the past from the present in a way we almost cannot stand when it comes to the Civil War. It is here that the quality of academic writing, for good and for ill, might most contrast with the dominant narrative of the Civil War. It is an open question for the field: "Is the history sufficient, and can it stand alone, with values embedded in the story we tell and not the definitive legal answers we provide?"

Yet this answer to the question of who was right on secession, I do not know, runs the risk of mischaracterizing the meaning of secession both at the time of the Civil War and today, and this brings me briefly to my second point. Secession may ultimately be most fundamentally not a close legal question, but rather a vessel for our questions about the meaning of slavery and emancipation. This is a historical question: "Was secession essentially a referendum on slavery?" This is the essential question that Stampp neglects in his constitutional inquiry. If the answer is yes, then Stampp, in his emphasis on constitutional thought standing alone, both sheds light on secession and also omits the centrality of slavery in the secession crisis.

Secession may be most important, then and now, as a symbol, a symbol of the legitimacy of the Confederacy and the fight to preserve slavery. Interestingly, it may be that the symbolic meaning of secession was embraced by both sides, an embrace of secession as essentially driven by states' rights and an embrace of states' rights that turned, in both North and South, largely on the question of the preservation and expansion of slavery. It is here that Stampp's legal focus leads us astray and presents us with an analytical frame we ought now reject—namely treating secession as primarily a legal question. This does not mean that the legal argument is irrelevant or that it was infinitely malleable at the time. This means only that a legal question turning on states' rights and the right to secede was at all times embedded in the debate over slavery and cannot be considered first as a legal question and then as a political or social question.

This is even more apparent when one examines the staying power of the symbolic meaning of secession. The legitimacy of secession was at the heart of the Lost Cause and remains a potent symbol today for those seeking to deny the centrality of slavery to secession. In this way, Stampp's frame, in its presentation of a contained legal question, seems to me to miss a defining aspect of secession. Stampp might well admit this, of course, but to my mind, he cannot make the claim that his only concern for purposes of this piece was the law and the Constitution. This is, I think, an untenable dichotomy and one that has largely, thankfully, collapsed. It is here that the presentist obsession with determining the ultimate legality of secession actually aids the history because it forces upon us the realization that our present concern for the place of slavery within secession was very much a concern of the Civil War era. It is a powerful reason why we still care so much about secession and why actors at the time did as well.

We do not have to choose, indeed, between the abstract question of the legality of secession and its contrast with the lived experience of secession. We can examine contemporaries' competing assessments of legal and constitutional doctrine even as we take the realities of race and slavery into account.

NOTES

1. Kenneth M. Stampp, *The Concept of a Perpetual Union,* J. Am. Hist., June 1978, *at* 5.

2. Some of the following argument is based on claims I made in *Getting Right without Lincoln,* 45 Tulsa L. Rev. (Symposium Issue) 715 (2010).

3. Stampp, *supra* note 1, at 5.

4. *Id.*

5. *Id.*

6. *Id.* at 6.

7. *Id.*

8. Texas v. White, 74 U.S. 700 (1869).

9. Stampp, *Concept,* at 12.

10. *Id.* at 13.

11. *Id.* at 19.

12. Andrew Jackson, *Proclamation, in* Committee on the Library, Gen. Court of Mass., State Papers on Nullification: Including the Public Acts of the Convention of the People of South Carolina, Assembled at Columbia, November 19, 1932, and March 11, 1833, The Proclamation of the President of the United States, and the Proceedings of the Several State Legislatures Which Have Acted on the Subject 75 (1834).

13. Stampp, *supra* note 1, at 32.

14. *Id.* at 33.

15. *Id.*

16. David Donald, *Getting Right with Lincoln, reprinted in* Lincoln Reconsidered (1961).

17. Matthew Pinsker, *Lincoln Theme* 2.0, J. Am. Hist., Sept. 2009, at 417.

18. Hamilton, *supra* note 2, at 715.

19. James G. Randall, Constitutional Problems under Lincoln (1926). It remains central in leading accounts of Civil War legal history. *See* 2 Michael Burlingame, Abraham Lincoln (2008); Mark E. Neely, Jr., The Fate of Liberty (1991).

20. Hamilton, *supra* note 2, at 715.

5 Secession and Breach of Compact
The Law of Nature Meets the United States Constitution

Stephen C. Neff, University of Edinburgh School of Law

In the crisis of 1860–61, the architects of Southern secession were determined to justify their drastic action in legal terms. Not for them was a resort to naked power politics, in which brute force would be its own badge of legitimacy. This firmly legalistic outlook on the part of Southern leaders had been building up over the preceding decades. An important early figure was Robert J. Turnbull of South Carolina, who became the principal intellectual mentor of John C. Calhoun. In 1827, in a book called *The Crisis* (assembled from a series of articles written over the previous year), Turnbull pointed to the steady excess of population growth in the free states relative to the slave states. This of course translated, with the passage of years, into a constant growth of the political strength of the former over the latter in the federal Congress. In addition, there was the continuing fear of a long-term alliance between the northeastern and midwestern states in the form of Henry Clay's proposed American System of protective tariffs and internal improvements. (An enthusiastic supporter of Clay and his American System was an ambitious Illinois lawyer and politician named Abraham Lincoln.) In the face of this growing challenge, the proper strategy for the South, Turnbull contended, was resolute insistence on respect for the sovereign rights of the states.[1] As will be seen, these rights of the states were asserted, in the secession crisis, not against the federal government, as such, but rather against the free states. Southerners, in short, held themselves to be on the firmest of legal grounds in referring to the conflict of 1861–65 as the 'War between the States.'

For the marshalling of the arguments in support of their action, the South possessed two particularly notable legal paladins. One was Alexander Stephens of Georgia, who served as Vice President of the Confederacy and (more notably for present purposes) wrote a detailed constitutional exposition of the Southern position shortly after the Civil War.[2] The other was Judah P. Benjamin of Louisiana, who served as Confederate Attorney-General at the start of the war (and later as Secretary of War and finally Secretary of State). He set out the Southern position with great care in a speech in the Senate on December 31, 1860, which was then published in pamphlet form.[3]

This discussion will briefly outline the legal arguments in favor of the secessionist position. The first section will survey four arguments that could, in theory, have been employed but that, in practice, were used either not at all or only marginally. The second section will survey, in greater detail, the principal argument that was advanced in 1860–61: that secession was a lawful remedy available to the Southern states in the face of material breaches of the constitutional compact of 1787 by the free states. It will be observed that, in this argument, general considerations of natural law and of the law of nations played a central role.

I. ARGUMENTS THAT MIGHT HAVE BEEN EMPLOYED

There were four basic arguments that might have played important roles in the legal justification of Southern secession but did not. They are worth some brief attention, though, for two reasons. First, some of them were the subject of public debate, even if those debates did not play a central role in the secession crisis. Second, they highlight, by contrast, the nature of the breach-of-compact argument which was advanced as the principal justification.

These four alternative or subsidiary arguments for secession do not have standard labels. They will be referred to here as: first, the inherent-right, or voluntary-Union thesis; second, the inherent-power position; third, the absence-of-federal-power argument; and fourth, the revolutionary argument. It will be seen that, strictly speaking, the second and third of these are not arguments in support of an actual *right* of secession, but are merely assertions of the ability of the Southern states effectually to bring about secession.

A. *The Inherent-Right-of-Secession (or Voluntary-Union) Argument*

The basis of the argument for an inherent right of secession on the part of the Southern states (or any other states for that matter) was the belief that the federal Union was a purely voluntary association of states, terminable at will by any party at any time. For this reason, it can be alternatively termed the voluntary-Union thesis. In all events, the basic contention was that, as a matter of their inherent sovereign rights, the states of the Union were entitled at any time, as an act of unilateral will, to withdraw from the federal Union.

This line of reasoning held the United States to be, in effect, an international organization (in modern terminology) of sovereign nation-states, along the lines of the League of Nations or the United Nations. In the League of Nations Covenant, explicit provision was made (perhaps unadvisedly) for withdrawal of member states on their own unilateral initiative—a right that was resorted to with disconcerting frequency. The UN Charter contains no analogous provision, nor is there any clear judicial authority on the matter. But the predominant opinion is that states do possess an inherent right of withdrawal from international organizations as an exercise of their normal sovereign rights.[4] The United States, it may be noted, has itself withdrawn from two organizations in the UN family: the International Labor Organization and UNESCO (although in due course it rejoined both).[5]

Concerning this inherent-right thesis, it remains to note only a curious development that has yet to be adequately explored or explained: the fact that, while the argument was not employed at the time of the secessions of 1860–61, it came to attract significant support in the course of the conflict. Confederate Attorney-General T.H. Watts, for example, asserted it in an opinion in 1862, holding that a state of the federal Union

> might, as a matter of right, secede, according to its will and pleasure, though every constitutional provision remained intact and unbroken, and though every law of the United States was in accordance with its will and pleasure.[6]

The following year, in a similar vein, he maintained that the states had retained their sovereign rights upon joining the federal Union in 1789—meaning that they were entitled at any time, as a matter of inherent sovereign prerogative, to rescind their membership of that Union.[7]

B. The Inherent-Power Argument

This argument is similar to the inherent-right argument, except that it focuses on power rather than on right. According to the inherent-right thesis, there is a permanent and standing entitlement on the part of member states of the federal Union to rescind their membership. The corresponding inherent-power argument is to the effect that, even if no such right exists, states nonetheless possess the *power* to reassert their full range of pre-Union sovereign rights and thereby to revert to the status of a fully independent nation-state. Even if that power is exercised contrary to legal right—that is, even if it constitutes an unjustified breach of a legally binding compact or treaty—it is nonetheless effectual in bringing about the end sought (withdrawal from the federal Union).

If the power was exercised in circumstances that entailed a breach of a legal obligation, then the parties to whom that obligation was owed thereby became legally entitled to reparation for any loss that they suffered. In principle, this would mean something along the lines of an action for money damages, comparable to damages for the breach of a contract when a remedy of specific performance was not available. In practice, of course, no court existed with jurisdiction to order such a remedy. But even if it did, the Union would nevertheless remain dissolved because no judicial authority could order a state to enter or reenter a Union with other states against its will (that is, a remedy of specific performance would not be available against a seceding state to force it back into the Union).

It does not appear that this argument was ever advanced, in any significant way, at the time of the secession crisis of 1860–61. Perhaps the distinction between right and power was not strongly on the collective minds of lawyers and political theorists at that time. It may be noted, though, if only in passing, that, after the war, this argument did win the explicit endorsement of a judge in the Georgia Supreme Court (though only in dissent, with the majority of the court holding otherwise on this point).[8]

C. *The Absence-of-Federal-Power Argument*

This argument is closely allied to the inherent-power argument just discussed, in being, as it were, the flip side of it. Whereas the inherent-power thesis was a positive one, focusing on the *possession* of power by the states to *effectuate* secession, this argument was a negative one, focusing instead on the *absence* of any power of the federal government to *prevent* secession.

This argument had been initially aired by Calhoun during the nullification crisis of the early 1830s. He conceded that the federal government had the power to act coercively against individuals—for example, for violation of federal criminal laws—but it had no power, he insisted, to take armed action against a state.[9] Calhoun was scornful of the value of a Union that could be held together only by force, invoking instead an alternative vision of a "harmonious aggregate of States, produced by the joint consent of all."[10]

Attorney-General Jeremiah S. Black took a similar position in an opinion on "The Power of the President in Executing the Laws," written in November 1860, just after the election of Lincoln to the presidency but before the secession of South Carolina.[11] Normally, Black noted, federal laws are executed by the courts, with marshals acting as the enforcement arm.[12] In unusual cases, though, the efforts of the marshals might require supplementation by additional manpower of some kind. But any such additional force, Black contended, must be ancillary to the normal operations of the federal courts. "There must be courts and marshals to be aided," he cautioned.[13] Otherwise, "to send a military force into any State, with orders to act against the people, would be simply making war upon them"—something that the President had no power to do.[14] The federal government, to be sure, possessed the right of self-defense, entitling it to use force to repel actual attacks against federal installations such as arsenals or forts. But this right could not be extended to allow the federal government to wage offensive war against states. Even Congress did not have the power to wage war against a state because the Congress's constitutional power to declare war referred, in Black's view, only to war against foreign countries, not against member states of the federal Union.[15]

Outgoing President James Buchanan took this advice to heart. In his final annual message to Congress, in December 1860, with the secession crisis looming, he expressly denied that the federal government possessed the power to exercise coercion against states.[16] He echoed Black's advice by holding that no branch of the federal government had the right or power to invoke force against a state.[17] "[T]he power to make war against a State," he asserted, "is at variance with the whole spirit and intent of the Constitution."[18]

A similar conclusion was reached by Chief Justice Roger B. Taney in some unpublished thoughts on the subject of potential federal legislation to institute military conscription. The federal government, thought Taney, "could not exercise forcibly any authority civil or military by its own officers within the territories of a State without its consent."[19]

D. The Revolutionary Argument

The fourth and final argument that might have played a central role in the secession debate was the revolutionary argument. Given the potential resonance with the patriots of 1776, it might be thought that this argument would have played a starring role in the legal drama of 1860–61. It is interesting to note that President Buchanan candidly conceded at least the potential validity of a revolutionary argument. "The right of resistance on the part of the governed against the oppression of their governments," he asserted in his final annual message to Congress, "cannot be denied. It exists independently of all constitutions, and has been exercised at all periods of the world's history."[20]

Judah Benjamin provided a characteristically more exact analysis of the legal nature of this right of revolution. It arose, he explained, in situations in which a government was exercising powers that it lawfully possessed but was exercising in an oppressive manner.[21] In such a case, remedies at law would, by the nature of the case, be lacking; so the only recourse of the suffering people was the extra-legal one of overthrowing the government by force.[22] Revolution, in other words, was the appropriate remedy against what would now be called an abuse of right on the part of a government.

The reason that this argument did not play an important part in the secession crisis may be stated briefly here: that the Southern leaders were not alleging oppression of the Southern states by the federal government. They could even be said to have been complaining of the very opposite: that the federal government was insufficiently powerful, that its policies—notably the enforcement of the Fugitive Slave Act[23]—were being thwarted by disruptive persons (and state governments) in the North. This contention will be expanded on presently.[24] Here, it is sufficient simply to note that the true legal grievances of the Southern states were not against the federal government, but rather against the Northern states, which (in the Southern view) were undermining the effectiveness of federal policies.

It may be noted that, in the course of the conflict, the South did find occasion to assert a revolutionary argument for secession. This was inspired by an act of the Union government which inspired particular loathing in the South: the arming and employment of former slaves as soldiers in the Union cause. One form that the Confederate reaction took was the insistence that black soldiers were (in modern parlance) unlawful combatants and that they would accordingly not be accorded prisoner-of-war treatment if captured. More to the point for present purposes, though, was the text of a manifesto on the war that was promulgated by the Confederate Congress in June 1864. Now echoing the Declaration of Independence of 1776, the Richmond Congress asserted "the right of a free people, when a government proves destructive of the ends for which it was established, to recur to original principles and to institute new guards to their security."[25]

II. THE BREACH-OF-COMPACT THEORY AND ITS IMPLICATION

The legal argument that was actually deployed by the Southern leaders in 1860–61 may be characterized as the breach-of-compact theory. Its essence is simple. The federal Union, properly understood, was an ongoing contractual union between sovereign states—states that retained all aspects of their sovereignty after entry into the Union, save those that they had expressly delegated to the federal government. That original constitutional contract—or compact—like any other contract, retained its legal validity only so long as the parties continued faithfully to adhere to it. Any breach of the compact by parties to it automatically entitled the innocent parties to withdraw from the arrangement.

Support for this line of argument in the text of the Constitution itself was altogether absent. There was no real question, therefore, of constitutional interpretation here. Instead, the argument rested on a certain understanding about the general character of the federal Union, fortified by arguments drawn from writings about general natural law.

More specifically, the breach-of-compact argument for secession relied for its credibility, in essence, on the establishment of four key propositions. The first three are points of law and the fourth a point of fact. First, the true nature of the federal Union was a compact between sovereign states rather than a single national government. Second, a material breach of the covenant gave rise to the lawful remedy of rescission. Third, self-judgment was necessary for the determination of the existence of such a breach. Fourth and finally, there was the application of these three legal principles to the facts of the particular situation of 1860–61, in the form of concrete evidence of actual violation of the federal compact by the Northern states.

A. *The Compact Theory of the Federal Union*

The first and most basic underlying component of the secessionist case was the thesis that the American federal Union was a Union of sovereign states rather than a single nation-state. This Union was, concededly, the creation of the people of the United States, but only in an indirect manner. The American people created the Union not by giving their approval as a single population of individual persons, but rather through the media of the various sovereign states into which they were then divided—and into which they continued to be divided for all purposes save those expressly transferred to the Union government. The case for and against this basic compact theory has been analyzed before, so that only its most salient points need be noted here.

The compact theory received its first systematic treatment at the hands of Calhoun.[26] The federal government, in his words, was "the government of a community of States, and not the government of a single State or nation."[27] The United States, in other words, must be regarded as a union of preexisting political communities and not as a single society of individuals, as was the case for a true nation-state. Moreover, these preexisting political communities retained their character as sovereign states even after forming the Union; as a result, they were bound together, as separate entities, in a continuing, ongoing contractual relationship. Calhoun insisted that sovereignty was, by its nature, single and indivisible and that sovereignty remained with the states. The federal Union was therefore not a sovereign entity in its own right, but a mere vehicle or tool of the states, created by them for the fulfillment of their purposes.

It must not be thought that Calhoun invented the compact theory out of whole cloth. It had at least a measure of support from the Founding Fathers themselves. James Madison, for example, in the *Federalist* No. 39, expressly described the establishment of the Constitution (though not the day-to-day operation of the federal government) as "not . . . a *national*, but a *federal* act."[28] The founding of the Union, Madison went on to say, was "the act of the people, as forming so many independent States, not as forming one aggregate nation."[29] The character of the Union as a compact of states was further evident, Madison pointed out. As in the case of contracts generally, adherence was purely voluntary on the part of each party—in sharp contrast to the position in a political society, in which the majority will would bind the minority.

Further support for the compact theory could be adduced from the Kentucky and Virginia Resolutions of 1798, drafted by Thomas Jefferson and James Madison, respectively. Madison's Virginia Resolution expressly described the powers of the federal government as "resulting from [a] compact,"[30] and it went on to lament any tendency "to consolidate the states by degrees, into one sovereignty."[31] Jefferson's Kentucky Resolution was similar in tone, proclaiming each state to have acceded "to this compact . . . as a State," with "its co-States forming as to itself, the other party" to the compact.[32]

The compact theory of the Union, not surprisingly, met with fierce opposition. And no opponent of it was fiercer than the redoubtable Senator Daniel Webster of Massachusetts. He asserted with characteristic force and eloquence, most notably in the famous Senate debate against Robert Hayne in 1830, that the compact theory was fundamentally unsound, asserting instead that the federal Union was "the independent offspring of the popular will" of the American people at large.[33] The Constitution, he insisted, was the creation "of the people of the United States, in the aggregate."[34]

Even the eloquence of Daniel Webster did not suffice to dislodge the Southerners from their attachment to the compact theory. They maintained it up to the Civil War and even beyond, with Stephens as their spokesman-in-chief.[35] The compact theory also received official support from the Confederate government. In 1863, Confederate Attorney-General Watts opined that the population of the United States "never constituted one and the same community," nor did the United States ever constitute a nation.[36]

B. The Remedy of Rescission for Breach of Compact under Natural Law

This second crucial proposition—that the remedy of termination of the compact (that is, of secession) was available in cases of breach—lay at the very core of the Southern case for lawful secession. It should be noted that this thesis is not logically entailed by the compact theory as such. It was possible to see the Union as a compact of states while holding at the same time that that Union was not terminable for any reason.[37] The issue of terminability of the Union is therefore conceptually distinct from the question of the underlying nature of the Union—a point that was clearly understood by all parties to the debates.

The issue over the terminability of the Union has sometimes been seen as a debate over whether or not the federal Union was, or was intended at its outset to be, a perpetual one.[38] That is a misleading way of putting it, because the word 'perpetual' may be understood in either of two quite distinct senses, which could be termed the 'strong' and the 'weak.' Perpetual in the strong sense means that the Union is indissoluble in any circumstance whatsoever—that is, upon joining the federal Union, a state thereby alienated, irrevocably and in perpetuity, all right and power to withdraw from the Union. Perpetual in the weak sense means that the Union is perpetual in principle, or that it was intended at the outset to be perpetual—but that this aspiration of perpetuity could be achieved in reality only by the continued adherence of the parties to the original arrangements over time. According to this weak view of perpetuity, then, a state, upon joining the Union, surrenders only its right to withdraw from the Union as a matter of unilateral sovereign will. It is left with the possibility of withdrawal as a lawful remedy for breach of the compact by the other parties to it.[39] The position of the advocates of secession in the 1860–61 crisis was that the Union was a perpetual one in the weak sense, but not in the strong sense.

On this subject too, the views of Benjamin are particularly instructive, as he addressed the question of the perpetual character of the federal Union very explicitly. He candidly conceded that, in principle, the federal Union was a perpetual one—though, crucially, in the weak sense rather than the strong one. "[N]o man pretends," insisted Benjamin, "that the generation of to-day is not bound by the compacts of the fathers."[40] But he went on to contend that the real issue at hand was not whether the Union had been envisaged as perpetual in the 1780s. It had been. The issue was whether, since that time, that Union had been irredeemably shattered by the failure of the Northern states to abide by their commitments under the original constitutional compact. The compact remained binding, Benjamin maintained, only so long as all parties continued to adhere to it.[41]

That it would be wrong to regard the secession advocates as enemies of perpetual unions per se is evident from no less authoritative a source than the Confederate Constitution itself. That document did not include a provision granting the states a right to secede at will. On the contrary, it explicitly stated in the preamble the intention of the Southern states "to form a permanent federal government"[42]—permanent, it is safe to conclude, in the weak rather than the strong sense.

The Southerners' proposition that the federal Union of 1787–89 was perpetual only in the weak sense (that is, it was terminable in the event of breach) was, however, nowhere to be found in the Constitution, which made no provision for breaches by states. To be sure, there was the Supremacy Clause. But that spoke to a different problem: the possibility of a clash between a state law and a federal law. It shed no light whatsoever on how to resolve a clash between the states over a breach of terms of adherence to the federal Union itself. Authority for the existence of this remedy of rescission would therefore have to be found outside the framework of the Constitution.

The justification for this remedy was duly found in natural law, which was an integral part of the mental universe of American lawyers in the early and midnineteenth century. It was one of the most venerable intellectual ornaments of Western civilization, older than Christianity itself. Its basic thesis was that law, in its most fundamental guise, was a set of statements of principles of universal and permanent validity. Its strictures prevailed in all countries and all civilizations and in all times. It was painfully obvious that its tenets were all too frequently violated in practice, but these violations, however frequent, could have no effect on the essential validity of this body of law. Natural law thought is therefore in sharp contrast with schools of legal philosophy (most notably the positivist one) which holds law to comprise the expression of the will of a given sovereign, expressed in the form of commands issued to a subject population and with the prospect of punishment for disobedience of those commands.[43] There were various theories as to how the tenets of natural law were to be discovered. But the most prominent one in the eighteenth and nineteenth centuries held natural law to be discoverable through the exercise of human reason. This was a doctrine put forcefully by Thomas Aquinas in the Middle Ages[44] and expounded by a line of writers in the centuries that followed. The most prestigious of these was Hugo Grotius[45] in the seventeenth century followed by the German writers Samuel Pufendorf[46] and Christian Wolff,[47] as well as by the Swiss writer Emmerich de Vattel.[48]

Most pertinent of these natural law writers for the American tradition was John Locke, in the late seventeenth century, whose writings were echoed by Jefferson and others among the Founders of the American Republic in the eighteenth century. In the tradition of his forebears of the rationalist tradition of natural law, Locke insisted that one of the important tenets of natural law was the duty to adhere to contracts.[49] This fundamental principle applies not only to individual persons, but also to political collectives and even to God Himself.[50]

This law of nature was applicable, in its purest form, to persons who were living in what was called a state of nature vis-à-vis one another. A state of nature, for this purpose, was, in essence, a condition in which no common sovereign existed over the persons in question—with the inevitable result that relations between them were governed solely by natural law. Once a political society was established (whether peacefully by contract or violently through coercion or conquest), natural law could be overridden or superseded by the commands of the established sovereign. The effect, then, was that natural law operated as a kind of continuous 'default law,' which would be applicable in any situation in which there was no holder of sovereign power to promulgate laws or adjudicate disputes.

Locke was also very clear in his exposition of another aspect of this question: what was to be done, under natural law, in the event that a party to a contract violated its duty of obedience. The remedy, Locke explained, was self-enforcement. This was the only possibility because, by definition, no sovereign power existed that could undertake the enforcement. As Locke put it, one of the key powers held by all persons in a state of nature (as defined above) was the power "to judge of, and punish the breaches of that law in others, as he is persuaded the offence deserves."[51] This could even go to the point of inflicting capital punishment on a miscreant (provided that such drastic punishment was duly proportionate to the wrong committed).[52]

In a political society, Locke maintained, this natural law power of self-judgment and self-execution was transferred from the ordinary citizens to the sovereign (whether by free will or by force, as the case may be). This was, in fact, for all practical purposes the very definition of a political society for writers in the natural law tradition. The inevitable logical corollary was that, wherever and whenever this transfer of natural-law power had not been effectuated, it remained in force. "[W]herever there are any number of men, however associated," Locke explained, "that have no such decisive power [that is, no sovereign] to appeal to, there they are still in the state of nature."[53] In such a state, each party must remain "judge for himself, and executioner" in the event that a dispute arose.[54]

The question, then, is what form this self-help action of enforcement could take. It could be argued that the innocent party, in a breach-of-contract scenario, could resort to force, on a sort of analogy with self-defense—that is, that could exert however much force (and no more) as was necessary under the circumstances to compel obedience from the recalcitrant party. More commonly, though, natural law writers spoke in terms of a right of rescission of the contract on the part of the innocent party. As Hugo Grotius explained in his treatise *On the Law of War and Peace,* "the individual terms of an alliance have the force of conditions"—with the effect that a violation by one party enables the other to withdraw.[55] In a similar vein, Pufendorf held:

> [W]hen one party does not perform what is agreed upon, the other is not obligated to perform what he agreed to in exchange and in consideration of the other's performance. For whoever promises another something by a pact, does so not absolutely and gratis, but in consideration of what the other has undertaken to perform; and so the performances of each for the other take on the form of a condition.... But it is fixed that whatever is built upon a condition falls to the ground when the condition does not appear.[56]

Similar, too, as well as more succinct, was Wolff: "If one party shall have violated a treaty," he pronounced, "the other party... can withdraw from it."[57] He agreed with Pufendorf that, in every treaty that contained mutual promises, the due performance of those promises by either party must be regarded as conditions for the reciprocal performance by the other. Jean-Jacques Rousseau, the French political philosopher, was also of this view. Each party to a contract, he contended, "would always have a right to renounce the contract, as soon as he found that the other had violated its terms."[58]

More directly familiar to American lawyers and political writers would have been Vattel, whose treatise *On the Law of Nations* of 1758 was widely known in American legal circles. A breach of a treaty by one party, Vattel asserted, entitled the other to resort to armed force to compel performance (that is, it was a cause for the waging of a just war, in the parlance of the time). But an alternative, and less drastic, remedy was rescission of the treaty:

> [I]t is at times more expedient for the [injured innocent] State to revoke its own promises and to break the treaty; it is unquestionably justified in doing so,

> since its own promises were made only on condition that the other State would carry out on its part the stipulations of the treaty.[59]

"Prudence and policy," he maintained, would decide which of the available options the injured state would choose on a given occasion.[60]

Closer still to home was the word of the American writer on international law (as well as Supreme Court reporter and diplomat) Henry Wheaton. Speaking in the context of treaties of peace, he echoed Vattel in holding that a violation by one party "abrogates the whole treaty, if the injured party so elects to consider it."[61] He went on to explain that the effect of this principle is that the violated treaty becomes "not absolutely void, but voidable at the election of the injured party."[62]

The application of this reasoning to the American situation in 1860–61 led adherents of the compact theory of the Union to a clear conclusion. On the basis of the compact theory, they insisted that the states retained their sovereign status even after entry into the Union and that, consequently, the federal government was not a sovereign with authority over the states. The federal government was merely a vehicle created by the sovereign states to carry out certain limited functions that had been entrusted to it in the original federal compact of 1787. Consistent with this view, Southern writers tended to insist that there was no such thing as citizenship of the United States. There was only citizenship of the individual states.[63]

As a result (went the argument on the compact theory), the states of the American Union must be regarded as being in a state of nature vis-à-vis one another. More specifically, the provisions of Article III of the Constitution, outlining the jurisdiction of the federal courts, contained no grant of jurisdiction over issues of the kind presented in the 1850s. It did grant the federal courts jurisdiction over "[c]ontroversies between two or more States."[64] But it appears to have been generally agreed that this referred to the adjudication of competing claims by states to rights of some kind, such as a dispute over a boundary or territory. It did not apply to accusations by one state that another one was impeding enforcement of federal law (that is, of the Fugitive Slave Act) within its territory.

The states, to be sure, were bound to adhere to agreements that they made. But it was general natural law that so bound them, rather than the commands of a sovereign federal government. By the same token, it was natural law that conferred the remedy of rescission in the event of violation of any such agreement. Alexander Stephens was very explicit on this point. The right of rescission, he explained, "comes not from any thing in the Constitution, but from the great law of Nations, governing all Compacts between Sovereigns."[65] This right of rescission, he went on to emphasize, finds its source in the general law of nations, which provides for "the right . . . to abrogate a treaty by either or any of the parties to it."[66] He conceded that this right (or rather remedy) "is seldom set forth in the treaty itself, and yet it exists, whether it be set forth or not. . . . [W]here no such provision is made, the right exists by the same laws of Nations which govern in all matters of treaties or conventions between Sovereigns."[67]

Several points about this remedy of rescission for breach of the federal compact should be noted with care. One was that it was generally agreed, in natural law writing, that this right of rescission in the event of a breach of a compact was subject to one marginal caveat: that it was open to the makers of a compact, at the time of contracting, expressly to exclude rescission as a remedy for breach. In terms of the federal Union, the effect of such an express arrangement would be to make the Union a perpetual one in the strong sense rather than the weak one. It was therefore necessary to the Southern thesis to insist that, in the case of the American Constitution, no such express provision had been made.

Another point to note is how different the legal quandary of the Southern states was from that of the American colonies in the 1770s, despite a certain amount of emotional appeal to the example of the Founders. The American colonists in the 1770s had alleged that they were oppressed by their lawful sovereign, the monarch of Great Britain. That is to say, they were reacting against an alleged abuse of powers by a political superior. Their action was therefore revolutionary in the strict sense that Benjamin had explained, in that it was an overthrowing a sovereign power that was prima facie lawful (though oppressive).

The Southern states were making a very different claim in 1860. They were not contending that the federal government was inflicting oppression upon them in the manner of King George III in days of old. It could even be said that they were making the very opposite claim: that the federal government, far from being an oppressor, was actually, in effect, itself a victim of wrongdoing by the Northern states. It was a victim in the sense that its attempts to enforce the law of the land (for example, the Fugitive Slave Act) were being thwarted by lawless elements in the Northern states, with the more or less active collaboration of the state governments.

The legal grievances of the Southern states therefore had remarkably little to do with the federal government per se. This may appear surprising in light of the fact that the Civil War, as it unfolded, became a gigantic effort by the federal government to bring the rebellious Southern states to terms. Similarly, the post–Civil War period witnessed a long-term (if often rather low-key) struggle between the federal government and the Southern states over issues of states' rights (most outstandingly, of course, concerning the civil and political rights of former slaves and their descendants in the Southern states). But it was only with the adoption of the 14th Amendment to the Constitution in 1870, with its grant to the federal government of a degree of supervisory power over the states, that the grand contest between federal rights and states' rights came to assume its familiar modern form.[68]

On the eve of the Civil War, the Southern leaders were champions of states' rights in a very different way. They were championing the rights not so much of the states vis-à-vis the federal government, but rather rights of one class of states against another class of states—that is, the rights of the class of law-abiding states against the class of nullifying states. Far from struggling against a usurpatious federal government—as had been the case in the nullification crisis of the 1830s—the Southern states were now staunchly on the side of that same federal government, seeking to prevent the Northern states from, in effect, following nullification policies of their own against the Fugitive Slave Act.

C. The Necessity of Self-Judgment

The third key conceptual pillar of the Southern argument for the lawfulness of secession lay in the right of parties to a dispute—still under the authority of general natural law—to determine for themselves when their own rights had been infringed. Few legal clichés would win readier consent than the proposition that a person should not be the judge in his or her own cause.[69]

In the natural law tradition, however, there was venerable authority for holding this proposition to be restricted in scope to disputes that occur in politically organized society. In those cases, it is the duty of the disputants to submit to the judgment of their sovereign. For persons in a state of nature (that is, in the absence of such a sovereign), however, this principle cannot apply because, by definition, there is no sovereign. In such a situation, there can be no alternative to allowing each party to a dispute to reach its own judgment as to when its rights have been violated. Rousseau expressed a similar view. In the absence of a judge with jurisdiction over a dispute, he posited, "the parties would be sole judges in their own cause."[70]

In his discussion of this point, Locke was under no illusion that this state of affairs was unsatisfactory, for the obvious reason that each party will naturally insist on the rightness of its own position.[71] It is for just such a reason that a politically organized society is preferable to a state of nature. But so long as the state of nature persists, there simply is no alternative to allowing self-judgment of disputes. The only consolation that Locke could offer was to assure his readers that persons in the state of nature who abused this prerogative would be "answerable for it to the rest of mankind."[72]

In the 1860–61 crisis, Benjamin articulated this position. Political disputes, he contended, are, in general, not justiciable—not necessarily because they are inherently incapable of being decided by courts, but rather because of the absence of any court possessing the requisite jurisdiction.[73] In this situation, Benjamin contended, "natural law and the law of nations" dictates that the state parties to the constitutional compact must judge their own injuries themselves.[74]

This characterization of the dispute between the slave and free states as a political question naturally calls to mind the political question doctrine in general constitutional jurisprudence. But there was an important difference. The political question doctrine in general constitutional law refers, basically, to issues that, by their nature, are not susceptible of judicial resolution. Such questions must therefore be hammered out by other branches of the government through normal political processes.[75] The dispute between the slave and free states in 1860–61 was not, however, of that character. As a straightforward claim of breach of compact, it would seem eminently suitable for judicial resolution—if, that is, a court were at hand with jurisdiction to hear the case. The general political question doctrine, in other words, requires an initial finding that a dispute, by its nature, is political, with the consequential effect that courts are then deprived of a jurisdiction they would otherwise have had. That is to say, courts lack jurisdiction because the issue at hand is political. In the secession crisis, the conceptual arrow of causation pointed in the opposite direction: the question of a breach of compact was a political one, not because of its intrinsic character, but only because of the absence of jurisdiction by courts, so that the issue became political by virtue of that absence of jurisdiction.

In all events, support for self-help action on the part of states that were victims of violations of the Constitution went as far back as the *Federalist Papers,* in which Hamilton had considered the hypothetical case of usurpation of state powers by either the federal government or the states.[76] The solution, he proposed rather vaguely, was that each of these political bodies would naturally "stand ready to check the usurpations" of the other.[77] The issue between them would be decided, ultimately, by "[t]he people," who would support one side or the other as they judged best.[78] Moreover, if the rights of the people were to be invaded by, say, the federal government, then the remedy (again rather vaguely) would be for the aggrieved people to "make use of" their state government to "adopt a regular plan of opposition" against the impending oppression.[79] Conversely, if the offending government was the state, then the people would react by lending their support to the federal government. If more than one state was a victim of federal encroachment, then the affected states could combine their efforts and thereby render resistance more effective.

The important point to note about Hamilton's thesis is that it envisaged political, rather than judicial, action against usurpations of power under the Constitution. He made no attempt to pretend that any court would have jurisdiction to resolve the matter. The basic theory, therefore, was one of countervailing political powers. In such a system, there was simply no alternative to self-judgment on the part of the contending parties. Each was necessarily left to determine for itself when its own rights had been infringed, and in the event of clashing opinions on the matter between different branches or levels of government, the decision must rest ultimately—somehow or other—with the people.

It is true that Hamilton's immediate concern was with a conflict between the federal government and one or more states (as in the case of the Nullification Crisis of the 1830s). But at the heart of his argument, if only implicitly, was the thesis that in the absence of jurisdiction by any court, a clash between governments within a federal system could be resolved only by political means—and this process inevitably and necessarily entailed self-judgment by the contending parties.

D. *Applying the Facts of 1860–61 to the Law*

As the fourth and final step in the making of the legal case for secession, it only remained to apply the facts of the case to the legal framework just outlined—that is, to establish that the terms of the federal compact had in fact been violated by the Northern states. In the eyes of the secession advocates, that was the easiest step of all. Foremost among the accusations against the Northern states were allegations of violation of the Fugitive Slave Act, that notorious centerpiece of the Compromise of 1850.

The 1850 act did not, of course, come out of a vacuum. The Constitution itself had made explicit provision on the subject, setting out the general principle that an escaping slave could not thereby be discharged from his "Service or Labour."[80] In other words, the act of escaping did not alter a slave's legal status as a slave or deprive the master of his rights incidental to ownership. The clause also provided that an escaping slave "shall be delivered up" upon claim by the master.[81] Only in 1850, though, did Congress enact legislation setting up a permanent system of commissioners charged specifically with the capture and return of slaves—a system that, crucially, operated in the territory of the free states.

The essence of the Southern case for secession, then, was that the Northern ones were in breach of the constitutional compact because of their attempts to nullify federal law by interfering with enforcement of the Fugitive Slave Act. With scrupulous exactitude, the Georgia politician Howell Cobb maintained that ten states of the Union "have interposed their strong arm to protect the thief, punish the owner [of slaves], and confiscate the property of a citizen of a sister State."[82] This amounted, he insisted, to "the plain and palpable violation of the constitutional compact" on the part of these ten "nullifying States" (as he bluntly designated them).[83] Stephens, in a similar vein, contended that thirteen of the Northern states had "openly and avowedly disregarded their obligations" under two key provisions of the Constitution: the Fugitive Slave Clause, and the Extradition Clause.[84] The result was that "by public law they [the Southern states] had a perfect right to withdraw" from the Union.[85] The Virginians were not to be outdone in this regard. R.M.T. Hunter accused the Northern states of waging "a regular warfare" against the Southern slave system, "the practical effect of which was to nullify the fugitive slave law."[86]

These same accusations appeared in official form in the declarations issued by several of the Southern states on the causes of secession. The *South Carolina Declaration*, for example, asserted that fourteen of the free states "have deliberately refused, for years past, to fulfill their constitutional obligations, and as a result, the laws of the General Government have ceased to effect the objects of the Constitution."[87] The declaration went on to state the legal essence of the Southern position with exquisite precision:

> We maintain [proclaimed the South Carolina secession convention] that in every compact between two or more parties, the obligation is mutual; that the failure of one of the contracting parties to perform a material part of the agreement, entirely releases the obligation of the other; and that, where no arbiter is provided, each party is remitted to its own judgment to determine the fact of failure, with all its consequences.[88]

The declaration of the causes of secession issued by Georgia was particularly eloquent on this subject. Claimants of fugitive slaves, it proclaimed, "are murdered with impunity; officers of the law are beaten by frantic mobs instigated by inflammatory appeals from persons holding the highest public employment in these States, and supported by legislation in conflict with the clearest provisions of the Constitution, and even the ordinary principles of humanity."[89] In broadly similar, if slightly more measured terms, Mississippi's declaration asserted that the hostility of Northern populations "has nullified the Fugitive Slave Law in almost every free State in the Union, and has utterly broken the compact which our fathers pledged their faith to maintain."[90] The Texas declaration solemnly asserted "that the federal constitution has been violated and virtually abrogated" by the Northern states.[91]

III. CONCLUSION

It remains only to make two final, and related, observations relating to some broader aspects and implications of the secession experience of 1860–61. The first concerns the fate of the compact theory of the federal Union, that essential conceptual foundation-stone of the secessionist case. In 1871, Justice Joseph P. Bradley of the federal Supreme Court pronounced it to have been "definitely and forever overthrown."[92] What Justice Bradley tactfully left unmentioned was that overthrow had taken place on the fields of battle rather than in the paneled rooms of courts or legislatures. The question of the nature of the federal Union, in event, proved to be neither a judicial nor a political question, but a military one.

The compact theory became, in other words, a sort of specialized juridical version of the Lost Cause of Southern independence in general. But there is a further and little noted parallel between the legal situation and the general political fate of the South. Just as Southerners regained much of their political strength after the war and Reconstruction—sufficient to delay the enjoyment of effective civil rights for Southern blacks for nearly a century—so also did at least some of their legal arguments live on for years to come.

In particular, appeals to natural law and related principles in support of existing social and economic arrangements, far from dying out after the Civil War, lived a long and robust life—no longer, of course, in support of the specific institution of slavery. But natural-law arguments continued to be regularly invoked as buttresses of the status quo—for example, in support of the principle of unlimited freedom of contract (against social-welfare legislation) and of the rights of property holders (against various forms of wealth redistribution and government regulation). This was in sharp contrast to the appeal to natural law by political liberals and revolutionaries in the seventeenth and eighteenth centuries—including, notably, the American colonies in their quest for independence. How it was that so dramatic a change occurred in so short a period of time is one of the yet-untold stories of the history of jurisprudential thought. The Southern arguments for the lawfulness of secession should therefore be seen, not as mere historical curiosities—interesting though they undoubtedly are in that regard—but as part of a far more general, and largely successful, effort to enlist the law of nature on the side of the forces of conservatism.

NOTES

1. Robert J. Turnbull, The Crisis, Or, Essays on the Usurpations of the Federal Government (1827).

2. *See* Alexander H. Stephens, A Constitutional View of the Late War between the States (2 vols. 1868–70).

3. *See* Judah P. Benjamin, *The Right of Secession, in* Southern Pamphlets on Secession, November 1860–April 1861, at 101–14 (Jon L. Wakelyn ed., 1996).

4. *See* N. Feinberg, *Unilateral Withdrawal from an International Organization,* 39 Brit. Y.B. Int'l L. 189–219 (1963).

5. The United States withdrew from the International Labor Organization in 1977 and rejoined in 1980. It withdrew from UNESCO at the end of 1984 and rejoined in 2003.

6. T.H. Watts, *Relation of Confederacy to the Former Union (Dec. 27, 1862), in* The Opinions of the Confederate Attorneys General 1861–1865, at 224 (Rembert W. Patrick ed., 1950).

7. T.H. Watts, *Pardon for a Deserter (Mar. 4, 1863), in* Patrick, *supra* note 6, at 231, 240.

8. Chancely v. Bailey, 37 Ga. 532 (1868).

9. John C. Calhoun, *A Discourse on the Constitution and Government of the United States, in* John C. Calhoun, Union and Liberty 79, 178 (Ross M. Lence ed., 1992) [hereinafter Calhoun, *Discourse*].

10. John C. Calhoun, *Speech on the Revenue Collection [Force] Bill* (Feb. 15–16, 1833), *in* Union and Liberty, *supra* note 9, at 401, 436 [hereinafter Calhoun, *Speech on the Force Bill*].

11. Power of the President in Executing the Laws, 9 Op. Att'y-Gen. 516 (1860).

12. *Id.* at 523.

13. *Id.*

14. *Id.*

15. *Id.* at 524.

16. 5 A Compilation of the Messages and Papers of the Presidents 1789–1897, at 635–36 (James D. Richardson ed., 1897).

17. *Id.*

18. *Id.*

19. *See* Roger B. Taney, Thoughts on the Conscription Law of the U[nited] States—Rough Draft Requiring Revision 3 (Philip G. Auchampaugh ed., n.d.).

20. Richardson, *supra* note 16, at 634.

21. Benjamin, *supra* note 3, at 107–8.

22. *Id.*

23. Act of Sept. 18, 1850, 9 Stat. 462.

24. *See* the text at note 82 infra.

25. Joint Res. Declaring the Dispositions, Principles and Purposes of the Confederate States in Relation to the Existing War with the United States, Joint Res. No. 13, June 14, 1864, *reprinted in* Statutes at Large of the Confederate States of America, 2d Cong., 1st Sess. 287 (1864).

26. *See* generally Calhoun, *Discourse, supra* note 9.

27. *Id.* at 82.

28. The Federalist No. 39 (James Madison).

29. *Id.*

30. Virginia Resolutions (Dec. 24, 1798), *in* Documents of American History 182 (Henry Steele Commager ed., 9th ed. 1975).

31. *Id.* at 178.

32. *Kentucky Resolutions* (Nov. 16, 1798), *in* Commager, *supra* note 30, at 178.

33. The Webster-Hayne Debate on the Nature of the Union 136, 153 (Herman Belz ed., 2000).

34. *Id.*

35. *See* 1 Stephens, *supra* note 2, at 477–522.

36. T.H. Watts, *Pardon for a Deserter* (Mar. 4, 1863), *in* Patrick, *supra* note 6, at 231, 239–40.

37. *See, e.g.*, Chancely v. Bailey, 37 Ga. 532 (1868).

38. *See, e.g.*, Kenneth Stampp, *The Concept of a Perpetual Union,* 65 J. Am. Hist. 5 (1978).

39. The informative discussion in Stampp, *id.*, is concerned only with perpetuity in the strong sense.

40. Benjamin, *supra* note 3, at 104.

41. *Id.*

42. *Constitution of the Confederate States of America* (Mar. 3, 1861), *in* Commager, *supra* note 30, at 376.

43. There is, surprisingly, no single treatment of natural law that traces its entire historical trajectory. *See,* however, Clarence J. Glacken, Traces on the Rhodian Shore (1967), a stimulating book with a wealth of information on key elements of natural law thought over a large part of its history.

44. For Aquinas's principal writings on natural law, *see* The Political Ideas of St. Thomas Aquinas 42–54 (Dino Bigongiari ed., 1953). *See also* A.P. D'Entreves, Natural Law 42–49 (2d ed. 1970); D.J. O'Connor, Aquinas and Natural Law (1967); and Anthony Lisska, Aquinas's Theory of Natural Law (1996).

45. Hugo Grotius, On the Law of War and Peace (Francis W. Kelsey trans., 1925) (1625).

46. Samuel Pufendorf, On the Law of Nature and Nations (C.H. & W.A. Oldfather trans., 1934) (1672).

47. Christian Wolff, The Law of Nations Treated According to a Scientific Method (Joseph H. Drake trans., 1934) (1749).

48. Emmerich de Vattel, The Law of Nations, Or, the Principles of Natural Law Applied to the Conduct and the Affairs of the Nations and Sovereigns (Charles G. Fenwick trans., 1916) (1758).

49. John Locke, *Second Treatise of Government, in* Two Treatises of Government 121–22, 214 (Mark Goldie ed., 1993). On the natural law duty to adhere to contracts, *see also* Thomas Hobbes, The Element of Law Natural and Politic 87–88 (J.C.A. Gaskin ed., 1994) (1650).

50. Locke, *supra* note 49, at 214.

51. *Id.* at 157.

52. *Id.* at 118.

53. *Id.* at 159.

54. *Id.* at 158.

55. Grotius, *supra* note 45, at 405. The fact that the reference was specifically to treaties of alliance is not crucial.

56. Pufendorf, *supra* note 46, at 788.

57. Wolff, *supra* note 47, at 225–26.

58. Jean-Jacques Rousseau, Discourse on the Origin of Inequality Among Men, and Is It Authorized by Natural Law? 97 (G.D.H. Cole trans., 1973) (1755).

59. Vattel, *supra* note 48, at 177.

60. *Id.*

61. Henry Wheaton, Elements of International Law 604 (Richard Henry Dana, Jr., ed., 1936) (1836).

62. *Id.* at 603–4.

63. *See* Calhoun, *Speech on the Force Bill, supra* note 10, at 443–44; and 2 Stephens, *supra* note 2, at 426.

64. U.S. Const. art. III, § 2.

65. 1 Stephens, *supra* note 2, at 500–501.

66. *Id.* at 501.

67. *Id.*

68. For a general historical survey of the 14th Amendment, *see* Raoul Berger, Government By Judiciary (2d ed. 1997).

69. *See* Thomas Hobbes, Leviathan, or the Matter, Forme and Power of a Commonwealth Ecclesiasticall and Civil 84–85, 93–103 (Michael Oakeshott ed., 1957) (1651). *See also* Thomas Hobbes, De Cive, of the Citizen 43–59 (Sterling Lamprecht ed., 1949) (1642).

70. Rousseau, *supra* note 58, at 96–97.

71. Locke, *supra* note 49, at 121.

72. *Id.*

73. Benjamin, *supra* note 3, at 107.

74. *Id.*

75. *See* Luther v. Borden, 48 U.S. (7 How.) 1 (1849). For the leading modern exposition of the doctrine, *see* Baker v. Carr, 369 U.S. 186 (1963).

76. The Federalist No. 28 (Alexander Hamilton).

77. *Id.*

78. *Id.*

79. *Id.*

80. U.S. Const. art. IV, § 2.

81. *Id.*

82. *Cobb, Letter... to the People of Georgia, in* Wakelyn, *supra* note 3, at 88, 90, 94.

83. *Id.*

84. 1 Stephens, *supra* note 2, at 497.

85. 2 Stephens, *supra* note 2, at 261–62.

86. Hunter, *Speech... on the Resolution Proposing to Retrocede the Forts... Delivered in the Senate of the United States, Jan 11, 1861, in* Wakelyn, *supra* note 3, at 262, 264.

87. *Declaration of the Immediate Causes Which Induce and Justify the Secession of South Carolina from the Federal Union* (Dec. 24, 1860), *in* Commager, *supra* note 30, at 372, 373.

88. *Id.* at 373.

89. Declaration of the Causes of Secession of Georgia, Jan. 29, 1861, 1 (ser. 4) OR 81–85.

90. *A Declaration of the Immediate Causes Which Induce and Justify the Secession of the State of Mississippi from the Federal Union* (Jan. 9, 1861), *in* Journal of the State Convention 86–88 (1861).

91. *A Declaration of the Causes Which Impel the State of Texas to Secede from the Federal Union* (Feb. 2, 1861), *in* Journal of the Secession Convention of Texas 61–66 (E.W. Winkler ed., 1912).

92. *See, e.g.*, the concurring opinion of Justice Bradley in *Knox v. Lee*, 79 U.S. (12 Wall.) 457, 555 (1871) (Bradley, J., concurring).

6 William Rawle and Secession
Legal Rights and Political Wrongs

H. Jefferson Powell, Duke University School of Law

The constitutional issue of secession is as dead as any once-live issue in U.S. constitutional law can be, buried beyond recall by "the constitutional experts on Missionary Ridge" who successfully fought a great Civil War to put down the Republic's one episode.[1] Even to understand what the issue involved in its antebellum heyday is a little tricky. Not only is the question obsolete, but so as well are some of the concepts that statesmen and lawyers used before and during the War in discussing it. Most critically, to understand their disagreements one must distinguish between 'secession' and 'revolution,' between the exercise of a legal right (one that the government denied it was legally obliged to respect) and the attempt to overthrow the existing government. The constitutional question was whether an attempt by a state or group of states to exit the Union could be lawful, and thus demand respect from the United States government as well as support from the citizens of the seceding state(s), or whether secession could only be a revolutionary act that the federal government might lawfully attempt to suppress and that loyalists might reject. In turn, answering this question involved consideration of other legal and moral issues as well—for example, how one should define the political community that is relevant to issues of secession and revolution—but this chapter shall omit the intellectual epicycles and focus on the point of practical debate: may an individual state secede from the Union, or is the only option that its citizens (or in practice, some subset of its citizens) attempt a revolution?

To begin with the debate's common starting point, everyone agreed that a people[2] has a moral or political right to rid itself of government by overthrowing it—how could they not, given the origins in revolution of the United States itself? As Abraham Lincoln—no supporter of secession—put it in his first inaugural address: "Whenever [the people] shall grow weary of the existing Government, they can exercise ... their revolutionary right to dismember or overthrow it."[3] The moral legitimacy of revolution was, Lincoln agreed, a political premise of the American system. At the same time, Lincoln and other antebellum nationalists regularly denied any logical connection between the principles animating the Declaration of Independence and a supposed legal or constitutional right on the part of individual states to secede from the Union. The right of revolution is simply the ultimate translation into action of the precept that all just government derives its authority from the consent of the governed. If the people decide it necessary to withdraw that consent, the government loses its legitimacy and either falls or becomes a tyranny; but by a necessity that is both legal and practical, such a radical reworking of the existing constitutional order cannot be the exercise of a legal right within that order. "It is safe to assert that no government proper ever had a provision in its organic law for its own termination," Lincoln insisted, and "in contemplation of universal law and of the Constitution the Union of these States is perpetual ... it being impossible to destroy it except by some action not provided for in the [Constitution] itself."[4] Rather than citizens exercising a constitutional right, the secessionists of 1860 and 1861 were mere rebels and lawbreakers, and the actions they took "against the authority of the United States are insurrectionary or revolutionary, according to circumstances."[5] The duty of those charged with exercising "the authority of the United States," including one A. Lincoln, was therefore to maintain that authority, not to respect some nonexistent constitutional right.

Thirty years before Lincoln spoke, Justice Joseph Story dismissed as mere dogma the claim that the legitimacy of the American Revolution necessarily implied the legality of state secession.

> The people of the United States have a right to abolish, or alter the constitution of the United States; but that the people of a single state have such a right, is a proposition requiring some reasoning beyond the suggestion, that it is implied in the principles on which our political systems are founded.[6]

The only colorable excuse for inferring the existence of a constitutional right of secession, Story continued, lay "in the notion of all governments being founded in *compact*, and therefore liable to be dissolved by the parties, or either of them; a notion which it has been our purpose to question." In his view, the idea that the American Union is the product of a compact among sovereign states, "having no foundation in the words of the constitution, is altogether a gratuitous assumption, and therefore inadmissible."[7] The Constitution, in truth, is "a permanent form of government" established by the same authority that alone has the right of revolution, the people, while the notion of lawful secession (like its close relative, state nullification of federal law) is a constitutional chimera, the product of "artificial reasoning founded upon theory" rather than law or fact.[8]

Without any doubt, the standard argument in 1860–61 for the legitimacy of secession was a mirror image of Lincoln's and Story's nationalism. For most secessionists, the Constitution was precisely what Story said it was not, a compact: a treaty or contract among sovereign states that, having created the compact by their own volition, were free to leave it at will. A former Confederate soldier named Alpheus Baker admirably summarized the secessionist position in his postwar petition for pardon: he "'had been taught from my youth upwards to believe . . . that the Union was a revocable compact, & Secession a constitutional right.'"[9] The interpretation of the Constitution as a compact among the states as independent sovereigns was almost as old as the Constitution itself, having been crafted by Thomas Jefferson and James Madison as part of their assault on the Alien and Sedition Acts of 1798.[10] "The American Blackstone," St. George Tucker, provided state compact theory legal legitimacy and national circulation within the legal profession, by adopting it in his widely used 1803 edition of Blackstone's *Commentaries on the Laws of England*.[11] Tucker taught a "strictly federal" view of the Union, by which he meant that the Constitution is quite literally a treaty (Latin *foedus*) among independent states.[12]

> The federal government, then, appears to be the organ through which the united republics communicate with foreign nations, and with each other. Their submission to its operation is voluntary: its councils, its sovereignty is an emanation from theirs, not a flame by which they have been consumed, nor a vortex in which they are swallowed up. Each is still a perfect state, still sovereign, still independent, and still capable, should the occasion require, to resume the exercise of its functions, as such, in the most unlimited extent.[13]

While Tucker willingly acknowledged the supremacy of the Constitution and of valid federal laws, in his view that supremacy was strictly conditional and dependent on the continuing "acquiescence" of the people of the several states, and he argued that the Constitution "furnishes the means of a peaceable dissolution of the government, if ever the crisis should arrive that may render such a measure eligible, or necessary."[14] Tucker himself thought of secession as a last resort in a situation of crisis, but his compact account of the Constitution set no constitutional limits on an individual state's discretion to dispense with the Union. In the political crisis of "secession winter" that followed Lincoln's election, Tucker's theory was tailor-made for those arguing that the slave states could not abide an antislavery president.

Not everyone who supported the withdrawal of the slave states from the Union in response to Lincoln's election was convinced that secession was the exercise of a legal right rather than the making of a second American revolution. One of the most famous Southern jurists of the time, retired Chief Justice Thomas Ruffin of North Carolina, flatly rejected the existence of any constitutional right of secession, although he adhered to the Confederacy after a state convention adopted "an ordinance to dissolve the union" and announced North Carolina's ratification of the Confederate constitution.[15] Rather than calling a special convention to consider secession, the Tennessee legislature approved a document that labeled itself a "Declaration of Independence and Ordinance dissolving the federal relations between the State of Tennessee and the United States"; expressly "waiv[ed] any expression of opinion as to the abstract doctrine of secession, but assert[ed] the right, as a free and independent people, to alter, reform, or abolish our form of government in such manner as we think proper"; and provided for a popular referendum on the document.[16] More subtly, the Confederacy's President, Jefferson Davis, attempted not to obscure but to reconcile the concepts of revolution and secession: Davis's intellectually creative effort underscores the complex nature of any satisfactory discussion of secession and constitutionality.

In the first of his two inaugural addresses,[17] Davis began a defense of the new republic's legitimacy by explaining that (in the words of the 1776 Declaration) secession "illustrate[d] the American idea that governments rest upon the consent of the governed, and that it is the right of the people to alter or abolish governments whenever they become destructive of the ends for which they were established." In seceding, he continued, the Confederate States had "merely asserted a right which the Declaration of Independence of 1776 had defined to be inalienable." Almost immediately afterward, however, Davis sounded the legal note first articulated by Tucker: secession was the exercise of a legal right reserved by and under the United States Constitution:

> The right solemnly proclaimed at the birth of the States . . . has been affirmed and reaffirmed in the bills of rights of States subsequently admitted into the

> Union of 1789 [which] undeniably recognizes in the people the power to resume the authority delegated for the purposes of government. Thus the sovereign States here represented proceeded to form this Confederacy, and it is by a gross abuse of language that their act has been denominated a revolution. They formed a new alliance, but within each State its government has remained.

Secession, then, was a legitimate but extralegal revolution against the old constitutional order *and* the exercise of a legal right preserved in and through that order. Secession was thus both like and unlike the Revolution of 1776, and Davis could rightly claim that the Confederacy's "present condition [has been] achieved in a manner unprecedented in the history of nations."[18]

Davis's description of the genesis of the Confederacy as somehow both extralegal and strictly constitutional was no doubt apologetic in intention: like the deliberately ambiguous ordinances of secession adopted by many state conventions, Davis's address was intended to appeal to orthodox Tucker-style secessionists as well as to supporters of the Confederacy like Chief Justice Ruffin who dismissed secession as a mirage and essentially agreed with Lincoln that the South was attempting a revolution against the lawful national government. However, I think that Davis's argument rose above a piece of political legerdemain meant to placate diverse constituents. Davis's own views on constitutional law were rather closer to Story's or Lincoln's than to Tucker's on many issues,[19] and he was concerned not to alienate European (and conservative Northern) public opinion by trumpeting the Confederacy's origins in the desire to perpetuate human chattel slavery.[20] It was doubly unsatisfactory from Davis's perspective simply to invoke as a justification for their actions the principle that the seceding states had concluded (in Tucker's words) that secession was an "eligible" measure of policy for the preservation of slavery.

In his inaugural address, Davis sought not to obscure the difference between legal secession and extralegal revolution but to show the inner relationship between the two in an American constitutional order based on the consent of the governed. The acts of secession of 1860 and 1861, Davis insisted, were legitimate not simply because states had chosen to exercise a legal right but because secession had become a moral and political necessity by the very terms of the existing constitutional system: the "transition from the former Union to the present Confederacy has not proceeded from a disregard on our part of just obligations, or any failure to perform every constitutional duty. . . . [W]e have vainly endeavored to secure tranquillity and to obtain respect for the rights to which we were entitled. As a necessity, not a choice, we have resorted to the remedy of separation."[21] Revolution had been forced on the South, and in response, the seceding states had acted within legal bounds as, implicitly, the revolutionaries of 1776 had not. In this delicately interwoven argument, Davis was attempting to invest the defense of secession's constitutionality with a moral dignity beyond the realm of lawyers' arguments, yet without conceding President Lincoln's charge that the Confederacy was a lawless rebellion. One may doubt his success—Davis's rhetorical skill could mask but not change the fact that without slavery there would have been no secession—but he was right to see that the constitutional question of secession demanded both a legal and moral answer.

Jefferson Davis was not the first American constitutional thinker to see that the constitutionality of secession was at one and the same time a moral and a legal question. Long before the events of 1860 and 1861, one of the first systematic constitutionalists, William Rawle, addressed the issue in a fashion that foreshadowed Davis's later argument in his treatise, *A View of the Constitution of the United States.*[22] Because Rawle was a Northerner, an opponent of slavery, and an associate of George Washington untainted by involvement in post-Founding Southern disunionism, Rawle's endorsement of the legality of secession dismayed antebellum nationalists and has provided support then and since for those arguing that secession was a legitimate constitutional option eliminated from the realm of plausible constitutional argument only by brute force.[23] In fact, Rawle's analysis of the question of secession was considerably more complex than a simple equation of his views with Confederate-style secessionism acknowledges.

The author of *A View* was prominent among lawyers and political figures in his day but has long needed a brief introduction.[24] William Rawle (1759–1836) belonged to a family that had been prominent in Pennsylvania and Philadelphia affairs since the early eighteenth century. Rawle's mother and stepfather (his father died in 1761) were loyalists during the American Revolution, and he spent most of the war in British-occupied territory or in Britain itself, where he studied law for several months at the Middle Temple. After the Crown acquiesced in American independence, Rawle returned to Philadelphia and seems to have had little trouble entering (or reentering) the elite social class to which his forebears had belonged. Despite his youth and loyalist connections, Rawle established personal relationships with leading figures of the Revolution, including Benjamin Franklin, Robert and Gouverneur Morris, Benjamin Rush, and most important of all, George Washington. In 1791, Washington appointed Rawle as United

States attorney for the district of Pennsylvania. In his near decade in that office, Rawle established a reputation as one of the leaders not only of the Philadelphia bar but of the legal profession nationally, and when he retired from political life in 1800 he remained a prominent figure in legal, cultural, and educational circles.

One motivation impelling Rawle to write a systematic examination of federal constitutional law was doubtless his well-known interest in higher education, but it is difficult not to see a political intention as well. After 1800, Rawle cultivated a reputation for high-minded nonpartisanship in electoral politics, but he made no secret of his allegiance to the nationalist political example of President Washington. *A View* repeatedly praised the views and the actions of "this great man," "whose character stamps inestimable value on all that he has uttered, and whose [political and constitutional opinions], springing from the purest patriotism and the soundest wisdom, ought never to be forgotten or neglected."[25] Rawle's interpretation of the Constitution was shaped by his conviction that it was Washington's practical construction of the instrument, in the very infancy of the Republic, that "proved that the excellencies of the Constitution consisted not merely in theory and contemplation, but could be realized in practice; that within its proper sphere no right was unprotected, and no evil unredressed." Rawle's fundamental constitutional doctrine was that "the principles of George Washington's administration [ought to be] faithfully followed,"[26] and constitutional arguments that he thought inconsistent with Washingtonian principle were plainly wrong. The state compact interpretation of the Constitution that St. George Tucker had propagated was such a fundamental error,[27] and throughout *A View*, Rawle consistently refuted not only the theory but even verbal expressions such as 'the federal courts' that might seem to give countenance to the theory: "In these quotations the author has retained, without approving of, the expression *federal*, frequently applied to the courts of the United States. The government not being strictly a federal government, its tribunals are not properly federal tribunals."[28]

In the light of Rawle's strong endorsement of Washington, Rawle's own consistent support for the authority of the national government, and his express disavowal of the state compact interpretation of the Constitution, the reader of *A View* is likely to share Justice Story's incredulity when, on reaching the final chapter in the book, entitled *Of the Permanence of the Union*, he or she finds a flat assertion that "[t]he states, then, may wholly withdraw from the Union."[29] Story refuted Rawle's inexplicable lapse into constitutional heresy by citing the *Feder-*

alist for the proposition that the Constitution is to be construed "as a permanent from of government, as a fundamental law, as a supreme rule, which no state was at a liberty to disregard, suspend, or annul." The unconstitutionality of secession thus asserted, Story continued that "[i]t is a matter of surprise, therefor, that a learned commentator should have admitted the right of any state, or of the people of any state, without the consent of the rest, to secede from the Union at its own pleasure."[30] Whatever can Rawle, an associate of the great Washington himself, have been thinking of?[31]

The answer is that Story read *A View*'s subtle discussion of the issue of secession too hastily: Story was so concerned with Rawle's unpalatable bottom line that he failed to attend to the nuances of Rawle's argument. That argument bears rereading, beginning with the title of the chapter: Rawle identified its topic as "the Permanence of the Union," not its dissolution, and elaborated the point in the chapter's first sentence, which announced that he intended to draw the reader's attention "to the principles of [the Union's] cohesion, and to the provisions it contains for its own duration and extension."[32] Much of the chapter is, in fact, devoted to establishing the authority of the national government over the states: "[T]he paternal power of the Union" is "authorized to oppose, and if possible, prevent every state in the Union from relinquishing the republican form of government," and if "a faction" should "endeavor to enforce [a rejection of republican government by a state] by violence . . . the Union is bound to employ its power to prevent it."[33] In parallel fashion, it is Congress alone, and not the states acting individually or as a group, that can enlarge the Union and in doing so impose geographically enlarged duties of reciprocity on the states.[34] Rawle concluded the chapter with a lengthy excerpt from Washington's famous *Farewell Address* in which the President commended "'the continuance of the Union'" to his fellow Americans, "'a name which belongs to you in your national capacity [and] must always exalt the just pride of patriotism, more than any appellation derived from local discriminations.'"[35] The long quotation from Washington ends with the warning that "'there will always be reason to distrust the patriotism of those who in any quarter may endeavor to weaken [the Union's] bands;'" immediately before introducing the quotation, Rawle spoke in his own voice of feeling "the deepest impression of a sacred obligation to preserve the union of our country" and of his conviction that "we must resist the attempt of its own citizens to destroy it, with the same feelings that we should avert the dagger of the parricide."[36] Secessionists as dubious patriots, secession as parricide, the preservation of the Union as a duty with religious force: if Rawle's discussion is a vindication of secession, it is an odd vindication indeed. Yet Rawle identified secession as a lawful act within the contemplation not just of American political principle but of the Constitution as law.

The government of the Union has the authority to use force, if necessary, to preserve republican government in the states, "[y]et it is not to be understood, that its interposition would be justifiable, if the people of a state should determine to retire from the Union" and take appropriate steps to actualize an "express intention of seceding": "It depends on the state itself... whether it will continue a member of the Union."[37] The ultimate basis of the right of secession lay in the moral and political foundations of the American Revolution—"To deny this right would be inconsistent with the principle on which all our political systems are founded, which is, that the people have in all cases, a right to determine how they will be governed"—but when properly exercised, secession would be the exercise of legal right that "must be considered as an ingredient in the original composition of the general government, which, though not expressed, was mutually understood."[38] Were a state to secede in a constitutional fashion, Rawle did indeed concede, "the previous ligament with the Union, would be legitimately and fairly destroyed" and the national government without lawful authority to reverse the state's decision.[39]

But if one is to recognize secession as potentially the exercise of a legal right, Rawle insisted that one must also recognize a "due process of secession:" the implied constitutional right is bounded by the principles and procedures that reason can infer from secession's status as the ultimate limit to the otherwise paramount authority of the Constitution and the "general government" it creates. No mere act of the state legislature can absolve a citizen from his duty of allegiance to the United States, and nothing short of a "deliberate, clear, and unequivocal" act of the state itself rather than its legislature could lawfully effect secession: "To withdraw from the Union comes not within the general scope of [the legislature's] delegated authority."[40] As a matter of constitutional law, "the people is the only moving force" in exercising secession as a legal right, and they must "distinctly and peremptorily declare[]" their will in "a solemn, serious act... manifested in a direct and unequivocal manner" if the national government's authority is to cease. "The powers of the general government cannot be defeated or impaired by an ambiguous or implied secession on the part of the state."

> [W]ithout plain, decisive measures of this nature, proceeding from the only legitimate source, the people, the United States cannot consider their legislative powers over such states suspended, nor their executive or judicial powers

> any way impaired, and they would not be obliged to desist from the collection of revenues within such state.[41]

The exercise of this right, furthermore, would give rise to legal duties on the seceding state's part to surrender its claim to representation in Congress, to pay its just "proportion of the national debt," and to accept its status as "a foreign country" no longer entitled to the benefits of United States law or the privileges of treaties between the United States and other nations.[42] Lawful secession, Rawle warned, would be a direct route to "jealousies and discord . . . internal war [and invasion by] foreign enemies," and Americans had a duty not only to themselves but also "to the world in general, anxiously and faithfully to preserve . . . [t]he first example which has been exhibited of a perfect self-government."[43]

Secession, in William Rawle's political judgment, was likely to be a moral and political disaster; in his legal judgment, it is clear that for a state to secede lawfully would be so difficult as to make the right as much an abstract limiting case to the supremacy of the national government than a practical reality. It is difficult to imagine that he would have approved of the protection of slavery as a proper ground for secession. Furthermore, if one applies to the circumstances of 1861 the conditions that Rawle thought an attempted secession must meet before the national government is obliged to accept its lawfulness, it is not entirely clear that he would have thought Lincoln wrong to maintain that the Union was unbroken. The latter informed Congress in his special message of July 4, 1861, that he "questioned whether there is to-day a majority of the legally qualified voters of any State, except, perhaps, South Carolina, in favor of disunion" and that he saw "much reason to believe that the Union men are the majority in many, if not in every other one, of the so-called seceded States."[44] Assuming that Lincoln was sincere, by Rawle's legal standards he had a strong argument that he had the authority and indeed the duty to treat the Confederate States as the "illegal organization" he labeled it and to uphold the Union's authority within the seceding states as constitutionally unimpaired.[45] Rawle is a remarkably poor choice if one is looking for constitutional authority supporting the legality of the one attempt at secession in American history.

This chapter began with the observation that the legality of secession is a dead issue in American constitutional law, and so it is: Whether one thinks Rawle or Tucker or Davis or Story most persuasive on the matter, the secession of a state from the United States is no longer within serious legal or political contemplation. It does not follow, I think, that the lines of reasoning these constitutionalists employed in thinking about secession have nothing to teach us. One of the most striking aspects of Rawle's discussion of secession is the way in which he refused to separate legal and moral or political issues in thinking about secession as a constitutional act.[46] Instead, Rawle treated legal and extralegal considerations as inextricably linked in thought about the constitutionality of secession, but he did so without eliding legal argument and moral and political judgment. This was not typical of nineteenth-century thinkers. Nationalists like Story and Lincoln shared with Tucker the compact theorist and with the ordinary secessionist of 1861 the assumption that the constitutional and the legal could be equated and that a sharp distinction should be drawn between legality and morality; they differed only in rejecting or accepting, respectively, the existence of a legal right of secession. Either an individual state possessed a technical legal right to secede, in which case secession was constitutional, or the concept was a legal mirage, in which case no constitutional issue could arise.

Rawle took a different approach. It would hardly make sense, from Rawle's perspective, to say that an act of secession was constitutional simply because it was technically lawful. The Constitution is not merely a set of legal rules but encompasses "the principles on which [American] government is formed and conducted."[47] The constitutionality of public action is distinct from, although it is certainly related to, its technical legality, and the faithful observance of the Constitution demands consideration of that action's conformity to the moral and political principles of the Constitution. Contrast this vision with that of Tucker. Tucker strongly objected to slavery as a moral evil and inconsistent with fundamental American political principle; he was, furthermore, "an active political fighter for emancipation,"[48] unlike most leading Founders in Virginia, who more typically left their antislavery convictions in the realm of theory. But Tucker drew a sharp line between political and moral convictions and issues of constitutional law, a line nowhere more clearly shown than in his authorship of the leading opinion in the Virginia high court decision that rejected the argument that slavery was presumptively unlawful under the Virginia bill of rights.[49] For Tucker, secession as a means of perpetuating slavery might be a grievous moral error, but its constitutionality if a state chose to exercise the right would be beyond dispute. One cannot know with certainty, of course, what Rawle (or Tucker, for that matter) would have thought if confronted with the circumstances of 1860 to 1861, but Rawle's understanding of what it means to discuss the constitutionality of secession would have invited or even demanded him to treat the political morality of secession's purpose as intrinsic to the question of its constitutionality.

William Rawle was a great lawyer, and his constitutional treatise was one of the first attempts to bring reasoned legal analysis to bear on the broad range of issues that make up constitutional law. His most lasting contribution, however, may be his passionate insistence that our Constitution is more than law narrowly defined and that great constitutional judgments may require wisdom more than the intellectual skills of the lawyer.

NOTES

1. This vivid description of the Union Army comes from the great constitutional lawyer Professor Charles L. Black, Jr. I do not have the original citation.

2. I pass by, for the moment, the question of whether the relevant 'people' are the several populaces of the individual states or the American people as a whole.

3. Abraham Lincoln, First Inaugural Address (Mar. 4, 1861), *in* 4 The Collected Works of Abraham Lincoln 249, 269 (Roy P. Basler et al. eds., 1953).

4. *Id.* at 264.

5. *Id.* at 265. Given the strongly nationalistic cast of the rest of his remarks, Lincoln's reference to the possibility that (some) secessionists might be acting in a revolutionary rather than insurrectionary manner is surprising: I assume that Lincoln thought that in the American context the 'people' who can properly lay claim to a revolutionary right to overthrow its government is the American people. He may simply have meant that if secession was in the end successful, it would be appropriate after the fact to categorize it as a revolution in the same way that the American Revolution, precisely because it succeeded, is celebrated as the founding of a republic rather than dismissed as a failed rebellion. It is also possible that Lincoln was subtly distinguishing the real firebrands, who were determined to destroy the Union and were simply engaged in lawless insurrection, from Southern moderates, whom Lincoln could view in a more conciliatory fashion as fellow-citizens temporarily caught up in a mistaken debate over the propriety of revolution. It is perhaps unfair to read too much legal precision into a political speech, but Lincoln was a careful wordsmith and experienced lawyer, and his *First Inaugural* was in part a surprisingly legalistic response to secession.

6. 1 Joseph Story, Commentaries on the Constitution of the United States § 359 (1833).

7. *Id.*

8. *Id.* §§ 352, 372.

9. Baker's petition is quoted in Cynthia Nicoletti's admirable article *The American Civil War as a Trial by Battle*, 28 L. & Hist. Rev. 71, 82 (2010).

10. Madison at least was no secessionist, and Justice Story happily (and correctly) cited Madison as an opponent of the Constitution-as-compact in any sense that legitimated nullification or secession. *See* 1 Story §§ 361, 366 (quoting Madison at length). On Jefferson's and Madison's creation of the compact theory, *see generally* H. Jefferson Powell, *The Principles of "98: An Essay in Historical Retrieval*, 80 Va. L. Rev. 689 (1994).

11. Tucker was a prominent figure in early American jurisprudence. He served as a judge on the Virginia General Court from 1788 to 1803 and then on the state's highest court until

his appointment as United States District judge in 1811, remaining in that office until his death in 1827. He was the second professor of law at William & Mary, where he taught from 1803 on.

12. *View of the Constitution of the United States with Selected Writings* 95 (1999) (originally 1 St. George Tucker, Blackstone's Commentaries appendix D (1803)). Tucker would not have recognized the Civil War era distinction between 'Federals' (soldiers of the National or Union Army) and 'Confederates.' For him, the distinction to be drawn was between the 'federal/confederate' view of the Constitution (adhering to the correct state compact theory) and the 'national' or 'consolidating' idea that there is a single American people and that supposedly led to such archetypal acts of tyranny as the Alien and Sedition Acts of 1798.

13. *Id.* at 136.

14. The quotations are from *id.* at 123, 257. The "means of dissolution" Tucker had specifically in mind was the ability of the states to dissolve the federal executive branch by declining to appoint presidential electors, but it is clear that he thought the states had the legal right to exit, or dissolve the Union, in other ways.

15. *See* John V. Orth, *Thomas Ruffin, in* The Yale Biographical Dictionary of American Law 472 (Roger K. Newman ed., 2009).

16. *See* http://www.constitution.org/csa/ordinances_secession.htm (reprinting the text of the May 6, 1861, resolutions approved by the Tennessee legislature). The convention of Kentucky secessionists that met in November 1861 to take that commonwealth out of the Union adopted an instrument that attempted to blend the distinct rhetorics of secession and revolution. *See id.* (reprinting the text of the Nov. 20, 1861, resolutions approved by a convention meeting in Russellville, Kentucky, declaring that "we do hereby forever sever our connection with the Government of the United States, and in the name of the people we do hereby declare Kentucky to be a free and independent State").

There is a vast literature on the difficult historical issues about political opinion on secession during the 1860–61 crisis. For a recent and powerful presentation of the argument that the Confederacy suffered from a delegitimating and ultimately fatal democratic deficit quite apart from its foundations in human chattel slavery, *see* Stephanie McCurry, Confederate Reckoning: Power and Politics in the Civil War South (2012).

17. Davis was inaugurated President of the provisional government of the Confederate States of America on February 18, 1861. He took the presidential oath under the permanent constitution of the Confederacy on February 22, 1862. In this chapter, I consider only his 1861 inaugural address, although nothing in the later speech contradicts his original argument.

18. Jefferson Davis, *Inaugural Address* (Feb. 18, 1861), *in* 7 The Papers of Jefferson Davis 45, 46 (Lynda Lasswell Crist et al. eds., 1992).

19. It is well known that President Davis's administration adopted in practice a robust view of Confederate government power far closer to Chief Justice Marshall's opinion in *McCulloch v. Maryland* than to the strict-construction perspective of compact theorists such as Tucker. *See* the classic statement by Emory M. Thomas in The Confederacy as a Revolutionary Experience 58–78 (1971). However, this was not simply a concession to "the demands of modern, 'total' warfare, as Professor Thomas concluded. *Id.* at 78. Whatever may have been the case with other Confederate leaders, Davis was a principled adherent to the Marshallian view of national authority. *See* David P. Currie, *Through the Looking Glass: The Confederate Constitution in Congress, 1861–1865*, 90 Va. L. Rev. 1257, 1282 (2004) ("President

Davis . . . thumpingly endorsed Marshall's expansive understanding of congressional authority."). *See also id.* at 1283 n.103 (quoting a hostile state governor asserting of Davis's views that "I am not aware that the proposition was ever stated more broadly in favor of unrestrained Congressional power by Webster, Story, or any other statesman or jurist of the Federal school.").

20. Davis made no direct mention of 'slavery' in his February 1861 speech or, indeed, in his 1862 inaugural address. *See* Jefferson Davis, *Inaugural Address* (Feb. 22, 1862), *in* 5 Jefferson Davis Constitutionalist: His Letters, Papers and Speeches 198 (Dunbar Rowland ed., 1923). In contrast, a month after Davis gave his 1861 address, Confederate Vice President Alexander H. Stephens proclaimed that the "corner-stone" of the Confederacy was its adherence to a doctrine of racial inequality: "This, our new government, is the first, in the history of the world, based upon this great physical, philosophical, and moral truth." Alexander Stephens, *The Corner Stone Speech* (Mar. 21, 1861), *in* Henry Cleveland, Alexander H. Stephens, in Public and Private. With Letters and Speeches, Before, During, and Since the War 717, 721 (1866).

21. Jefferson Davis, *Inaugural Address* (Feb. 18, 1861), *in* 7 The Papers of Jefferson Davis 45, 47–48 (Lynda Lasswell Crist et al. eds., 1992).

22. Rawle published the book in 1825 and put out a slightly revised edition in 1829. All citations to *A View* are to this second edition. *See* William Rawle, A View of the Constitution of the United States of America (H. Jefferson Powell ed., 2009) (photographic reproduction of 1829 edition with introduction and notes) [hereinafter, Rawle, A View].

23. We can leave to one side the legendary but often-repeated claim that Rawle's book was an official textbook at West Point for many years and was directly responsible for inculcating the idea that secession was constitutional in a generation of graduates of the United States Military Academy. In fact, it appears that *A View* was officially used at the academy for at most one or two academic years, in 1825 and 1826, after which James Kent's treatise (which characterized secession as illegal) was adopted, although some cadets may have read Rawle on their own. On the (non-)role of A View in shaping the secessionist views of some Southern graduates of West Point, *see* Jacob Kobrick, *No Army Inspired: The Failure of Nationalism at Antebellum West Point*, at 3–4, www.publications.villanova.edu/Concept/2004/No%20Army%20Inspired.doc. Jefferson Davis (West Point graduating class of 1828) recalled that he "did not use the Rawle text but was taught using Kent's *Commentaries*." Patrick Finnegan, *The Study of Law as a Foundation of Leadership and Command: The History of Law Instruction at the United States Military Academy at West Point*, 181 Military L. Rev. 112, 113 n.15 (2004).

24. Detailed citations to sources for Rawle's life can be found in my introduction to the Carolina Academic Press edition of A View, especially at pages xi–xix of the editor's introduction.

25. Rawle, A View, at 308 n.* and 308.

26. *Id.* at 198.

27. Rawle's title tracked the separate heading that Tucker gave to the lengthy constitutional appendix to his Blackstone (View of the Constitution of the United States) and may also allude to a book by another compact theorist, John Taylor of Caroline. *See* Taylor, New Views of the Constitution of the United States 276 (1823) (arguing that the Union is "[a] federal compact, and not an American nation"). I argue that A View was intended to be a

sustained refutation of Tucker's compact theory in pages xxi–xxviii of the editor's introduction to the 2009 republication of Rawle's book.

28. *Id.* at 252 n.* It is ironic that the quotations in question were from *Osborn v. Bank of the United States*, 22 U.S. (9 Wheat.) 738, 819–23 (1824), and thus the writer whom Rawle was chastising for dangerously Tuckeresque language was Chief Justice John Marshall.

29. Rawle, A View, at 297.

30. 1 Story, Commentaries § 359. Story cited without specific quotation numbers 15–20, 38, 39 and 44 of the *Federalist*, and Rawle's chapter *Permanence of the Union* with a number of specific page citations.

31. Decades later, the defenders of the Confederacy would attempt the difficult task of enlisting Washington in the cause of secession, but in the period of Rawle's A View and Story's Commentaries, there was little doubt that Washington stood for the permanence and paramount claim to allegiance of the Union over all regionalist or divisive loyalties. Rawle's friend Peter S. Du Ponceau published a short book on the Constitution in 1834 and omitted any discussion of the issue of secession, explaining that if he even raised the question he "feared lest the shade of Washington should frown upon me." *See* Elizabeth K. Bauer, Commentaries on the Constitution 1790–1860 299–300 (1952) (quoting Du Ponceau).

32. Rawle, A View, at 295.

33. *Id.* at 296, 299. Nor are "[t]he power and duty of the United States to interfere with the particular concerns of a state . . . limited to the violent efforts of a party to alter its constitution"; it lies with the national government to maintain "the internal peace and order of the state" if its government cannot do so, to prevent interstate conflict or aggression, and to "carr[y] into effect" by force if necessary the decisions of "the judicial power of the Union" in controversies between state and state. *Id.* at 299–300.

34. *Id.* at 300–302.

35. The quotations from Washington are found at 310 and 308.

36. *Id.* at 310, 307.

37. *Id.* at 296.

38. *Id.*

39. *Id.* at 303.

40. *Id.* at 296–97 (referring to the earlier discussion of allegiance in *id.* at 96–97), 302. Rawle conceded the possibility that the people of a state could delegate the power to secede to the legislature by "an express provision to that effect inserted in the state constitution[]" while plainly counseling against entrusting a "matter so momentous" to the ordinary legislative process. *Id.* at 302.

41. The quotations are from *id.* at 303 and 305.

42. *Id.* at 305–6.

43. *Id.* at 306–7.

44. Abraham Lincoln, *Message to Congress in Special Session* (July 4, 1861), *in* 4 The Collected Works of Abraham Lincoln 421, 437 (Roy P. Basler et al. eds., 1953).

45. *Id.* at 423. South Carolina, where Lincoln grudgingly conceded that a majority of voters

probably did favor secession, compromises a Rawlesian defense of Lincoln's actions. Lincoln is usually thought to have consistently overestimated the extent of active Union sentiment in the South, although *if* we ask about the views of Southerners generally rather than 'the legally qualified voters' (a group all male, all white, and in many states effectively exclusive of many poor white males as well) *and* if we take into account the role that coercion and chicanery of various sorts played in several states, the argument that secession had majority popular support in the states generally thought to have seceded becomes a good deal shakier. *See, e.g.*, McCurry, *supra* note 16.

46. To be fair, Davis similarly declined to separate the legal and the moral/political in his 1861 inaugural address. Rawle might have criticized Davis's constitutional reasoning as nevertheless fundamentally flawed because Davis could not deny, although he labored to avoid mentioning, the causative relation between the intent to maintain slavery (a moral and political evil in Rawle's view) and secession 1861-style.

47. Rawle, A View, at 9.

48. Robert M. Cover, Justice Accused 54 (1975).

49. Hudgins v. Wright, 11 Va. (1 Hen. & M.) 134 (1806). Tucker joined a unanimous court in reversing the revered Chancellor George Wythe, who had concluded in the trial court that under the Virginia bill of rights all persons regardless of race or color were entitled to a presumption that they were free. That presumption, the court of appeals concluded, did not apply in the case of persons appearing to be African in ancestry. Tucker explained in his opinion that the constitutional rules laid down by the bill of rights were "notoriously framed with a cautious eye to this subject" of slavery and that they could not properly be construed "by a side wind to overturn the rights of property." *Id.* at 141. *Hudgins,* and Tucker's ironic role in writing racially defined slavery into the Virginia bill of rights, are discussed in H. Jefferson Powell, A Community Built on Words: The Constitution in History and Politics 100–10 (2002).

III

Impact of the 14th Amendment

7 The 14th Amendment and the Unconstitutionality of Secession

Daniel A. Farber, University of California, Berkeley

April 18, 1861, was a fateful day in American history. On that day, a talented fifty-four-year-old army officer was offered the command of the Union Army.[1] But on the same day, he learned that his home state of Virginia had decided to secede from the Union.[2] Although a Southerner, he was not enthusiastic about the institution of slavery.[3] He opposed secession, saying that the Framers would never have "exhausted so much labor, wisdom, and forbearance" in forming the Union "if it was intended to be broken up by every member of the [Union] at will."[4] Yet, in the end, he decided that his primary allegiance was to his state, proclaiming, "I cannot raise my hand against my birthplace, my home, my children."[5] Five days later, the officer—one Robert E. Lee—became the Commander in Chief of the Virginia military, and within a month he was a Confederate general.[6] If he had accepted the offer to head the Union Army, the course of the Civil War might have been far different.

Robert E. Lee's decision exemplified the choice facing Southerners at the start of the Civil War: Was their primary allegiance to their home states or to the United States of America? According to the foremost historical study of the constitutional evolution of citizenship, "the Civil War was a struggle over the nature of the community created in 1789—a bloody contest over allegiance."[7] Thus, "[t]he lines now were sharply drawn between those who stressed the primacy of the state communities of allegiance and those who insisted that the Union had created one nation and one people."[8] After the enactment of the 14th Amendment, however, the status of Americans "with respect to the states depended upon this national statute and upon their own choice of residence, and it could not be impeached or violated by state action."[9] In short, the Civil War itself and the ensuing 14th Amendment resolved the previously contested issue of the relative priority of state and national allegiance.[10]

A corollary flows naturally from this observation. Any remaining constitutional question about rights of states to secede was laid to rest: if allegiance to the national government was primary, action by states could not cut the bond between Americans and the national government. The text of the 14th Amendment is explicit. First, anyone born or naturalized within the jurisdiction of the United States is a citizen of the United States and of the state in which he or she resides.[11] State citizenship is derivative and cannot be controlled by the state itself. Second, no state can deprive any American citizen of the privileges or immunities of citizenship—which means, for example, that the state cannot deprive a citizen of U.S. citizenship by seceding.[12] The Privileges or Immunities Clause explicitly prohibits a state from depriving citizens of their federal rights, and secession would be a blatant violation of that prohibition.

The implications of the Citizenship Clause and the Privileges or Immunities Clause for secession should be obvious to anyone who understands how sovereignty, citizenship, and the right to national protection were interwoven in antebellum thought. But even among constitutional scholars, such knowledge is not universal, and the law review literature does not directly address this point.

The broader significance of the 14th Amendment for the nature of the Union—and specifically, for the issue of secession—has been insufficiently appreciated by constitutional scholars. For instance, one leading constitutional scholar has pointed to the secession issue as a key example of the irrelevance of constitutional text:

> Before the Civil War, there was a lively and inconclusive debate over whether the Constitution permitted states to secede. There is no longer any such debate; the issue was settled by the Civil War. No one today would seriously advance the position that the Constitution permits secession, at least the kind that the Confederacy attempted. Where is the text that settled this question? The answer, of course, is that this question, like other important constitutional questions, is decided by something other than the text.[13]

It is true, of course, that the Civil War resolved the issue and crystallized a new conception of the nature of the Union. It is wrong, however, to see the resolution as completely nontextual. In fact, the 14th Amendment enshrines the Civil War's political transformation of the Union into constitutional text.

In part, the victory of nationalism was embodied in the Citizenship Clause of the 14th Amendment. Seth Kreimer gives a cogent explanation of this point:

> At the time the United States was founded, one could conceive of American citizenship as derived from a more basic identification with each of the component states, but the time has long past when the "United States of America" was a plural construction. . . . As a political matter the Civil War resolved the issue by force of arms, and the resolution was embodied in the Citizenship Clause of the Fourteenth Amendment: persons born or naturalized in the United States are indissolubly citizens of the United States, and only derivatively or contingently citizens of the "State wherein they reside."[14]

Similarly, a federal judge remarked in 1871 that "[b]y the original constitution citizenship in the United States was a consequence of citizenship in a state" but that under the 14th Amendment, "this order of things is reversed."[15] Thus, the Citizenship Clause implies that a state has no right to sever the bond between a U.S. citizen and the national government through secession or otherwise.

The 14th Amendment does not, however, leave the issue of state power to implication. Although the Citizenship Clause is part of the 14th Amendment's resolution of the issue of secession, the Privileges or Immunities Clause is equally important. While the Citizenship Clause makes it clear that citizens owe their primary allegiance to the federal government, the Privileges or Immunities Clause makes it clear that states have no power to interfere with the rights attaching to citizenship. Section 5 of the 14th Amendment then completes the picture, giving Congress the power to enforce the rights of citizenship against the states. In short, the 14th Amendment creates a duty on citizens of allegiance toward the United States while giving the citizen certain rights in return, a prohibition on state interference with those rights, and a federal power of enforcement against the states.

One reason why the 14th Amendment's invalidation of secession is important is that there has been something of a revival of interest in the topic in recent years. Most notably, in April 2009, Texas Governor Rick Perry came close to threatening secession, reportedly suggesting that "Texans might at some point get so fed up they would want to secede from the union," though he also said, "[H]e sees no reason why Texas should do that."[16] He added:

> There's a lot of different scenarios. . . . We've got a great union. There's absolutely no reason to dissolve it. But if Washington continues to thumb their nose at the American people, you know, who knows what might come out of that. But Texas is a very unique place, and we're a pretty independent lot to boot.[17]

At the other end of the political spectrum, Thomas Naylor, a retired economics professor, published a book in 2005 advocating that Vermont withdraw from the Union.[18] Academic discussion of the secession issue has also increased.[19] Although occasional uses of secessionist rhetoric should probably not be taken as serious advocacy for fragmenting the nation, they do highlight the need to clarify the nature of our constitutional order.

To understand fully the relevance of the first two clauses of the 14th Amendment to secession, we need to examine the antebellum disputes about citizenship and sovereignty, the subject of part II below. Issues about citizenship arose in the context of specific disputes about naturalization, expatriation, and the rights of freedmen, but they implicated conflicts over the seat of allegiance and the nature of the Union.

Part III turns to the Reconstruction debates and shows how they reflect a fundamentally nationalistic view of citizenship. The Reconstruction Amendments to the Constitution were connected with a powerful vision of national citizenship and its implications for federal and state power. Under this vision, the national government had the first claim to the loyalty of citizens and in return was obligated to protect their rights as American citizens against state interference. An effort by a state to secede would directly imperil the status of its residents as American citizens, and both the federal government and the residents themselves had a duty to resist this interference with their constitutional rights. The two clauses in the 14th Amendment dealing most directly with citizenship embody this vision.

I. ANTEBELLUM CONCEPTIONS OF CITIZENSHIP AND THE NATURE OF THE UNION

It might seem obvious today that state law cannot control who is or is not a U.S. citizen. But it was not always so clear, for reasons that were related to the ultimate crisis of the constitutional order during the Civil War. Understanding the connection between citizenship and secession requires an examination of the conflicting theories of the Union that led to the secession crisis and their connection with antebellum conceptions of citizenship. Part A will briefly describe antebellum constitutional theories, part B investigates conceptions of citizenship, and part C ties the two topics together.

A. *Secession and the Nature of the Union*

Today, the Supreme Court's view of the nature of the Union holds that the Constitution transformed a loose association of states into a true national government that derived its power directly from the people. This view was expressed by the majority opinion in the *Term Limits* case, in which Justice John Paul Stevens's majority opinion lays out the conventional modern view of state and federal sovereignty.[20] Under the Articles of Confederation, according to Justice Stevens, "the States retained most of their sovereignty, like independent nations bound together only by treaties."[21] The new Constitution "reject[ed] the notion that the Nation was a collection of States, and instead creat[ed] a direct link between the National Government and the people of the United States."[22] Under this view, secession by a state would have been appropriate before the ratification of the Constitution as a form of treaty revocation, but after the Constitution, the states became subordinate sovereigns who had no right to interfere with the relationship between the federal government and people.

Before the Civil War, there were a variety of views on this issue. Abraham Lincoln was at the nationalist end of the spectrum, and his view went further than the *Term Limits* majority in affirming American nationhood. According to Lincoln, the "Union is much older than the Constitution."[23] Instead of viewing the Articles of Confederation as a federation between independent state sovereigns, he argued that the Union actually predated the formation of the states themselves.[24] From this perspective, the Constitution was simply another step in the evolution of the nation's government, being merely a revised framework to govern an already existing nation.

In effect, Lincoln's vision of nationalism made the Declaration of Independence, rather than the Constitution, the foundational national document. Thus, Lincoln displaced the Constitution from center stage, tying national identity much more closely to the Declaration as the initial collective statement of American nationhood. This may or may not be good history, but it surely accords with conventional Fourth of July rhetoric, which ties the Declaration not merely to the independence of individual states from Britain but more importantly to the creation of the United States.

Indeed, Lincoln insisted that that the Union was formed by the Articles of Association in 1774, even before it was "matured and continued by the Declaration of Independence in 1776."[25] Because the states never had any independent existence, secession was legally impossible. As Lincoln said, "The States have their *status* in the Union, and they have no other *legal status*. If they break from this, they can only do so against law, and by revolution."[26]

Lincoln made this constitutional vision the centerpiece of his opposition to secession. After the fall of Fort Sumter, Lincoln's message to Congress traced the

Union back to 1774 and then to the Declaration of Independence: "Our States have neither more, nor less power, than that reserved to them, in the Union by the Constitution—no one of them ever having been a State *out* of the Union. The original ones passed in the Union even *before* they cast off their British colonial dependence."[27]

Thus, according to Lincoln, in the Declaration of Independence,

> [T]he 'United Colonies' were declared to be 'Free and Independent States'; but, even then, the object plainly was not to declare their independence of *one another*, or of the *Union*; but directly the contrary, as their mutual pledge, and their mutual action, before, at the time, and afterwards, abundantly show.[28]

A few years after independence, Lincoln said the Union was strengthened by the Articles of Confederation, which were declared to be perpetual, and then by the Constitution, which sought a "more perfect union."[29] From this hypothesis, he deduced that secession was unconstitutional: "But if the destruction of the Union, by one, or by a part only, of the States, be lawfully possible, the Union is *less* perfect than before the Constitution, having lost the vital element of perpetuity."[30]

If the Confederation was perpetual, and if the Constitution created a more perfect union, then the Constitution had to provide for a perpetual bond. Moreover, because the only true sovereign government was national, Lincoln's view implied that citizenship was predominantly a national rather than state status; thus, allegiance was owed primarily to the federal government.

Lincoln's nationalist view contrasted sharply with the state-centered constitutional theory held by many Southerners. In defending the constitutionality of secession, Jefferson Davis affirmed a long-standing Southern view of the nature of the Union. During the American Revolution, Davis said, the British threat to American liberty had led to an alliance under which each state expressly retained its sovereignty.[31] Davis's narrative continued with a Constitutional Convention by state-appointed delegates who negotiated what he called "a compact between independent States."[32] State sovereignty, Davis said, was then explicitly reaffirmed in the 10th Amendment.[33] But a heresy arose in the North, according to Davis—a heresy holding that that Constitution did not create a compact of states but a national government.[34]

Note that Lincoln did not exactly endorse this 'heresy'—instead, he viewed nationhood as predating the Constitution. So, by Davis's standards, Lincoln's view was even worse than the Northern heresy; it was practically infidel. It is little wonder that Lincoln failed to persuade Southerners of his views.

The theory advanced by Davis was hardly original. John Calhoun was perhaps the most articulate spokesman for the Southern theory of the Union. He claimed that the states had separately become sovereign when they declared independence from England.[35] This sovereignty remained intact through the Articles of Confederation, and in the Constitution, all the states had done was appoint the federal government as their agent to perform certain functions.[36] According to Calhoun, the "government is a federal, in contradistinction to a national government—a government formed by the States; ordained and established by the States, and for the States—without any participation or agency whatever, on the part of the people, regarded in the aggregate as forming a nation."[37] (Notice the language "By the states . . . and for the states," and contrast that language with Lincoln's at Gettysburg.) There is, Calhoun said, "no such community, politically speaking, as the people of the United States, regarded in the light of, and as constituting one people or nation."[38] In short, he said, the Constitution created "the government of a community of States, and not the government of a single State or nation."[39] In a community of states, clearly the allegiance of citizens runs directly to their own state and only derivatively to the community as a whole.

Calhoun and Davis were important historical figures, but they did not evolve their theories on their own. Both drew on a larger tradition of Southern constitutionalism traceable to Thomas Jefferson. Well before Calhoun, the Southern vision of the Union had begun to emerge in the Virginia and Kentucky resolutions.[40] The *Kentucky Resolutions*, based on a draft by Jefferson, began with a strong affirmation of the compact theory. The states created the general government for special purposes, reserving to each state all remaining power. The resolutions maintained that the federal government, as a creature of the compact, was not final judge of the extent of its own powers. Instead, each party to the contract had to judge for itself whether the terms of the agreement had been violated.[41] The resolutions did not speak of secession, but the logical implication was that a party to the compact could withdraw in case of a breach or repudiation of the agreement by other parties.

Thus, by the onset of the Civil War, the South already had held an antinationalist, state-centered theory of the Constitution for over half a century. Indeed, according to a recent history of secession, the states' rights theory had become so familiar to Southerners by 1860 as to be boring:

> Secessionists' potentially saving state's rights creed started as a legalistic bore. The 1860 secessionists (and their fathers and grandfathers) had grown up listening to endless disquisitions on how the states came before the nation, on how the states had ratified the U.S. Constitution, on how the ratifying bodies

> retained reserved rights and especially the right to withdraw their ratification, and how the original parties to a contract can rescind the document if its terms were violated.[42]

So familiar was this theory that Southerners were outraged "when federal agents coercively violated the (white) people of a state's sovereign right to shift consent to another government."[43] This theory became invaluable in bringing the Upper South to secede after Fort Sumter. States like Virginia had not found Lincoln's election a sufficient basis to secede, but "[i]f the federal agency coerced the people of a single state who had claimed their state's right to remove their consent and never to be enslaved, the state's rights justification could bring other southern states charging to the rescue, whatever they thought of the expediency of the first secession."[44]

Even today, remnants of the antebellum Southern constitutional vision occasionally surface. Speaking for four members of the U.S. Supreme Court fifteen years ago, Justice Clarence Thomas invoked a similar conception of federalism. In his *Term Limits* dissent, he said that the "ultimate source of the Constitution's authority is the consent of the people of each individual State, not the consent of the undifferentiated people of the Nation as a whole"—adding that "the people of the several States are the only true source of power."[45] He seemed to indicate that state sovereignty remains primary today: "[T]he people of each State retained their separate political identities,"[46] and the "very name 'congress' suggests a coming together of representatives from distinct entities."[47]

Thus, although so far as we know no current Justice endorses a right to secede, elements of the antebellum Southern view linger in some present-day quarters. One implication of this article is that the 14th Amendment completed the work of the Constitution itself in consolidating the original colonies into a true nation. Thus, the *Term Limits* dissenters were embracing a theory that had lost whatever validity it ever had by 1867.

B. Federalism and Citizenship in the Antebellum Period

Justice Thomas oversimplified the issue in his *Term Limits* dissent, but the historical record does reflect considerable uncertainty and dispute about whether the United States was truly a nation. The question of "whether the Revolution had created one community of allegiance or many" remained unresolved.[48]

As an important part of this larger confusion, the relationship between states and national citizenship was unclear before the Civil War. Just three weeks after the Declaration of Independence, the Continental Congress passed a resolution providing that "all persons residing within any of the United Colonies, and deriving protection from the laws of the same, owe allegiance to the said laws, and are members of such colony."[49] The states quickly adopted their own naturalization laws,[50] but their power over citizenship was the source of confusion.

One reason for the confusion was that citizenship in a single state had significance in other states. Each state's citizens became entitled to equal treatment in all other states under the Articles of Confederation's precursor to what is now the Privileges and Immunities Clause of Article IV.[51] As James H. Kettner writes, "Although the primary locus of allegiance throughout the Confederation period was still in the individual sovereign state, the idea that citizens belonged to a larger national community surfaced frequently, never fully articulated or theoretically explored, but persuasive—almost instinctive—in certain contexts."[52] For instance, it was unclear whether a person who had been naturalized by a state under the articles was thereby a citizen of the United States for purposes of qualifying to sit in the United States Senate.[53]

Before the Civil War, the dispute over sovereignty was tied to a dispute over the meaning of citizenship. During the nullification crisis, South Carolina insisted that the "[A]llegiance of the citizens . . . is due to the . . . State, and . . . obedience only, and not allegiance, is due . . . to any other power or authority, to whom a control over them has been or may be delegated by the state."[54] The state legislature then passed a law requiring all militia officers to swear that they had "faithful and true allegiance" to the state.[55] The law was held unconstitutional by the state appellate court, with a dissenting nullifier arguing that only the state government could command a citizen's ultimate allegiance.[56]

Southerners also argued that a national statute governing expatriation (abandonment of citizenship) would be unconstitutional because it was not within any express congressional power and therefore left the matter to the states.[57] As a U.S. representative from Virginia put it, "The relation to the State government was the basis of the relation to the General Government, and therefore, as long as a man continues a citizen of a State, he must be considered a citizen of the United States."[58]

On the eve of Civil War, the dominant Southern view was that allegiance to state government was primary. However, adherence to the primacy of state citizenship was not absolute. In the name of protecting the power of Southern states to exclude free blacks from other states, Southerners were also willing to limit the power of other states to make blacks citizens for purposes of federal law. Allowing Northern states to make blacks into citizens would have led to the unpalatable conclusion that their status as citizens in Northern states would have been entitled to recognition in Southern states under the Privileges and Immunities Clause.

Chief Justice Roger B. Taney's opinion in *Dred Scott* contended that the Framers considered blacks "a subordinate and inferior class of beings, who had been subjugated by the dominant race, and, whether emancipated or not, yet remained subject to their authority, and had no rights or privileges but such as those who held the power and the Government might choose to grant them."[59] Justice Peter V. Daniels managed to exceed even Justice Taney's level of offensiveness with his dictum: "That in the establishment of the several communities now the States of this Union, and in the formation of the Federal Government, the African was not deemed politically a person."[60] Note, however, that the Constitution refers to slaves as "*persons* held to servitude,"[61] as Justice John McLean pointed out in his dissent.[62] It is also significant that citizenship had never been completely limited to whites: Indians were eligible for citizenship, and some Southern courts held that free blacks automatically became state citizens.[63]

James Madison himself took the view that emancipated blacks were entitled to the right of citizenship.[64] Moreover, an 1803 federal statute banned ships from bringing any black into the country who were not "a native, a *citizen*, or registered seaman of the United States."[65] That statute clearly implies that a black could be a citizen of the United States, and in 1807, Americans had been outraged by British seizure of four "American citizens," two of whom were black.[66]

In dissent, Justice McLean pointed out that Justice Taney's historical exegesis was remarkably one-sided: "[W]hile I admit the government was not made expecially [*sic*] for the colored race, yet many of them were citizens of the New England States, and exercised the rights of suffrage when the Constitution was adopted."[67] In Massachusetts, for example, a proposed 1778 state constitution went down to defeat in part because it excluded blacks from the right to vote.[68] This may not prove that free blacks were regarded as U.S. citizens, but it does rebut Justice Taney's assertion that blacks were incapable of being members of the political community or of having legal rights that others were required to accept.[69]

One reason for the relative paucity of evidence about the Framers' definition of citizenship is that they were rarely required to consider it. Citizenship is an important legal concept but not necessarily a decisive one in a broad range of contexts. In many respects, personhood is the more important concept under the U.S. Constitution. In the Constitution itself, citizenship is mostly mentioned as a job qualification for elected federal office.[70] But there is no constitutional requirement of citizenship for appointed office as a member of the judiciary or the cabinet nor any limitation of the franchise to citizens.

Moreover, the Constitution allowed free blacks to participate in the selection of members of Congress, provided that the state allowed them to vote or hold office. Article I, Section 2, provides that voters for House members "have the Qualifications requisite for Electors of the most numerous Branch of the State Legislature," so blacks could vote in federal elections if they could vote in state elections, regardless of whether they were citizens.[71] Under Article I, Section 3, members of the Senate are chosen by state legislatures, with no stated restriction on who can serve in such a legislature. [72]

Apart from the qualifications for political office, only a few provisions bore directly on citizenship. Article I, Section 8, Clause 4, gives Congress the power to "establish a uniform Rule of Naturalization . . . throughout the United States."[73] Otherwise, citizenship shows up only in Article III's definition of diversity jurisdiction[74] and in Article IV's Privileges and Immunities Clause.[75] Only in these two clauses and in the requirements for election to the Senate is state citizenship rather than federal citizenship mentioned. Notwithstanding Justice Taney's effort to restrict Article III diversity jurisdiction to whites, there was no constitutional barrier to blacks bringing suit under Article III's admiralty or federal question jurisdiction because the Constitution does not tie these to the identity of the parties.

Citizenship seemed to have less relevance to possession of rights than mere legal personhood. Article III, Section 2, Clause 3 provides a right to a jury in the "Trial of all Crimes, except in Cases of Impeachment," without reference to citizenship.[76] Article I, Section 9 prohibits bills of attainder and ex post facto laws without any reference to the citizenship of the defendant.[77] Some provisions of the Bill of Rights refer to "the people," which by Justice Taney's reasoning might not have included blacks.[78] But the 5th and 6th Amendments, governing due process, property confiscation, and criminal procedure, are not so limited, nor is the right to jury trial in civil cases of the 7th Amendment.

C. *Citizenship, Sovereignty, and Secession*

More vexing before the Civil War than the legal dimension of U.S. citizenship was its significance in terms of political obligation. Was Robert E. Lee an American citizen who owed allegiance to the United States first and foremost? If so, he was guilty of treason in taking up arms against the U.S. government and giving aid and comfort to its enemies.[79] Or was he a citizen of Virginia first and foremost, in which case he was bravely defending his country (Virginia) against a foreign enemy?

These citizenship issues had an obvious link with competing visions of the Union. The constitutionality of secession turned on whether the United States was a confederation of states (so that American citizenship derived from being a state citizen), or whether the United States was a genuine nation (so that American citizenship was primary). Even today, these viewpoints have left remnants in historical terminology. The former view is implicit in references to the Civil War as 'the war between the states,' whereas under the latter view, it was a Civil War between the United States and Southern rebels.

Before the Civil War, the answer to this question was debatable, but the Constitution itself was more nationalist than many people then or now seem to realize. To begin with, there is the Preamble's intention to create "a more perfect Union"[80] than the Articles of Confederation, which were supposed to be perpetual.[81] Other provisions of the Constitution, however, also speak volumes about the desire to create a powerful national government, not just an agent for a confederation of independent sovereigns. Besides granting the federal government broad powers over the economy, including control of all interstate commerce, exclusive power to coin money, and the bankruptcy power,[82] the Constitution invested the powers of war and peace as well as the power to make treaties, in the United States. It explicitly denied those powers to the states.[83] It also allowed the federal government to intervene in the internal political affairs of a state if it considered the state's form of government not to be "Republican" in nature.[84]

In addition, federal laws are "the Supreme Law of the Land" and override state constitutions, meaning that the people of the states gave up their plenary power to draft constitutions to suit themselves.[85] The federal government also controls naturalization and hence limits the power of a state to determine who counts as a citizen. All of these provisions seem well beyond the terms of a mere confederation. The states did retain control of purely local affairs, but that role seems decidedly subordinate to the sweeping constitutional powers of the federal government to address issues of national and international importance.

To see the degree to which the Constitution created something more than a mere confederation, it may be helpful to consider a modern-day analogy. Imagine a proposal to give "the United States of All the Americas (USAA)" the power to replace the U.S. dollar with a new currency, while disbanding the U.S. Army in favor of a military controlled by a President elected by North and South Americans. The USAA also controls all international trade in the Americas and takes over control of immigration issues. On top of this, the laws of the USAA override the U.S. Constitution. It is hard to imagine that anyone would think this organization was just a federation of existing states like NATO or that the USAA was merely acting as an agent for individual governments like the IMF or World Bank today.

Even more than the extensive national powers given to the U.S. government, the title of the document speaks strongly of nationhood. Its predecessor was called the Articles of Confederation. Eschewing this term, the new title is "Constitution of the United States." According to the Preamble, this national constitution is "ordain[ed] and establish[ed] . . . for the United States of America" by "We the People of the United States" in order "to form a more perfect Union."[86] This language sounds very much like the creation of a nation—as the union of Scotland and England created the United Kingdom.[87]

Notably, the Constitutional Convention sent the Continental Congress a letter explaining its efforts.[88] The letter spoke of the need to place key powers "fully and effectually" in the federal government, which admittedly would require some sacrifice of state sovereignty.[89] Moreover, the letter says: "In all our deliberations on this subject we kept steadily in our view, that which appears to us the greatest interest of every true American, the consolidation of our Union, in which is involved our prosperity, felicity, safety, perhaps our national existence."[90] The references to "consolidation" and to "our national existence" are inconsistent with the notion of a confederation. The letter closes with the hope that the Constitution "may promote the lasting welfare of that country so dear to us all, and secure her freedom and happiness"—rather than the "welfare of the countries dear to each of us."[91] This is nationalist language, not the language of a compact between independent sovereigns.

Still, the case of American nationhood (and with it, the case against secession) cannot be considered ironclad before the Civil War. As Madison pointed out in *Federalist* No. 39, the structure of the government contained ambiguities.[92] Madison pointed to nationalist features of the Constitution, such as the operation and extent of federal powers.[93] Yet the governance structure relied heavily on the states as separate entities (such as the election of senators by state legislatures), and the ratification process was by state conventions rather than a national vote.

II. CITIZENSHIP, RECONSTRUCTION, AND PROTECTION AGAINST STATE ACTION

In short, although the Constitution bears strong marks of nation building, there was no smoking-gun proof of the nature of the Union in the constitutional text that could decisively prevent Southerners from adopting a states' rights vision. As part III will explain, that smoking gun was supplied by the 14th Amendment. What was arguably still an open question in 1860 was answered in no uncertain terms in 1866 with the adoption of the 14th Amendment.

The relevant portions of the 14th Amendment are familiar, but their significance is obscure today, because we have lost the historical context that made issues of U.S. citizenship so foundational to the constitutional regime. The first sentence of the amendment provides, "All persons born or naturalized in the United States, and subject to the jurisdiction thereof, are citizens of the United States and of the State wherein they reside."[94] Only with the passage of this amendment did it become incontestable that state citizenship was merely a geographic by-product of federal citizenship. Correspondingly, the second sentence of the amendment prohibits states from interfering with the privileges and immunities of national citizenship.[95] The upshot of these sections is that the United States establishes a direct relationship between the federal government and citizens that is beyond any form of interference by the states, which enjoy only a secondary right to allegiance from their residents. While the two clauses may seem to deal only with some narrowly defined legal issues relating to citizenship, the implications were much broader.

Part III discusses the implications of this change for the issue of secession. The right to secede is a natural feature of a confederation in which citizens owe allegiance to their own individual local governments, but it is out of place in a nation that demands the primary allegiance of its citizens and in turn promises to protect their rights from interference by local governments.

Part A begins by examining the reciprocal relationship between a citizen's allegiance to the sovereign and the right to protection by the sovereign. Part B shows how these ideas entered the Reconstruction view of the Article IV Privileges and Immunities Clause. Then, part C shows how concepts of allegiance and protection were put to use in the Reconstruction debates to support the right of American citizens to national protection against infringement by their own state governments. Finally, part D shows how the Supreme Court viewed the relationship between citizenship and rights after the Civil War. Although the Court took a narrow view of what rights inhered in national citizenship, it clearly understood that national citizenship was primary and beyond the reach of state authority.

A. *Protection and Allegiance*

According to legal historian Philip Hamburger, "The reciprocal relation of allegiance and protection . . . became a foundation of American government."[96]

This concept was deeply embedded in the common law and in the thinking of the Republicans who passed the 14th Amendment. It implied that if residents of seceding states remained U.S. citizens, they were entitled to the protection of the U.S. government against would-be secessionists and to enforcement of their rights under federal law.

The connections between citizenship, allegiance, and government protection went back in English law at least to the time of Lord Coke, who faced such issues in the context of determining the rights of citizens of Scotland under English law during the reign of James I.[97] James had become king of both England and Scotland, but the countries had separate parliaments, so it was not clear how their citizenships related.[98] Fundamental to Coke's analysis was the proposition that the "bond between the subject and the sovereign . . . involved reciprocal obligations" of allegiance and protection that attached at birth.[99] The duty of allegiance to the king and the correlative rights to "the King's legal protection" were explicit in the case.[100] Because Scots born after the Union received the protection of James, who was monarch of both Scotland and England, they acquired a duty of allegiance to both states and hence citizenship in both parts of the realm.

In the American Civil War, both sides claimed entitlement to allegiance, in each case implying that violations of allegiance would constitute treason. Based on the theory that individual allegiance flowed fundamentally to the states, the Confederacy maintained that no change in allegiance took place at secession. Thus, unlike the American Revolution, in which individuals were considered to have a period in which to choose allegiance, the allegiance of Southerners automatically remained with the existing states when those state governments chose to sever their relationship with the federal government.[101] Hence, after secession, Southern Unionists were subject to the law of treason. A similar situation would arise today if the United States decided to leave the United Nations or NATO. Such a decision would clearly have no effect on the status of U.S. citizens, who would remain citizens of the United States, not citizens of NATO, and Americans who chose to side with NATO against the United States in a military conflict would be guilty of treason. For the same reason, according to Confederate legal theory, Southerners who decided to side with the North after secession were guilty of treason.[102]

As might be expected, Northerners took a different view. The significance attached to national citizenship and allegiance in the North became evident in the early days of the war. In the *Prize Cases*,[103] for example, the Supreme Court was required to determine not only the President's power to impose a blockade but also the relationship of Southerners to the federal government after the outbreak of the war.[104] The Court strongly affirmed presidential power to react to the emergency without waiting for congressional approval or a declaration of war. When war broke out, the Court said, "[t]he President was bound to meet it in the shape it presented itself, without waiting for Congress to baptize it with a name; and no name given to it by him or them could change the fact."[105] As to the question of the status of the citizens in the South, the Court said, "They have cast off their allegiance and made war on their Government, and are none the less enemies because they are traitors."[106] In an affirmation of nationalism, the Court also said that citizens owe "supreme allegiance" to the federal government but only "qualified allegiance" to their states.[107] Note that this holding anticipates the view ultimately enshrined in the Citizenship Clause of the 14th Amendment.

B. *Citizenship and Rights*

Given the emotional significance of allegiance during the sectional conflict and the expansion of national power under the stress of war, it is not remarkable that Republicans used the concept of national citizenship to justify their support for the Civil Rights bill. Republicans invoked the Privileges and Immunities Clause in Article IV, Section 2, of the original Constitution because they believed that the clause had already established the connection between United States citizenship and fundamental rights.

Congressional Republicans had their own theory of citizenship, based in part on the Privileges and Immunities Clause of Article IV. Section 2 of Article IV provides that "[t]he citizens of each State shall be entitled to all Privileges and Immunities of Citizens in the several States."[108] This language is somewhat unclear. One reading is that "in the several states" tells us both where the rights are protected and which rights exist (those created severally—that is separately—in particular states). On this reading, the clause prohibits states from discriminating against citizens of other states. But the other reading is that the "privileges and immunities of citizens" are national in scope rather than being defined by particular state. Every law student today learns the antidiscrimination meaning of the clause, which may well be the correct interpretation. But Republicans, as we will see, often favored the national rights interpretation.

The Republican interpretation of this clause relied heavily on *Corfield v. Coryell*.[109] In *Corfield*, Justice Bushrod Washington said that the Comity Clause protected "those privileges and immunities which are, in their nature, fundamental; which belong, of right, to the citizens of all free governments; and which have, at all times, been enjoyed by the citizens of the several states."[110] Among these rights were "[p]rotection by the government; the enjoyment of life and liberty, with the right to acquire and possess property of every kind, and to pursue and obtain happiness and safety; subject nevertheless to such restraints as the government may justly prescribe for the general good of the whole."[111]

This interpretation of the Privileges and Immunities Clause figured prominently in the debates on the 1866 Civil Rights bill. One purpose of the 14th Amendment was to constitutionalize the Civil Rights Act, so the debates on that statute are particularly relevant to understanding the amendment.

In the Senate debate on the 1866 act, Senator Lyman Trumbull referred to the Privileges and Immunities Clause to support the constitutionality of federal civil rights legislation at a time when the 14th Amendment did not yet exist. He argued that

> [t]he rights of a citizen of the United States were certain great fundamental rights, such as the right to life, to liberty, and to avail one's self of all the laws passed for the benefit of the citizen to enable him to enforce his rights; inasmuch as this was the definition given to the term as applied in that part of the Constitution, I reasoned from that, that when the Constitution had been amended and slavery abolished, and we were about to pass a law declaring every person, no matter of what color, born in the United States a citizen of the United States, the same rights would then appertain to all persons who were clothed with American citizenship.[112]

In the House, Representative Henry Wilson argued that the rights protected in the bill were not new because they were already contained in the Comity Clause as construed in *Corfield*. In his view, that clause represented a "general citizenship" that "entitles every citizen to security and protection of personal rights."[113] He argued that the bill protected rights belonging to "citizens of the United States, as such."[114]

Representative William Lawrence discussed the role of the Comity Clause in great detail in his response to the President's veto of the bill. He stated:

> I maintain that Congress may by law secure the citizens of the nation in the enjoyment of their inherent right of life, liberty, and property, and the means essential to that end, ... to enforce the observance of the provisions of [the Comity Clause], and the equal civil rights which it recognizes or by implication affirms to exist among citizens of the same State.[115]

Representative Lawrence concluded, after a discussion of some of the cases and writings dealing with the Comity Clause, that it embodies "equal fundamental civil rights for all citizens."[116]

Thus, even before the 14th Amendment, advocates of Reconstruction saw Congress as having the power to protect the rights of citizens from violation by state government. They rooted this understanding in the clause protecting the "privileges and immunities of citizens in the several states." When it came time to ensure that their constitutional views were entrenched in the constitutional text, they chose similar, but more explicit, language relating to the "privileges or immunities of citizens of the United States."

C. Protecting the Rights of Citizens against the States

Another concept played an important role in the debates over the Civil Rights Act: the idea that citizens owe allegiance to their government in exchange for the government's grant of protection to them. Thus, one of the most important rights of citizenship is the right to receive such protection. This concept served not only as a possible source of rights but also as a power to protect the rights of citizens that might arise from other sources, such as the Privileges and Immunities Clause.

Early in the debates on the Civil Rights Act, Senator Reverdy Johnson raised the argument that the federal government had a duty to protect its citizens from state interference with their rights:

> If I am right . . . that we can authorize them [blacks] to sue, authorize them to contract, authorize them to do everything short of voting, it is not because there is anything in the Constitution of the United States that confers the authority to give to a negro the right to contract, but it is because it is a necessary, incidental function of a Government that it should have authority to provide that the rights of everybody within its limits shall be protected, and protected alike.[117]

Senator Johnson concluded that it "would have been a disgrace to the members of the [Constitutional] Convention" if they had foreseen the abolition of slavery and "had denied to the Congress of the United States the authority to pass laws for the protection of all the rights incident to the condition of a free man."[118] His argument was echoed by Senator Lot Morrill.[119]

A similar argument was made in the House by Representative John Broomall. He made a sweeping, nontextual argument:

> But throwing aside the letter of the Constitution, there are characteristics of Governments that belong to them as such, without which they would cease to be Governments. The rights and duties of allegiance and protection are corresponding rights and duties. . . . [Wherever] I owe allegiance to my country, there it owes me protection, and wherever my Government owes me no protection I owe it no allegiance and can commit no treason.[120]

Representative Broomall attacked the idea that such protection could be left to the states, inasmuch as "everybody knows that the rights and immunities of citizens were habitually and systematically denied in certain States to the citizens of other States: the right of speech, the right of transit, the right of domicil [*sic*], the right to sue, the writ of habeas corpus, and the right of petition."[121] He also argued that the necessity for the bill was not limited to blacks because loyal whites were being denied their basic rights in the South.[122]

Representative James Wilson made one of the most forceful arguments based on the duty to protect. He argued that the bill did not establish new rights, but instead protected and enforced those which already belonged to every citizen. In his opinion, the Comity Clause entitled every citizen to protection of personal rights. He summarized his defense of congressional power as follows:

> If a citizen of the United States should go abroad, and while within the jurisdiction of a foreign Power be despoiled of his rights of personal security, personal liberty, or personal property contrary to the due course of law of the nation inflicting the wrong, this Government would espouse his cause and enforce redress even to the extremity of war.[123]

From the power to protect U.S. citizens from foreign powers by war, Representative Wilson deduced as a lesser-included case the power to protect citizens from their own state governments by peaceful means:

> [I]f all the terrible powers of war may be resorted to for the protection of the rights of our citizens when those rights are disregarded and trampled on beyond our jurisdiction, is it possible that our Constitution is so defective that we have no power under it to protect our citizens within our own jurisdiction through the peaceful means of statutes and courts?[124]

Thus, he concluded, the federal government had the inherent power to prevent states from violating the rights of U.S. citizens:

> I assert that we possess the power to do those things which Governments are organized to do; that we may protect a citizen of the United States against a violation of his rights by the law of a single State; . . . that this power permeates our whole system, is a part of it, without which the States can run riot over every fundamental right belonging to citizens of the United States; that the right to exercise this power depends upon no express delegation, but runs with the rights it is designed to protect.[125]

Likewise, Representative Samuel Shellabarger stressed that because citizens owe their primary allegiance to the federal government, the government's primary duty correspondingly was to protect them. Like Representative Wilson, Shellabarger argued that if the states could abridge those rights which the United States is bound to protect, even by a declaration of war in the case of violations by foreign governments, then "the United States is no nation."[126]

After President Andrew Johnson's veto of the Civil Rights bill, Senator Trumbull made an important speech in the Senate defending the bill against Johnson's charges. He asserted:

> To be a citizen of the United States carries with it some rights; . . . They are those inherent, fundamental rights which belong to free citizens or free men in all countries, such as the rights enumerated in this bill, and they belong to them in all the States of the Union.[127]

In short, he said, "the right of American citizenship means something."[128] That is a truism today, but would have been contested by Southerners before the war, who viewed American citizenship as nothing but a proxy for citizenship in Virginia or some other state.

Trumbull stated that citizens are entitled to protection within the states as well as abroad. He asserted that "American citizenship would be little worth" if it did not carry protection with it:

> How is it that every person born in these United States owes allegiance to the Government? Everything that he is or has, his property and his life, may be taken by the Government of the United States in its defense . . . and can it be that . . . we have got a Government which is all-powerful to command the obedience of the citizen, but has no power to afford him protection? Is that all that this boasted American citizenship amounts to? . . . Sir, it cannot be.[129]

Trumbull staunchly rejected this limited view of the nature of citizenship:

> Such is not the meaning of our Constitution. Such is not the meaning of American citizenship. This Government, which would go to war to protect its meanest—I will not say citizen—inhabitant . . . in any foreign land whose rights were unjustly encroached upon, has certainly some power to protect its own citizens in their own country. Allegiance and protection are reciprocal rights.[130]

The right to protection was embodied in the 14th Amendment, which prohibited states from interfering with the rights of citizens or any inhabitant to due process and equal protection. Yet secession truncates the rights of national citizenship for any citizens who remain in the state. Under the 14th Amendment, states do not have the power to impair these rights of national citizenship, and

Section 5 of the amendment explicitly gives Congress the power to take any necessary action to deal with the situation.[131]

D. Citizenship and the Slaughterhouse Cases

When it came time for the Supreme Court to interpret the Reconstruction Amendments, the significance of national citizenship was not overlooked. The appellants in the *Slaughterhouse Cases* argued that

> [t]he doctrine of the "States-Rights party," led in modern times by Mr. Calhoun, was, that there was no citizenship in the whole United States, except *sub modo* and by the permission of the States. According to their theory the United States had no integral existence except as an incomplete combination among several integers. The fourteenth amendment struck at, and forever destroyed, all such doctrines. . . . By it the national principle has received an indefinite enlargement. The tie between the United States and every citizen in every part of its own jurisdiction has been made intimate and familiar.[132]

This argument reflected a clear understanding of how the 14th Amendment solidified the bond between citizens and the national government.

Similarly, in his dissent, Justice Stephen Field also clearly articulated the import of the amendment for national citizenship and its accompanying rights. He began by demonstrating his awareness of the past confusion on this topic:

> The first clause of this amendment determines who are citizens of the United States, and how their citizenship is created. Before its enactment there was much diversity of opinion among jurists and statesmen whether there was any such citizenship independent of that of the State, and, if any existed, as to the manner in which it originated. With a great number the opinion prevailed that there was no such citizenship independent of the citizenship of the State. Such was the opinion of Mr. Calhoun and the class represented by him.[133]

After recounting the holding in *Dred Scott,* Field explained how the 14th Amendment settled the question of who possessed citizenship as well as that of the significance of citizenship as a source of rights:

> The first clause of the fourteenth amendment changes this whole subject, and removes it from the region of discussion and doubt. . . . A citizen of a State is now only a citizen of the United States residing in that State. The fundamental rights, privileges, and immunities which belong to him as a free man and a free citizen, now belong to him as a citizen of the United States, and are not dependent upon his citizenship of any State.[134]

Of course, the views of the advocates and the dissenters are less significant than that of the majority. While the majority opinion rejects the sweeping vision of national rights advocated by Justice Fields and the respondent's attorneys, it reflects a clear understanding of the primacy of national citizenship and of the fact that this citizenship carries with it genuine rights.[135]

Like the dissent, the majority opinion displays an awareness of the prewar confusion regarding citizenship. Justice Samuel Miller recounted the antebellum disputes about citizenship. First, he said, there was confusion over the status of individuals born within the United States but not in any state:

> It had been said by eminent judges that no man was a citizen of the United States, except as he was a citizen of one of the States composing the Union. Those, therefore, who had been born and resided always in the District of Columbia or in the Territories, though within the United States, were not citizens. Whether this proposition was sound or not had never been judicially decided.[136]

More significant, however, was the issue of black citizenship. *Dred Scott* was not forgotten:

> But it had been held by this court, in the celebrated Dred Scott case, only a few years before the outbreak of the civil war, that a man of African descent, whether a slave or not, was not and could not be a citizen of a State or of the United States. This decision . . . had never been overruled; and if it was to be accepted as a constitutional limitation of the right of citizenship, then all the negro race who had recently been made freemen, were still, not only not citizens, but were incapable of becoming so by anything short of an amendment to the Constitution.[137]

Justice Miller explained how the Citizenship Clause resolved these issues:

> The first observation we have to make on this clause is, that it puts at rest both the questions which we stated to have been the subject of differences of opinion. It declares that persons may be citizens of the United States without regard to their citizenship of a particular State, and it overturns the Dred Scott decision by making *all persons* born within the United States and subject to its jurisdiction citizens of the United States.[138]

Miller then listed some privileges and immunities of national citizenship that are protected against state interference. The rights on his list are, at least today, quite uncontroversial, but one should keep in mind that a state's secession would have deprived each of its citizens of every right on the list except to the extent that some later treaty might allow foreigners from the seceded state to exercise these rights. Justice Miller's list included the following:

> [T]he right of the citizen of this great country, protected by implied guarantees of its Constitution, "to come to the seat of government to assert any claim he may have upon that government, to transact any business he may have with it, to seek its protection, to share its offices, to engage in administering its functions. He has the right of free access to its seaports, through which all operations of foreign commerce are conducted, to the subtreasuries, land offices, and courts of justice in the several States."[139]
>
> Another privilege of a citizen of the United States is to demand the care and protection of the Federal government over his life, liberty, and property when on the high seas or within the jurisdiction of a foreign government.[140]
>
> The right to peaceably assemble and petition for redress of grievances, the privilege of the writ of *habeas corpus*, are rights of the citizen guaranteed by the Federal Constitution.[141]
>
> The right to use the navigable waters of the United States, however they may penetrate the territory of the several States, all rights secured to our citizens by treaties with foreign nations, are dependent upon citizenship of the United States, and not citizenship of a State.[142]
>
> [A] citizen of the United States can, of his own volition, become a citizen of any State of the Union by a *bonâ fide* residence therein, with the same rights as other citizens of that State.[143]
>
> To these may be added the rights secured by the thirteenth and fifteenth articles of amendment, and by the other clauses of the fourteenth.[144]

Most of these rights relate to American nationhood—the citizen's connection with the federal government and the right to recognition of national citizenship by every state. Secession would obviously interfere with these rights—for instance, no longer would citizens of another state retain the right to enter and become citizens of the seceded state or to use the navigable waters in that state, nor would the citizens of the seceded state retain their rights as American citizens. The Privileges or Immunities Clause of the 14th Amendment makes it clear that no state has the power to deprive U.S. citizens within its borders of these rights.

III. CONCLUSION

School children today pledge allegiance "to the flag of the United States of America, and to the republic for which it stands, one nation, under God, indivisible, with liberty and justice for all." Much of constitutional import is captured by this pledge: that allegiance is to the United States as 'one nation,' not a confederation; that the nation is 'indivisible,' not subject to being divided by secession; and that all of this is tied with a national guarantee of 'justice for all,' which is to say protection of the rights of individuals.

Before the Civil War and the 14th Amendment, none of this could have been said with complete assurance. Southerners, and a significant number of Northerners, would have thought it more correct for the pledge to refer to the flag and "to the republics for which it stands, one Confederation, divisible at the will of any state, with liberty and justice for all white men."

This hypothetical pledge would have encapsulated the Southern constitutional vision for the benefit of school children. Prior to the Civil War, the state governments were primarily responsible for meeting the basic needs of American citizens. The national government had little impact on the daily lives of most Americans. Consequently, before the war, state citizenship was usually paramount in practical importance and arguably of paramount legal importance as well. From this premise, it was a small step to the conclusion that allegiance to the state came before allegiance to the federal government, as Southerners like Robert E. Lee reluctantly decided. But such concepts obviously could not survive the Civil War, a war fought in large part over the primary allegiance of the citizen. The decision to defeat secession by force necessarily implied that the citizen's relationship to the national government took precedence over his or her relationship to the state.

How far the nation has come from the antebellum Southern view of the Union was illustrated during former Alaska Governor Sarah Palin's 2011 bus tour. Although Palin is no friend of federal power,[145] her bus touted the indivisibility of the American Republic: "You'll never guess the colors of the Palin bus. In huge letters it has the closing Pledge of Allegiance line: 'One nation, under God, indivisible with liberty and justice for all.' Plus an image of the Declaration of Independence with the words 'We the people.'"[146] 'Indivisible,' of course, means that the nation cannot be divided through secession.

Under the 14th Amendment, it is clear that today's pledge is correct: we owe our primary allegiance to the United States, which is a nation rather than a confederation, and which in return offers us protection for our rights as citizens. Correspondingly, states, as building blocks of the nation, have only second place in our allegiance, with state citizenship being defined by the 14th Amendment as only a geographic marker of where an American citizen happens to reside at any given time.

Today, then, there would be no doubt about the choice facing a modern-day Robert E. Lee. He could live up to his obligations as a citizen of the indivisible

United States, or by joining an unconstitutional armed rebellion, he could attempt to assist a state in destroying the privileges and immunities of national citizenship for its own residents. In using force on behalf of this effort, he would have to make war against the United States and give aid and comfort to the enemy. For him to claim that his primary allegiance was to his home state rather than to the national government would be to profoundly mistake the nature of the post–Civil War constitutional order. In Lee's time, perhaps there was some basis for good faith confusion on this point, but after the Civil War and the 14th Amendment, there can be no question about the unconstitutionality of secession.

NOTES

1. James M. McPherson, Battle Cry of Freedom 280–81 (1988).

2. *Id.* at 281.

3. *Id.*

4. *Id.*

5. *Id.*

6. *Id.* at 280–81.

7. James H. Kettner, The Development of American Citizenship, 1608–1870, at 340 (1978). *The Development of American Citizenship* remains the leading historical treatment of the subject. Douglas Bradburn, *The Citizenship Revolution* (2009), adds a valuable perspective on the development of nationalism during the early years of the Republic.

8. Kettner, *supra* note 7, at 340.

9. *Id.* at 343.

10. *See* Eric Foner, The Fiery Trial 93 (2010) ("Until after the Civil War, there existed no commonly agreed understanding of citizenship or of the rights it entailed."). Of course, this is not to say states have lost all significance to Americans. As Bruce Ackerman says:

> No need to exaggerate. I don't suggest that Americans think of themselves as citizens of a unitary nation-state on the model of, say, nineteenth-century France. We remain Pennsylvanians or Oregonians as well as Americans, but the textual promise of the Fourteenth Amendment has finally become a living reality: we are Americans first.

Bruce Ackerman, *The Living Constitution*, 120 Harv. L. Rev. 1737, 1749–50 (2007).

11. "All persons born or naturalized in the United States, and subject to the jurisdiction thereof, are citizens of the United States and of the State wherein they reside." U.S. Const. amend. XIV, § 1. This language derives from the Civil Rights Act of 1866, 14 Stat. 27 (1866), with a change from excepting persons "subject to any foreign power" and "Indians not taxed" to those "not subject to the jurisdiction of the United States." Many supporters of the statute believed that the 13th Amendment made blacks citizens when it abolished slavery. *See* Robert J. Kaczorowski, *Revolutionary Constitutionalism in the Era of the Civil War and Reconstruction*, 61 N.Y.U. L. Rev. 863, 899 n.157 (1986) (*citing* United States v. Rhodes, 27 F. Cas. 785 (C.C.D. Ky. 1867) as exemplifying this view). For example, Senator Benjamin Wade

said: "I have always believed that every person, of whatever race or color, who was born within the United States was a citizen of the United States; but by the decisions of the courts there has been a doubt thrown over that subject; and if the Government should fall into the hands of those who are opposed to the views that some of us maintain, those who have been accustomed to take a different view of it, they may construe the provision in such a way as we do not think it liable to construction at the time, unless we fortify and make it very strong and clear." Cong. Globe, 39th Cong., 1st Sess. 2768 (1866) (remarks of Sen. Wade). The Framers of the 14th Amendment shared this view but wished to eliminate any remaining doubt on the question. *See* Richard L. Aynes, *Unintended Consequences of the Fourteenth Amendment and What They Tell Us about Its Interpretation*, 39 Akron L. Rev. 289, 295–97 (2006). For a review of the legislative history, *see* Garrett Epps, *The Citizenship Clause: A "Legislative History,"* 60 Am. U. L. Rev. 331 (2010).

12. "No State shall make or enforce any law which shall abridge the privileges or immunities of citizens of the United States." U.S. Const. amend. XIV, § 1.

13. David A. Strauss, *The New Textualism in Constitutional Law*, 66 Geo. Wash. L. Rev. 1153, 1155–56 (1998). Strauss has made the same argument elsewhere:

> In the decades leading up to the Civil War, respected political and legal figures advanced serious legal arguments, claiming descent from Jefferson's Kentucky Resolutions, in support of the right to secede. *No amendment adopted after the Civil War settled this question, either expressly or by any reasonably direct implication.*
>
> Yet the question has, without doubt, been settled. The person on the street would say that the Civil War settled it, and that person would be right. The Civil War settled it, even though no formal amendment was added to the Constitution.

David A. Strauss, *The Irrelevance of Constitutional Amendments*, 114 Harv. L. Rev. 1457, 1486 (2001) (emphasis added). Strauss is probably right that as a practical matter, the Civil War would have banished any serious claims about the right to secede even without a formal amendment. The 14th Amendment can be seen as memorializing a constitutional shift that had already taken place, at least inasmuch as it can be considered to be the cause of the shift. But as a legal matter, the 14th Amendment incorporated the newly entrenched vision of the Constitution and gave it a textual home.

14. Seth F. Kreimer, *Lines in the Sand: The Importance of Borders in American Federalism*, 150 U. Pa. L. Rev. 973, 983 (2002).

15. United States v. Hall, 26 F. Cas. 79, 82 (C.C.S.D. Ala. 1871) (No. 15282).

16. *Governor Says Texans May Want to Secede from Union but Probably Won't*, FoxNews.com, Apr. 15, 2009, http://www.foxnews.com/politics/2009/04/15/governor-says-texans-want-secede-union-probably-wont/.

17. *Id.*

18. Thomas H. Naylor, The Vermont Manifesto (2005); Robert C. Black, Book Note, *If at First You Don't Secede, Try, Try Again*, 39 New Eng. L. Rev. 839, 842 (2005) (reviewing Naylor, *supra*). *See also* Joseph Curl, *Blue States Buzz over Secession*, Wash. Times, Nov. 9, 2004, at A1 (describing blue state buzz over secession after George W. Bush's successful reelection, some of it serious, some of it merely rhetorical).

19. *See, e.g.*, Cynthia Nicoletti, *The American Civil War as a Trial by Battle*, 28 Law & Hist. Rev. 71 (2010) (arguing that the Civil War did not resolve the legal question of the secession's constitutionality); Peter Radan, *Lincoln, the Constitution and Secession*, *in* Secession as an

International Phenomenon 56–75 (Don H. Doyle ed., 2010) (critiquing Lincoln's arguments against secession); Michael Stokes Paulsen, *The Civil War as Constitutional Interpretation,* 71 U. Chi. L. Rev. 691, 703–15 (2004) (endorsing Lincoln's view of secession); Akhil Reed Amar, *Abraham Lincoln and the American Union,* 2001 U. Ill. L. Rev. 1109 (2001) (critical discussion of Lincoln's view).

20. U.S. Term Limits, Inc. v. Thornton, 514 U.S. 779 (1995).

21. *Id.* at 803.

22. *Id.*

23. Abraham Lincoln, *First Inaugural Address, in* 4 The Collected Works of Abraham Lincoln 265 (Roy P. Basler ed., 1953) [hereinafter Collected Works].

24. For a defense of Lincoln's view, *see* Murray Dry, *Born on the Fourth of July,* Legal Affairs, Nov./Dec. 2005, at 66.

25. Lincoln, *supra* note 23, at 265.

26. Abraham Lincoln, *Special Message to Congress, July 4, 1861, in* 4 Collected Works, *supra* note 23, at 434.

27. *Id.* at 433.

28. *Id.*

29. Lincoln, *supra* note 23, at 265.

30. *Id.*

31. Jefferson Davis, *Message to Congress April 29, 1861* (Ratification of The Constitution), *available at* http://avalon.law.yale.edu/19th_century/csa_m042961.asp.

32. *Id.*

33. *Id.*

34. *Id.*

35. John C. Calhoun, *A Discourse on the Constitution and Government of the United States, in* Union and Liberty 84 (Ross M. Lence ed., 1992).

36. *Id.* at 83–84.

37. *Id.* at 116.

38. *Id.*

39. *Id.* at 82.

40. Stanley Elkins & Eric McKitrick, The Age of Federalism 719 (1993).

41. *Kentucky Resolutions of 1798 and 1799, in* 4 The Debates in the Several State Conventions 540, 544 (Jonathan Elliot ed., 1891). On the difference between Jefferson and Madison regarding the precise nature of the federal compact, *see* H. Jefferson Powell, *The Principles of '98: An Essay in Historical Retrieval,* 80 Va. L. Rev. 689, 717–18 (1994).

42. William W. Freehling, Road to Disunion 346 (2007).

43. *Id.* at 349.

44. *Id.* at 351.

45. U.S. Term Limits, Inc. v. Thornton, 514 U.S. 779, 846–47 (1995) (Thomas, J., dissenting).

46. *Id.* at 849.

47. *Id.* at 857–58.

48. Kettner, *supra* note 7, at 209.

49. *Id.* at 179.

50. *Id.* at 214–19.

51. *Id.* at 220.

52. *Id.* at 224.

53. *Id.* at 234–35. For an overview of immigration policy prior to the Constitution, *see* James E. Pfander & Theresa R. Wardon, *Reclaiming the Immigration Constitution of the Early Republic: Prospectivity, Uniformity, and Transparency*, 96 Va. L. Rev. 359, 371–85 (2010).

54. Kettner, *supra* note 7, at 265.

55. *Id.*

56. *Id.* at 267.

57. *Id.* at 282–83. Justice William Paterson had taken a contrary view in the lead opinion in *Talbot v. Jansen*, 3 U.S. (3 Dall.) 133 (1795):

> The act of the legislature of Virginia, does not apply. Ballard was a citizen of Virginia, and also of the United States. If the legislature of Virginia pass an act specifying the causes of expatriation, and prescribing the manner in which it is to be effected by the citizens of that state, what can be its operation on the citizens of the United States? If the act of Virginia affects Ballard's citizenship, so far as respects that state, can it touch his citizenship so far as it regards the United States? Allegiance to a particular state, is one thing; allegiance to the United States is another. Will it be said, that the renunciation of allegiance to the former implies or draws after it a renunciation of allegiance to the latter? The sovereignties are different; the allegiance is different; the right too, may be different.

Id. at 153–54. For background on the case, *see* Bradburn, *supra* note 7, at 116–22.

58. Kettner, *supra* note 7, at 283.

59. Dred Scott v. Sandford, 60 U.S. 393, 404–5 (1856). Don Edward Fehrenbacher, *The* Dred Scott *Case* (1978), is a classic treatment of the historical context, legal complexities, decisional process, and impact of the case. It is more readily available in an abridged paperback, Don Edward Fehrenbacher, *Slavery, Law, & Politics* (1981). Another useful treatment is Paul Finkelman, Dred Scott v. Sandford (1997), which also contains excerpts from the long, meandering opinions and reprints the responses of Northern and Southern papers to the decision. For a brief introduction to the case and its effects, *see* Richard H. Sewell, *A House Divided* 57–61 (1988).

60. *Dred Scott*, 60 U.S. at 481.

61. The Fugitive Slave Clause provides:

> No Person held to Service or Labour in one State, under the Laws thereof, escaping into another, shall, in Consequence of any Law or Regulation therein, be discharged from such Service or Labour, but shall be delivered up on Claim of the Party to whom such Service of Labour may be due.

U.S. Const. art. IV, § 2, cl. 3. The point is that while slaves may have been property, they were also persons for some constitutional purposes. Whether status as property could be squared with the right to due process created by the 5th Amendment is a question that may have had no satisfactory resolution before the issue was rendered moot by the Civil War.

62. *Dred Scott*, 60 U.S. at 537 (Mclean, J., dissenting).

63. Kettner, *supra* note 7, at 316–19.

64. Bradburn, *supra* note 7, at 259.

65. *Dred Scott*, 60. U.S. at 587 (Curtis, J., dissenting).

66. Bradburn, *supra* note 7, at 235–36.

67. *Dred Scott*, 60 U.S. at 537.

68. Bradburn, *supra* note 7, at 245. Bradburn believes that free blacks were close to treatment as citizens at the time of the Revolution but then were gradually demoted to the status of "denizens" in the early nineteenth century. *Id.* at 239–40.

69. The *Dred Scott* case continues to attract interest today, as seen by recent scholarship such as Gerald Leonard, *Law and Politics Reconsidered: A New Constitutional History of* Dred Scott, 34 Law & Soc. Inquiry 747 (2009); Harry V. Jaffa, Dred Scott *Revisited*, 31 Harv. J. L. & Pub. Pol'y 197 (2008); Jack M. Balkin & Sanford Levinson, *Thirteen Ways of Looking at* Dred Scott, 82 Chi.-Kent L. Rev. 49 (2007); Sarah H. Cleveland, *Foreign Authority, American Exceptionalism, and the* Dred Scott *Case*, 82 Chi.-Kent L. Rev. 393 (2007); Sam Erman, *An "Unintended Consequence":* Dred Scott *Reinterpreted*, 106 Mich. L. Rev. 1157 (2008).

70. *See* U.S. Const. art. I, § 2, cl. 2 (members of the House must have been citizens of the United States for seven years); U.S. Const. art. I, § 3, cl. 3 (Senators must have been citizens of the United States for nine years and citizens of the state at the time of election); U.S. Const. art. II, § 1, cl. 5 (the President must be "a natural born Citizen, or a Citizen of the United States, at the time of the Adoption of this Constitution"). Note that the requirements for Senators clearly distinguish between United States citizenship and citizenship in a particular state.

71. U.S. Const. art. I, § 2, cl. 1.

72. U.S. Const. art. I, § 3, cl. 1.

73. U.S. Const. art. I, § 8, cl. 4.

74. Article III provides:

> The judicial Power shall extend to . . . Controversies . . . between a State and Citizens of another State;—between Citizens of different States; between Citizens of the same State claiming Lands under Grants of different States, and between a State, or the Citizens thereof, and foreign States, Citizens or Subject.

U.S. Const. art. III, § 2.

75. The Privileges and Immunities Clause of Article IV states that the "Citizens of each State shall be entitled to all Privileges and Immunities of Citizens in the several States." U.S. Const. art. IV, § 1.

76. U.S. Const. art. III, § 2, cl. 3.

77. U.S. Const. art. I, § 9, cl. 3.

78. For instance, the 4th Amendment provides that the "right of the people to be secure in their persons, houses, papers, and effects, against unreasonable searches and seizures, shall not be violated." U.S. Const. amend. IV.

79. U.S. Const. art. III, § 3, cl. 1 provides that "[t]reason against the United States, shall consist only in levying War against them, or in adhering to their Enemies, giving them Aid and Comfort."

80. U.S. Const. pmbl.

81. As the Supreme Court said in *Texas v. White*, 74 U.S. 700 (1968):

> The Union of the States never was a purely artificial and arbitrary relation. It began among the Colonies, and grew out of common origin, mutual sympathies, kindred principles, similar interests, and geographical relations. It was confirmed and strengthened by the necessities of war, and received definite form, and character, and sanction from the Articles of Confederation. By these the Union was solemnly declared to "be perpetual." And when these Articles were found to be inadequate to the exigencies of the country, the Constitution was ordained "to form a more perfect Union." It is difficult to convey the idea of indissoluble unity more clearly than by these words. What can be indissoluble if a perpetual Union, made more perfect, is not?

Id. at 724–25. In dissent, Justice Robert C. Grier refused to opine on the constitutionality of secession and said that the issue had been settled through "trial by battle." *Id.* at 740.

82. U.S. Const. art. I, § 8, cl. 3 (commerce power); cl. 4 (bankruptcy); cl. 5 (control of the money supply). Other economic powers include control of intellectual property rights, art. I, § 8, cl. 8; the taxing and spending powers, cl. 1; and control of weights and measures, cl. 5.

83. U.S. Const. art. I, § 10, cl. 1, 3.

84. U.S. Const. art. IV, § 4.

85. U.S. Const. art. VI, § 2.

86. U.S. Const. pmbl.

87. On the resemblance between the formation of the UK and the Constitution, *see* Akhil Reed Amar, *Architexture*, 77 Ind. L.J. 671, 683 (2002) ("The phrase 'perfect Union' in fact echoes language from the Union of England and Scotland in 1707, as Publius reminds his readers in The Federalist No. 5.").

88. The text of the letter can be found in Daniel A. Farber, *The Constitution's Forgotten Cover Letter: An Essay on the New Federalism and the Original Understanding*, 94 Mich. L. Rev. 615, 649–50 (1995).

89. *Id.* at 649.

90. *Id.*

91. *Id.* at 650.

92. The Federalist No. 39, at 239 (James Madison) (Henry Cabot Lodge ed., 1888).

93. *Id.*

94. U.S. Const. amend. XIV, § 1.

95. *Id.*

96. Philip Hamburger, *Beyond Protection*, 109 Colum. L. Rev. 1823, 1853 (2009).

97. Kettner, *supra* note 7, at 16–17.

98. *Id.* at 16.

99. *Id.* at 18.

100. *See* Polly J. Price, *Natural Law and Birthright Citizenship in* Calvin's Case *(1608)*, 9 Yale J.L. & Human. 73, 88–89 (1997). Francis Bacon's argument for the plaintiff insisted that allegiance was due under the law of nature. *Id.* at 109–10. Coke accepted this theory. *Id.* at 113, 115.

101. Kettner, *supra* note 7, at 335.

102. *Id.*

103. Prize Cases, 67 U.S. (2 Black) 635 (1862).

104. *Id.* at 640–41. In attempting to uphold the blockade, the federal government was put in a difficult position. On the one hand, it was committed to the position that secession was legally void and that Southerners remained citizens of the United States subject to American municipal law. The implication of this view was that the Civil War was in effect a police action against a band of criminals. But such a police action would not give the United States the right under the law of nations to impose a blockade on neutrals on the high seas, nor would it give the government the right under the Constitution to seize the property of citizens who were not proved to be members of the criminal group. Those remedies were available only against enemy aliens. Republicans uneasily straddled these conflicting theories.

105. *Id.* at 669.

106. *Id.* at 674.

107. "Under the very peculiar Constitution of this Government, although the citizens owe supreme allegiance to the Federal Government, they owe also a qualified allegiance to the State in which they are domiciled." *Id.* at 673.

108. U.S. Const. art. IV, § 2.

109. Corfield v. Coryell, 6 F. Cas. 546 (C.C.E.D. Pa. 1823) (No. 3,230). *See also* Douglas v. Stephens, 1 Del. Ch. 465, 469–74, 476–77 (1821). *Corfield* has some resemblance to the Supreme Court's current view of the Comity Clause, which also uses a fundamental rights analysis, although the modern Court uses the idea of fundamental rights as a limitation on the antidiscrimination prohibition rather than viewing it as the core of the clause's meaning. For a critique of *Corfield* and its use as a limitation on the clause, *see* Stewart Jay, *Origins of the Privileges and Immunities of State Citizenship under Article IV, available at* http://ssrn.com/abstract=185377.

110. *Corfield*, 6 F. Cas. at 551–52.

111. *Id.* For a more in-depth discussion of the case, *see* David R. Upham, Note, Corfield v. Coryell *and the Privileges and Immunities of American Citizenship*, 83 Tex. L. Rev. 1483 (2005).

112. Cong. Globe, 39th Cong., 1st Sess. 600 (1866). *See also id.* at 476 (bill protects "fundamental rights belonging to every man as a free man"). Trumbull used somewhat similar language in connection with the Freedmen's Bureau bill. *See id.* at 319, 322.

113. *Id.* at 1118.

114. *Id.* at 1294.

115. *Id.* at 1835.

116. *Id.* at 1836. *See also id.* at 1263 (remarks by Rep. Broomall listing free speech as one of

the "rights and immunities of citizens"); *id.* at 1266 (remarks of Rep. Raymond listing "right to bear arms" as a right of citizens); *id.* at 1293–94 (remarks of Rep. Shellabarger, right of petition is an "indispensable" right of citizenship).

117. *Id.* at 530. *See also* Johnson's expostulation in response to a contrary argument by Sen. Henderson. *Id.* at 572.

118. *Id.* at 530.

119. *Id.* at 570 (remarks of Sen. Morrill).

120. *Id.* at 1263.

121. *Id.*

122. *Id.*

123. *Id.* at 1119. Wilson reiterated essentially the same argument. *Id.* at App. 157, 1294.

124. *Id.* at 1119.

125. *Id.* A similar view was articulated by Rep. Shellabarger. *Id.* at 1293.

126. *Id.*

127. *Id.* at 1757.

128. *Id.*

129. *Id.*

130. *Id.*

131. Section 5 provides that "[t]he Congress shall have power to enforce, by appropriate legislation, the provisions of this article." U.S. Const. amend. XIV, § 5.

132. The Slaughter-House Cases, 83 U.S. 36, 52–53 (1872).

133. *Id.* at 94.

134. *Id.* at 95.

135. *Texas v. White*, 74 U.S. 700 (1868), also tangentially touches upon citizenship. In the first half of the decision, the Court held that Texas never seceded from the United States: "The Constitution, in all its provisions, looks to an indestructible Union, composed of indestructible States." *Id.* at 725. In considering whether the actions of the Texas rebel legislature were valid, the Court held that citizens' individual obligations to the Constitution were preeminent over their obligations to their state:

> Obligations often remain unimpaired, while relations are greatly changed. The obligations of allegiance to the State, and of obedience to her laws, subject to the Constitution of the United States, are binding upon all citizens, whether faithful or unfaithful to them; but the relations which subsist while these obligations are performed, are essentially different from those which arise when they are disregarded and set at nought. And the same must necessarily be true of the obligations and relations of States and citizens to the Union. . . . The government and the citizens of the State, refusing to recognize their constitution obligations, assumed the character of enemies, and incurred the consequences of rebellion.

Id. at 727.

136. *The Slaughter-House Cases*, 83 U.S. at 72–73.

137. *Id.* at 73.

138. *Id.*

139. *Id.* at 79.

140. *Id.*

141. *Id.*

142. *Id.* at 79–80.

143. *Id.* at 80.

144. *Id.*

145. *See, e.g.*, Robert Faturechi, *Palin Takes Jabs, Makes No Promises*, L.A. Times, May 2, 2011, at AA2 (Palin delivers "searing critique of big government").

146. Andrew Malcolm, *Sarah Palin and Her "One Nation" Bus Tour, Coming to a Town Near Voters Soon*, L.A. Times, May 26, 2011, http://latimesblogs.latimes.com/washington/2011/05/sarah-palin-bus-tour-memorial-day-.html.

IV

Contemporary Views of Interposition, Nullification, and Secession

8 Interposition

An Overlooked Tool of American Constitutionalism

Christian G. Fritz, University of New Mexico

The 150th anniversary of American secession is an appropriate time to revisit the idea of interposition, a doctrine that was misconstrued and stigmatized not only in the period leading up to the Civil War but long afterward. Inevitably linked with the discredited constitutional heresy of nullification (and, by extension, secession), interposition as a legitimate aspect of American constitutionalism has been a casualty of politics and sloppy history. Interposition is largely lost to us today because of the political controversy over nullification in the 1830s during which both doctrines were depicted as handmaidens to secession. This reputation survived the Civil War and has been perpetuated by many historians ever since.

In the heat of sectional debates in the 1830s, James Madison's explanation of the constitutional role and dimensions of interposition were brushed aside. Few contemporaries paid attention to Madison's explanation distinguishing his and Jefferson's authorship of the Virginia and Kentucky resolutions protesting the Alien and Sedition Acts in the late eighteenth century with the doctrine of nullification advanced by South Carolina in the 1830s to resist a detested tariff. Indeed, not only contemporaries of Madison but historians since his time have failed to appreciate the constitutional tool of interposition that emerged before passage of the Alien and Sedition Acts and that was well understood before the Nullification Crisis.[1] Instead, Madison's explanations in the 1830s have been depicted as a problematic effort to distance himself from the implications of nullification that were allegedly planted by the Virginia and Kentucky resolutions. To complicate matters, one of Kentucky's resolutions identified "nullification" as a "rightful remedy" for acts "unauthorized" by the Federal Constitution.[2] Notwithstanding that terminology, regarding interposition as synonymous with nullification was incorrect at the time, and it remains a widespread but mistaken scholarly assumption that obscures a historical understanding of those two doctrines.[3]

The historiography of interposition (and, by definition, nullification) reveals two principal reasons why interposition has been misunderstood: an overwhelming tendency to see the doctrine as an issue of federalism pertinent only to the sectional conflict leading to the Civil War and an unfortunate presentism that cannot imagine how interposition might function as a constitutional tool today. Before attempting to recover the concept of interposition, the historiographical stumbling blocks that lie in the way of such an understanding should be identified.

Initially, it is important to acknowledge that the Virginia and Kentucky resolutions and the Nullification Crisis clearly raised a central question of federalism: the respective powers of state governments and the national government. Equally important, however, is an appreciation that those episodes were not exclusively about federalism. They also raised key questions of constitutionalism: Who were 'the people' that underlay the national constitution and how could that sovereign act and be recognized in action. Questions of constitutionalism, it should be emphasized, did not involve matters of constitutionality or the conformity of given actions or decisions with a written constitution. Rather, the term constitutionalism as used in this chapter pertains to the underlying authority of the Federal Constitution—the people—and their relationship with government.[4] A failure to recognize this second dimension of these controversies has miscast interposition and the Nullification Crisis as implicating only a struggle over states' rights.[5] Even more problematic is the assertion that the origins of American constitutionalism justify nullification.[6]

Confusion over these issues—among later scholars as well as Americans at the time—is not surprising. As many have noted, the language around discussions of interposition and nullification was inherently ambiguous and subject to multiple understandings. Moreover, the politics of the day emphasized the practical consequences of a compact theory of states' rights. The dominance of that political question simply overshadowed the questions of constitutionalism that were part of James Madison's careful thought about the theoretical foundation of the Constitution. Madison's views about the constitutional implications of governments resting on a collective sovereign were easily overlooked—then as well as today.

The second historiographical stumbling block is that contemporary constitutional theory has no place for the concept of interposition, contributing to its neglect as a subject of interest and relevance to American constitutional history. From the viewpoint of contemporary theory, interposition—like nullification and secession—simply seems beyond the constitutional pale. Interposition flies in the face of the current reality in which the United States Supreme Court plays a principal, if not monopolistic, role in monitoring the operation of government under the Constitution. Interposition rejected the idea that the Supreme Court was the obvious, much less the sole, interpreter of whether the national government acted in conformity with the constitution from which it drew its legitimacy. As such, interposition is at odds with the well-established norm of judicial review in today's American constitutional order. The historical practice of the doctrine of interposition posited a radically different process and responsibility for assessing the constitutionality of acts of the national government than that which we now take for granted.

That lawyers and legal scholars might greet the doctrine of interposition with skepticism, if not hostility, is not wholly unanticipated, but a similar response by historians is more surprising. Rejecting historical evidence of an understanding of interposition on the ground that earlier generations of Americans could not have seriously entertained them simply because those ideas are not viable under today's conventional constitutional theory is strikingly ahistorical. While it may seem to be an archaic pretension about how to write history, for many that activity has long been framed in terms of taking the past on its own terms. The instinct to make history 'relevant' and to find a 'useable past' is powerful and understandable. However, such a focus is more appropriate for would-be shapers of today's policies than for those seeking to understand the past without imputing contemporary views to that history. Ultimately, what gave interposition legitimacy long before its discussion in the context of the Nullification Crisis of the 1830s was a concept of constitutionalism far different from the one Americans embrace today.

I. INTERPOSITION AND THE SHARED RESPONSIBILITY OF MONITORING GOVERNMENT

Monitoring the operation of government was a central issue after the adoption of the Constitution in 1787 (just as it was when state constitutions created new governments after Independence). Each of America's first four Presidents—Washington, Adams, Jefferson, and Madison—confronted the issue. Their struggles revealed a fundamental disagreement among Americans about their country's unique governments and the day-to-day relation of those governments to the acknowledged sovereign in America, the people. Americans wrestled with the puzzle at the heart of the new federal system: what did rule by a collective sovereign mean under a national constitution when the people who held this sovereignty also served as the sovereign of their individual state governments? Overlooked in standard treatments of the Virginia and Kentucky resolutions and the Nullification Crisis is how the American sovereign could—as the concept of the people's sovereignty called for—monitor the constitutional operation of the national government.

These two controversies saw Americans using a tool invoked before the Civil War but little seen today: the right of interposition. Although confused and wrongly associated with nullification, interposition facilitated a vigilance of government that accorded with American constitutionalism in the aftermath of the Revolution. Interposition sought reversal of national laws that some people thought unconstitutional or simply wrongheaded. It involved many potential instruments and actions to maintain the proper functioning of the Constitution by the people. It could involve individual citizens or groups of citizens. It also could involve the state legislatures, acting not as the sovereign, but as an instrument of the people to communicate concerns about the national constitution.

Interposition as a constitutional tool received its first prominent articulation by Alexander Hamilton—a fact somewhat ironic, given Hamilton's undisguised contempt for the common man. In the course of the debates over the ratification of the Constitution, Hamilton sought to allay the concerns of New Yorkers about the authority the proposed constitution gave Congress over military matters in times of peace. In *Federalist* No. 26 he argued that political parties in Congress formed a first line of scrutiny of the new national government. According to Hamilton, "[T]he public attention will be roused" by the "party in opposition" if the issue of a military establishment arose. Beyond this partisan check, however, the state legislatures would act as "jealous guardians of the rights of the citizens." In the new federal system, the state legislatures, observed Hamilton, would always "sound the alarm to the people" whenever the national government exceeded its rightful powers.[7]

Public opinion, petitions, and protests as well as instructions to political representatives were some of the ways interposition could 'sound the alarm' about unconstitutional actions and thereby secure the Constitution's faithful execution. Interposition might also seek to resolve constitutional controversies by revising the Constitution. James Madison described these options as "the several constitutional modes of interposition by the States against abuses of powers." The word 'interposition' did not carry the meaning implied by some today and by some during the sectional debates preceding the Civil War—that interposition nullified a law. Rather, what Madison and his contemporaries meant by interposition seemed to come from its classic sense. As used in astronomical and scientific texts of the period, interposition described the movement of something between two other things in a relationship, so as to interrupt and bring attention to the essence of that relationship.[8]

In a constitutional mode, interposition usually involved action by a third party coming between the people as the sovereign and the sovereign's agent, the government. This interposition was not a sovereign act, since it was not the people as the collective sovereign that took that step. It did not break the ties between the people and their government, as did nullification, for example. Rather, the interposer—through public opinion, protests, petitions, or even state legislatures acting as an instrument of the people—focused attention on whether the government was acting in conformity with the people's mandates as expressed in their constitutions. A successful interposition occurred when either the government backtracked, conceding that it had overstepped constitutional limits as asserted by the interposition, or when the people in light of the interposition chose to change the constitutional order.

From our modern perspective, it is difficult to understand the need for interposition. Unlike the regularized, if not full–time, operation of state legislatures today in an age of instant communication, earlier legislatures met less frequently and at varying times. Thus, there were significant barriers to learning about the proceedings of Congress as well as to responding (much less coordinating a collective response) to laws being considered and even passed by that body. Given an inevitable time lag, interposition served as a useful communication mechanism to share the sentiments of citizens and their state legislators with legislators in other states as well as with national lawmakers in Washington.

The underlying logistic impetus for the tool of interposition due to the constraints of communication and transportation naturally lessened with the appearance and expansion in the nineteenth century of an infrastructure of canals, telegraphs, and railroads. However, the demise of interposition came principally from its stigmatization along with the discredited doctrine of nullification. Yet the practice of interposition by state legislatures expressing their views on national measures they deemed unconstitutional or impolitic persisted long after the Nullification Crisis and the Civil War.

Since the agent of interposition was not 'the people' acting as the sovereign, the interposer's action alerted the people but did not affect the legitimacy of the challenged action of government. The people, in considering the claims of the interposer, were not limited to the forms of change provided in the Constitution. Because the sovereign had "ultimate authority" outside the "purview and forms" of the Constitution, they could act, as Madison put it, to "explain, amend, or remake" the Constitution. As the Constitution's sovereign creator, the people were not subordinate to their creation, the national government. The people had final authority. The Constitution was "a description of those powers which the people have delegated to their Magistrates, to be exercised for definite purposes." Interposition alerted the people to question whether the government, their agent, was acting in conformity with constitutional dictates. It remained an open question whether the people could not only monitor the constitutional order as interposition envisioned but also directly invoke their constitutional authority to nullify acts of Congress. As Madison stated, it was up to the people as the collective sovereign whether to resolve matters by exercising their final or, as he put it, "ultimate" authority, which could also be exercised outside the "purview and forms" of the Constitution.[9] The theoretical possibility that the collective sovereign of the Constitution might act outside the normal channels of interposition raised the elusive question of just who that collective sovereign was.

II. THE PUZZLE OF IDENTIFYING THE FEDERAL CONSTITUTION'S COLLECTIVE SOVEREIGN

The Constitution divided governmental power between the national and state governments, a division that created a puzzle in identifying the sovereign of the Constitution. This perplexing question did not arise under state constitutions, whose sovereign was logically composed of the people of a given state. The Federal Constitution, however, initially invited two different views of the identity of the collective sovereign that underlay that constitution. First, the sovereign of the Constitution could be considered the people of the discrete states acting collectively. Alternatively, that sovereign people could be seen as one undifferentiated national American people. Both positions were plausible, but mutually inconsistent.

During the federal convention and the ratification debate Madison argued that the sovereign was the people in the discrete states acting collectively. Similarly, in 1798, fellow Virginian John Taylor considered the need for federal constitutional amendments and described "the people in state conventions" as "incontrovertibly the contracting parties" behind the Constitution capable of effecting such changes. In 1800, Madison described "the people composing" the political societies of their respective states acting "in their highest sovereign capacity" as creating the Constitution. Others also described the foundation of the Constitution as resting on the consent of "the people of the several states, separately, and independently taken, and expressed."[10]

In contrast, other Americans described one undifferentiated national people as the sovereign, not the people of the discrete states acting collectively. The idea that a national people created the Constitution gained currency when Daniel Webster described the formation of the American nation not by the people in separate states but rather by "the People of the United States, in the aggregate" rising together to create a government.[11]

The concept of American constitutions as instructions by the sovereign people logically supported either view of the Founding: that it was a national people or the people identified with individual states acting collectively. Arguably, the idea of the people collectively acting through the agency of their particular states better reflected American constitutionalism before 1787. The manner in which the Federal Constitution was ratified exemplified a model of the people within individual states acting collectively through conventions in the states in which they lived. Even those who thought the Constitution granted broad national powers to the federal government, such as Chief Justice John Marshall, described the Founding in a voice much closer in tone to Madison's than Webster's.[12]

Because the people who created the national government could act, as a practical matter, only through the agency of their states, the term 'the states' introduced a complexity that confused Americans at the time and has confounded later observers as well. Like many Americans of his day, Madison could describe the sovereign who gave life to the national government as 'the states.' But like those other Americans, Madison could have been referring to any of three different things. Madison acknowledged that "the term 'States'" was ambiguous. First, the states, Madison noted, could mean individual state governments. Second, it could mean the people within a state as the sovereign of that state. Third, it could mean the people of the nation who lived in the different geographic areas known as 'states.' Madison's definition of the national sovereign encompassed this third meaning of the people in "the 'States.'"[13]

These different meanings of the term 'the states' dictated how one might understand the Constitution as a compact among the states.[14] Under the first meaning attributed to 'the states,' the Constitution could mean a compact of individual state governments.[15] The second meaning implied the sovereign people of an individual state compacting with the sovereign people of other states to adopt the Constitution.[16] For Madison, in using the third meaning of the term, the Constitution was a compact reflecting an agreement by the people of the individual states acting as the collective sovereign of the national government they were creating. The collective people of the nation—while still identified in terms of the individual states in which they lived—was a sovereign different from that formed when those people acted as the sovereign of their respective states. This collective sovereign was the sovereign that created the Federal Constitution, and only a majority of that collective sovereign could alter or abolish the Constitution.[17]

Madison's terminology illustrated the point that calling the Constitution a compact did not necessarily acknowledge individual state governments or the sovereign people of individual states as the parties who created that constitution. Rather, in describing 'the states' as parties to the federal compact, Madison envisioned a collective sovereign that eluded definition in solely individual state terms or in purely national terms. In the political climate of the 1830s, the distinction Madison had long maintained positioned his view between a states' rights understanding of the Constitution as a compact and a nationalistic view of the Constitution as the product of an undifferentiated American people.

Because a states' rights position became associated with the assertion of unilateral action by individual states as parties to the federal compact, some Americans rejected the use of the word 'compact' in describing the Constitution. For example, in denying that the Constitution was a compact, Daniel Webster insisted that a national people and not the states had created the Constitution. From that position, the subtlety of Madison's view was overlooked—not only by many of his contemporaries but by subsequent scholars as well.[18]

Different views about the relationship of the collective sovereign to the national government persisted in disputes arising after the formation of the Constitution. These differences tend to be analyzed today as reflecting understandings about states' rights and competing compact theories of the Federal Constitution. But as Madison's efforts after the adoption of the Constitution illustrated, these differences also cast light on a second national division. This second division did not involve the relationship of various governments within a federal system or issues of federalism but rather the relationship of the people to their various governments. The people's relationship to government also involved the authority of the sovereign to oversee the operation of the government it had created.[19]

III. PRACTICING INTERPOSITION: THE VIRGINIA AND KENTUCKY RESOLUTIONS

Many federal Framers—including George Washington—expected that the people would be more subordinate and deferential to their national governors and that they would assume a passive role as the sovereign after the adoption of the Constitution. Yet attempts to collect the national government's first tax on a domestic product, an excise on whiskey, met stiff resistance. Those tax protests reflected a wider and persistent debate over the people's relationship to that government.[20]

Washington ultimately crushed the so-called Whiskey Rebellion, but this victory did not quell growing concerns about the relation of the people to their government. Washington's successor, John Adams, faced his own crisis in 1798 when Federalists in Congress passed several laws in a climate of agitation for war against France because of its interference with American shipping. One law, the Alien Act, allowed the President to deport aliens whom he deemed "dangerous to the peace and safety" of the nation or suspected of "treasonable or secret machinations." Its companion, the Sedition Act, permitted punishment of "false, slanderous, and malicious writing" that brought the President or members of Congress into "contempt or disrepute."[21]

Critics of Federalist policy were likely targets of both acts, but particularly of the Sedition Act. Consequently, Republicans considered this legislation a political attack. The Federalist bias of the American press diminished in the 1790s, as more newspapers emerged that took a Republican slant. The Sedition Act threatened the Republicans' use of newspapers to counter their Federalist opponents. Besides the acts' political impact, they appeared to subvert the federal constitutional order. Republicans asserted that the Alien Act exceeded Congress's constitutional powers, while the Sedition Act violated the 1st Amendment. Jefferson complained to Madison that the acts showed "no respect" for the Constitution. Madison called the Alien Act "a monster" that would "for ever disgrace its parents," the Federalists. The act denied the people the "right of freely examining public characters and measures."[22]

The Alien and Sedition Acts prompted Madison and Jefferson to orchestrate protests. Most dramatic were the resolutions they drafted to be adopted by the legislatures of Virginia and Kentucky. Madison authored Virginia's resolutions, and the resolutions that Jefferson drafted after learning of the passage of the Sedition Act were eventually adopted in modified form by Kentucky's legislature. In passing the resolutions, both legislatures expressed their view that the two federal laws were unconstitutional. Kentucky's resolutions instructed the state's congressional representatives to seek repeal of the acts. The governor was asked to transmit copies to other state legislatures in the hope that those bodies would adopt similar measures. Likewise, Virginia's resolutions were sent to the state's congressional representatives and other state governors.[23]

Some contemporaries assumed (as have numerous subsequent scholars) that the resolutions sought to nullify the operation of the two objectionable federal laws in Virginia and Kentucky. This assumption discounts the resolutions' express purpose—to stimulate a coordinated national effort to repeal the laws through congressional action. (Indeed, if the resolutions were understood as having nullified the Alien and Sedition Acts, no point would have been served in seeking their repeal through agitation stimulated by the resolutions.) In fact, the resolutions embodied a distinction between a legislature's opinion of the constitutionality of national laws and action by the sovereign people to render those laws unenforceable. Virginia's resolutions called the acts "unconstitutional," while Kentucky's described them as "not law but utterly void and of no force." Even Federalists who took issue with the resolutions recognized that they merely represented the opinion of the two state legislatures.[24]

James Madison later reiterated that the resolutions merely underscored the legislature's view of the acts. They did not constitute a nullification of the acts. Neither Virginia's nor Kentucky's legislature had asserted that their resolutions made the acts a dead letter (they were not passing a 'law'), nor did either state take any action to resist the enforcement of the acts. The resolutions, as Madison pointed out, did not "annul the acts" because they came "from the Legislature only, which was not even a party to the Constitution." Only collective action by the people as the sovereign source of the Federal Constitution could nullify the acts.[25]

Kentucky's 1798 resolutions asked its "Co-states" to declare the acts "void and of no force." Virginia's resolutions identified "the states" as the "parties" to the Constitution who could "interpose" to stop unconstitutional acts. The resolutions were an interposition of each state legislature's offering of its constitutional opinion. They were obviously not an ultimate intervention by the people of the states themselves.[26]

Upon receiving the Kentucky legislature's resolutions, Jefferson forwarded a copy to Madison. Opponents of the acts nationwide should "distinctly affirm" the Kentucky resolutions' "important principles" in the hope that this would avoid their taking matters "to extremities." As Jefferson wrote Virginia legislator John Taylor before Virginia's resolutions passed, it was premature to contemplate the ultimate step by the people. "[F]or the present," he told Taylor, "I should be for resolving the alien & sedition laws to be against the constitution & merely void." Virginia should ask other states to make "similar declarations."[27]

Taylor agreed with Jefferson's request, recognizing that if the state and national governments came into conflict, it might force "the people in convention" to settle the matter. This approach reflected Taylor's belief that when the people met in "a general convention" they were "the only genuine and legitimate fountain of power" and the ultimate "corrector of unconstitutional" acts of the government.[28]

Five days after Virginia's legislature acted, Madison expressed his belief that an individual state legislature did not have the constitutional authority to nullify a national law. Unlike the political arrangement under the Articles of Confederation, state governments did not form the Federal Constitution. Meetings of state conventions, like those that ratified the Federal Constitution, were the appropriate means by which the people might invoke their "ultimate" right to correct "infractions" by the national government. This was "especially" true, noted Madison, since the people in "a Convention was the organ by which the Compact was made."[29]

It is worth reminding ourselves that Madison's and Hamilton's understanding of what 'the people' might do was informed by a perspective significantly different from that of the generation of Americans who came after the revolutionary era. Despite their different reactions to the people's invoking their sovereignty, both Madison and Hamilton had personally experienced how such a collective sovereign could act directly in justifying a revolution and establish new governments in its wake. Such knowledge was theoretical or at best secondhand for many Americans who debated nullification in the 1830s (and entirely so for later generations of Americans).

The Virginia and Kentucky resolutions acknowledged the ultimate authority of the people to assess the constitutionality of acts of the government. Interposition by state legislatures operated differently from such final action by the people as a matter of last resort. Legislative interposition sought the repeal of unconstitutional laws by focusing attention on them. As Madison pointed out in the Virginia resolutions, legislators were doing their "duty" to "watch over and oppose every infraction" of constitutional principles. Virginia's and Kentucky's legislatures were acting as Alexander Hamilton suggested they would during the ratification debate. During those debates, Hamilton also noted that after identifying excesses of "national authority," those legislatures could "communicate with each other" and "at once adopt a regular plan of opposition."[30]

Many Americans considered the guardianship of the federal constitutional order an obligation extending well beyond state legislators and legislative action.

Ensuring that governments operated constitutionally was the responsibility of individual citizens as well as of state legislators.[31]

IV. REACTION TO THE RESOLUTIONS AND COUNTERREACTION

Instead of rallying other legislatures to protest the Alien and Sedition Acts, the Virginia and Kentucky resolutions stimulated Federalist attacks. George Washington dismissed criticism of the acts as party politics. Washington's fears were echoed by other Federalists. For example, Massachusetts Federalist Theodore Sedgwick believed the resolutions were "a declaration of war," while his colleague Timothy Pickering thought they implied "a right to disobey" national laws.[32]

No other state legislature formally joined the protests of Virginia and Kentucky. Three months after the two states had issued their resolutions, American state legislators revealed no "unanimity" about them. The negative responses of state legislatures to the resolutions reflected Federalist legislative majorities but also obscured a frequently sizable Republican dissent. As such, the formal replies of states to the Virginia and Kentucky legislatures exaggerate the opposition to the resolutions.[33]

Legislative responses reflected the view—by no means universally held—that constitutional interpretation was "exclusively vested" in the federal courts and especially the Supreme Court. Federalists thought the legislatures of Virginia and Kentucky had no business assessing the constitutionality of the acts. State legislative opinions were "unwarranted" and threatened to destroy the Union, undermine the national government, and introduce "discord and anarchy."[34]

On the other hand, Republicans questioned whether the judiciary was the sole interpreter of the Constitution. Keeping the national government within constitutional bounds was the responsibility of the state legislature as well as of private citizens. Indeed, Republican legislators in Vermont thought the resolutions were among "the most pressing" duties of citizens "to guard with a watchful scrupulosity" against breaches of the Constitution. The defense of that constitution could not be left to the federal government or its judiciary. Indeed, just a few years earlier, the Virginia Republican John Taylor had insisted that the people of "the nation itself must watch over the constitution" and "preserve it from violation." Republican legislators were now being denied a right "daily exercised by individual citizens."[35]

The negative reactions stimulated a reaffirmation of the earlier position from both Virginia's and Kentucky's legislatures, aided by Madison and Jefferson. Kentucky's legislature passed a resolution in November 1799 clarifying that it had not intended to secede or "disturb the harmony" of the Union. Kentucky's legislature suggested that "the several states" (and by implication the people of the several states) had the "unquestionable right" to judge infractions of the Federal Constitution and "that a nullification by those sovereignties of all unauthorized acts done under color of that instrument, is the rightful remedy." Such a step could be exercised by the people as the sovereign who created that constitution. Kentucky's legislative response to the Alien and Sedition Acts was a "solemn protest" intended to bring attention and corrective action. The state legislature recognized that those acts were "laws of the Union" and would "bow" to such laws despite opposing them in a "constitutional manner." Kentucky's *Resolution of 1799* was silent on the issue of secession. However, despite distinguishing interposition from nullification, the appearance of the word "nullification" in that resolution inevitably muddied the two concepts.[36]

Initially, Jefferson was more willing to contemplate secession than was Kentucky's legislature. In August 1799, Jefferson wrote Madison about the right to dissent from actions of the national government. He even imagined disunion (what he called "scission") if the government persistently ignored "the true principles" of the Constitution. In contemplating secession, Jefferson reflected a states' rights compact theory of the Federal Constitution despite the fact that he—along with Madison—understood that the sovereign basis of American constitutions rested on the authority of the people. Jefferson calmed down, perhaps by a reminder of what he had written a year earlier when he opposed talk of Virginia's and North Carolina's potential separation from the Union. In "every free & deliberating" society, Jefferson wrote, political differences were inevitable. But if temporary dominance of one side justified the other in seceding, "no federal government" could "ever exist." Better, he counseled, to "keep together," "have patience," and gain political ascendancy. Madison evidently persuaded Jefferson to heed his own advice, since Jefferson's draft for Kentucky's rejoinder omitted any reference to secession.[37]

V. MADISON'S REPORT OF 1800

In drafting Virginia's response, Madison sought to correct the "misconception" in the formal replies of state legislatures that Virginia's resolutions threatened the Union. He insisted that states had a "right to interpose a *legislative* declaration of opinion on a constitutional point." Published in 1800, Madison's *Report* justified the resolutions as legitimate and appropriate interposition to monitor the Constitution.[38]

In his *Report,* Madison explained that Virginia's resolutions only "communicat[ed]" to the other states its view that the acts were "unconstitutional." This communication was not improper, unconstitutional, or hostile to the Union. The resolutions reflected the "intermediate existence" of state governments "between the people" and the national government. Virginia's legislators were exercising a right defended by the Constitution's supporters—the right of scrutiny. Madison recalled that in 1788, Federalists had insisted that the "vigilance" of state governments "would sound the alarm" at the first signs of "usurpation" by the national government. Virginia's legislature did its "duty" by signaling the people about these "alarming infractions of the constitution" represented by the Alien and Sedition Acts.[39]

Madison's *Report* surveyed the American practice of interposition. This practice was not a "novelty" for either individuals or state legislatures. Protests and declarations—by citizens or legislatures—were merely "expressions of opinion" to prompt "reflection" on the government's actions. Virginia's resolutions were only one form of interposition. All Americans shared a responsibility to maintain constitutional limits on government and vigilantly defend constitutional principles. There were many other legitimate means of interposing to preserve the Constitution. In addition to state legislatures, "private citizens" could interpose to object to acts of the government they believed were unwarranted by the Constitution.[40]

Declaring the acts unconstitutional did not exhaust the legislature's powers of interposition. State legislatures could have made a "direct representation" to Congress, explained Madison, either seeking the repeal of the "two offensive acts" or a revision of the Constitution by amendment or through a constitutional convention. Interposition included all of these approaches for influencing the operation of the national government. They were some of the "several means . . . constitutionally open for consideration" as a legislative protest. Still, "the first and most obvious" step for Virginia's legislature was issuing its resolutions.[41]

The interposition by Virginia's legislature did not preclude the sovereign—the people of the states that included, but was not limited to, those in Virginia—from using other "farther measures that might become necessary and proper." Among the "farther measures" for responding to unconstitutional laws was the sovereign's right to dictate a final constitutional solution based on the fact that, in America, "The people, not the government, possess the absolute sovereignty." The sovereign for the purpose of the Federal Constitution was the people of the states. As the "sovereign parties" to the Constitution, they supplied that constitution's "genuine source" of legitimacy.[42]

For purposes of identifying who gave life to the Constitution (what Madison referred to as its "legitimate and solid foundation") the term 'the states' meant "the people composing those political societies, in their highest sovereign capacity." Such a meaning was clear because that was how the Constitution was "submitted to the 'States'" for adoption. The people of each state formed the sovereign of their respective state constitutions but could not constitute the sovereign underlying the Federal Constitution. The sovereign people of one ratifying state needed co-ratification by the people of other states for the federal constitutional compact to take effect.[43]

States' rights advocates asserting that state legislatures were the parties to the federal compact displayed "inaccuracies" in understanding the sovereign basis of the Constitution, concluded Madison. Since the people of the states had ratified the Constitution as a collective body, they and not the state legislatures were the "parties to the compact" that granted the national government its rightful authority. Whether to exercise the ultimate right of constitutional judgment under the Constitution rested, therefore, with "the American public."[44]

The constitutionalism reflected by the resolutions presumed that the sovereign who adopted a written constitution had the final word on the constitutionality of government actions. For many Americans, as for Madison, this was "a plain principle, founded in common sense, illustrated by common practice, and essential to the nature of compacts." Because "resort can be had to no tribunal superior to the authority of the parties, the parties themselves must be the rightful judges in the last resort, whether the bargain made, has been . . . violated."[45]

According to Madison, an "interposition of the parties, *in their sovereign capacity*" (emphasis added) was justified only when unconstitutional acts of government "deeply and essentially affect[ed] the vital principles of their political system." This final resolution of the Constitution by the people should not occur "in a hasty manner, or on doubtful . . . occasions." Virginia's resolutions referred to a right and duty of the people of the states "to interpose" collectively in cases of the national government's "deliberate, palpable and dangerous exercise" of powers not granted to it by the Constitution. Madison's analysis of the acts provided a justification for such ultimate interposition.[46]

The people of the states "as co-parties to and creators of the constitution" could exercise their ultimate authority by amending the Constitution or finding other ways to express their constitutional understanding. Madison later conceded that the resolutions and his *Report* lacked precise explanations about how "the States could interpose in their collective character as parties to the Constitution." However, given "the object and reasoning" of those documents, specifics were "not necessary": "It was sufficient to show that the authority to interpose existed, and was a resort beyond that of the Supreme Court of the United States." If the sovereign people invoked their ultimate right to intervene, how they did so was their "own choice."[47]

VI. MADISON'S VIEW OF THE ROLE OF THE SUPREME COURT AS CONSTITUTIONAL INTERPRETER

Madison's *Report* rejected the Supreme Court as the Constitution's "sole expositor" and the view that the judiciary was the only branch of government that could authoritatively shape the Constitution. Madison articulated two concepts of how the Constitution was to be applied. The first was a broad view of who could authoritatively construe the Constitution. The second identified certain areas in which the court was the expositor whose construction would prevail as the final word, "in the last resort."[48]

During the ratification debates and during his service in the First Congress, Madison considered each of the three branches of the national government equally entitled to construe the constitutional authority of its own branch. In *Federalist* No. 49, Madison asserted that since no branch could "pretend to [have] an exclusive or superior right of settling the boundaries between their respective powers," the ultimate ability to rectify constitutional "encroachments" among the branches of government was an "appeal to the people themselves." The people as the sovereign "can alone declare" the constitution's "true meaning and enforce its observance." This view did not change after the Constitution's adoption.[49]

Madison's concept of "departmental review" of the Constitution had wide and continuing support.[50] It was consistent with an American constitutionalism that did not cede to the courts a monopoly in constitutional interpretation.[51] Even the emerging acceptance of judicial review was not inconsistent with the insistence that many other Americans—be they citizens or legislators—retained the right and duty to express their views about the constitutionality of actions of the government and to participate in the guardianship of the Constitution.[52]

The growing acceptance of judicial review was consistent with interposition. For instance, even Hamilton's advocacy for the doctrine in *Federalist* No. 78 depicted judicial review as a process of interposition that kept the constitutional order in check. Hamilton identified the federal courts as "an intermediate body between the people and the legislature . . . to keep the latter within the limits assigned to their authority." Judicial review at the state level was often described as a process of interposition. As a delegate to the New York constitutional convention in 1820 suggested, by invalidating unconstitutional acts, the state judiciary formed a "shield between the rights of citizens and the encroachments of legislative power."[53]

That the Supreme Court was not the sole expositor of the Constitution was not inconsistent with Madison's second concept of how the Constitution was to be applied. Under certain circumstances, the Court was to be the expositor of "last resort." However, the Court's power here was limited. It could exercise its authority only in cases properly before it. In deciding those cases, the Court indeed had the final word on the Constitution. Madison thought it appropriate for the Supreme Court to interpret the Constitution "in the ordinary course of Government." In the *Report of 1800*, Madison elaborated on the limits of judicial review and the necessity of review beyond the Supreme Court in certain "great and extraordinary" cases. One limitation of judicial review involved unconstitutional acts of another branch that did not arise in a case "within the control of the judicial department." Another situation involved the Judicial Department itself—if ever the judiciary "exercise[d] or sanction[ed] dangerous powers beyond the grant of the constitution."[54]

In these cases, only the sovereign could determine whether the national government exceeded the people's grant of authority in the Constitution. The people of the states who formed "the parties to the constitution" and not the departmental agents to whom they "delegated authority" retained "the ultimate right . . . to judge whether the compact has been dangerously violated." This action by the sovereign people served as a check beyond judicial review. Their agents—public officials, representatives, and judges—could not exercise such authority for the sovereign. No single branch, including the judiciary, could make a decision to supersede "the authority . . . the sovereign parties to the constitution" might exercise.[55]

Madison's understanding that the Supreme Court did not hold a monopoly in interpreting the Constitution was well within the mainstream of American thought at the time. The doctrine that only the Court could consider the constitutionality of national laws, wrote one Republican contributor in 1799 to a Boston newspaper, took "from the people the ultimate sovereignty" and conferred it on their "agents." Another Republican contributor argued that if the people were truly America's sovereign, it was "difficult" or even contradictory to credit the Federalists' argument that the people "*have no right to decide on any invasion of [their] constitutional powers.*"[56]

Historians often deem the Virginia and Kentucky resolutions a failure because no other state issued similar resolutions. Yet the interposition by these two states in 1798 and 1799 focused attention on the Alien and Sedition Acts, as interposition was designed to do. Against that backdrop, American voters went to the polls in 1800 and chose between candidates who took opposing positions on those acts. Jefferson made "violations of the true principles" of the Constitution a major issue of his campaign. His election to the presidency and that of his Republican followers to Congress reflected public opinion about the constitutionality of the acts. Madison later concluded that the resolutions achieved "a triumph over the obnoxious acts, and an apparent abandonment of them forever."[57]

Following the lead of the first generation of Americans who lived under the Constitution, subsequent generations employed interposition in response to national legislation they believed violated the Constitution. But as the revolutionary generation began to die off, the next generation lost sight of the legitimate tradition of interposition.

VII. THE NULLIFICATION CRISIS

In the late 1820s, another controversy divided the Union when Southern critics declared a tariff on imports imposed by Congress in 1828 unconstitutional because it primarily aided Northern manufacturers rather than advanced a proper constitutional purpose of raising revenue for the nation. The tariff's protectionist motive and its tendency to make imports more expensive reduced government revenue as people bought less of the goods subject to the tariff. For tariff opponents, particularly in South Carolina, this demonstrated that Congress lacked a proper purpose in imposing the tariff and had exceeded its constitutional authority. For many Southerners it represented a perversion of the Union—a transfer of the earnings of Southern agriculture to Northern manufacturers.[58]

The protests against the tariffs initially followed the traditional patterns of interposition, seeking the repeal of laws deemed unconstitutional. The effort was not limited to South Carolina. Protests came from counties, such as from Madison's neighbors in Orange County, as well as from state legislatures, such as Georgia, seeking relief. Eventually, tariff opponents organized a national convention, the so-called Free Trade Convention, held in Philadelphia in September and October 1831. South Carolina sent a large delegation reflecting the view adopted by its legislature in 1825 that the tariff was unconstitutional. Many other states, Northern as well as Southern, attended the convention. The convention adopted a memorial asking Congress to adjust the tariff. Congress ignored the memorial, and from the perspective of many in South Carolina, the convention itself had avoided the central issue—it failed to address the concern that the tariff was only an example of what Southern states would face in the future if the constitutional balance of the federal system were not restored.[59]

Years of trying to repeal the tariff brought little relief. Many South Carolinians concluded that the traditional tools of protest through interposition had failed. Petitions, remonstrances, and the multistate convention were well-known means of interposition to review and protest governmental action. Their ineffectiveness on this occasion was frustrating. By late 1831, John C. Calhoun, then the Vice President of the United States, observed that South Carolinians had "petitioned, remonstrated and resolved" for years against the tariff. South Carolina's legislature did its duty in bringing attention to the tariff's "unequal and unconstitutional burden." Meeting with "other States" at the Philadelphia Free Trade Convention was South Carolina's "last effort at redress." For tariff opponents, the convention's failure made other steps necessary.[60]

One new approach promised to redress not only the constitutional imbalance represented by the tariff but also later federal measures that might unconstitutionally disadvantage the South. For Calhoun, the Constitution provided "checks against the abuse of power on the part of the absolute majority." The current tariff crisis stemmed not from a flaw in the Constitution's design but from the neglect of Southern states to apply "the proper remedy." For advocates of the next step, the logical move was the use of the individual state veto.[61]

The names proponents used to describe the state veto seemed innocuous at first—the veto was a state's "protest," its "interposition," or its exercise of "reserved rights." As the heat of the national debate intensified, other, more dire names came into use. Proponents of the state veto were now embracing "nullification, secession, disunion, and revolution." What distinguished the state veto from earlier proposals to rebalance the federal constitutional order was its national effect. The state veto proposed in the 1820s and 1830s allowed any individual state to invalidate a national law for the Union as a whole. The state veto also was advocated by prominent figures on the national stage rather than simply by local or regional leaders.[62]

The theory justifying the single state veto came from the pen of John C. Calhoun. Calhoun considered the 1828 tariff to affect the South disproportionately, insufficiently promoting the general welfare and raising national revenue. In November 1828, at the request of his state's legislature, Calhoun anonymously drafted what became known as the *South Carolina Exposition*, published by the legislature. Like Madison's *Report of 1800* for Virginia's legislature, South Carolina's *Exposition* examined the national government's power. The *Exposition*'s justification of a state veto stirred national debate over whether the Constitution included such a check on the national government. That debate reintroduced many questions that had arisen during the controversy over the Virginia and Kentucky resolutions. In addition, the veto debate raised other sensitive and unsettled issues in American constitutionalism.[63]

One key question went to the core of American constitutionalism: the extent to which Americans were united—and still divided since the Revolution—about the meaning of a government in which the people were the sovereign. The scope of the controversy is best illustrated by several participants in the debate over the state veto—principally John Calhoun, its chief theorist. Opposing the state veto was Daniel Webster, U.S. Senator from Massachusetts. Another, at times reluctant, participant was James Madison, in retirement at Montpelier. Both sides of the debate claimed that Madison's writings justified their positions. Madison struggled to set the record straight. His efforts to clarify that he had not justified a state veto were undermined by the heated debate.

Calhoun's *Exposition* asserted that the veto was a specific remedy justified by the Constitution. It could be exercised when a power of the Constitution granted the national government to achieve "one object" was used "to advance another" and in so doing sacrificed the proper object to which that power was to be directed. This was a "perver[s]ion" of the Constitution, and according to Calhoun, the 1828 tariff presented just such an example. Congress had used its authority to enact a tariff. However, that tariff was not for the legitimate purpose of raising government revenue. Instead, it was designed to benefit Northern manufacturing states by burdening Southern agricultural states.[64]

Calhoun described his theory as an interposition, something both envisioned and exercised by the Constitution's founders. Proponents of the state veto justified their reading of the Constitution by identifying the words and actions of the federal Framers that they felt demonstrated a recognition of such a veto. Like other political mechanisms operating within the constitutional framework of the national government, such as political parties or the presidential cabinet system, important devices for sustaining the Constitution did not have to be specified in the text. They could be fairly implied from how the founding generation had acted under the Constitution. Calhoun found just such proof for his theory in the Virginia and Kentucky resolutions and Madison's *Report of 1800*. Calhoun credited the resolutions and the *Report* as "the basis" of his discovery of the state veto. He cast the state veto as an interposition as equally justified as that taken by Virginia's and Kentucky's legislatures in 1798.[65]

Calhoun's concept of a single state veto provoked a storm of controversy, in part because it invoked the authority of Madison and Jefferson. Learning of such arguments, Madison felt compelled to enter the fray. Madison insisted that neither he nor Jefferson bore responsibility for nullification, a doctrine with a "fatal tendency." Rather than protecting the diverse interests of the Union, Madison believed nullification put "powder under the Constitution and Union, and a match in the hand" of any faction, leaving it to their whim whether "to blow them up." Secession was a "twin" to the "heresy" of nullification, warned Madison. Both doctrines sprang "from the same poisonous root." What grew from this root would bring "disastrous consequences." By 1832, he noted how inexpressibly "painful" it was that Calhoun's doctrine might cause the Constitution to be "broken up and scattered to the winds."[66]

VIII. VISIONS OF THE FEDERAL SOVEREIGN CONTRASTED: CALHOUN VERSUS WEBSTER

What made the 'poisonous root' of the state veto and nullification so toxic was that it drew on the same principle that underlay American constitutionalism: that in America, the people were the sovereign. A half century after Americans had established their governments on this principle, the concept remained as elusive as when it first energized the Revolution. The problem was that Americans remained divided on precisely how that sovereign could give effect to an expression of its will.

For purposes of the national government, all agreed that the people were the sovereign—but how could they exercise their sovereignty? Proponents of the state veto, such as Calhoun, argued that the sovereign for purposes of the Constitution was the people of each individual state. As he explained, the Constitution "when formed, was submitted for ratification to the people of the several States; it was ratified by them as States, each State for itself; each by its ratification binding its own citizens." Although each state independently bound itself to the Union, that did not mean they lost their independence.[67]

For Calhoun, the people were unquestionably the sovereign, yet this sovereign expressed itself through organization into independent states. The people were the sovereign who created the independent states, but those states in turn were the sovereign of the national government. Calhoun dismissed the Preamble's declaration that the Constitution was "ordained by the people of *the United States*." Those words did not make a national people but rather made the individual states the sovereign. Irrespective of the Preamble's language, Calhoun noted that the Constitution's "article of ratification" provided that "when ratified, it is declared '*to be binding between the States so ratifying.*'" This made "the conclusion . . . inevitable, that the Constitution is the work of the people of the States, considered, as separate and independent political communities—that they are its authors—their power created it—their voice clothed it with an authority—that the Government it formed is in reality their agent—and that the Union, of which it is the bond, is a Union of States, and not of individuals."[68]

Opponents of the state veto, including Daniel Webster, dismissed such arguments. In refuting Calhoun's concept of the sovereign, Webster described a different arrangement. This sovereign was also 'the people.' The Constitution was not "the creature of the States," observed Webster. It was created by a much greater entity—"The people of the United States." The American people "in the aggregate" formed the Federal Constitution.[69]

By their act as the national sovereign, the American people henceforth bound themselves to the terms of that Constitution. Thereafter, any alteration of the constitutional order required "submission to the laws" by compliance with the revision provisions of Article V, Webster argued. The attempt to change the operation of the Constitution through other means—as, for example, by the theory of the state veto—necessarily relied on the natural law right of resistance to tyranny. There was no "middle course," no alternative between the government's complying with the Constitution's procedural requirements or the people's exercise of the natural law right of revolution. Nullification gave each state a veto and, in Webster's mind, represented "revolution or rebellion;" it could never amount to "constitutional resistance."[70]

As Webster's position illustrated, how one described the sovereign that created the Constitution shaped one's understanding of the nature of the federal union. The sovereigns envisioned by Webster and Calhoun were each different from the sovereign recognized by the Constitution's founder, James Madison. Madison thought both their concepts of the sovereign shared a "not uncommon" mistake about the "true character" of the Constitution. Both Calhoun and Webster thought that only one of two options was possible—America had either "a consolidated Government" or "a confederated Government."[71]

IX. MADISON'S UNDERSTANDING OF THE SOVEREIGN BASIS OF THE FEDERAL CONSTITUTION

Madison explained that the Constitution created neither. It was not formed "by the governments of the component States" like the Articles of Confederation, as Calhoun maintained. Individual states were not the sovereign of the national government. "[N]or was it formed by a majority of the people of the United States, as a single community, in the manner of a consolidated Government," as Webster maintained. Therefore, the people in the individual states retained constitutional significance. As Madison explained, the Constitution was "a mixture of both" consolidated and confederated governments. Neither Webster's claim that the American people in "the aggregate" were the sovereign who formed the Constitution nor Calhoun's position that individual sovereign states were the parties creating the Constitution accurately described the federal founding. Rather, "the undisputed fact is, that the Constitution was made by the people . . . as imbodied into the several States . . . and, therefore, made by the States in their highest authoritative capacity."[72]

When the sovereign people of each state acted individually, they did not maximize their expression of sovereignty. According to Madison, a state acted in its "highest sovereign capacity" only when the sovereign people of a state acted in combination with the sovereign people of other states. Nearly thirty years after he had drafted the *Virginia Resolutions*, Madison remained unshaken in his belief that the people of the states in their collective capacity created the Constitution and were the sovereign of the national government. Nonetheless, much to his frustration, Americans in the 1830s began (and would continue) to describe the Constitution in the binary terms of either a consolidated or a confederated government, ignoring Madison's concept of the Constitution's formation.[73]

Madison distinguished the Virginia and Kentucky resolutions from South Carolina's "nullifying process." South Carolina, Madison noted, did not distinguish the constitutional "right of *the parties* to the Constitution" to nullify national laws from the revolutionary act of "a *single* party" withdrawing from the Union. "[T]he *plural* term *States*," observed Madison of his *Report of 1800*, "was invariably used in reference" to actions taken by states collectively and not by a single state. This meant that the collective sovereign, acting through the people in the states, could cancel a national law regardless of Article V's requirements for amending the Constitution. This constitutional authority of the collective sovereign that had created the Constitution was obviously not available to an individual state and hence could not justify an individual state's veto. Any state could, however, abdicate its constitutional obligations by withdrawing from the Union "in extreme cases of oppression." This drew on a right of resistance, or what Madison called a right to "cast off the yoke" of tyrannical government by exercising "original rights." That last step was revolutionary and outside the bounds of American constitutionalism.[74]

Madison was appalled by how veto proponents used his *Report*. That *Report* explained and justified the interposition by the Virginia and Kentucky legislatures but did not suggest that the people of a single state could constitutionally veto a national law. In response to Calhoun's inference of this position this from the *Report of 1800*, Madison wrote that he had consistently referred to "the 'States'" when describing "the people . . . in their highest sovereign capacity" who had ratified the Constitution. Likewise, he made the same reference when identifying the people's constitutional right to intervene in extraordinary circumstances when the actions of government had gone hopelessly amiss. Madison's use of the plural—that it was the people of the states who were a collective sovereign—crucially distinguished his views from Calhoun's concept of a confederation of states, in which each individual state was a sovereign party to the Constitution.[75]

Calhoun assumed that when Madison's *Report* and the *Virginia Resolutions* referred to the powers of the sovereign who created the Constitution, Madison meant powers exercised by the people within a single state. Reading the *Report* in this way affirmed Calhoun's belief that "a sovereign State as a party to the Con[stitutiona]l comp[ac]t" could nullify an unconstitutional federal law. Calhoun's theory asserted that each state was a sovereign of the national government and thus could act authoritatively and independently of the others and veto unconstitutional laws. Calhoun used Madison's description that the collective people of all the states were the sovereign to justify a single state's veto. That argument failed to recognize that Madison identified the people of the states acting collectively—and not independently within individual states—as the sovereign of the national government.[76]

The fact the Constitution provided means for resolving constitutional questions, however, did not and could not preclude the people from collectively deciding the constitutional issue for themselves. Even after a decision by the judiciary or other branch of the federal government, the sovereign—the people of the states as "the parties to the Constitution"—might still exercise their "authority *above* that of the Constitution itself" (emphasis added). Their authority to interpose existed regardless of "the decisions of the judicial as well as other branches of the Government." This was simply a matter of the unlimited power of the collective sovereign. As "the last resort of all" for challenging the proper meaning of the Constitution, explained Madison, there could be no "tribunal above" the people in the states when they acted as the sovereign. As the "parties to the constitutional compact," they collectively could "decide whether" the constitutional compact they made had been "violated."[77]

Madison described both the Court and the sovereign people as having ultimate authority regarding the Constitution's meaning in "the last resort." This was not a contradiction. For Madison, the Constitution allowed the judicial branch, using the forms and procedures established by the Constitution, to check and balance the exercise of authority by the national executive and legislature. Even so, the sovereign who gave life to the Constitution did not limit its own powers as the sovereign in adopting the Constitution. The sovereign could use the forms and procedures of the Constitution to redress any challenged exercise of government power. The interposition of the Virginia and Kentucky resolutions provided one such example—an attempt to get the people to use the rights of petition, speech, and the franchise to reverse ill-conceived government action. In the exercise of these forms of the Constitution, the judiciary properly and ultimately interpreted the scope of the Constitution. However, if the people acted outside the Constitution's forms and exercised their power as the collective sovereign, the judiciary's determinations could not prevail.[78]

As a practical matter, the Supreme Court was the "surest expositor" of the Constitution. The judiciary could act relatively quickly to construe the Constitution under the forms and procedures for the operation of that branch of government. In contrast, action by the ultimate authority over the meaning of the Constitution, the people collectively, was much more gradual. For example, it had taken that sovereign nearly two years to put in place the Federal Constitution in 1789. Simply because there were logistical challenges in manifesting an authentic action by that collective sovereign did not preclude the power of that sovereign to act on constitutional questions.[79]

X. RESOLUTION OF THE NULLIFICATION CRISIS

The key was authenticating an act of the sovereign. In November 1832, delegates for the people of South Carolina gathered in a convention and purported to nullify the tariff as unconstitutional. They did not rely on "what are called our natural rights, or the right of revolution," but insisted they were acting under "a constitutional right." Under Madison's theory of constitutionalism, had the people of South Carolina acted with the people of the other states rather than as an individual state, their nullification would have been an act of the sovereign that created the national Constitution. Although occurring outside the 'forms' of the Constitution, if joined by the collective action of the people of other states, that nullification would have had constitutional legitimacy. This conclusion reflected Madison's long-held view that the people of the states in their collective capacity constituted the sovereign of the national government. Only when the people of a given state acted in combination with the sovereign people of other states could there be a legitimate claim of the ultimate sovereign authority of 'the people.'[80]

As unilateral defiance by one state, South Carolina's nullification presented the dire prospect of disunion. Linking nullification with disunion dealt a heavy blow to the concept of the people as a meaningful monitor of the federal constitutional order, as President Andrew Jackson's swift response to South Carolina's declaration made clear. He issued a proclamation that, while acknowledging the people's "indefeasible right of resisting acts which are plainly unconstitutional and too oppressive to be endured," declared that South Carolina had taken "the strange position" that a single state could "declare an act of Congress void" and "prohibit its execution." This was "*incompatible with the existence of the Union*" and "*destructive*" of the Constitution because the Union was not a "compact between sovereign States." Jackson concluded, as did Webster, that a national American people as the sovereign formed the basis of national government. Madison disagreed with both Jackson and Webster on that point. Nonetheless, Madison agreed with Jackson that nullification through a single state's veto, like secession, was a "revolutionary act," not a constitutional right.[81]

In early January 1833, some Virginians suggested that their state might mediate the dispute between the national government and South Carolina. Virginia "should re-assert in the most emphatic terms our Resolutions of '99," especially where Madison proclaimed "the right of the States to judge and interpose for arresting" potential constitutional "evil." "[A]t the same time," the state should declare "that the South Carolina doctrine is an illegitimate and dangerous inference from this resolution." Ultimately, Andrew Jackson in that same month engineered a congressional resolution to the crisis by suggesting a lower tariff with greater enforcement power. Congress passed a Force Bill (enhancing presidential authority to collect federal revenues) as well as a Compromise Tariff (reducing tariff rates). After Jackson signed both bills, South Carolina nullified the Force Bill but accepted the Compromise Tariff. These joint maneuvers and symbolic gestures effectively ended the confrontation between South Carolina and the national government. Later that year, Calhoun judged the attempted nullification a "success" and "indeed a triumph" because a political majority had responded to the grievances of a minority.[82]

XI. CONCLUSION

For many Americans of Madison's generation, monitoring the constitutional operation of government was an active responsibility of all citizens, not just their elected officials. As the sovereign, the collective people who created the Constitution were its final arbiter. Properly understood, interposition was inherent in American constitutionalism because, as Madison put it, the sovereign could always—in the end—act outside the "purview and forms" of the Constitution. For Madison, the collective sovereign consisting of the people of the states exercised constitutional authority, even while circumventing such procedures. This was distinctly different, Madison argued, from an individual state independently deciding to nullify a national law, a step constituting a revolutionary act.

Madison carefully distinguished interposition by groups of citizens or state legislatures that identified unconstitutional laws from any effort by individual states to nullify such laws. A single state lacked constitutional authority to nullify national laws or secede from the Union, Madison maintained. He considered the people of the states the ultimate judge of the constitutionality of acts of the government, and at the end of the day, that collective sovereign had constitutional authority to render national laws void or give constitutional text its final meaning.

Because American constitutions expressed the voice of the people as the sovereign, the people could also directly weigh in on whether government acted consistent with their directions. Some Americans asserted that the Supreme Court was the sole authority to determine questions of constitutionality, but for eighteenth- and nineteenth-century Americans, such a monopoly was neither obvious nor inevitable. Before the Civil War, many Americans believed that individual citizens, state legislatures, various branches of the national government, and ultimately the people themselves—and not just the federal judiciary—played a significant role in ensuring the Constitution's proper functioning. Interposition was a tool for scrutinizing the national government to ensure that it acted as intended.

Interposition supplemented other devices structurally embedded in the Constitution to keep the government responsive to the sovereign, such as periodic elections. Like elections, interposition could reflect the will of the people. Unlike elections, interposition served to clarify issues that went beyond simply voting for one candidate or another. Interposition could bring voters' attention to matters that might help focus the exercise of the suffrage. The constitutional guarantee of voting did not preclude the use of more informal means such as interposition.

While interposition could be used to express a view on the constitutionality of a law, it did not preclude the role of the Court as interpreter of the Constitution. The judicial branch continued to play an important role in monitoring the operation of the national government. Supplementing more formal and informal institutions of government, interposition was a sporadic tool available to the people when circumstances warranted the exercise of that authority. This informality gave it no less a role than other informal devices such as political parties in a conception of constitutionalism shared by Madison and many other Americans before the Civil War.

Whether Madison's concept of interposition remains a viable and appropriate mechanism today is a question beyond the scope of historical inquiry.[83] Ultimately, that question is one that the present generation of Americans must answer. At the very least, however, Madison would have approved of a vigilant citizenry participating in monitoring the federal constitutional order.

NOTES

1. While this chapter focuses on the use of interposition in the context of the Alien and Sedition Acts, the tool of interposition was used both before and after that episode. For example, Virginia's legislature in 1790 passed two resolutions seeking the cooperation of other state legislatures, one to alter the constitutionally questionable practice of closing the Senate's debates to the public, and the other challenging the national government's power to assume state debts. *See* Elizabeth G. McPherson, *The Southern States and the Reporting of the Senate Debates, 1789–1802*, 12 J. So. Hist. 229 (1935); *Virginia Resolutions on the Assumption of State Debts* (Dec. 16, 1790), *in* Documents of American History, 155 (Henry Steele Commager ed., 8th ed. 1968). In early 1791, Pennsylvania's legislature passed resolutions raising concerns about a proposed national excise tax and noting that such efforts "ought to attract the attention of this house." *See* Gaz. of the U.S., Feb. 5, 1791. Moreover, in 1794, Pennsylvania manufacturers sought "a seasonable interposition" of their state legislature to oppose a proposed excise tax on their products by Congress. *See* Daily Advertiser, Sept. 10, 1794. And for questions of the constitutionality of the Jay Treaty raised by Virginia's legislature in 1795, *see* Thomas J. Farnham, *The Virginia Amendments of 1795: An Episode in Opposition to Jay's Treaty*, 75 Va. Mag. Hist. & Biog. 75–88 (1967).

A decade after the Virginia and Kentucky resolutions, Federalist opposition to the embargo against Britain that culminated in the Hartford Convention in 1814 illustrated the widespread use of interposition in New England. *See* Christian G. Fritz, American Sovereigns 210–18 (2008).

By 1824, a Maryland commentator noted, "The right of state legislatures to express their approbation or disapprobation of the proceedings and policy of the federal government has been claimed, exercised, and conceded . . . from the establishment of the federal government to the present day." *See Curtius to The Freeman of Maryland*, Easton Gaz., Jan. 1, 1825.

Indeed, even during the height of the Nullification Crisis, a Virginia newspaper editor suggested that Virginia might serve as a mediator between the South Carolina nullifiers and President Andrew Jackson. While sympathizing with the protests against the tariff, the editor emphasized the importance of both rejecting the supposed "remedy of Nullification" and at the same time reaffirming "the right of the States to judge and interpose for arresting the evil" of the tariff. Interposition and nullification were two different things. The *Virginia Resolutions* of 1799 had defended the right of interposition, while "the South Carolina doctrine" of nullification was "an illegitimate and dangerous inference from this resolution." *See* Rich. Enquirer, January 3, 1833.

2. *Kentucky Resolutions of 1799* (Nov. 14, 1799), *reprinted in* Ethelbert Dudley Warfield, The Kentucky Resolutions of 1798 125–26 (1894) ("nullification" to "rightful remedy").

3. For the tendency to conflate "nullification" and "interposition," *see, e.g.*, Adrienne Koch & Harry Ammon, *The Virginia and Kentucky Resolutions: An Episode in Jefferson's and Madison's Defense of Civil Liberties*, 5 Wm. & Mary Q. 162 (1948) (arguing that Jefferson, but not Madison, embraced nullification by an individual state); Richard E. Ellis, The Union at Risk 4 (1987) (describing the Virginia and Kentucky resolutions as asserting the right of states to "'interpose' or nullify' an act of Congress"); Merrill D. Peterson, The Great Triumvirate 177 (1987) (endorsing the description of nullification as the asserted power of a single state to "interpose and nullify" national acts deemed unconstitutional); John Niven, John C. Calhoun and the Price of Union 160 (1988) (describing Calhoun's solution as "interposition, state veto, or, as it came to be called, nullification"); David N. Mayer, The Constitutional Thought of Thomas Jefferson 201 (1994) (asserting that Jefferson's *Kentucky Resolutions* were "more radical" in "expressing the principle that the states might nullify—that is, treat as void—acts of Congress that they deemed unconstitutional"); Kevin R. Gutzman, *From Interposition to Nullification: Peripheries and Center in the Thought of James Madison, in* 36 Essays in Hist. 104 (1994) (questioning any difference between nullification and interposition); Gary Wills, A Necessary Evil 148, 152 (1999) (calling Madison "an abettor" of nullification for using the "strong" and active word "interpose"); William J. Watkins, Jr., Reclaiming the American Revolution 75 (2004) (asserting that Jefferson "declared that a single state could nullify acts of Congress"); Thomas E. Woods, Jr., Nullification 3 (2010) (alluding to "the Jefferson remedy of state interposition or nullification").

For some exceptions to this tendency, *see* Diane Tipton, Nullification and Interposition in American Political Thought 7 (1969) (distinguishing nullification as the purported power of an individual state to veto a national law because of its unconstitutionality from interposition, conceived as a broader range of actions taken to reverse such laws); H. Lee Cheek, Jr., Calhoun and Popular Rule 51 (2001) (detecting a difference between how Madison understood interposition and nullification); Bradley D. Hays, *A Place for Interposition? What John Taylor of Caroline and the Embargo Crisis Have to Offer Regarding Resistance to the Bush Constitution*, 67 Md. L. Rev. 200–221, 202 (2007) (describing John Taylor's understanding of state legislative interposition, but erroneously calling Taylor "the father of interposition").

4. For the distinction between "questions of constitutionalism" and "constitutional questions" *see* Fritz, *supra* note 1, at 6, 9, 175, 192, 274, 286.

5. For the focus on federalism in the debates over the theory of the Union before the Civil War, *see* Wayne D. Moore, *Reconceiving Interpretive Autonomy: Insights from the Virginia and Kentucky Resolutions*, 11 Const. Comment. 315–54 (1994); Kevin R. Gutzman, *A Troublesome Legacy: James Madison and "The Principles of '98,"* 15 J. Early Republic 571 (1995) (considering "the radical southern states' rights tradition" as "firmly based" on the writings of Jefferson and Madison and especially the resolutions of 1798); David F. Ericson, *The Nullification Crisis, American Republicanism, and the Force Bill Debate*, 61 J. So. Hist. 255 (1995) (attributing to Southern Senators the perception that the resolutions were "glorious reassertions of states-rights principles"); Keith E. Whittington, Constitutional Construction 72–112 (1999) (analyzing the Nullification Crisis mainly as an issue of federalism); Lawrence M. Anderson, *The Institutional Basis of Secessionist Politics: Federalism and Secession in the United States*, 34 Publius 1–18 (2004) (examining the influence of federalism on the secession movement leading to the Civil War); Watkins, *supra* note 3, at 55 (seeing in the resolutions "insights

into the American experiment with self-government" that "remain instructive as we continue to debate the proper roles of the state and national governments").

6. *See, e.g.*, 1 W. Kirk Wood, Nullification, A Constitutional History, 1776–1833, at xvi–xvii (2008) (advancing an "alternative history of America and the South . . . that makes the anti-Federalists the real framers of our federal republic, Nullification constitutional, and the South (and John C. Calhoun and Jefferson Davis) the real heirs to the principles of 1776 and 1787"); Woods, *supra* note 3.

7. The Federalist No. 26, at 168–69 (Hamilton) (Jacob E. Cooke, ed., 1961) ("the public attention" to "sound the alarm").

8. James Madison, *To "A Friend of Union and State Rights"* (1833), *in* 4 Letters and Other Writings of James Madison 335 (William C. Rives & Philip R. Fendall eds., 1865) (hereinafter ML) ("the several constitutional modes"). For the sense of 'interpose' and 'interposition' as something placed or put between two other things, *see* Samuel Johnson, A Dictionary of the English Language (1786–1787); 7 The Oxford English Dictionary 1130–31 (2nd ed. 1989); 1 Jedidiah Morse, The American Universal Geography 37 (1796) ("Only a small part of the convex[ity of the globe is interposed between us and the sun."); Noah Webster, An American Dictionary of the English Language (1828) ("The interposition of the moon between the earth and the sun occasions a solar eclipse").

9. Madison, *To 'A Friend,'* and *On Nullification* (1835/1836), *in* 4 ML, *supra* note 8, at 335 ("ultimate authority" and "purview and forms") and 417 ("explain"); Address upon Presenting President Jefferson a Gift on New Year's Day in 1802, Cheshire, Massachusetts, *reprinted in* L. H. Butterfield, *Elder John Leland, Jeffersonian Itinerant*, 62 Proc. Am. Antiquarian Soc'y 224 (1952) ("a description").

10. 1 The Records of the Federal Convention of 1787, at 314 (Max Farrand ed., revised ed. 1966) (hereinafter RFC) (Madison); The Federalist No. 39, *supra* note 7, at 254 (Madison); Letter from John Taylor to Thomas Jefferson (June 25, 1798), *in* 30 The Papers of Thomas Jefferson 434 (Julian P. Boyd et al. eds., 1950–) (hereinafter JP) ("the people in state conventions"); *Report of 1800, in* 17 The Papers of James Madison 309 (William T. Hutchinson et al. eds., 1962–1991) (hereinafter MP) ("the people composing" to "sovereign capacity"); St. George Tucker, View of the Constitution of the United States with Selected Writings 34 (Clyde N. Wilson ed., 1999) ("the people of the several states"). *See also* William Rawle, A View of the Constitution of the United States of America 25 (1825) (identifying the "people of the states" as establishing the national government).

11. *Speech of Daniel Webster* (Jan. 26–27, 1830), *in* The Webster-Hayne Debate on the Nature of the Union 153 (Herman Belz ed., 2000) ("the People of the United States"). *See also* James Wilson, *Pennsylvania Convention* (Dec. 4, 1787), *in* 2 Documentary History of the Ratification of the Constitution 472 (Merrill Jensen ed., 1976–) (hereinafter, DHRC) (identifying the sovereign as the people acting as "one great community"); Chief Justice John Jay in *Chisholm v. Georgia*, 2 U.S. 419, 470 (1793) (identifying "the people, in their collective and national capacity" as giving life to the Constitution); Joseph Story, 1 Commentaries on the Constitution of the United States 319 (1833) ("The people of the *United States* not the distinct people of a *particular state*" created the Constitution.).

12. Most scholars suggest that Marshall viewed the Federal Constitution's framing as resting on a national people, but a careful reading of his defense of *McCulloch v. Maryland* (1819) reveals his more consistent endorsement of the view that the people of the states

framed the constitution. *See* Martin S. Flaherty, *John Marshall, McCulloch v. Maryland, and "We the People": Revisions in Need of Revising*, 43 Wm. & Mary L. Rev. 1339–97, 1389 (2002) (observing that "as Marshall had been at pains to point out, 'the people of the United States' is properly understood to mean the peoples of the several states in their highest sovereign capacity"). For the scholarly tendency to attribute the federal Founding to a national people, *see* Jack N. Rakove, Original Meanings 163 (1996) (concluding that James Wilson, who endorsed a view of a national people as the basis of the constitution, was a "better historian" than Luther Martin, who advanced the idea that sovereign states created the federal Union); Akhil Reed Amar, America's Constitution 33 (2005) (asserting that the Federal Constitution "would shape a new continental nation whose sovereign would be a truly continental people").

13. For Madison's distinctions of the meaning attributable to "states," *see Report of 1800*, *in* 17 MP, *supra* note 10, at 308–9 ("the term 'States'"). *See Speech of John Rowan* (Feb. 4, 1830), *in* Belz, *supra* note 11, at 269 (noting, "[m]uch confusion has arisen from the indiscriminate application of the word State to different and distinct subjects. Sometimes it is used to mean the government of the State, instead of the people in their political capacity.").

14. While Americans were familiar with contract theories of government and offered different compact theories to describe the Federal Constitution, the use of contract analogies became problematic—at least as a theoretical matter—in post-revolutionary America. With the Revolution, Americans embraced the concept that governments were an expression of a sovereign people rather than a bargain between a king and his subjects. America's first federal constitution—the Articles of Confederation—more naturally lent itself to a concept of individual states as parties, given the organization and operation of the Continental Congress. The Constitution of 1787, however, was understood (and its creation justified) as resting on the sovereignty of the people. *See* Fritz, *supra* note 1, at 15, 21–22, 138–41.

15. For example, when Patrick Henry challenged Federalists during the Virginia ratifying convention to explain why the Constitution's Preamble spoke of "*We, the People*, instead of *We, the States*," he suggested "the States" were "the agents of this compact," thus implying state governments as the actors forming the Constitution. Patrick Henry, June 4, 1788, Virginia Convention, *in* 9 DHRC, *supra* note 11, at 930.

16. For example, when John C. Calhoun asserted that an individual state could unilaterally nullify a national law, he described that action as taking place through a convention that would represent the sovereign people of that state. *See Rough Draft of... the South Carolina Exposition* (completed ca. Nov. 25, 1828), *in* 10 The Papers of John C. Calhoun 510 (Robert L. Meriwether et al. eds., 1959–2003) (hereinafter JCP) (noting that while a state legislature—composed of governmental agents for the people—did not embody the sovereignty of the people of the state, it was clear "that a convention, fully represents" such sovereignty).

17. For overlooking the divergent meaning that "the states" possessed for contemporaries and that Americans at the time were often unclear about which possibility they were considering, *see, e.g.*, Andrew C. Lenner, The Federal Principle in American Politics, 1790–1833, at 63 (2001) (asserting that "the extensive role of the states in the formation of the Constitution" proved to Jefferson and John Taylor that the states "remained sovereign"); Akhil Reed Amar, *Of Sovereignty and Federalism*, 96 Yale L. J. 1452 (1987) (assuming that pre–Civil War descriptions of a "federal compact" necessarily entailed an understanding that "the People of each state were sovereign"). *But see* H. Jefferson Powell, *The Principles of '98: An Essay in*

Historical Retrieval, 80 Va. L. Rev. 738 (1994) (recognizing in "compact theory" both an inherent ambiguity and an intent to vindicate the people's sovereignty and to reject its reduction "to a theoretical premise of republican government of no pragmatic significance").

18. *See, e.g.*, Edmund S. Morgan, Inventing the People 267 (1988) ("Madison was inventing a sovereign American people to overcome the sovereign states."); Saul Cornell, The Other Founders 242 (1999) (assuming that Madison and Jefferson were talking about only "the rights of the state legislatures to judge constitutional matters"); Forrest McDonald, States' Rights and the Union 82 (2000) (asserting that in the *Virginia Resolutions* Madison claimed that the Federal Constitution "had been created by the states as states").

In part, the challenge of understanding Madison's constitutional thought comes from his often complex, if not convoluted, manner of expression (his contributions to the *Federalist Papers* being a notable exception). Only by carefully parsing his prose is it possible to piece together and offer a clear statement of his views on the nature of the sovereign underlying the Federal Constitution and how the people as the sovereign could act as the ruler as well as the ruled. If this "de-construction" of Madison's prose offers a clarity lacking in his original iteration, it is submitted that the explanation of his thought offered in this chapter is consistent with and remains faithful to what he wrote.

19. For examples of scholarship exclusively equating "compact theory" to a states' rights justification for nullification and issues of federalism, *see* G. Edward White, with the aid of Gerald Gunther, The Marshall Court and Cultural Change, 1815–1835, at 486–94 (abridged ed. 1991); Stanley Elkins & Eric McKitrick, The Age of Federalism 719 (1993) (asserting that both the Virginia and Kentucky resolutions embraced "a view of the Constitution as a compact among the several states"); Kurt T. Lash, *James Madison's Celebrated Report of 1800: The Transformation of the Tenth Amendment*, 74 Geo. Wash. L. Rev. 186 (2006) (seeing a basic divide between "those who sought to construe the Constitution as a compact between the federal government and the states (and not the undifferentiated American people)"); 1 The Papers of Daniel Webster, Speeches and Formal Writings 571 (Charles M. Wiltse ed., 1986–88) (hereinafter Web (SFW)) (editors identifying the "dogma" of nullification as deriving "from an interpretation of the Constitution as a compact between sovereign states").

20. *See* Fritz, *supra* note 1, at 153–89.

21. The four separate laws composing the so-called Alien and Sedition Acts are reprinted in James Morton Smith, Freedom's Fetters 438 ("dangerous" to "secret machinations") and 442 ("false" to "disrepute") (1956). For additional background on the acts, *see* Michael Kent Curtis, Free Speech, "The People's Darling Privilege" 58–79 (2000); David Jenkins, *The Sedition Act of 1798 and the Incorporation of Seditious Libel into First Amendment Jurisprudence*, 45 Am. J. of Legal Hist. 154–213 (2001); Marc Lendler, "*Equally Proper at All Times and at All Times Necessary": Civility, Bad Tendency, and the Sedition Act*, 24 J. Early Rep. 419–44 (2004).

22. Letter from Thomas Jefferson to James Madison (June 7, 1798), *in* 7 Writings of Thomas Jefferson 267 (Andrew A. Lipscomb ed. 1903–1904) ("no respect"); letter from James Madison to Thomas Jefferson (May 20, 1798), *in* 30 JP, *supra* note 10, at 359 ("a monster"); *Virginia Resolutions of 1798*, *in* 17 MP, *supra* note 10, at 189–90 ("right of freely"). For newspaper coverage during the framing of the Federal Constitution, *see* John K. Alexander, The Selling of the Constitutional Convention (1990); Jeffrey L. Pasley, "The Tyranny of Printers" (2001).

23. Before the resolutions, Jefferson and Madison anonymously drafted several petitions protesting Federalist use of federal grand juries in Virginia to intimidate Republicans. They

sought 'redress' from the state's legislature, prompting a resolution in support by the legislature's lower house. For these parallel efforts of interposition and the genesis of the better known resolutions, *see* Koch & Ammon, *supra* note 3, at 145–76, 153 ("redress"); Mayer, *supra* note 3, at 199–201. Long after their appearance, the genesis and authorship of the two sets of resolutions remained shrouded in mystery and misinformation. *See* Editorial Note, *The Kentucky Resolutions of 1798*, *in* 30 JP, *supra* note 10, at 529–35. Jefferson and Madison kept their authorship of the resolutions secret, in part because "the very act of drafting these Resolutions was in violation of the Sedition Act." Mayer, *supra* note 3, at 357 n.66.

24. Frank Maloy Anderson, *Contemporary Opinion of the Virginia and Kentucky Resolutions*, 5 Am. Hist. Rev. 45–63, 225–52 (1899–1900); *Virginia Resolutions* (Dec. 21, 1798), *in* 17 MP, *supra* note 10, at 190 ("unconstitutional"); *Kentucky Resolutions Adopted by the Kentucky General Assembly* (Nov. 10, 1798), *in* 30 JP, *supra* note 10, at 552 ("not law"); Robert Goodloe Harper (Feb. 10, 1799), *in* 2 Circular Letters of Congressmen to Their Constituents, 1789–1829, at 147 (Noble E. Cunningham, Jr. ed., 1978) (Federalist member of the House of Representatives from South Carolina informing his constituents that Virginia's legislature was merely "denouncing the Alien and Sedition acts as unconstitutional and void"). At the time, the sponsor of the *Kentucky Resolutions*, John Breckinridge, emphasized that Kentucky's legislators were simply "firmly express[ing]" their "opinions" and asking other states to "examine" the laws. John Breckinridge, legislative speech recorded in the Frankfurt Palladium (Nov. 13 and 20, 1798), *in* Warfield, *supra* note 2, at 95.

25. Letter from James Madison to James Robertson (Mar. 27, 1831), *in* 4 ML, *supra* note 8, at 166 ("annul the acts"). New Hampshire's U.S. Senator and future U.S. Supreme Court Justice Levi Woodbury agreed with Madison in 1830 when he observed that any state "may express her convictions on the nullity or unconstitutionality of a law or decision of the General Government" in the hopes of changing public opinion. *See* Register of Debates, 21st Cong., 1st Sess. (Senate), Feb. 24, 1830, 186.

26. *Kentucky Resolutions Adopted by the Kentucky General Assembly* (Nov. 10, 1798), *in* 30 JP, *supra* note 10, at 555 ("Co-states" and "void"); *Virginia Resolutions*, Dec. 21, 1798, *in* 17 MP, *supra* note 10, at 189 ("the states" to "interpose").

27. Letter from Thomas Jefferson to James Madison (Nov. 17, [1798]) and letter from Thomas Jefferson to John Taylor (Nov. 26, 1798) *in* 30 JP, *supra* note 10, at 580 ("distinctly affirmed" to "extremities"), 589 ("For the present" to "similar declarations").

28. Letter from John Taylor to Thomas Jefferson (before Dec. 11, 1798), *in* 30 JP, *supra* note 10, at 601 ("the people in convention"); John Taylor, An Enquiry into the Principles and Tendency of Certain Public Measures 54 ("a general convention"), 49 ("the only genuine"), and 53 ("corrector") (1794).

29. Letter from James Madison to Thomas Jefferson (Dec. 29, 1798), *in* 30 JP, *supra* note 10, at 606.

30. *Virginia Resolutions* (Dec. 21, 1798), *in* 17 MP, *supra* note 10, at 189 ("duty" to "every infraction"); The Federalist No. 28, *supra* note 7, at 180 (Hamilton) ("national authority" to "opposition").

31. During the protests against the Alien and Sedition Acts, some argued that juries played a crucial role in determining the constitutionality of federal laws. *See* Kathryn Preyer, United States v. Callender: *Judge and Jury in a Republican Society*, *in* Origins of the Federal Judiciary 173–95 (Maeva Marcus ed., 1992). For individual and locally organized opposition to

the Alien and Sedition Acts, *see* James Morton Smith, *The Grass Roots Origins of the Kentucky Resolutions*, 27 Wm. & Mary Q. 221–45 (1970). For the geographical range of petitions sent to Congress, *see* letter from Thomas Jefferson to James Madison (Jan. 30, 1799) *in* 30 JP, *supra* note 10, at 665–66; Elkins & McKitrick, *supra* note 19, at 615 (noting petitions "from everywhere" coming to Congress in early 1799 bearing "thousands of signatures").

32. Letter from George Washington to Bushrod Washington (Dec. 31, 1798) and letter from George Washington to Patrick Henry (Jan. 15, 1799), *in* 37 The Writings of George Washington from the Original Manuscript Sources, 1745–1799, at 81, 89 (John C. Fitzpatrick ed., 1931–44); letter from Theodore Sedgwick to Rufus King (Mar. 20, 1799) and letter from Timothy Pickering to Rufus King (Dec. 14, 1798), *in* 2 The Life and Correspondence of Rufus King 581 ("a declaration") and 493 ("a right") (Charles R. King ed., 1894–1900) (hereinafter RKC).

33. Letter from Theodore Sedgwick to Rufus King (Mar. 20, 1799), *in* 2 RKC, *supra* note 32, at 581 ("unanimity"). For the split votes in repudiating the resolutions and the acts, *see* Anderson, *supra* note 24, at 46–47 (Maryland; House rejected *Kentucky Resolutions* 58 to 14, *Virginia Resolutions* 42 to 24), 53 (New Jersey; House perfunctorily dismissed the resolutions 20 to 15), 57 (New York; motion in House to declare sedition laws unconstitutional defeated 50 to 43, Senate rejected resolutions 31 to 7), and 232 (Vermont; Legislature rejected *Virginia Resolutions* 104 to 52, *Kentucky Resolutions* 101 to 50). For the seven formal legislative responses of Delaware, Rhode Island, Massachusetts, New York, Connecticut, New Hampshire, and Vermont to the resolutions, *see* 4 The Debates in the Several State Conventions, on the Adoption of the Federal Constitution 532–39 (Jonathan Elliot ed., 2nd ed.1861). For legislative responses omitted by Elliot because they were not directed to be sent back to the Virginia and Kentucky legislatures (including those from Maryland, Pennsylvania, and New Jersey), *see* Anderson, *supra* note 24, at 52–54, 244–52.

34. *See* Anderson, *supra* note 24, at 46 (quoting Committee Report of Maryland House of Delegates describing the *Kentucky Resolutions* as containing "*sentiments and opinions unwarranted by the Constitution of the United States*"), 245 (resolutions of Pennsylvania House of Representatives declaring that "the people of the United States . . . have committed to the supreme judiciary of the nation the high authority of ultimately and conclusively deciding upon the constitutionality of all legislative acts"), and 247 (resolutions of Connecticut General Assembly describing the *Kentucky Resolutions* as "calculated to subvert the Constitution and to introduce discord and anarchy"); Elliot, 4 Debates, *supra* note 33, at 533 (Rhode Island General Assembly) (describing "the very unwarrantable resolutions" of Virginia) 534 (Massachusetts Senate) ("exclusively vested"), 538 (New York Senate) (doctrines of the Virginia and Kentucky resolutions were "destructive to the federal government"), and 539 (New Hampshire House of Representatives) (constitutional interpretation "is properly and exclusively confided to the judicial department").

35. *Quoted in* Anderson, *supra* note 24, at 252 ("the most pressing" to "watchful scrupulosity"); Taylor, *supra* note 28, at 54 ("the nation" to "violation"); *quoted in* Anderson, *supra* note 24, at 251 ("daily exercised").

36. *Kentucky Resolutions of 1799* (Nov. 14, 1799), *in* Warfield *supra* note 2, at 125–26 ("disturb the harmony" to "constitutional manner"). Madison, elected to the Virginia legislature in the spring of 1799, formulated Virginia's response, while Jefferson shared his views with Kentucky legislators. Madison and Jefferson collaborated by letter and in person about how to respond. *See* Koch & Ammon, *supra* note 3, at 155–60.

37. Letter from Thomas Jefferson to James Madison (Aug. 23, 1799), *in* 17 MP, *supra* note 10, at 258 ("scission" to "true principles"); Letter from Thomas Jefferson to John Taylor (June 4, 1798), *in* 17 JP, *supra* note 10, at 388 ("every free" to "ever exist") and 389 ("keep together" and "have patience"). For the argument that Madison exercised a moderating influence on Jefferson, *see* Koch & Ammon, *supra* note 3, at 165–69.

38. *Report of 1800* (Jan. 7, 1800), *in* 17 MP, *supra* note 10, at 349 ("misconception"); James Madison, *To A Friend of Union and States Rights* (1833), *in* 4 ML, *supra* note 8, at 335 ("right to interpose"). *See also* letter from James Madison to Thomas Jefferson (Dec. 29, 1799), *in* 17 MP, *supra* note 10, at 297 (reporting on "the job of preparing a vindication of the Resolutions"). The seven formal replies are collected in Elliot, 4 Debates, *supra* note 33, at 532–39.

39. *Report of 1800* (Jan. 7, 1800), *in* 17 MP, *supra* note 10, at 349 ("communicat[ed]" to "unconstitutional") and 350 ("intermediate existence" to "infractions of the constitution").

40. *Id.* at 348 ("novelty" to "private citizens").

41. *Id.* at 349 ("direct representation" to "most obvious").

42. *Id.* at 349 ("farther measures"), 336–37 ("The people, not the government"), 310 ("sovereign parties"), and 311 ("genuine source").

43. *Id.* at 309 ("legitimate" to "submitted to the states").

44. Madison's marginal notes on Memorandum from an Unidentified Correspondent (ca. Jan. 2, 1800), *id.* at 302 n.4 ("inaccuracies"), 309 ("parties to the compact"), and 312 ("American public").

45. *Id.* at 309 ("a plain principle" to "violated").

46. *Id.* at 310 ("the interposition" to "occasions"); *Virginia Resolutions of 1798*, *in* 17 MP, *supra* note 10, at 189 ("to interpose" and "deliberate").

47. James Madison, *On Nullification* (1835/1836), *in* 4 ML, *supra* note 8, at 413 ("as co-parties" to "own choice").

48. *Report of 1800*, *in* 17 MP, *supra* note 10, at 311 ("sole expositor" and "in the last resort").

49. The Federalist No. 49, *supra* note 7, at 339 (Madison) ("pretend" to "observance"); Annals of Congress, House of Reps., 1st Cong., 1st Sess., (June 17, 1789), 520 (James Madison) (in questions over the "constitutional boundary" between branches of government, Madison did "not see that any one of these independent departments has more right than another to declare their sentiments on that point"). *See also* James Madison, *Helvidius* 2 (Aug. 31, 1793), *in* 15 MP, *supra* note 10, at 83 (describing all three branches of the federal government as having "a *concurrent* right to expound the constitution").

50. On views of "departmental review," *see* Donald Morgan, Congress and the Constitution (1966); Kermit L. Hall, The Supreme Court and Judicial Review in American History 4 (1985) (describing a theory in which "the political branches had responsibility for political-constitutional controversies within their spheres, and the judicial branch assumed the role of settling legal-juridical questions, overseeing the rule of law"). Both Thomas Jefferson and Andrew Jackson embraced a departmental theory of judicial review. *See* letter from Thomas Jefferson to Spencer Roane (Sept. 6, 1819), *in* 10 Writings of Thomas Jefferson 141 (Paul Leicester Ford ed., 1892–99) (describing his understanding that under the Federal Constitution "each department is truly independent of the others, and has an equal right to decide for itself what is the meaning of the constitution in the cases submitted to its action");

Andrew Jackson, *Veto Message* (July 10, 1832), *in* 2 A Compilation of the Messages and Papers of the Presidents 582 (James D. Richardson ed., 1896–99) (hereinafter MPP) ("It is as much the duty of the House of Representatives, of the Senate, and of the President to decide upon the constitutionality of any bill or resolution which may be presented to them for passage or approval as it is of the supreme judges when it may be brought before them for judicial decision."). For the argument that America's constitutional history supports a departmental theory of constitutional review featuring "the people themselves," *see* Larry D. Kramer, The People Themselves (2004).

51. During the Nullification Crisis, Martin Van Buren denied that the Supreme Court was "the exclusive expositor of the Constitution," especially in conflicts between the state and the federal government. In those instances, "it is the right of each party to judge for itself; not for the Federal Government exclusively." *See Resolves of the Legislature of New York, in* State Papers on Nullification 140 ("the exclusive") and 147 ("it is the right") (1834). Moreover, in his *First Inaugural Address,* Abraham Lincoln questioned the Supreme Court's interpretive finality because such power undermined the sovereignty of the people. *See First Inaugural Address* (Mar. 4, 1864), *in* 4 The Collected Works of Abraham Lincoln 268 (Roy P. Basler ed., 1953) (observing that "if the policy of the government, upon vital questions, affecting the whole people, is to be irrevocably fixed by decisions of the Supreme Court . . . the people will have ceased, to be their own rulers, having, to that extent, practically resigned their government, into the hands of that eminent tribunal").

See also Pauline Maier, *The Road Not Taken: Nullification, John C. Calhoun, and the Revolutionary Tradition in South Carolina*, 82 So. Carolina Hist. Mag. 10 (1981) (noting that some nineteenth-century Americans "yielded to the Supreme Court their role as guardian of the constitution," but others did not); Phillip Shaw Paludan, *Hercules Unbound: Lincoln, Slavery, and the Intentions of the Framers, in* The Constitution, Law, and American Life 2 (Donald G. Nieman ed., 1992) (offering the reminder that "the practice of making the Court the final arbiter in constitutional interpretation did not gather momentum until after the Civil War"); John J. Dinan, Keeping the People's Liberties (1998) (describing a wide-ranging conception of nonjudicial guardianship of constitutional rights in America before the twentieth century); McDonald, *supra* note 18, at 224 (describing the notion of the Court as "the sole and final arbiter of constitutional controversies" the "truly revolutionary consequence" of the Civil War); Kramer, *supra* note 50, at 8 (arguing that for most of American history "American constitutionalism assigned ordinary citizens a central and pivotal role in implementing their Constitution" and that "courts no less than elected representatives were subordinate to their judgments").

52. For the contingent and contested meaning of judicial review before the Civil War, *see* Tony A. Freyer, Producers versus Capitalists (1994); Powell, *supra* note 17, at 740 (describing the "universe" of those deemed to hold constitutional interpretative authority as including "legislatures, juries, private citizens, and 'the people in their highest sovereign capacity'"). *See also* Gerald Gunther, *Judicial Hegemony and Legislative Autonomy: The Nixon Case and the Impeachment Process,* 22 UCLA L. Rev. 34 (1974) (arguing that the decision in *Marbury v. Madison* "intended" not "to announce that every constitutional issue requires final adjudication on the merits by the judiciary" but that many constitutional issues are left to other branches); David E. Engdahl, *What's in a Name? The Constitutionality of Multiple "Supreme" Courts,* 66 Ind. L. J. 457–510 (1991) (identifying eighteenth-century terminology and practice that calls into question the modern assumption that a "supreme" court necessarily implied judicial finality).

53. The Federalist No. 78, *supra* note 7, at 525 (Hamilton) ("an intermediate"); Peter Livingston *quoted in* John J. Dinan, The American State Constitutional Tradition 102 (2006) ("shield"). On early attitudes toward judicial review, *see* Maeva Marcus, *Judicial Review in the Early Republic, in* Launching the "Extended Republic" 25–53 (Ronald Hoffman & Peter J. Albert eds., 1996); Gordon S. Wood, *The Origins of Judicial Review Revisited, or How the Marshall Court Made More out of Less,* 56 Wash. & Lee L. Rev. at 798–99 (1999) (suggesting that for many Americans in the 1790s, judicial review "remained an extraordinary and solemn political action, akin perhaps to the interposition of the states that Jefferson and Madison suggested in the Kentucky and Virginia resolutions of 1798—something to be invoked only on the rare occasions of flagrant and unequivocal violations of the Constitution"); William Michael Treanor, *Judicial Review Before Marbury,* 58 Stan. L. Rev. 455–562 (2005).

54. *Report of 1800, in* 17 MP, *supra* note 10, at 310 ("last resort") and 311 ("great and extraordinary" to "grant of the constitution"); Annals of Congress, House of Reps., 1st Cong., 1st Sess., (June 17, 1789), 520 (James Madison) ("in the ordinary").

55. *Report of 1800, in* 17 MP, *supra* note 10, at 311.

56. Boston Chronicle (Feb. 25, 1799) and Boston Chronicle (Feb. 18, 1799), *in* Anderson, *supra* note 24, at 58 ("doctrine" to "agents") and 62 ("difficult" to "*constitutional powers*").

57. Letter from Thomas Jefferson to James Madison (Nov. 26, 1799), *in* 17 MP, *supra* note 10, at 280 ("violations"); James Madison, *On Nullification* (1835/1836), *in* 4 ML, *supra* note 8, at 415 ("a triumph"). *See also* Amar, *supra* note 17, at 1502 (arguing that public reaction to the acts "effectively transformed" the election of 1800 into "a popular referendum" on them).

58. *See* William W. Freehling, Prelude to Civil War 25–86, 138–40 (1965).

59. *South Carolina on Internal Improvements and the Tariff* (Dec. 16, 1825), *in* Herman V. Ames, State Documents on Federal Relations 140 (1906, reprinted 1970) ("unconstitutional"). For the campaign against the tariff, *see* Freehling, *supra* note 58, at 134–259; Chauncey Samuel Boucher, The Nullification Controversy in South Carolina 1–45 (1916, reprinted 1968). On the "Free Trade" convention, *see Memorial of a Committee Appointed by the Free Trade Convention, Held in Philadelphia in September and October, 1831, upon the subject of the present tariff of duties,* Jan. 30, 1832, House Document No. 82, 22nd Cong., 1st Sess.

60. John C. Calhoun, *Draft Report on Federal Relations* (ca. Nov. 20, 1831), *in* 11 JCP, *supra* note 16, at 508 ("petitioned" to "last effort at redress"). For the perceived failure of the Philadelphia convention, *see* letter from John C. Calhoun to Francis W. Pickens (Mar. 2, 1832), *in* 11 JCP, *supra* note 16, at 558–59.

61. *Rough Draft of . . . the South Carolina Exposition* (completed ca. Nov. 25, 1828), *in* 10 JCP, *supra* note 16, at 496 ("checks against the abuse" and "the proper remedy").

62. *South Carolina Protest* (Dec. 19, 1828) and *Rough Draft of . . . the South Carolina Exposition* (completed ca. Nov. 25, 1828), *in* 10 JCP, *supra* note 16, at 535 ("protest") and 512 (asserting "the Constitutional right of the States to interpose in order to protect their powers"); letter from John C. Calhoun to A. Griffin and Five Others (May 14, 1832), *in* 11 JCP, *supra* note 16, at 585 ("reserved rights"); Daniel Webster, *The Constitution Not a Compact* (Feb. 16, 1833), *in* 1 Web (SFW), *supra* note 19, at 619 ("nullification").

63. *See Rough Draft of . . . the South Carolina Exposition* (completed ca. Nov. 25, 1828), *in* 10 JCP, *supra* note 16, at 444–534.

64. *Id.* at 446.

65. Letter from John C. Calhoun to William Campbell Preston (Nov. 6, 1828), *in* 10 JCP, *supra* note 16, at 431 ("the basis").

66. *Speech of Robert Y. Hayne* (Jan. 25, 1830), Webster-Hayne Debate, *supra* note 11, at 73 (tracing the single state veto to Madison's "celebrated 'Virginia Resolutions'"); letter from James Madison to Henry Clay (Oct. 9, 1830), letter from James Madison to Edward Coles (Aug. 29, 1834), letter from James Madison to Nicholas P. Trist (Jan. 18, 1833), letter from James Madison to Joseph C. Cabell (Sept. 16, 1831), letter from James Madison to Mathew Carey (July 27, 1831), and letter from James Madison to Nicholas P. Trist (May 1832), *in* 4 ML, *supra* note 8, at 117 ("fatal tendency"), 357 ("powder" to "blow them up"), 268 ("twin" and "heresy"), 196 ("poisonous root"), 192 ("disastrous consequences"), and 218 ("painful" and "broken up").

67. Letter from John C. Calhoun to James Hamilton, Jr. (Aug. 28, 1832), *in* 11 JCP, *supra* note 16, at 615 ("when formed").

68. *Id.* at 616 ("ordained by the people" to "not of individuals").

69. *Second Reply to Hayne* (Jan. 26–27, 1830), *in* 1 Web (SFW), *supra* note 19, at 330 ("the people" to "people of the United States"); *Speech of Daniel Webster* (Jan. 26–27, 1830), *in* Webster-Hayne Debate, *supra* note 11, at 153 ("the aggregate").

70. *Second Reply to Hayne* (Jan. 26–27, 1830), *in* 1 Web (SFW), *supra* note 19, at 329 ("submission to the laws" to "constitutional resistance").

71. Letter from James Madison to Edward Everett (Aug. 1830), *in* 4 ML, *supra* note 8, at 95 ("not uncommon" to "confederated Government").

72. *Id.* ("by the governments" to "a mixture of both"); *Speech of Daniel Webster* (Jan. 26–27, 1830), *in* Webster-Hayne Debate, *supra* note 11, at 153 ("the aggregate"); letter from James Madison to Daniel Webster (Mar. 15, 1833), *in* 4 ML, *supra* note 8, at 293 ("the undisputed fact"). Like Webster, Calhoun characterized the dispute over the Federal Constitution as a matter of "two opposite views," whether a "consolidated" as opposed to "federal" government was established. *Rough Draft of an Address to the People of South Carolina* (ca. Dec. 1, 1830), *in* 11 JCP, *supra* note 16, at 266.

73. Letter from James Madison to Edward Everett (Aug. 1830), *in* 4 ML, *supra* note 8, at 95 ("highest sovereign capacity"). Scholars have cast the formation of the Federal Constitution in binary terms of either a national people or the people of individual states. *See, e.g.*, Gordon S. Wood, The Creation of the American Republic, 1776–1787, at 532–36 (1969) (describing the Federalists' identification of "the people" as the foundation of the Federal Constitution, implicitly assuming such a reference meant a national people without considering an alternative basis for ratification other than individual states); Henry Paul Monaghan, *We the People[s], Original Understanding, and Constitutional Amendment*, 96 Colum. L. Rev. 121, 129 (1996) (asserting that the constitution as created rested on "'We the People' (nationally understood) *and* the several states (i.e., 'We the People' thereof) as independent political communities"). An example of this binary tendency among Supreme Court justices is *U.S. Term Limits v. Thornton*, 514 U.S. 779, 846 (1995) ("The ultimate source of the Constitution's authority is the consent of the people of each individual State, not the consent of the undifferentiated people of the Nation as a whole.") (Thomas, J., dissenting).

74. Letter from James Madison to C. E. Haynes (Aug. 27, 1832) and letter from James Madison to Edward Livingston (May 8, 1830), *in* 4 ML, *supra* note 8, at 224 ("nullifying process"), 80 ("right of *the parties*" to "a *single* party"), and 225 ("[T]he *plural* term" to "original rights").

75. *Report of 1800* (Jan. 7, 1800), *in* 17 MP, *supra* note 10, at 309 ("the 'States'" and "the people . . . in their highest sovereign capacity"). After the *Exposition,* Madison reiterated that a determination of constitutionality beyond that of the U.S. Supreme Court would "necessarily derive its authority from the whole, not from the parts; from the States in some collective, not individual capacity." Letter from James Madison to Nicholas P. Trist (Feb. 15, 1830), *in* 4 ML, *supra* note 8, at 63.

76. *Rough Draft of . . . the South Carolina Exposition* (completed ca. Nov. 25, 1828), *in* 10 JCP, *supra* note 16, at 520 ("a sovereign State").

77. Sketch enclosed in letter from James Madison to W. C. Rives (Oct. 21, 1833), *To "A Friend of Union and State Rights"* (1833), and letter from James Madison to Nicholas P. Trist (Dec. 1831), *in* 4 ML, *supra* note 8, at 318 ("the parties" to "the Constitution itself"), 335 ("to interpose" to "branches of the Government"), and 205 ("the last resort of all"); *Report of 1800, in* 17 MP, *supra* note 10, at 310 ("tribunal above"), 309 ("parties to the constitutional compact"), and 310 ("violated").

78. Letter from James Madison to Nicholas P. Trist (Dec. 1831) and letter from James Madison to unknown correspondent (1834), *in* 4 ML, *supra* note 8, at 205 ("the last resort").

79. Letter from James Madison to Nicholas P. Trist (Dec. 1831) and letter from James Madison to unknown correspondent (1834) *in* 4 ML, *supra* note 8, at 350 ("surest expositor"). In 1821, Madison endorsed the national judiciary as the appropriate interpreter of the Federal Constitution, instead of "the States in their individual characters." Letter from James Madison to Spencer Roane (June 29, 1821), *in* 3 ML, *supra* note 8, at 223.

80. *Journal of the Convention of the People of South Carolina: Assembled at Columbia on the 19th November, 1832, and Again, on the 11th March, 1833* (Columbia, SC, 1833), 60 ("what are called" to "CONSTITUTIONAL right").

81. Andrew Jackson, [Nullification] *Proclamation* (Dec. 10, 1832), *in* 2 MPP, *supra* note 50, at 641 ("indefeasible right" to "execution"), 643 ("*incompatible*" to "*destructive*"), 648 ("compact"), and 649 ("revolutionary act"); letter from James Madison to Edward Coles (Aug. 29, 1834), *in* 4 ML, *supra* note 8, at 196 (rejecting the idea "that although a State could not nullify a law of the Union, it had a right to secede" and describing both doctrines as springing "from the same poisonous root").

82. Rich. Enquirer, January 3, 1833 ("should re-assert" to "this resolution"); letter from John C. Calhoun to Maximilian LaBorde and others (Mar. 27, 1833), *in* 12 JCP, *supra* note 16, at 150 ("success" to "triumph").

83. For an argument that state interposition should be revived today, *see* Hays, *supra* note 3.

9 Originalism's Limits

Interposition, Nullification, and Secession

Lee J. Strang, University of Toledo College of Law

Conventional wisdom on interposition, nullification, and secession has two components: First, prior to the Civil War, it was a plausible—though not necessarily the strongest—claim that states were constitutionally permitted to use the 'tools' of interposition, nullification, and secession;[1] and second, following the Civil War, that claim became false.[2] In this chapter, I use these two facets of conventional wisdom to exemplify an originalist approach to questions of constitutional interpretation and, more importantly, some of originalism's limits.

Specifically, I argue that, prior to the Civil War, originalism had little to offer regarding two of the most common arguments[3] for and against the constitutional validity of interposition, nullification, and secession. After the Civil War, however, the concept of constitutional construction provided originalism with the means to definitively evaluate the legitimacy of these same arguments. The Civil War itself, coupled with the decisions of each branch of the federal government and the state governments, constructed the Constitution's meaning to make the two most common arguments used for the constitutional validity of interposition, nullification, and secession, frivolous.[4] Furthermore, I suggest that the Civil War may constitute a binding constitutional precedent that today's government officials must respect.

I. THE LIFE, DEATH, AND RESURRECTION OF INTERPOSITION, NULLIFICATION, AND SECESSION

A. *Introduction*

Claims that states have the constitutional authority to interpose, nullify, and secede have ebbed and waned over the centuries.[5] The exact contours of these three concepts are hazy, as advocates and critics have drawn upon various conceptions at various times. The most frequently employed conception of nullification is that each state has the authority to ascertain whether an act of the federal government is constitutional.[6] If a state determines that an act is unconstitutional, that state may, among other remedies, interpose its authority—that is, preclude the operation of that unconstitutional federal act within the state.[7] Secession involves a state's withdrawal from membership in the United States, often as a mechanism of last resort to enforce a state's attempted nullification and interposition.[8]

I wish to focus on two aspects of antebellum claims for and against nullification and secession. First, arguments both for and against nullification and secession failed to focus on the Constitution's text and original meaning. Instead, advocates nearly always resorted to more generalized arguments and treated text-based arguments as either superfluous to or supportive of their main philosophical argument. This phenomenon primarily manifested itself in the form of two opposing claims: The Constitution was a compact among the states, or it was the constituting act of one national people. Second, those text-focused arguments that were made, were not powerful. Rather, they tended to be strained readings and frequently mere assertions.

Building on these two points, in part II, I show that originalism's limits make it difficult to say that originalism had the resources, prior to the Civil War, to definitively evaluate these two claims. I then show that, after the Civil War, the situation was different and that originalism could utilize the concept of constitutional construction to definitively say that the primary arguments in favor of the constitutional validity of nullification and secession were frivolous. Additionally, I briefly suggest that the Civil War constituted a precedent that bound later interpreters to reject the two primary arguments in favor of nullification and secession.

B. *Compact or "One People"?, and Textual Hooks*

Arguments for and against nullification and secession came in three basic forms; I will concentrate on two:[9] (1) whether the Constitution was a compact formed by independent states who retained the sovereignty to authoritatively judge for themselves the Constitution's meaning and to leave the compact;[10] and (2) whether the Constitution's text and/or structure authorized states to authoritatively interpret the Constitution and leave the Union.[11] The compact-noncompact distinction dominated these debates.[12] Below I provide a sampling of these two forms of argument.[13]

The earliest prominent employment of these arguments occurred in the *Kentucky Resolutions* and the *Virginia Resolutions*,[14] issued in response to the Alien and Sedition Acts.[15] Drafted by Thomas Jefferson and James Madison, respectively, the resolutions provided the foundation for subsequent nullification and secession advocates.[16] The resolutions' core conclusion was that each state's interpretation of the U.S. Constitution had at least as much authority as federal court interpretations.[17] This claim was premised on a common, though contested, theory of the Constitution: the compact theory.[18] On this view, the Constitution was a contract among coequal parties who retained their independent authority to interpret the contract, including breaches thereof, by the federal government.[19]

The compact theory was one major theory on the nature of the Constitution.[20] But others held a different view, a nationalist view exemplified by the tepid and in many cases hostile responses accorded the Kentucky and Virginia resolutions.[21] For example, Massachusetts rejected the compact theory relied upon by Kentucky and Virginia and instead asserted that one national people—"the people themselves"—had delegated interpretative authority to the federal government and reserved only one interpretative role for the states: the amendment process.[22] Massachusetts claimed that individual state interpretative authority would lead to anarchy as various states, with varying interpretations, vied with one another, and with the federal government, for supremacy.[23]

Some responses to the resolutions made superficial appeals to the Constitution's text to support their positions. Rhode Island, for instance, argued that Article III vested the federal Supreme Court with "exclusive[]" and "ultimat[e]" interpretative authority.[24] Massachusetts, using a similar argument, contended that the federal judiciary was "exclusively vested by the people" with the authority to interpret the Constitution.[25]

To counter arguments against the first resolutions, Kentucky adopted a second *Kentucky Resolution* that, for the first time, raised nullification as a mechanism to keep federal constitutional *mis*interpretations in check.[26] Virginia also responded via Madison's famed *Report of 1800*.[27] This *Report*, issued by the Virginia House of Delegates, defended the *Virginia Resolutions*. Virginia reiterated that the Constitution was "a compact to which the states are parties."[28] Virginia argued that the Constitution had been ratified by the states, which were "political societies, in their highest sovereign capacity."[29] The states, as parties to the compact, were each qualified to judge whether the compact was violated.[30]

Virginia also rejected the text-focused claim that Article III gave the federal judiciary final interpretative authority over the Constitution's meaning. Virginia argued that the federal judiciary may have the final word so far as the three federal branches are concerned.[31] However, because it holds only power delegated by the sovereign states, the federal judiciary could not have the final say over the state-parties to the constitutional compact.[32]

Contrary to common impression, Northerners also, though less frequently, advocated nullification and secession.[33] The most prominent early instance is the *Report and Resolutions of the Hartford Convention* of 1815.[34] There, New England Federalists met to respond to the Embargo Law,[35] the War of 1812, and the United States' acquisition of western land from which Congress was carving new states.[36] The *Hartford Report* urged states to interpose their authority "to protect the citizens of said states from the operation and effects of all acts which have been or may be passed by the Congress . . . not authorised by the constitution of the United States."[37] Paraphrasing Madison's *Report of 1800*, the *Hartford Report* argued that nullification was legitimate because the states were the final interpreters of the Constitution because they were parties to the constitutional compact.[38]

The Supreme Court, guided by Chief Justice John Marshall, also waded into the debates over nullification and secession by articulating the nationalist position on the nature of the Constitution. In *McCulloch v. Maryland*, for example, the Court argued that the Constitution was ratified by one American people, not thirteen separate peoples.[39] Therefore, the national government was supreme when acting within its constitutionally authorized powers.[40] Similarly, in *Martin v. Hunter's Lessee*, the Supreme Court ruled that Article III granted it jurisdiction over state court civil appeals.[41] It again relied on the claim that "[t]he constitution of the United States was ordained and established, not by the states in their sovereign capacities, but emphatically, as the preamble of the constitution declares, by 'the people of the United States.'"[42]

The South Carolina Nullification Crisis provided the next stage for the development of arguments regarding nullification and secession.[43] The crisis began when Congress passed a tariff—labeled the Tariff of Abominations by critics—that increased the tax on many imported goods.[44] In response, the most prominent[45] antebellum proponent of nullification, John C. Calhoun,[46] drafted *The*

South Carolina Exposition and Protest.[47] Building on earlier arguments from the Kentucky and Virginia resolutions,[48] South Carolina argued that the Constitution was a compact of sovereign states.[49]

Furthermore, federal court interpretative supremacy was incorrect because the Constitution did not grant such authority to the federal courts[50] and because these courts were part of the federal government and therefore inclined to rule in its favor and against state interests in cases of alleged breaches of the compact.[51] Calhoun argued that nullification by the state-members of the compact was therefore a necessary tool to maintain the federal-state balance: to maintain a federal government of limited and enumerated powers.[52]

Calhoun explicitly recognized that his conclusion—that state nullification was constitutionally legitimate—was not clearly articulated in the Constitution's text.[53] Though Calhoun made arguments from text and structure,[54] the clear weight of his conclusion rested on the compact theory of the Constitution.

In the Senate, Daniel Webster responded to South Carolina's nullification claims by articulating the nationalist position.[55] Webster argued that the Union preceded the Constitution, and that the Constitution, therefore, created and empowered a true sovereign government that was supreme when it acted within the scope of its delegated powers.[56] Webster claimed that Article III made the federal courts the proper body to resolve questions concerning the national constitution.[57] Otherwise, state interpretative authority would lead to anarchy.[58]

To avert a constitution crisis, Congress modified the tariff schedule in 1832.[59] In response, South Carolina called a state convention that adopted the *South Carolina Ordinance of Nullification*, which purported to prohibit operation of the 1832 tariff in South Carolina.[60] The *Ordinance* also raised the stakes by stating that, if the federal government attempted to enforce the tariff, South Carolina would secede.[61]

President Andrew Jackson issued a detailed rebuttal to South Carolina's arguments.[62] Jackson argued that nullification would lead to bad consequences, such as disharmony and dissolution of the Union.[63] More importantly for our purposes, Jackson, more clearly than other nationalists before him,[64] went beyond familiar claims and argued that the Constitution's Preamble showed the fallacy of nullification.[65] The Constitution, made by one American people, was "more Perfect" than the Articles of Confederation because it made the national government supreme. He also contended that Article II's grant of power to the President to "take Care that the Laws be faithfully executed,"[66] established the supremacy of the national government's constitutional interpretations.[67]

Justice Joseph Story wrote and published his famous *Commentaries on the Constitution of the United States* in this tense context.[68] The *Commentaries* "advocat[ed] nationalism and suppl[ied] the theoretical framework to attack the theories of state rights."[69] Story argued that the Constitution constituted a national government of one American people.[70] He relied on historical background, the Constitution's text, and the ratification debates.[71] Similarly, he argued that the Supreme Court's constitutional interpretations were final.[72]

President Abraham Lincoln later carried forward Jackson's arguments.[73] He most prominently defended the nationalist position in his *First Inaugural Address*.[74] President Lincoln first claimed that perpetuity of the Union "is implied, if not expressed" in the Constitution.[75] Lincoln tied this claim to a general rule of contract law that rescission of a contract required the assent of all the contracting parties.[76]

Lincoln asserted that the Constitution was adopted by one people, the people of the United States of America.[77] The American people[78]—the Union—Lincoln argued, predated the Constitution and the states.[79] This fact was borne out, Lincoln claimed, by the Preamble's promise of a "more perfect Union."[80] A union is less perfect if it is not perpetual.[81]

From this premise, Lincoln argued that the federal government's actions and constitutional interpretations were supreme (in the federal government's sphere of authority delegated to it by the American people).[82] States, on this reading of the Constitution's origins, did not have a unique status that made their constitutional judgments binding on, for instance, the U.S. Supreme Court.[83]

One last note on the widespread advocacy of nullification and secession: prior to the Civil War, Americans of vastly different ideological stripes argued for nullification and secession. Abolitionists used multiple mechanisms of nullification in many Northern states, especially in the context of fugitive slaves.[84] For example, in response to a U.S. marshal's arrest of Sherman Booth for violating the 1850 Fugitive Slave Act, the Wisconsin Supreme Court ordered his release via writ of habeas corpus.[85] Later, Booth was convicted in federal district court of violating the act, and again the Wisconsin Supreme Court ordered his release via writ of habeas corpus.[86] The U.S. Supreme Court acknowledged that it faced attempted state nullification of federal law[87] and ruled that the Wisconsin Supreme Court's action violated the Supremacy Clause.[88]

That was not the end of Wisconsin's nullification efforts, however. The Wisconsin legislature issued a resolution stating that the U.S. Supreme Court's decision was "without authority, void, and of no force."[89] The resolution relied on the central nullificationist argument. The Constitution is a state compact, so the states, and not the federal government, each have ultimate interpretative authority within their respective jurisdictions:[90] "[T]he several States which formed the instrument, being sovereign and independent, have the unquestionable right to judge of its infractions."[91]

The Civil War silenced nullification and secession advocates.[92] Conventional wisdom held that the Civil War eliminated whatever plausibility these claims might once have had.[93] The conventional law school curriculum bears this out. Nullification and secession either are not mentioned or are described as claims silenced by the Civil War.[94] Other than a brief upsurge in nullification and secession rhetoric during the Civil Rights Era,[95] these issues were rarely raised in the political or legal literature.[96]

C. *Revival of Claims for Nullification*

Recently, however, nullification and secession have regained a place in public debates over the scope of federal power.[97] The Tea Party movement arose in response to the unprecedented expansions—both actual[98] and proposed[99]—of federal control over individuals and states.[100] Most importantly, Tea Party movement members challenged the federal government's authority to enact the Patient Protection and Affordable Care Act (PPACA).[101]

Two prominent facets of the Tea Party movement's claims are important for my purposes: First, the Tea Party movement claimed that originalism is the only correct interpretative methodology;[102] and, second, many Tea Party movement members argued that states had the constitutional authority to nullify[103] an unconstitutional federal law, such as the PPACA.[104]

The Tea Party movement is the first popular movement—for at least a generation—to define itself in terms of fealty to the Constitution.[105] What makes the Tea Party movement even more interesting is its commitment to originalism.[106] Tea Partiers argue that the central cause of America's problems is its departure from the Framers' Constitution.[107] The sole path of redemption for the United States, in their view, is to return to its founding commitments embodied in the Constitution's original meaning.[108]

Perceiving a long, deep drift away from the original Constitution,[109] the Tea Party movement has searched for mechanisms to restore the 'Lost Constitution.'[110] One tool that has gained some following is nullification. Particularly in response to the PPACA, Tea Party members have proposed that states pass statutes and constitutional amendments to block or limit operation of the PPACA within their respective jurisdictions.[111]

The most sustained scholarly articulation of this position is Dr. Thomas E. Woods, Jr.'s, *Nullification*.[112] Woods argued that the federal government routinely exerts its power unconstitutionally and that the mechanisms usually advanced to prevent unconstitutional federal activity, such as judicial review, have failed.[113] Woods then claimed that nullification is faithful to the Constitution and to American history, and that it would be an effective mechanism to limit unconstitutional federal action.[114] According to Woods, the "most important question of all" is whether the Constitution is a compact entered into by independent states or a unitary nation-state created by one American people.[115]

The combination of the Tea Party's advocacy of originalism and its proposal of nullification raises the question of whether the former supports the latter and, by extension, secession. Below, I describe the analysis used by an originalist to determine whether the Constitution authorizes nullification or secession. I focus on whether the Constitution was a compact and on textual arguments made by antebellum Americans.

I conclude that the originalist answer is that the Constitution's original meaning did not determinatively accept or reject these two arguments. I also show that, postbellum, constitutional constructions of the Supremacy Clause, "judicial Power," and the nature of the Constitution, preclude nullification and secession. These constructions, I argue, remain authoritative until undermined by significant political change. At this point, the antinullification and antisecession constructions remain politically dominant. Last, I offer the possibility that the Civil War constituted a precedent that today's interpreters must follow.

II. ORIGINALISM'S LIMITS

A. *Originalism's Sources: Text, Structure, History, and Principles*

Though originalists today are divided along many axes,[116] most originalists typically look at the same interpretative data to ascertain the Constitution's authoritative meaning.[117] Originalists look initially to the Constitution's text and structure.[118] For example, to ascertain the meaning of 'Commerce,' an originalist will first study the terms in the Commerce Clause[119] and the usage of the term 'Commerce' elsewhere in the Constitution.[120] The originalist will also note that the term appears both in Article I, Section 8[121] of the Constitution, which delegates power to Congress, and in Article I, Section 9,[122] which limits federal power.

Then, an originalist will review conventional usage of the term 'Commerce' in the framing and ratification debates.[123] The originalist's goal is to uncover the contemporary linguistic conventions into which the Constitution's text fits.[124] This goal is further aided by the next steps: reviewing the broader societal debate over the text in question[125] and, finally, consulting the background cultural, philosophical, and economic commitments of the society.[126] Professor Randy Barnett, for instance, reviewed these sources and concluded that 'Commerce' originally meant "the trade or exchange of goods including the means of transporting them."[127]

What should be clear from this brief description is that the originalist enterprise[128] is textcentric and that the goal is to ascertain the meaning of the constitutional text. Free-floating meaning, unrooted in the Constitution's text, does not fit easily, if at all, within originalism.

One facet of originalism that is potentially in tension with its textcentric focus is the drive to ascertain and flesh out the Constitution's meaning from its structure. The most common examples of this tendency tap the structural principles of federalism[129] and separation of powers.[130] Typically, originalists appeal to the Constitution's structure to provide greater determinacy to the Constitution's text.

Resort to constitutional structure to ascertain constitutional meaning—and the assumption that structure conveys information about the text's meaning—is consistent with originalism. The Framers carefully and intentionally chose the Constitution's structure, including the particular location of text within that structure, with the goal of making the text's meaning more perspicuous. For instance, the fact that the Necessary and Proper Clause is in Article I, Section 8, is additional evidence that it delegates power to the federal government.[131] Perhaps the scholar most adept in this method of wringing meaning from the Constitution's organization is Akhil Reed Amar.[132]

However, originalists' use of some principles is subject to more criticism than others. For instance, both nonoriginalists[133] and originalists[134] have criticized the Supreme Court's broad statement of state sovereign immunity in the line of cases running from *Seminole Tribe v. Florida*[135] to *Alden v. Maine*.[136] The Court majority, purporting to use an originalist methodology,[137] concluded that there is a constitutional principle of state sovereign immunity not limited by or tied to any particular text.[138] Indeed, the Court acknowledged that its principle went far beyond the 11th Amendment's text and argued that the 11th Amendment was itself only an example of the broader principle.[139]

By contrast, the principle that the federal government is one of limited and enumerated powers has much more to recommend it. It fits with the enumeration in Article I, Section 8; it fits the original meaning of the Necessary and Proper Clause;[140] and there is overwhelming historical evidence that the principle was embraced by the Framers and Ratifiers.[141]

B. Questions Originalism Can and Cannot Answer

Originalism has limits because of its textcentric focus. There are many questions that the theory does not answer,[142] for a host of reasons. This chapter focuses on two types of questions that originalism cannot answer. The primary distinction between these two categories is that originalism has nothing to say about the first set of questions, while is does provide at least some information on the second set.

The first involves issues outside originalism's subject matter. Originalism is primarily a theory about the Constitution's meaning; it is an interpretative methodology whose purpose is to articulate, describe, and elucidate the meaning of the constitutional text.

There are numerous subjects that lie beyond the text's original meaning and about which originalism will have nothing to say. To take a lighthearted example, originalism has nothing to say about which cartoon character, Mickey Mouse or Bugs Bunny, is better. Pertinent to my purposes is the central question that divided antebellum Americans on the issues of nullification and secession: whether the Constitution was a compact among states or the constituting moment of one American people.

The second category of issues that originalism cannot answer lies within originalism's subject matter—the Constitution's meaning—but involves constitutional underdeterminacy.[143] There is some evidence of what the Constitution's original meaning is, but the evidence is insufficient to determine—that is, fully answer—a concrete legal question. Originalism may have more or less to say on a particular subject and still not provide a definitive answer to a question of constitutional meaning. Originalism may narrow the list of plausible answers to two, in some situations, while in others, it may not narrow the list much at all.

For instance, the Republican Guarantee Clause in Article IV assures "a Republican Form of Government."[144] The clause's original meaning is determinate on many points; for instance, a Communist-style dictatorship would not constitute a "Republican Form of Government." However, the clause is also underdetermined on many issues including, for example, whether statehouse representation with interdistrict variation violates the clause.[145]

When the Constitution's original meaning is underdetermined, the Supreme Court[146] must 'construct' constitutional meaning. Originalists label this phenomenon constitutional construction. As I describe below, many of the text-based arguments to bolster claims for and against nullification and secession fall into the "construction zone."[147]

C. *Antebellum, Originalism Did Not Definitively Determine Whether Nullification or Secession Was Legitimate*

1. *INTRODUCTION*

The two categories of arguments on which I have focused were, for two different reasons, within an area of constitutional underdeterminacy. As a result, originalism could not definitively answer them.

2. *CONSTITUTIONAL COMPACT OR "ONE PEOPLE"?*

Prior to the Civil War, originalism did not answer whether the Constitution was a compact entered into by continuing state sovereigns or whether it was a consolidated nation entered into by one national American people.[148] This issue was the central focus of antebellum debate.[149] Advocates for nullification and secession supported the claim that the Constitution was a compact among equal states, and their opponents supported the claim that the Constitution was authorized by one American people.

These arguments are in the category of questions that, in principle, originalism cannot answer.[150] They are not claims regarding the Constitution's original meaning.[151] Instead, they focus on a different subject: the nature of the Constitution. Pro- and anti-secession arguments began with conflicting foundational premises. Originalism did not have available to it the resources to determine which of the two premises was correct.[152]

Even if the Constitution's nature was an issue that originalism could, in principle at least, resolve, the evidence contained in the Constitution is indeterminate.[153] There is no explicit textual statement, like that contained in the Articles of Confederation,[154] that evidenced the Constitution's nature.[155] What little evidence there is from the ratification debates on this point is conflicting.[156] Vigorous debate over the Constitution's nature continued, with increasing intensity, up to the Civil War.[157] Many of the arguments marshaled to support both positions were plausible.[158] Many intelligent Americans, in good faith, relied on this evidence to support both conceptions of the Constitution.[159] Lastly, the fact that it took the Civil War's decisive elimination of state sovereignty arguments is evidence that the arguments were plausible before the war.[160]

3. *ISSUES OF CONSTRUCTION*

In addition to the core dispute over the nature of the Constitution, participants in the antebellum debates also used arguments from the Constitution's text, structure, and original meaning to bolster their respective positions. These arguments are of the type that, in principle, originalism can answer. That is, they are claims regarding the text's original meaning.

Nationalists, for instance, resorted to relatively implausible textual arguments. Rhode Island's claim that "judicial Power" gave the federal courts interpretative supremacy was unsupported by historical evidence and, on its merits, was weak. Article III does provide that the Supreme Court is authorized to interpret the Constitution in its case-deciding function.[161] That limited original meaning does not, however, determine whether the Supreme Court's constitutional interpretations are binding on the other branches of the federal government,[162] nor does it determine that states must follow the Court's interpretations.[163]

The absence of compelling text-based arguments is made more clear by comparing America's experience with that of Canada. Antebellum Americans had no clear textual hook from which to support or criticize nullification and secession. As a result, they resorted primarily to broader normative and political claims and to implausible textual arguments.

This argumentative move stands in sharp contrast to the Canadian constitution, which contains an explicit textual home for nullification: the Notwithstanding Clause.[164] The Notwithstanding Clause authorizes a provincial legislature to declare that one of its laws is operative 'notwithstanding' its inconsistency with the Canadian Charter of Rights and Freedoms and any court decisions pursuant to the Charter.[165]

4. *CAUTIONARY NOTE*

In the brief space of this chapter, I cannot do justice to the richness and depth of the historical record and the constitutional arguments deployed by parties to the debates over secession and nullification. It may be that, upon further research, it would become clear that the Constitution did determine one or both of the arguments in the two identified categories. I address this possibility below in my discussion of the Civil War-as-precedent.

D. Postbellum, Nullification and Secession are Unconstitutional

1. *THE CIVIL WAR AS CONSTITUTIONAL CONSTRUCTION*

The Civil War resulted in three textual changes to the Constitution generally known as the Reconstruction Amendments.[166] The text of the Reconstruction Amendments is best read not to reject state authority to nullify or secede.[167] Review of the provisions in the Reconstruction Amendments reveals that they responded to discrete social and legal problems that preceded or were caused by the Civil War. Section 1 of the 14th Amendment, for instance, overruled *Dred Scott v. Sandford*[168] in its first clause[169] and placed the 1866 Civil Rights Act on a firm constitutional footing in its second clause.[170]

Further evidence that the Reconstruction Amendments themselves did not affect secession or nullification is found in the major Supreme Court pronouncement on the constitutionality of secession, *Texas v. White.*[171] *Texas v. White* was the post–Civil War test case regarding the constitutionality of secession.[172] The existence of a test case that made its way to the Supreme Court itself shows that the arguments for secession were not affected by adoption of the amendments.

The Supreme Court in *Texas v. White* did not rely on the amendments to justify its rejection of the constitutionality of secession. Instead, Chief Justice Salmon P. Chase adopted the most common pre–Civil War nationalist claim: the United States predated the individual states, and when states joined or were created by that Union, they were indissolubly members of that Union.[173] The Union's indissolubility came from the Articles of Confederation's statement that it was "perpetual"[174] combined with the Constitution's goal of a "more perfect Union."[175]

In fact, the Radical Republicans who controlled Congress rejected calls to amend the Constitution to explicitly prohibit state authority to nullify or secede. They did so for two related reasons. First, many of them rejected, on the merits, the nullification and secession arguments.[176] Second, many of them were concerned that an amendment would acknowledge that nullification and secession once had been legitimate.[177]

At the same time, any plausibility that the nullification and secession arguments might have possessed antebellum entirely collapsed.[178] The federal government's organs each repudiated those arguments, and in both the political and legal realms, nullification and secession claims became extinct.[179] The executive and legislative branches rejected secession and nullification by prosecuting the Civil War to a successful conclusion. The Supreme Court ratified[180] this constitutional construction in *Texas v. White.*[181] Likewise, the Northern states, through their participation in the Civil War, rejected the validity of state authority to secede or nullify.

The Southern states that had joined the Confederacy also accepted that the Civil War eliminated the viability of claims for secession and nullification.[182] Of course, the Southern states rejoined the Union, though that, by itself, does not necessarily show rejection of the claims. However, postwar accounts written by numerous Southerners show that the South accepted that the Civil War eliminated the viability of secession and nullification.[183] As summarized by Professor Cynthia Nicoletti's survey of this literature: "[E]mploying th[e] trial by battle metaphor made it possible for defeated ex-Confederates . . . to console[] themselves with the knowledge that the logical rationale for the right of secession had not been repudiated, even though the war had made exercise of the right impossible. At the same time, triumphant Unionists likened the Civil War to a trial by battle in order to lend the imprimatur of a legal action to the violent turmoil of war."[184]

Originalism accounts for this dichotomous situation—robust assertion of nullification and secession before the war and acknowledged unviability of the concepts after the war—with the concept of constitutional construction, described above. The Civil War resulted in a political settlement—participated in by the major governmental actors, political parties, and American citizens—that states could not nullify federal law or secede from the Union. As a construction, it was and remains deep and wide, in dramatic contrast to the pre–Civil War openness to nullification and secession.

The concept of constitutional construction has the benefit of providing a reasoned explanation for respecting the Civil War's result. Instead of the mysterious and unsatisfying metaphor of trial by battle,[185] constitutional construction places the post–Civil War unviability of secession and nullification in the context of a broad political settlement. That settlement eliminated the previously existing underdeterminacy and substituted a political construction of the Constitution.

The constitutional construction that obviated both nullification and secession performed two functions. First, it resolved (some of) the vagueness in the Constitution's text, structure, and original meaning that operated prior to the War. For example, the post–Civil War construction of Article III "judicial Power" determined that Supreme Court constitutional interpretations would bind states.[186]

Second, it determined the extraconstitutional issue of the nature of the American Union, the central point of contention in the debates over nullification and secession.[187] The advocates of nullification and secession argued that the United States was a confederation of separate peoples brought together under the constitutional compact, while the nationalist bloc claimed that there was one American people that ratified the Constitution. The Civil War and subsequent political settlement settled the debate and determined that the latter conception of the United States was authoritative.

The constitutional construction against nullification and secession is deep. It has fundamentally structured legal and political discourse. In the legal realm, the process of federal interpretative supremacy culminated in *Cooper v. Aaron* in 1958.[188] In the political realm, Americans no longer look to their states as the primary source of their political identity.[189] The construction is not unchallengeable, and many scholars have argued, for instance, that *Cooper*'s grandiose claims of the Supreme Court's authority themselves violate the Constitution's determinate original meaning,[190] though few scholars challenge the narrower claim that federal constitutional interpretations trump state interpretations.

The constitutional construction against nullification and secession is also wide. Since the Civil War, it has been unquestioned by the federal government, nearly all state governmental actors, and the public generally.[191] Legal claims that state constitutional interpretations trump federal ones are rarely raised and, if raised, inevitably fail. And, prior to the recent rise of the Tea Party movement, political challenges to federal interpretative supremacy were rarely made.

Constitutional construction does not necessarily foreclose raising a particular claim or argument. This is especially true with claims like these that, at least prior to the Civil War, were raised so regularly and vigorously—and plausibly—to support nullification and secession. Construction is an extralegal[192] process: it is relatively open, with many participants providing input regarding a construction. The process of construction is political. It requires the buy-in of the federal political branches and most of the states to give a construction staying power. Like all constructions, however, the post–Civil War construction against nullification and secession is politically defeasible if a critical mass of legal and political actors commit themselves to the legitimacy of nullification and secession.

Given the current constitutional construction's significant entrenchment, opponents would have to exert tremendous and longstanding political energies. Working within the extant political and legal system, opponents would have to capture one or both major political parties, control the elected branches of the federal government along with a critical mass of states. Additionally, opponents would have to eliminate Supreme Court loyalty to the current constitutional construction by, for instance, replacing recalcitrant justices.

A similar process occurred during the New Deal.[193] The New Deal coalition exerted powerful and continuous pressure to change the dominant legal landscape.[194] This pressure came in the form of new statutory norms and executive action inconsistent with the existing legal doctrine. It also encompassed changes to Court personnel and challenges to existing legal doctrines. Importantly, the pressure was augmented and pushed forward by continual electoral victories by the New Deal coalition across the country.

2. THE CIVIL WAR AS PRECEDENT

I argued above that, prior to the Civil War, the Constitution's original meaning did not determinatively settle whether it was a compact or constitution, or the validity of common textual claims. In this subsection, I offer two further, tentative possibilities: (1) if the Constitution's original meaning left open the questions of secession or nullification, then the Civil War, and the subsequent political settlement, constitute a precedent that fixed these initial indeterminacies; and (2) assuming that the Constitution's original meaning was *not* indeterminate on these questions—instead, that the Constitution *was* a compact and that the original meaning *did* authorize nullification and secession—I offer the possibility that the Civil War, and subsequent political settlement, play a role analogous to *non*originalist precedent.

Most originalists agree that precedent, broadly conceived to include both judicial and nonjudicial precedents, can eliminate original underdeterminacies. The most thorough explanation of this is found in Professor Caleb Nelson's *Originalism and Interpretative Conventions*.[195] There, Nelson argued that a widely accepted interpretative convention at the time of the Framing and Ratification was that judicial and political actions could 'fix'—make determinate—original underdeterminacies.[196] Applied to the questions presented by secession and nullification—and assuming that the Constitution was originally indeterminate on the questions of whether it was a compact and whether the original meaning authorized nullification and secession—the Civil War and subsequent political settlement are a precedent that eliminated—fixed—this indeterminacy.[197]

Viewing the Civil War as an originalist constitutional precedent that constructed the Constitution means that the Supreme Court must follow the precedent, at least until the political branches alter it.[198] As a precedent, the Civil War can form the basis for later decisions and will exert "gravitational force" on other areas of the law.[199]

More tentatively, I raise the possibility that the Civil War, and the subsequent political settlement it engendered, is a nonoriginalist precedent. I argued in an earlier piece that Article III requires federal judges exercising "judicial Power" to give nonoriginalist *judicial* precedent significant respect.[200] My conclusion was based on the original meaning of "judicial Power."[201]

One could make a similar argument here in at least two ways: (1) argue that the original meaning of "legislative Power[],"[202] "executive Power,"[203] and "judicial Power,"[204] requires federal officers exercising those respective powers to give significant respect to nonoriginalist precedent, broadly conceived to include nonjudicial precedents; or (2) more narrowly argue that federal judges must follow *Texas v. White*[205] as a nonoriginalist precedent that held that the Union was permanent and indissoluble.

The first approach would require significant research beyond the scope of this chapter. There are, however, indications that a conception of precedential respect—possibly relatively weak and narrow—formed part of all three types of federal governmental powers.[206]

For instance, one of the most contested constitutional disputes in the early Republic was the constitutionality of a national bank.[207] James Madison argued during the initial push to charter a national bank in the House of Representatives that the Constitution did not authorize Congress to incorporate such an institution.[208] Madison lost that debate, and Congress chartered the First Bank of the United States. After the First Bank's charter expired, however, President Madison signed the bill incorporating the Second Bank of the United States.[209] Madison appeared to believe that, even though the Constitution's original meaning determinatively settled the question in the negative, as President, he was obliged to accept the long-standing and publicly accepted First Bank as a nonoriginalist precedent for the Second Bank.[210]

If, as Madison appeared to believe, federal officers of all stripes were required to give (at least some) precedential respect to nonjudicial nonoriginalist precedents, then post–Civil War federal officers would likewise have to respect the Civil War.[211] Post–Civil War federal officers must reject nullification and secession on this reading of the Civil War as binding nonoriginalist precedent.

Relatedly, but more narrowly, one could argue that *Texas v. White* requires the Supreme Court to reject nullification and secession. This could have an effect similar to that of the broader argument made above, depending on the extent to which the other federal branches must respect Supreme Court precedent.

Viewing the Civil War as a nonoriginalist precedent opens it to reversal or narrowing[212] and limits its ability to affect other areas of law. However, it is unlikely in the extreme that the Supreme Court would overrule the Civil War's legal settlement.

III. CONCLUSION

In this chapter, I reviewed two prominent categories of antebellum arguments that permeated nullification and secession debates: (1) the Constitution's nature; and (2) text-based claims. I argued that, prior to the Civil War, originalism could not accept or reject either argument first, because the Constitution's nature is beyond originalism's purview and second, because the text-based arguments were underdetermined by the Constitution's original meaning. Then, I argued that the Civil War dramatically altered the landscape by constructing the Constitution's meaning. The Civil War determined that the Constitution created one national people and rejected the text-based arguments in favor of nullification and secession. Lastly, I suggested that the Civil War may also play the role of a constitutional precedent that binds later interpreters.

NOTES

1. *See* Daniel Farber, Lincoln's Constitution 3 (2003) (describing the issue of secession as "more complex than modern readers sometimes assume"). Professor Farber's book is one of the best discussions of these issues. For thoughtful reviews, *see* Craig S. Lerner, *Saving the Constitution: Lincoln, Secession, and the Price of Union,* 102 Mich. L. Rev. 1263 (2004) (book review); Michael Stokes Paulsen, *The Civil War as Constitutional Interpretation,* 71 U. Chi. L. Rev. 691 (2004) (book review).

2. For an overview of nullification in constitutional argument, *see* Keith E. Whittington, Constitutional Construction 72–93 (1999).

3. As discussed more fully below, the two issues upon which I focus are: (1) was the Constitution a compact among states or the constituting action of one national people?; and (2), did the Constitution's text determinatively permit or proscribe interposition, nullification, and secession?

4. *See* Jack Balkin, *Randy Barnett Wants Us to Know That His Commerce Clause Argument Is Not Frivolous* (July 19, 2010), *available at* http://balkin.blogspot.com/2010/07/randy-barnett-wants-us-to-know-that-his.html (articulating the concept of "off-the-wall" claims and equating them with frivolousness).

5. *See* Farber, *supra* note 1, at 7–114 (describing and evaluating these debates prior to the Civil War); Kenneth M. Stampp, *The Concept of Perpetual Union,* 65 J. Am. Hist. 5 (1978) (providing the classic review of the history of arguments for and against secession and nullification).

6. Black's Law Dictionary 1095 (7th ed., 1999).

7. *Id.* at 824. Hereafter, I treat interposition as a subset of the broader concept of nullification. *See also* Arthur S. Miller & Ronald F. Howell, *Interposition, Nullification and the Delicate Division of Power in a Federal System,* 5 J. Pub. L. 2, 18 (1956) (struggling to distinguish these two concepts).

8. Black's Law Dictionary, *supra* note 6, at 1353.

9. The argument I do not review is whether the Framers and Ratifiers subjectively believed that nullification or secession were permitted or prohibited by the Constitution. *See* Stampp, *supra* note 5, at 6 (noting this line of argument).

10. Whittington, *supra* note 2, at 76 ("Numerous states, North and South, used legislative resolutions to reaffirm the compact theory of the Union."). *See also* Lerner, *supra* note 1, at 1268 ("The secession argument hinges in part on the claim that the states were independent

sovereigns prior to ratifying the Constitution and that they should therefore be able to reclaim their political independence.").

11. *See also* Lerner, *supra* note 1, at 1266 ("From the earliest days of the republic, Americans debated whether the states had the right to nullify federal laws or, more dramatically, secede from the Union.").

12. *See* Miller & Howell, *supra* note 7, at 9 (describing the two dominant contending "views of the nature of the government set up by the Constitution").

13. For an earlier review of the history of nullification see *id.* at 4–20. For a classic piece, from a nationalist perspective, see Edward S. Corwin, *National Power and State Interposition 1787–1861*, 10 Mich. L. Rev. 535 (1911).

14. *Kentucky Resolutions* (1798), *in* Documents of American History 178 (Henry Steele Commager ed. 1962); *Virginia Resolutions* (1798), *in* Documents of American History 182 (Henry Steele Commager ed. 1962).

15. The Alien and Sedition Acts, 1 Stat. 566, 570, 577, 596–97 (1798).

16. Stampp, *supra* note 5, at 21–22.

17. *See Kentucky Resolutions, supra* note 14, at 178–79 ("[I]n all . . . cases of compact among parties having no common judges, each party has an equal right to judge for itself, as well of infractions."); *Virginia Resolutions, supra* note 14, at 182 (stating that "the states, who are parties thereto, have the right and are in duty bound to interpose for arresting the progress of" misinterpretations).

At this point, nullification had yet to be employed. Instead, both Kentucky and Virginia urged other states and their collective representatives in the federal government to repeal the Alien and Sedition Acts. *Kentucky Resolutions, supra* note 14, at 181–82; *Virginia Resolutions, supra* note 14, at 183.

18. *See Kentucky Resolutions, supra* note 14, at 178–79 (labeling the Constitution a "compact among parties"); *Virginia Resolutions, supra* note 14, at 182 (same); *see also* Miller & Howell, *supra* note 7, at 14 ("[F]or the first time the concept of the Constitution as a compact made by mutual agreement of the states was articulated.").

19. *See Kentucky Resolutions, supra* note 14, at 178–79; *Virginia Resolutions, supra* note 14, at 182.

20. *See* Farber, *supra* note 1, at 30–31 (describing three positions on the nature of the Constitution); *see also* Corwin, *supra* note 13, at 536–42 (arguing that the Framers and Ratifiers rejected the compact view). My description simplifies the debate by placing two of Farber's categories—the nationalist and transformative views—into the nationalist camp.

21. *The State of Rhode Island and Providence Plantations to Virginia* (1799), *in* Documents of American History 184 (Henry Steele Commager ed., 1962); *New Hampshire Resolution on the Virginia and Kentucky Resolutions* (1799), *in* Documents of American History 185 (Henry Steele Commager ed., 1962).

22. *Commonwealth of Massachusetts* (1799), *in* The American Republic 403–4 (Bruce Frohnen ed., 2002).

23. *Id.* at 404.

24. *The State of Rhode Island and Providence Plantations to Virginia, supra* note 21, at 184. Unlike Kentucky and Virginia, however, Rhode Island did not offer any support for this

claim other than the potential negative consequences that would flow from states interpreting the Constitution. *See The State of Rhode Island and Providence Plantations to Virginia* (1799), *in* The American Republic 403 (Bruce Frohnen ed., 2002) (arguing that state constitutional interpretation would "blend[] together legislative and judicial powers," potentially cause "civil discord" among the states, and result in "less competent tribunals" deciding constitutional questions); *see also The State of New Hampshire in the House of Representatives* (1799), and *State of Vermont in the House of Representatives* (1799), *in* The American Republic 407 (Bruce Frohnen ed., 2002) (asserting, without support, the exclusive jurisdiction of the federal judiciary over constitutional interpretation).

25. *Commonwealth of Massachusetts*, *supra* note 22, at 403, 404.

26. *The Kentucky Resolutions of 1799* (1799), *in* Documents of American History 183 (Henry Steele Commager ed., 1962).

27. *Report of Virginia House of Delegates* (1799), *in* The American Republic 408 (Bruce Frohnen ed., 2002).

28. *Id.* at 408–9.

29. *Id.* at 409.

30. *Id.*

31. *Id.* at 410.

32. *Id.*

33. Lerner, *supra* note 1, at 1267.

34. *Report and Resolutions of the Hartford Convention* (1815), *in* Documents of American History 209 (Henry Steele Commager ed., 1962).

35. An Act Laying an Embargo on all ships and vessels in the ports and harbors of the United States, 2 Stat. 451 (1807).

36. Miller & Howell, *supra* note 7, at 14–15.

37. *Report and Resolutions of the Hartford Convention*, *supra* note 34, at 211.

38. *Report of the Hartford Convention* (1815), *in* The American Republic 447, 450 (Bruce Frohnen ed., 2002).

39. McCulloch v. Maryland, 17 U.S. (4 Wheat.) 316 (1819).

40. *Id.* at 403.

41. Martin v. Hunter's Lessee, 14 U.S. (1 Wheat.) 304 (1816). *See also* Miller & Howell, *supra* note 7, at 5–8 (surveying state opposition to the U.S. Supreme Court's rulings).

42. *Martin*, 14 U.S. (1 Wheat.), at 324. *See also* United States v. Peters, 9 U.S. (5 Cranch) 115, 136 (1809) ("If the legislatures of the several states may, at will, annul the judgments of the courts of the United States, and destroy the rights acquired under those judgments, the constitution itself becomes a solemn mockery; and the nation is deprived of the means of enforcing its laws by the instrumentality of its own tribunals. So fatal a result must be deprecated by all; and the people of Pennsylvania, not less than the citizens of every other state, must feel a deep interest in resisting principles so destructive of the union, and in averting consequences so fatal to themselves.").

43. *See* Whittington, *supra* note 2, at 74 (describing the South Carolina Nullification Crisis

as "the culmination of some thirty years of political thought on the nature of states' rights"). *See also* Miller & Howell, *supra* note 7, at 9–10 (describing the *Exposition* as "the most elaborate development of that theory ever made").

44. *See* Paul Johnson, A History of the American People 346–47 (1997) (providing background on the tariff controversy)

45. Calhoun was Vice President when he anonymously wrote the *Exposition.*

46. *See* Whittington, *supra* note 2, at 79 ("John C. Calhoun developed the most sophisticated version of what may be called 'radical federalism.'"). *See also* Calvin R. Massey, *The Locus of Sovereignty: Judicial Review, Legislative Supremacy, and Federalism in the Constitutional Traditions of Canada and the United States*, 1990 Duke L.J. 1229, 1248–55 (describing Calhoun and his claims).

47. *The South Carolina Protest against the Tariff of 1828* (1828), *in* Documents of American History 249 (Henry Steele Commager ed., 1962). *See also* Miller & Howell, *supra* note 7, at 10 (summarizing Calhoun's core arguments).

48. John C. Calhoun, *The South Carolina Exposition and Protest, in* Union and Liberty 349–50 (Ross M. Lence ed., 1992). *See also* Whittington, *supra* note 2, at 80.

49. Calhoun, *supra* note 48, at 344; Miller & Howell, *supra* note 7, at 10. *See also* 11 The Papers of John C. Calhoun 495 (Clyde N. Wilson ed., 1978) ("[T]he truth is that the very idea of an American people, as constituting a single community, is a mere chimera. Such a community never, for a moment, existed, neither before, nor since the decn of Independence.").

50. Calhoun, *supra* note 48, at 346.

51. *Id.* at 345–47.

52. *Id.* at 348–50. *See also* Lerner, *supra* note 1, at 1271 (arguing that "Calhoun's nullification theory was self-consciously offered as an improvement upon the Constitution, rather than a realization of its original understanding, by providing additional assurances against the tyranny of the majority").

53. Calhoun, *supra* note 48, at 352.

54. *Id.* at 342–43, 355–56.

55. Miller & Howell, *supra* note 7, at 10–11.

56. Daniel Webster, *Second Speech on Foot's Resolution, in* 6 The Writings and Speeches of Daniel Webster 65–66 (1903). *See also* Stephen C. Neff, Justice in Blue and Gray 12 (2010).

57. Webster, *supra* note 56, at 67–68.

58. *Id.* at 67–69.

59. Miller & Howell, *supra* note 7, at 11.

60. *The South Carolina Ordinance of Nullification* (1832), *in* Documents of American History 261 (Henry Steele Commager ed., 1962).

61. *Id.* at 262.

62. Andrew Jackson, *Proclamation to the People of South Carolina* (1832), *in* Documents of American History 262 (Henry Steele Commager ed., 1962). For a more detailed analysis of President Jackson's position and a nuanced comparison with Webster's, *see* Whittington, *supra* note 2, at 85–88.

63. Jackson, *supra* note 62, at 263–64.

64. *See* Stampp, *supra* note 5, at 31 (describing President Jackson's proclamation as "stand[ing] above the rest for its incisiveness, coherence, and comprehensiveness").

65. Jackson, *supra* note 62, at 264.

The South Carolina Nullification Crisis ended through a legislative compromise guided by Senator Henry Clay and agreed to by South Carolina's congressional representatives, and the South and West more generally. The compromise lowered tariff rates and included the Force Bill. Miller & Howell, *supra* note 7, at 11–12.

66. U.S. Const. art. II, § 3.

67. Jackson, *supra* note 62, at 267.

68. Joseph Story, Commentaries on the Constitution of the United States (1833).

69. Ronald D. Rotunda & John E. Nowak, *Joseph Story and the Commentaries on the Constitution*, *in* Joseph Story, Commentaries on the Constitution of the United States xi (1833). *See also* H. Jefferson Powell, *Joseph Story's Commentaries on the Constitution: A Belated View*, 94 Yale L.J. 1285, 1301–4 (1985) (describing Story's nationalist arguments).

70. Story, *supra* note 68, at §§148–62.

71. *Id.*

72. *Id.* at §§163–77.

73. For an overview of President Lincoln's constitutional views, *see* Akhil Reed Amar, *The David C. Baum Lecture: Abraham Lincoln and the American Union*, 2001 U. Ill. L. Rev. 1109.

74. *See* Farber, *supra* note 1, at 78–79 (reviewing some of President Lincoln's arguments). *See also* Paulsen, *supra* note 1, at 704–7 (explaining President Lincoln's address and evaluating Farber's review of the address).

75. Abraham Lincoln, *First Inaugural Address* (1861), *in* Documents of American History 385 (Henry Steele Commager ed., 1962).

76. *Id.*

77. *Id.*

78. *See also* A. E. Dick Howard, *The Indeterminacy of Constitutions*, 31 Wake Forest L. Rev. 383, 398–99 (1996) (arguing that "We the People" was an example of an incompletely theorized agreement).

79. Lincoln, *supra* note 75, at 385. *See also* Paulsen, *supra* note 1, at 707 ("[T]he First Inaugural does not directly engage the elaborate theoretical constructs of John Calhoun and others concerning state sovereignty."); compare Amar, *supra* note 73, at 1126 (expressing disagreement with President Lincoln's claim).

80. Lincoln, *supra* note 75, at 385; Amar, *supra* note 73, at 1124–25.

81. Lincoln, *supra* note 75, at 386. Professor Amar found the secessionist description of American constitutional history more accurate but ultimately accepted Lincoln's conclusion based on Article VI's Supremacy Clause. Amar, *supra* note 73, at 1123–24. Amar followed Professor Farber's position that state ratification of the Constitution converted independent states into one national society. *Id.* at 1124.

82. Lincoln, *supra* note 75, at 386.

83. *See also* Paulsen, *supra* note 1, at 713 (reading Lincoln's argument to "assume[] the position that a very serious breach of the Constitution by the national government would provide just cause for state resistance").

84. *See* Miller & Howell, *supra* note 7, at 15–16 (providing an overview of Northern recalcitrance in the face of federal proslavery legislation).

85. Ableman v. Booth, 62 (21 How.) U.S. 506, 507–8 (1858).

86. *Id.* at 511.

87. *See id.* at 513–14 ("[T]he Supreme Court of the State of Wisconsin . . . claimed and exercised the right to supervise and annul the proceedings of a commissioner of the United States. In the second case, the State court has gone a step further, and claimed and exercised jurisdiction over the proceedings and judgment of a District Court of the United States, and upon a summary and collateral proceeding, by habeas corpus, has set aside and annulled its judgment.").

88. *Id.* at 517.

89. *Wisconsin Defies the Federal Courts, in* State Documents on Federal Relations 304 (Herman V. Ames ed., 1906)

90. *Id.* at 304–5.

91. *Id.* at 305.

92. *See* Cynthia Nicoletti, *The American Civil War as a Trial by Battle,* 28 Law & Hist. Rev. 71, 76 (2010) (arguing that the Civil War's practical resolution of the legal question of secession provoked a "crisis" that prompted reflection on how to reconcile the two).

93. *See* Paulsen, *supra* note 1, at 691 ("The outcome of Grant v Lee resolved the most important issue of antebellum constitutional dispute—the nature of the Union—in favor of the nationalist view of sovereignty and against the South's sovereignty view."); Stampp, *supra* note 5, at 6 ("[T]he Union's perpetuity was rather firmly established at Appomattox and has rarely been disputed since.").

94. For example, the very popular casebook by Dean Erwin Chemerinsky does not mention nullification or secession. Erwin Chemerinsky, Constitutional Law (3d ed. 2009). *See also* Paulsen, *supra* note 1, at 693 (arguing that scholars have paid "little attention" to the "Civil War as an event of constitutional interpretation").

95. For a contemporary account and criticism of arguments to nullify *Brown v. Board of Education,* 347 U.S. 483 (1954), *see Miller & Howell, supra* note 7, at 2.

96. *Id.* at 17.

97. The most popular scholarly manifestation and partial catalyst of this move is Thomas E. Woods, Jr., Nullification (2010).

98. Patient Protection and Affordable Care Act, 124 Stat. 119 (2010), amended by the Health Care and Education Reconciliation Act of 2010, 124 Stat. 1029 (2010).

99. For instance, the proposed cap and trade legislation. American Clean Energy and Security Act, H.R. 2454, 111th Cong. (2009).

100. *See* Randy Barnett, *The Tea Party, the Constitution, and the Repeal Amendment,* 105 Nw. U.L. Rev. Colloquy 281, 282 (2011) (describing the Tea Party movement's belief that the "federal government has greatly exceeded its constitutional powers").

101. Patient Protection and Affordable Care Act, 124 Stat. 119 (2010). *See also* Barnett, *supra* note 100, at 282 (finding that the Tea Party movement's big government "concern was accentuated by the year-long run up to the enactment of the Affordable Care Act in March of 2010").

102. *See* Jared A. Goldstein, *The Tea Party Movement and the Perils of Popular Originalism*, 53 Ariz. L. Rev. 827, 828 (2011) ("[T]he Tea Party movement purports to be an originalist movement."); Rebecca E. Zietlow, *Popular Originalism?: The Tea Party Movement and Constitutional Theory*, 64 Fla. L. Rev. 483, 484 (2012) ("The Tea Party movement is . . . engaged in 'popular originalism.'").

103. I am leaving to one side the related but distinct issue of whether states have the constitutional authority to secede because few, if any, Tea Party members urge its use.

104. For instance, Ohio amended its constitution to prevent application of the PPACA's individual mandate in Ohio. Ohio Const. Art. I, § 21.

105. *See* Barnett, *supra* note 100, at 282 (describing the Tea Party movement as initiating "more grassroots interest in the Constitution than has existed in my lifetime, and perhaps in over a century"); Goldstein, *supra* note 102, at 288 ("More than any political movement in recent memory, the Tea Party movement is centrally focused on the meaning of the Constitution.").

106. *See* Goldstein, *supra* note 102, at 288 ("Tea Party supporters believe that the nation is facing a crisis because it has abandoned the Constitution, and they seek to restore the government to what they believe are its foundational principles.").

107. *Id.*

108. *Id. See also* Lee J. Strang, *The Declaration of Independence: A Unique Role in Constitutional Interpretation?*, 111 Penn St. L. Rev. 413, 457–58 (2006) (describing how, in times of crisis, Americans have frequently turned to the Founding, such as the Declaration of Independence, to reground the nation).

109. The original Constitution is the Constitution interpreted using originalism.

110. *See* Randy E. Barnett, Restoring the Lost Constitution (2004) (making the case that the Constitution has been lost and needs to be restored through originalist constitutional interpretation); Barnett, *supra* note 100, at 283–86 (describing Professor Barnett's cooperation with the Tea Party movement, in the form of amendment proposals, with the goal "to restore some features of the original Constitution that had been altered").

111. *See* Woods, *supra* note 97, at 1–19 (noting the unconstitutional expansion of the federal government, including the PPACA, and proposing nullification as a mechanism to restrain unconstitutional federal action).

112. Woods, *supra* note 97.

113. *Id.* at 1–58.

114. *Id.* at 21–143.

115. *Id.* at 87.

116. For instance, originalists are divided into original intent and original meaning contingents; some accept the concept of constitutional construction, while others do not; and some originalists accept the continuing vitality of nonoriginalist precedent, while others reject it.

117. *See* Richard S. Kay, *Original Intention and Public Meaning in Constitutional Interpretation*, 103 Nw. U.L. Rev. 703, 712–14 (2009) (arguing that because original intent and original meaning originalists look to the same evidence to ascertain the Constitution's meaning, they will infrequently diverge).

118. For an example of this facet of originalist inquiry *see* Akhil Reed Amar, *Intratextualism*, 112 Harv. L. Rev. 747 (1999).

119. For an earlier and excellent review of the clause's original meaning, *see* Richard A. Epstein, *The Proper Scope of the Commerce Power*, 73 Va. L. Rev. 1388 (1987).

120. *See* Barnett, *supra* note 110, at 278–79 (doing both of these tasks).

121. U.S. Const. art. I, § 8.

122. U.S. Const. art. I, § 9.

123. Barnett, *supra* note 110, at 280, 282–89.

124. *Id.* at 289.

125. *Id.* at 280–81.

126. *See* Robert G. Natelson, *The Legal Meaning of "Commerce" in the Commerce Clause*, 80 St. John's L. Rev. 789, 843 (2006) (pointing to the Framers' and Ratifiers' general knowledge of economics to bolster an originalist claim).

127. Barnett, *supra* note 110, at 280–97.

128. *See* Gary Lawson & Guy Seidman, *Originalism as a Legal Enterprise*, 23 Const. Comm. 47, 48 (2006) (describing how the "reasonable American person of 1788 determines . . . the meaning of the federal Constitution").

129. *See* Epstein, *supra* note 119, at 1395–99 (relying on multiple structural principles to support a proffered original meaning of "Commerce").

130. *See* Gary Lawson & Patricia B. Granger, *The "Proper" Scope of Federal Power: A Jurisdictional Interpretation of the Sweeping Clause*, 43 Duke L.J. 267, 333 (1993) ("The Sweeping Clause is the textual vehicle by which those principles find expression in the Constitution: a 'proper' law for carrying into execution the powers of any department of the national government must confine that department to its peculiar jurisdiction.").

131. *See* McCulloch v. Maryland, 17 U.S. (4 Wheat.) 316, 419 (1819) (using this argument to interpret the Necessary and Proper Clause).

132. *See* Amar, *supra* note 118, at 793–95 (explaining the facet of "intratextualism" that ascertains constitutional meaning from patterns in the Constitution).

133. *See* 1 Laurence H. Tribe, American Constitutional Law 529–34 (3d ed. 2000) (summarizing the criticism of the Court's historical claims).

134. *See* Michael B. Rappaport, *Reconciling Textualism and Federalism: The Proper Textual Basis for the Supreme Court's Tenth and Eleventh Amendment Decisions*, 93 Nw. U.L. Rev. 819, 868–69 (1999) ("In this area, the Supreme Court has drawn inferences, especially based on the Eleventh Amendment, that are inconsistent with textualism.").

135. Seminole Tribe v. Florida, 517 U.S. 44 (1996). Many critics trace the Supreme Court's errors almost a century earlier, to Hans v. Louisiana, 134 U.S. 1 (1890), where the Court held that a state was immune from suit in federal court by a citizen of that state.

136. Alden v. Maine, 527 U.S. 706 (1999).

137. *Id.* at 713 (stating that the principle of sovereign immunity is evidenced by the Constitution's structure and history).

138. *Id.* ("[T]he States' immunity from suit is a fundamental aspect of the sovereignty which the States enjoyed before the ratification of the Constitution, and which they retain today.").

139. *Id.*

140. Lawson & Granger, *supra* note 130, at 315–26.

141. *See* Tribe, *supra* note 133, at 795–96 ("The Constitution, in granting congressional power, thus simultaneously limits it.").

142. By "does not answer," I mean that originalism may not provide any information on a particular question or that originalism provides an inconclusive amount of information.

143. *See* Lawrence B. Solum, *On the Indeterminacy Crisis: Critiquing Critical Dogma*, 54 U. Chi. L. Rev. 462, 473 (1987) (providing the seminal discussion of underdeterminacy).

144. U.S. Const. art. IV, §4.

145. *See* Samuel B. Johnson, *The District of Columbia and the Republican Form of Government Guarantee*, 37 How. L.J. 333, 358–63 (1994) (reviewing the history and jurisprudence of the Republican Guarantee Clause). It is this underdeterminacy that led the Supreme Court to rule that Republican Guarantee Clause cases were nonjusticiable political questions. Luther v. Borden, 48 U.S. (7 How.) 1, 36 (1849).

146. The elected branches also construct constitutional meaning.

147. *See* Lawrence B. Solum, *We Are All Originalists Now, in* Robert W. Bennett & Lawrence B. Solum, Constitutional Originalism, A Debate 23 (2011) (using this description).

148. *See* Lerner, *supra* note 1, at 1268 (describing President Lincoln's argument against secession in his July 4, 1861, special message to Congress, as "turn[ing] on a legal/political definition of sovereignty and a historical account of the nature of the states prior to the Constitution's adoption").

149. *See* Nicoletti, *supra* note 92, at 72 ("[T]he constitutionality of secession remained an open question throughout the antebellum period.").

150. *See* Miller & Howell, *supra* note 7, at 17 ("The United States began life under the Constitution with the nature of the federal union an unanswered question and in the absence of agreement as to where final authority rested to maintain the federal system.").

151. *See* Farber, *supra* note 1, at 44 ("[T]he Constitution never expressly invokes the concept of sovereignty, [and] it is only indirectly relevant to constitutional interpretation.").

152. *See* Lerner, *supra* note 1, at 1274 ("[T]he text of the U.S. Constitution is silent on the question of a state's right to secede.").

153. This claim assumes the absence of a closure rule. If, as Professors John McGinnis and Michael Rappaport have argued, originalism includes closure rules, then originalism may have definitively resolved both the nature of the Constitution and state interpretative authority prior to the Civil War. John O. McGinnis & Michael B. Rappaport, *Original Methods Originalism: A New Theory of Interpretation and the Case Against Construction*, 103 Nw. U. L. Rev. 751, 773 (2009).

154. *See* Articles of Confederation, Preamb. ("Articles of Confederation and perpetual Union between the states of New Hampshire, Massachusetts-bay, Rhode Island and Providence Plantations, Connecticut, New York, New Jersey, Pennsylvania, Delaware, Maryland, Virginia, North Carolina, South Carolina and Georgia."); *id.* Art. II ("Each state retains its sovereignty, freedom, and independence, and every power, jurisdiction, and right, which is not by this Confederation expressly delegated to the United States, in Congress assembled.").

155. Some nationalists, such as Presidents Lincoln and Jackson, relied on the Preamble's goal of a "a more perfect Union" as a textual "hook" for their claim that states were not sovereign. U.S. Const. pmbl. For a review of these sorts of arguments *see* Farber, *supra* note 1, at 81–86; Lerner, *supra* note 1, at 1274–76.

156. *See* Lerner, *supra* note 1, at 1276–77 (describing one statement by Alexander Hamilton in the New York Ratification Convention and noting that three states, in their ratifications of the Constitution, reserved the right to rebel).

157. *See* Nicoletti, *supra* note 92, at 72 ("[M]ost historians have acknowledged that a robust debate about the nature of the Union and the ultimate locus of sovereignty flourished in American political discourse until 1861.").

158. *See* Farber, *supra* note 1, at 33–44 (describing common arguments for and against retained state sovereignty). *See also* Lerner, *supra* note 1, at 1277–78 (describing competing hypotheticals regarding the implicit understanding of the Framers and Ratifiers regarding the constitutional permissibility of secession).

159. Even President Lincoln, on some accounts, supported the legality of secession in extreme circumstances. *See* Paulsen, *supra* note 1, at 713 ("Lincoln appears to concede the theoretical legitimacy of secession for grave constitutional breaches.").

160. *See id.* at 703 ("[T]he Civil War holds that individual states are not sovereign.").

161. Marbury v. Madison, 5 U.S. (1 Cranch) 137, 177–78 (1803); Saikrishna B. Prakash & John C. Yoo, *The Origins of Judicial Review*, 70 U. Chi. L. Rev. 887, 890 (2003).

162. *See* Paulsen, *supra* note 1, at 711 n.55 ("The argument that the Constitution designates the Supreme Court, by implication, as the single authoritative interpreter of the Constitution is hard to square with the most natural reading of the Constitution's text, structure, and history.").

163. *Cf. id.* (arguing that the Constitution's original meaning precluded states from authoritatively judging for themselves "whether the national government has committed a material breach of the Constitution").

My claim in the text—that antebellum debate participants utilized implausible originalist arguments to argue for federal or state interpretative supremacy—fits with Professor Paulsen's narrower claim that originalism supports "state interpretative legitimacy and deni[es] . . . federal interpretative supremacy." *Id.* at 710–711.

164. Canadian Charter of Rights and Freedoms, Part I of the Constitution Act, 1982, Schedule B of the Canada Act 1982, (U.K.), ch. 11. For a comparison of the Notwithstanding Clause and American federalism, *see* Massey, *supra* note 46, at 1229.

165. Canadian Charter of Rights and Freedoms, Part I of the Constitution Act, 1982, Schedule B of the Canada Act 1982, (U.K.), ch. 11. *See also* Massey, *supra* note 46, at 1270 ("[I]n contemporary Canada, unlike Calhoun's America, the sectional brake is a textual part of the Constitution and is thus harder to deny.").

166. Other subconstitutional legal changes also occurred, including federal statutes such as the 1866 Civil Rights Act.

167. *See* Paulsen, *supra* note 1, at 691–92 (arguing that the Civil War constituted the "decisive legal interpretative event" that "reject[ed] state sovereignty and embrac[ed] instead national government authority").

168. Dred Scott v. Sandford, 60 U.S. (19 How.) 393 (1856).

169. U.S. Const. amend. XIV, § 1.

170. *Id.*

Professor Daniel Farber has recently argued that the 14th Amendment's Citizenship and Privileges or Immunities Clauses make secession unconstitutional. Daniel A. Farber, *The Fourteenth Amendment and the Unconstitutionality of Secession*, 45 Akron L. Rev. 479 (2012). Farber's argument proceeded in two steps: (1) the Citizenship Clause made national citizenship paramount to state citizenship; and (2) state secession would violate the privileges or immunities of national citizenship. *Id.* at 480–81, 510. Farber's claims could be in tension with my argument that the Civil War was an instance of constitutional construction because Farber claimed a textual—and therefore an instance of constitutional interpretation, not construction—resolution to antebellum indeterminacy regarding the nature of the Constitution. There are, however, at least two reasons why Farber's claims do not undermine my argument. Given space constraints, I will summarize these reasons briefly.

First, there is a distinction between the question on which I am focused—the nature of the Union—and Farber's claims. Farber's focus is on citizenship and the change in (or clarification of) citizenship contained in Section 1. Therefore, Farber may be correct that the 14th Amendment altered the nature of citizenship, but it is not a necessary implication that the nature of the Union was also thereby changed. *See id.* at 482 n.13 (stating that "the Civil War would have banished any serious claims about the right to secede even without a formal amendment"). In fact, Farber recognized that his argument needed an additional step to tie the 14th Amendment's alteration of citizenship to the alteration of the nature of the Union. *See id.* at 480 (stating that the change in the nature of the Union is a "corollary [that] flows naturally from" the change in citizenship).

Second, my argument focuses on the effects of the Civil War itself, independent of the 14th Amendment. I argue that the Civil War, accompanied by the political acceptance of its result, constituted a constitutional construction. Farber appears to acknowledge that the Civil War, by itself, had such an impact. *See id.* at 480 (distinguishing between the Civil War's and the 14th Amendment's effects on citizenship and the nature of the Union); *id.* at 482 n.13 (stating that the "Fourteenth Amendment can be seen as memorializing a constitutional shift that had already taken place").

171. Texas v. White, 74 U.S. (7 Wall.) 700 (1868). The abortive federal prosecution of ex-Confederate President Jefferson Davis was an attempted test case of the legality of the Civil War and secession. *See* Cynthia Nicoletti, *Did Secession Really Die at Appomattox?: The Strange Case of* U.S. v. Jefferson Davis, 41 U. Tol. L. Rev. 587 (2010) (describing the case).

172. *See* David K. Watson, *The Trial of Jefferson Davis*, 24 Yale L.J. 669 (1915) (describing the treason trial of Jefferson Davis, which presented the question of the constitutionality of secession and which, for that reason, did not go to trial). *See also* Case of Davis, 7 F. Cas. 63 (C.C.D. Va. 1867–1871) (No. 3621) (collecting the various legal materials associated with Davis' case).

173. *White*, 74 U.S. (7 Wall.) at 724–26.

174. The Articles of Confederation, Preamb. (1781), *in* Documents of American History 111 (Henry Steele Commager ed., 1962).

175. U.S. Const. pmbl.

176. *See* Akhil Reed Amar, America's Constitution 379 n.63 (2005) (summarizing scholarship on this point).

177. *Id.*

178. Paulsen, *supra* note 1, at 703. *See also* Nicoletti, *supra* note 92, at 587 (summarizing the scholarly consensus). *But see id.* at 588 ("[T]he Civil War did not fully resolve the constitutionality of secession.").

179. Paulsen, *supra* note 1, at 716 ("Appomattox settled for all time the question of the constitutional validity of secession, against the position of the South.").

180. Compare 2 Bruce Ackerman, We the People: Transformations 350–75 (1998) (detailing the Supreme Court's incorporation of the New Deal's constitutional principles into precedent).

181. Texas v. White, 74 U.S. (7 Wall.) 700 (1868).

182. Paulsen, *supra* note 1, at 703.

183. *See* Nicoletti, *supra* note 92, at 71 (describing the postwar consensus, both North and South, that the Civil War was a "trial by battle" of the issues of secession and that the verdict went against secession). *See also* Paulsen, *supra* note 1, at 691–92 (stating that the "outcome of Grant v Lee resolved the most important issue of antebellum constitutional dispute—the nature of the Union").

184. Nicoletti, *supra* note 92, at 76.

185. *See* Woods, *supra* note 97, at 84 (arguing that the brute fact of the Civil War's resolution could not settle whether nullificationist arguments were invalid). As my comments in the text make clear, my claim is that post–Civil War political changes eliminated the plausibility of nullificationist arguments via constitutional construction.

186. *See* Paulsen, *supra* note 1, at 703 ("[T]he Civil War holds that . . . the states, as states, [are not] the final and exclusive judges, for themselves, of the meaning of the Constitution.").

187. *Id.* at 691.

188. *See* Cooper v. Aaron, 358 U.S. 1, 18 (1958) ("This decision declared the basic principle that the federal judiciary is supreme in the exposition of the law of the Constitution, and that principle has ever since been respected by this Court and the Country as a permanent and indispensable feature of our constitutional system.").

189. *See* Amar, *supra* note 176, at 381 ("The [Citizenship Clause of the Fourteenth Amendment] codified a profound nationalization of American identity.").

190. *See* Saikrishna Prakash & John Yoo, *Against Interpretative Supremacy*, 103 Mich. L. Rev. 1539, 1554–63 (2005) (book review) (arguing that the interpretative authority of judicial judgments, not opinions or reasoning, binds other legal actors).

191. *See* Lerner, *supra* note 1, at 1264 ("It is difficult for Americans today to take seriously the legal claims in favor of a right of secession.").

192. Though still constrained by law.

193. The processes are somewhat dissimilar because the Civil War, and the political alterations that occurred contemporaneously and following it, constructed constitutional meaning in an area of original indeterminacy, while major portions of the New Deal changed constitutional interpretations.

194. A prominent description of this process is found inAckerman, *supra* note 180, at 279–382.

195. Caleb Nelson, *Originalism and Interpretative Conventions*, 70 U. Chi. L. Rev. 519, 525–53 (2003).

196. *See* Randy E. Barnett, *Trumping Precedent with Original Meaning: Not as Radical as It Sounds*, 22 Const. Comm. 257, 267–69 (2005) (accepting Nelson's conclusion with some reservations). *See also* Lee J. Strang, *An Originalist Theory of Precedent: The Privileged Place of Originalist Precedent*, 2010 BYU L. Rev. 1729, 1784–86 (describing how originalist judicial precedent plays this role).

197. *See* Paulsen, *supra* note 1, at 703 ("[T]he Civil War holds that individual states are not sovereign in the sense that any of them, acting singly or together, has a constitutional right to secede from the Union . . . ; nor are the states, as states, acting singly or together, the final and exclusive judges, for themselves, of the meaning of the Constitution.").

198. Strang, *supra* note 196, at 1785–86.

199. *Id.*

200. Lee J. Strang, *An Originalist Theory of Precedent: Originalism, Nonoriginalist Precedent, and the Common Good*, 36 N.M. L. Rev. 419, 452 (2006). *See also* John O. McGinnis & Michael B. Rappaport, *Reconciling Originalism and Precedent*, 103 Nw. U. L. Rev. 803, 806 (2009) (coming to a similar conclusion).

201. Strang, *supra* note 200, at 447–71.

202. U.S. Const. art. I, § 1, cl. 1.

203. *Id.* art. II, § 1, cl. 1.

204. *Id.* art. III, § 1, cl. 1.

205. Texas v. White, 74 U.S. (7 Wall.) 700 (1868).

206. *See, e.g.*, The Federalist No. 37 (James Madison) ("[A]ll new laws . . . are considered as more or less obscure and equivocal, until their meaning be liquidated and ascertained by a series of particular discussions and adjudications"); Letter from James Madison to Spencer Roane (Sept. 2, 1819), in 3 Letters and Other Writings of James Madison 145 (1865) ("It could not but happen, and was foreseen at the birth of the Constitution, that difficulties and differences of opinion might occasionally arise in expounding terms and phrases necessarily used in such a charter; . . . and that it might require a regular course of practice to liquidate and settle the meaning of some of them."). *See also* Barnett, *supra* note 196, at 267–69 (limiting the role of precedent to resolving original ambiguities).

207. For a general review of the controversy, *see* Leonard W. Levy, Original Intent and the Framers' Constitution 7–11 (1988).

208. *Id.* at 10.

209. *Id.* at 21. The Supreme Court, in *McCulloch v. Maryland*, famously upheld the constitutionality of the Second Bank. McCulloch v. Maryland, 17 U.S. (4 Wheat.) 316 (1819).

210. Levy, *supra* note 207, at 20–21.

211. Again, assuming that the Civil War manifested an incorrect interpretation of the Constitution, and hence was nonoriginalist.

212. *See* Strang, *supra* note 200, at 473 (listing three factors used to determine whether to overrule a nonoriginalist precedent).

V

Critical Views of Federalism, States' Rights, and Memories of Secession

10 Union and States' Rights 150 Years after Sumter

Some Reflections on a Tangled Political and Constitutional Conundrum

Sanford V. Levinson, University of Texas School of Law

Several years ago I published a piece with a question as the title: *Is Secession the Achilles Heel of "Strong" Federalism?*[1] That essay was far from the 'last word,' so I want to return to some of the issues that I explored then, which have been supplemented, of course, by subsequent developments. What do I mean by 'strong federalism'? It is, I believe, essential to distinguish *federalism*, whether weak or strong, from *decentralization*. The latter is merely a technique of either creating or implementing policies. It is readily obvious that a constitutionally unitary government can, for excellent reasons, choose to decentralize certain policy issues. Indeed, many contemporary analysts suggest that both China and France, in their own ways the very models of strong unitary government, have nonetheless adopted a highly decentralized approach in many policy areas. The point, though, is that neither country can be said to be under any constitutional obligation to do so and could presumably reverse the move toward decentralization should the national leadership come to the conclusion that centralization would, in fact, be better policy.

Unlike decentralization, best understood as a contextual political choice, *federalism* is a distinctly *legal* notion. This is the case even if one can easily argue that the initial decision, at the stage of drafting a constitution, reflects political facts on the ground and *not* the adoption of some abstract theory of government from behind a veil of ignorance. Constitutions are drafted by people with highly sensitive political antennae, and decisions reflect idealized theoretical conceptions less than they do submission to the demands of political adversaries one is trying to inveigle into an agreement on basic structures of government. This is the essence of constitutional federalism. In a widely cited article, political scientist Alfred Stepan suggests that federalism arises when one is trying either to bring together geographically differentiated preexisting communities of interest (think of the United States) or to hold together such communities, at least one of which is threatening secession from an existing unitary framework of government (think of modern Spain or Belgium).[2] Constitutional federalism requires, at the very least, the presence within a political system of a subnational unit that has some degree of guaranteed autonomy with regard to at least some significant issue(s). That is, the leaders of the national government do not have complete legal discretion as to whether to adopt a centralized or decentralized model of governance depending on political or technocratic considerations. The subnational unit has the legal authority to veto at least certain national requests on the basis that the constitutional agreement establishing the federal political order set out a protected domain of subnational control. Without some such division, it is hard to know exactly what one might mean by describing a political system as federal.

One must therefore always be sensitive to the historically contingent factors that explain the emergence of federalism in a given country. Consider the frequency with which geographically dispersed populations having distinctive racial, ethnic, religious, or other cultural attributes—not to mention significantly different reserves of natural resources, such as coal, oil, diamonds, or rare-earth metals—contemplate the feasibility of establishing or maintaining a federal association. Almost by definition, these groups may not entirely trust one another, even as they agree that each would be better off in some kind of political union.

There is, however, enough concern that the union is subject to capture by a coalition of potential political or cultural adversaries that great pains are taken during the negotiating process leading to the formation of the new system both to limit the powers of the national government and to reserve certain especially important powers to the subnational unit. These preexisting communities, and the political systems they may already have created prior to establishing the new political order, often intuitively adopt Ronald Reagan's famous dictum, "Trust but verify."

If one accepts the premise that the origins of federalism lie in mutual mistrust as well as whatever degree of mutual affection may be necessary to achieve a minimal national unity, then an obvious issue is how the subnational units can secure the federal bargain and guarantee the level of verification that was necessary to gain their assent to a union in the first place. One possibility, of course, is to write down certain understandings, which thereby assume the status of solemn promises that are expected to be honored even when, as is inevitable, the national government is tempted to overreach or the subnational units to shirk on their own commitments. James Madison was decidedly skeptical about the plausibility of relying on what he frequently dismissed, both in correspondence and in *Federalist* No. 48—the topic of which was that particular form of divided power called federalism—the 'parchment barriers' that could so easily be transgressed. Reagan was obviously unwilling to trust any promises made by the Soviet Union, even as he proved far more willing to deal with the Gorbachev government than many other anti-Communists were comfortable with. Words were cheap. More was necessary.

I. WHAT DOES THE UNITED STATES CONSTITUTION GUARANTEE THE STATES?

One of the odd features of the U.S. Constitution, it is worth noting, is the relative paucity of explicit guarantees of state autonomy. The states were asked to rely much more on the central promise that the new national government would be a limited government of assigned powers[3]—though, of course, it is also a notorious truth that the 1787 Constitution, prior to the Bill of Rights, contained extremely few explicit limitations on national power beyond those set out in Article I, Section 9. What do we find if we read the Constitution very carefully with regard to the kind of policy autonomy that distinguishes truly federal systems? The surprising answer is not very much, especially if we are motivated to look at the Constitution because of contemporary disputes about the extent of state autonomy. Instead, what we discover are the following textual assignments of authority to state governments.

A. *Managing Elections*

It is no small matter that states are given the responsibility for actually running elections, including elections for national office. Whether this is a feature or a bug of the American system can certainly be debated. Some observers have suggested that a number of our states are in some respects little better than most so-called underdeveloped or third-world nations in the way they conduct elections. One might believe, for example, that independence and detachment from raw politics are attributes at least as important with regard to those who conduct elections as to those we hire to judge cases. Yet in many states, the elections are presided over by highly partisan officials, sometimes elected, sometimes appointed, but always with clear partisan identities. A most spectacular example was Kathleen Harris, the Secretary of State of Florida and the official in charge of the recount in the 2000 presidential election even as she also served as the state cochair of the Bush-Cheney election committee. To be sure, state autonomy with regard to elections has been significantly limited by a number of congressional statutes and constitutional amendments, at least with regard to the ability of states to deprive people of the right to participate in elections, but much autonomy *does* remain, for better or, quite likely, for worse, thanks to decisions made in 1787.

B. The Original Senate

The original decision to place the power to appoint Senators in the hands of state legislatures (as well as the role that state legislatures were thought to be likely to play in choosing presidential electors) could be viewed as an *indirect* protection of state autonomy. After all, those seeking the approval of the legislatures might be expected to support their claims to residuary powers. Even with regard to the original conception of the Senate, however, the appointing legislature had no power to set senatorial salaries, which came from the national treasury, or more importantly, to *recall* Senators whose votes were seen as betrayals of the state's interests. There was, in fact, a lively debate at the end of the eighteenth century as to whether representatives were subject to instruction from their constituents or whether they could instead exercise independent judgment. One way of enforcing an instruction model is to allow the de facto firing of political agents by recall (instead of waiting until the next election). But that power doesn't exist in the American system. Moreover, Mikhail Filippov and his colleagues, authors of the marvelous book *Designing Federalism,* argue that one important reason for the six-year terms of Senators is to assure them a certain freedom from the response of those who had appointed them because, in many state legislatures, the appointing officials would be out of office by the time of the next election.[4] (As a matter of fact, most Senators themselves were content to serve only one term; it was not until the end of the nineteenth century that Senators often returned for multiple terms.) Even if a Senator antagonized those who held majority power, it was always possible that they would be succeeded by a new majority more compatible with the representative's views.

But the 17th Amendment and the requirement of popular election substantially defederalized the Senate. The excessive weight given to the interests of small states in the Senate—like the distortions of the Electoral College that similarly benefit specific states—has literally nothing to do with protecting what is thought to be important about federalism, which is state autonomy. Pandering to the residents of Ohio is entirely different from pledging to strengthen the powers of the Ohio legislature or, even more strongly, to support the prerogatives of that legislature against what it might perceive as an overweening national government. If one is serious about the Senate as a protector of state interests, one might look to Germany, where the second house, the Bundesrat, is composed of state officials, just as one might expect far more 'federalism friendly' executives if electors chosen directly by state legislatures were charged with picking presidents.

One other aspect of the Senate should be mentioned in this context. There can be no change in the equal access of voting power by states in the Senate without the de facto unanimous consent of the states, and there is no reason whatsoever to believe that any state would ever consent to its having diminished power in that body.

C. *The Guaranteed Status of State Boundaries*

Article IV, Section 4 provides that "no new State shall be formed or erected within the Jurisdiction of any other State; nor any State be formed by the Junction of two or more States, or Parts of States, without the Consent of the Legislatures of the States concerned as well as of the Congress." This means that California or Texas, to name the two most obvious examples, cannot decide that they would be better off splitting into smaller states, for Congress would have to approve such a division. And why is it almost certain that Congress would refuse to approve such changes? The answer is that they would effectively multiply the representation of the geographical territories encompassed by those states in the Senate. Thus Northern and Southern California would have a total of four Senators, just as the states of East, West, and South Texas would have six Senate seats. Why would the rest of the country consent to *that*? It's hard to see this clause, as applied to the hypothetical (but sensible) desire of California and Texas to split into smaller units, as protecting federalism as such. What *is* protective of federalism, presumably, is the fact that Congress could not force the altogether sensible joinder of the Dakotas into one state or the dissolution of Delaware into parts of New Jersey, Pennsylvania, and Maryland, since the affected states (including Delaware) would have a veto over such proposals. In any event, whatever interesting questions might be suggested for classroom discussion, it is hard to view this clause as a truly major protection of twenty-first-century federalism.

D. State Militias

States are also guaranteed, by the 2nd Amendment, the right to have their own state militias. As a practical matter, this might be the most important protection of federalism in the original Constitution, for it involves recognition of the importance of control of the means of violence to the actualities of politics. I shall discuss this at far greater length below, with regard to secession (which suggests that this protection is of far more of historical than contemporary importance).

E. Extradition and Alcohol

Perhaps it's worth mentioning the promise that states make to one another, in Article IV, to return certain fugitives who have fled from one state to another. Historically, the most important such commitment involved the compulsory return of *fugitive slaves,* but the additional promise to return "[a] Person charged in any State with Treason, Felony, or other Crime, who shall flee from Justice; and be found in another State" upon the "Demand" of the governor of the state from which the person fled remains significant. Although not so disruptive to social harmony as the so-called Fugitive Slave Clause, extradition can nonetheless generate controversy, either when the two states differ on the substantive merits of making particular conduct illegal or when there are deep suspicions on the part of one state about the fairness of the procedures that led to the charge in the other. This was most obviously the case in the past with regard to Northern suspicions of the procedural fairness of cases involving African Americans. Thus, from the perspective of the returning state, this may be viewed as a *burden* on state autonomy, a *price* of national union rather than a benefit (at least until that particular state demands extradition from another state that might have its own reluctance about following the Constitution's mandate).

There is also the 21st Amendment, which on its face seems to guarantee the states absolute control over the regulation of alcohol within their own territory, though some recent decisions of the Supreme Court have challenged the scope of state authority in this realm. But even if the ability of the state to regulate alcohol were complete, that would be small beer, as it were, when compared to such issues, for example, as education, the environment, or family law, none of which is explicitly reserved to the states and all of which are increasingly subject to regulation by institutions of the national government. Imagine, for example, a constitution that explicitly reserved such important subject matter areas or policy domains to the states for their own autonomous decisions. There are *no* such provisions in the Constitution. Still, there are implicit, even if decidedly nontextual, understandings about the nature of the balances struck between the national and state levels of government. How are those deals, whether explicit or implicit, to be maintained?

II. MAINTAINING THE DEAL(S)

A. *Trust, Mistrust, and Federalism*

Recall the basic argument that the most plausible empirical explanation of federalism is the presence of conflicting groups who do not sufficiently trust one another to enter into a *unitary* polity that, by definition, would arrogate all power to whatever political coalition could gain control of the national government. Whether this coalition might plausibly claim to represent a majority of the populace is irrelevant if one is a member of a vulnerable minority worried that the majority will be indifferent to your claims (or will become so as soon as that appears politically costless).

All federal constitutions exemplify deals among mistrustful groups, almost always organized in some significant measure along geographical lines, in which the groups first agree to give the central government some important powers but then agree as well to reserve other powers to the constituent subunits. Along the way, they might also agree to *limit* the powers of state governments in certain respects, but the easiest way to limit such powers is by establishing a unitary government able to pull the plug on decentralization gone wrong.

So what is the most obvious good that a central government provides? It is defense against external threats—the strength of unity. But at the same time, the new and more empowered national government must assure the subunits that its power won't be used to deprive the states of autonomy with regard to issues of vital interest to them. As the perception of outside threats wanes, so might one expect that the enthusiasm of the subunits for a strong national government might diminish as well. This tension was at the core of the call for a new constitutional convention in 1787.

Let's look for a moment at some important political realities of the 1780s that generated the call for reform and the strengthening of the national government. A fundamental reality is that the national government, such as it was, was nearly broke. Under the Articles of Confederation, the purportedly national government could only issue requisitions, basically pleading with the states to tax their own citizens and then convey the proceeds to the central government. Calvin Johnson has noted that the requisition of 1786, the last under the old regime, asked the states to remit approximately $3.8 million, of which a grand total of $663 was actually received.[5] As Alexander Hamilton argued in *Federalist* No. 15, what were intended to be solemn, even sacred, obligations of the states had been reduced to "mere recommendations," indeed "pompous petitions for charity."[6] The year 1786 surely represented the utter collapse of the requisition system, but it had never functioned well in the first place. In her book on federalism, Jenna Bednar includes an illuminating table noting that the thirteen original states paid a range between 64 percent (New York) and 0 percent (Georgia) of the requisitions asked of them. Massachusetts ponied up 42 percent, which ran well ahead of its neighbors—Rhode Island contributed 5 percent, New Hampshire 18 percent, and Connecticut 14 percent.[7] No national government can function under such conditions.

It was also the case, incidentally, that the government established by the Articles of Confederation could not raise its own armies. Here, too, it had to call on the constituent units to send troops (and the money to pay them). Fortunately for the cause of independence, here the states complied at a higher rate than with regard to taxes, but the figures still send decidedly mixed messages. With regard to the requisitions for troops between 1777 and 1783, New York was again in first place with a rate of 77 percent, and Connecticut was very narrowly behind at 75 percent. No other states, however, crossed the 70 percent threshold, and the two Carolinas tied for the low at 26 percent.

In many ways, the two most important parts of the new Constitution involved the explicit assignment of the power to tax (and spend) for the general welfare and to raise a national standing army that would not be dependent on the states. It should be clear that the new Constitution was defended not primarily as a device for protecting individual rights but as an instrument for creating a government that could adequately protect Americans against perceived dangers.

There were other, more internal, dangers as well. Many of the Philadelphia delegates defined as dangerous the passage of debtor relief legislation by Rhode Island and other states, which they believed would threaten the economy. This explains the presence of the Contract Clause in Article I, Section 10, designed explicitly to prevent such legislation, as well as other assignments of power to the national government as set out in Article I, Section 8. So what we see is a system that consists of a national government with new assignments of powers, some of them quite broad, and state governments that are at once *prohibited* from doing certain things (see Article I, Section 10) *and* at the same time promised that they will retain their traditional autonomy with regard to a variety of issues of special importance, even though almost none are spelled out. The only specific prohibitions on the national government in the original Constitution are found in Article I, Section 9; however important they might be, they scarcely speak to the central concerns of those suspicious of the new government.

The problem, then, is obvious: What will ensure that the multiple deals necessary to achieve a federation will, in fact, be kept? One can obviously write down specific promises, what Filippov and his colleagues call 'level one' protections of a federal bargain. But there are at least two problems. The first is that developments over time will diminish the importance of much that was written down and highlight the importance of other policy domains that were left unaddressed (and where no promises were made). The second scenario was classically stated by Madison in *Federalist* No. 48: "Will it be sufficient to mark with precision the boundaries of these departments in the constitution of the government, and to trust to these parchment barriers against the encroaching spirit of power?"[8] The answer is no. Part of the problem, as Madison (following John Locke) demonstrated in the remarkable passage in *Federalist* No. 37, involves the almost inevitable indeterminacies of language that leave the reader unclear as to the precise content of the promises. But even if the language *is* on occasion suitably precise, it still constitutes only a mere promise that could all too easily be broken when to do so was in the interest of one or another government.

Thus, even if the Constitution included more explicit reservations of state decisional autonomy than it does, these might turn out to be relatively unimportant. There are two great dangers: The first is encroachments by the national government. But one should be equally concerned about shirking by the states with regard to their own promises of subordination, even if not total, to the new national government. The breakdown of the requisition system is the best example of such shirking. Free riding is the favored term among economists to refer to those who enjoy the benefits of deals without actually paying for them. But, in addition to shirking, there is also the danger that states will adopt policies that impose costs on their neighbors in the absence of a sufficiently strong national government. What sort of arrangements can be counted on to preserve the *federal* system that exquisitely balances both state and national interests?

Filippov and his colleagues suggest the importance of supplementing the level-one promises spelled out in texts with level-two institutional structures. These could, of course, include a Senate appointed by state legislatures and a judiciary that, presumably, would be willing and able to monitor both state and national governments to make sure that they faithfully complying with the deals as originally made. A perhaps fatal problem with looking to the national judiciary as the umpire of federalism is that the appointment process—nomination by the President and confirmation by the Senate—seems more likely to guarantee the presence of judges with nationalist loyalties than state-oriented ones. Relying on state courts, of course, would generate the opposite problem.

B. So What Will Preserve State Autonomy, According to Madison? The Political Sociology of Federalist No. 46

There is also a body of 'level-three' *cultural and ideological values* that will reinforce—or call into question—the maintenance of federalism. They are at the heart of James Madison's argument in *Federalist* No. 46 as to why opponents of the new Constitution ought not be very concerned about the new national government—and its enhanced powers—that ratification of the Constitution entails. Devotees of state autonomy might be especially worried if they were aware, as we are, of what Madison and Hamilton, among others, had said in the secrecy of the Philadelphia Convention about the (ir)responsibility of state governments and the need for a strengthened national government. What could (and was) said in private and what could be articulated in public, though, might be quite different, especially once the task was no longer simply writing a constitution, but rather gaining its ratification in thirteen separate state conventions.

The *Federalist* essays are not abstract exercises in political theory presented to a seminar; they are, instead, propaganda, even if of an extraordinarily high quality, designed to justify the Constitution to those who might be doubtful. Among the most doubtful were strong proponents of what we would today call 'states' rights.' *Federalist* No. 46 is Madison's (and the *Federalist*'s) most extended response to the all-important question concerning why states should rely on the national government to preserve state autonomy. Madison insists, plausibly or not, that the new Constitution offers only a limited "sphere of jurisdiction" to the new national government. But his primary argument is one of *political sociology* and not one based on the raw text of the Constitution, which scarcely supports in any unequivocal way a reading of significantly limited national powers. Thus, he emphasizes that crucial reality that "the first and most natural attachment of the people will be to the governments of their respective states." That is, ordinary citizens will naturally identify with their state governments and view the national government as a fairly remote and possibly mistrusted entity. The image he sketches of the United States in *Federalist* No. 46 is almost like that one might apply to the United Nations, which no one would confuse with a world government—not only because the various states ratifying the United Nations Charter most certainly did not intend to give up much, if any, of their preexisting legal authority as sovereign states but also, and perhaps more fundamentally, because almost no one identifies him- or herself primarily as a 'citizen of the United Nations' instead of a citizen of one of the member states. One doesn't need complex social science evidence of this last point. One need only look into one's own consciousness and ask what constitutes a primary sociopolitical identity.

In effect, Madison seems to suggest that what is the case today for almost all of us with regard to the United Nations is substantially true for citizens of the United States, at least as of 1787. Perhaps he was reflecting his own knowledge of his home state of Virginia. Madison could not have known that some seventy-two years after publication of *Federalist* No. 46, Robert E. Lee, the West Point–trained general who had been offered command of the Union armies by Abraham Lincoln, would in effect vindicate his sociological observation by giving priority to his identity as a Virginian: Lee was obviously not alone in rejecting national in favor of state identity.

Indeed, Madison should have been unsurprised by the events of 1861 for yet another reason. He predicted, after all, that "ambitious encroachments of the federal government, on the authority of the state governments, would not excite the opposition [only] of a single state or of a few states." Instead, there would be a "general alarm" throughout the country, and "[e]very government would espouse the common cause." This indeed had happened in 1774–76, when what turned out to be a disastrously overreaching British policy toward the single colony of Massachusetts following the Boston Tea Party in fact incited a revolutionary response in all of the colonies.[9] This kind of universal response may have been lacking in 1860–61, but there was certainly enough to lead presumptively reasonable leaders to believe that they had legitimate grounds to withdraw from the Union and that they could make a go of it as an independent Confederate States of America. Finally, they were encouraged in this perception by the existence of state militias. It is these state militias that, in a very deep sense, comprise the most important level-two reinforcements of the federal bargain, at least from the perspective of the states, should the national government prove overbearing.

C. *Level-Two Institutional Protection*

1. *THE LEGISLATURE AND THE EXECUTIVE*

Before turning more fully to militias (and, ultimately, to secession), one might wonder why other level-two protections broke down by 1860. The Senate, given its mode of selection, might be expected to be attentive to general issues of state autonomy, but this might end up undercutting sufficient concern for preserving the Union itself. If federalism is explicable in part because of the importance of what might be termed 'deep diversity,' what happens if a particular issue that divides us, culturally and politically, also takes a strongly territorial dimension? This, of course, is slavery, which *did* ultimately become strongly defined along territorial lines. The compromise, rotten or otherwise, that created the Union in 1787 might have been maintained had there been no expansion of the United States. The five free states that would be created out of the territories that were the subject of the Northwest Ordinance—Ohio, Indiana, Michigan, Illinois, and Wisconsin—would be neatly counterbalanced by the southwest states that would shortly enter the Union as Kentucky, Tennessee, Alabama, and Mississippi. So long as population growth in the new United States was spread relatively equally between North and South, the federal bargain regarding slavery would almost certainly stick, for better and, for millions of people, distinctly for worse.

What changes this? The answer is the Louisiana Purchase, which, as historian William Freehling suggests, should really be called the Midwest Purchase.[10] The United States in 1803 more than doubled its territory, ranging from New Orleans, the point of the original negotiations, to what is now eastern Montana. Many new states would be created, and it mattered greatly whether they would be slave states or free states, especially in the Senate, with its principle of equal voting power among the states. Given that every single member of the House and Senate is elected *locally,* rather than in a truly national (or even regional) election, it is not surprising that Senators will represent the views of their constituents, who may be disinclined to compromise with other states and regions whom they view as engaging in immoral conduct. Thus, we see the increasing polarization of views in both the Senate and the House throughout the 1850s, when Senators became ever more dedicated to pro- or antislavery positions. What might be called a level-three culture of "bi-sectional accommodation" was breaking down.[11] Abolitionists were never more than a minority, but the new Republican Party, created out of the wreckage of the Whigs, did define slavery as one of the "twin relics of barbarism" and pledged to prevent any further expansion into the territories, which would assure that any future states would be admitted as free states.[12]

Just as important, patterns of population growth ended up favoring the free part of the United States, with consequences for the House of Representatives. To be sure, the slave states were still far better off than they might otherwise be, because of the three-fifths compromise, but they were increasingly nervous about what political scientists would call the self-maintaining features of the Constitution. The Electoral College had worked wonderfully, overall, to protect the interests of what was often called 'the slavocracy;' but that came to a dramatic end in 1860, when Abraham Lincoln gained the White House with a majority of electoral votes while winning less than 40 percent of the popular vote (and, as one might predict, gaining no electoral votes in any of the fifteen slave states, eleven of which would attempt to secede).

2. *WHAT ABOUT COURTS?*

Let's look once more at courts and their adequacy to maintain the federal bargain. As almost all political scientists recognize, the presence of judicial review is strongly correlated with federalism, for courts are assigned the role of the impartial third party who can adjudicate disputes between the national government and the states when they accuse each other of failing to implement the terms of the bargain. But this requires one to view the courts as genuinely impartial and worthy of trust.

Consider one of the most famous episodes in the history of the early United States, the Federalist enactment of the Alien and Sedition Acts that made it a crime, among other things, to criticize the President of the United States. (Interestingly enough, it was not a crime to criticize the Vice President, who just happened to be the Federalists' adversary Thomas Jefferson.) Jeffersonians uniformly thought that the Sedition Act was an encroachment by the national government. After all, the 1st Amendment provided that Congress shall make no law abridging freedom of speech.

Jefferson's response was to float the idea of the nullification by states of national legislation that they viewed as violating the federalist bargain. Madison was more moderate. The years 1798 and 1799 saw the passage by the Kentucky and Virginia legislatures of resolutions challenging the act, with accompanying justificatory reports written by Jefferson and Madison. Both states relied, among other things, on the compact theory of Union, which allowed the compacting states, the people of whom were represented in their own state legislatures, to declare the legislation offensive to the Constitution and, for proponents of nullification like Jefferson, null and void.

Why not rely on courts to make the definitive judgments about constitutionality? Madison offered his answer in the *Virginia Report* defending the resolution of 1798. First, it is possible that there "may be instances of usurped power, which the forms of the Constitution would never draw within the control of the judicial department." That is, if courts have only *limited* jurisdiction, then by definition there will be some issues that will not come before them even if they raise deep questions about constitutional fidelity. But Madison also writes of the impropriety of raising "the decision of the judiciary . . . above the authority of the sovereign parties to the Constitution"—that is, the states themselves. "[T]he decisions of the other departments must be equally authoritative and final with the decisions of that department." This is especially important with regard to

> those great and extraordinary cases, in which all the forms of the Constitution may prove ineffectual against infractions dangerous to the essential rights of the parties to it. The [Virginia] resolution supposes that dangerous powers, not delegated, may not only be usurped and executed by the other departments, but that the judicial department also may exercise or sanction dangerous powers beyond the grant of the Constitution; and, consequently, that the ultimate right of the parties to the Constitution, to judge whether the compact has been dangerously violated, must extend to violations by one delegated authority, as well as by another; by the judiciary, as well as by the executive, or the legislature.[13]

And, frankly, why should one put such faith in a judiciary whose members are appointed (and paid) by the national government? The system, Madison is suggesting, does not justify the level of trust that some would place in it. Similar arguments, whether or not justified by close analysis of Madison's text, would be made much more strongly, of course, by John C. Calhoun and ultimately by Jefferson Davis.

3. AUTONOMY AND MILITIAS

So if national institutions like the legislature and the courts lose their luster with regard to keeping to the federal bargain of limited government, what is next? One ominous response is to threaten withdrawal from the federation itself, by secession. Before examining the constitutional arguments with regard to any such claimed right, we should look at another level-two autonomy right found in the amended Constitution, which is the 2nd Amendment and its apparent guarantee (at least) to each state to have its own militia.

This is no small matter, even if debates about the right to bear arms today focus more on alleged individual rights. Why might a state *want* to have its own militia? A militia would be useful in quelling certain kinds of local troublemakers or providing order in a city ravaged by a hurricane. Indeed, one historical analysis of the origins of the 2nd Amendment emphasizes the relevance of slave patrols in the South. But another potential use for a militia might be defending a state against what is perceived as the tyranny of the national government. Consider in this context the fact that the governors of both Pennsylvania and Virginia threatened to call out their state militias and send them to Washington if the Federalists didn't acquiesce to the election of Thomas Jefferson to the presidency in 1800 (as they finally did on the thirty-sixth ballot of the House of Representatives within three weeks of the March 4, 1801 inauguration day).

The German sociologist Max Weber famously defined the state, among other things, as possessing a monopoly over the legitimate use of violence. It's easy enough to figure out what this means, analytically, if one is referring to a unitary government, defined as one with a clearly supreme authority over any and all territorial subunits (and individual citizens). But it is considerably more difficult to figure out the meaning if we refer to truly *federal* systems. Given the predictable difficulty, within any federal systems, of securing the bargain, especially with regard to preventing encroachments by the national government, isn't it reasonable for states to believe that having the ability to maintain armies, called militias, might be useful in warding off certain kinds of attacks on their residual sovereignty? To be sure, the Constitution is ambiguous on what might be termed the Weberian argument. Thus Article I, Section 10, explicitly prohibits a "State, without the Consent of Congress," from "keep[ing] Troops, or Ships of War, in time of Peace." Yet that same section in fact empowers states to "engage in War" if suffering not only "actual invas[ion]" but also "such imminent Danger as will not admit of delay." Perhaps one should view Congress's willingness to propose what became the 2nd Amendment—it was, numerically, originally the 4th Amendment, but the first two failed of ratification at the time—as implicit consent that the states should keep troops.

Consider very carefully a paragraph in *Federalist* No. 46, written by Madison, on the importance of an armed citizenry and the ultimate protection that it offers against even a "federal government [that] may previously accumulate a military force for the projects of ambition." Madison asserts that "[t]he highest number to which, according to the best computation, a standing army can be carried in any country," would lead to a national army of no more "than twenty-five or thirty thousand men. To these would be opposed a militia amounting to near half a million of citizens with arms in their hands, officered by men chosen from among themselves, fighting for their common liberties, and united and conducted by governments possessing their affections and confidence." He evokes "the last successful resistance of this country against the British arms" as evidence of the power of a citizen-militia. So the ultimate second-level defenses are, in effect, "the advantage of being armed, which the Americans possess over the people of almost every other nation [and] the existence of subordinate governments, to which the people are attached." Both assure that the "free and gallant citizens of America" are "able to defend the rights of which they would be in actual possession."[14]

There is, incidentally, a side argument as to whether this should be read as requiring that any such militia be firmly in the hands of the states or, instead, under more communal control. After all, if one can imagine a potentially oppressive national government that might need disciplining by the states, one might also imagine state governments that might profit from a similar show of force by an aroused citizenry. And Madison in *Federalist* No. 10 had made the classic argument as to why one might, as a member of a vulnerable minority, feel greater concern at the state than at the national level. These are not pleasant questions to contemplate. But it is a fundamental mistake to view constitutionalism as unconnected with the means of violence. After all, the debate about the President's power as Commander in Chief is ultimately a debate about who has the power to inflict violence and even death (and to accept the reality of those events with regard to those defending the United States).

So let me direct the following question to you: Imagine that you are consulting with *any* of the various groups in Iraq, Afghanistan, or Libya regarding the creation of a suitable constitution for those ethnically and religiously divided countries. Would you advise your clients to hand over their arms and disband their militias and, therefore, place their trust in the new central government that the constitution is creating? Or, on the contrary, would you demand their right to keep and bear arms, at least until enough verification had taken place, possibly over many years, to engender sufficient trust in a Weberian state? Does whatever answer you give for those three decidedly unhappy countries have any implications at all for the responses you might make with regard to the modern United States or any other countries you might think of?

Consider in this context the comments of Sharron Angle, the 2010 Republican candidate for the Senate in Nevada:

> Our Founding Fathers, they put that Second Amendment in there for a good reason, and that was for the people to protect themselves against a tyrannical

> government. In fact, Thomas Jefferson said it's good for a country to have a revolution every 20 years. I hope that's not where we're going, but you know, if this Congress keeps going the way it is, people are really looking toward those Second Amendment remedies."[15]

It is unlikely that many readers of this book agree with Ms. Angle's particular assessment of contemporary American politics and her specific reasons for sharing the widespread dissatisfaction with the direction the country is going.[16] But she makes an important point about the provenance of the 2nd Amendment. If one *did* agree with her about the tyrannical nature of the national government, would it be frivolous to suggest that a given state, committed to the importance of a nontyrannical view of politics, might mobilize itself against the centralized oppression? One might well wonder if there is a truly shared baseline for determining what is tyrannical or nontyrannical, but that question raises yet other problems in trying to assess *any* political institutions for their propensity to achieve the public good.

4. *SECESSION*

And so (at last) we come to secession and its constitutional status. Is it crystal clear what the United States Constitution permits or prohibits with regard to this most vital of all issues? There is, after all, no hard-and-fast piece of text that provides a yea-or-nay answer to the question, "Do states in the United States have a constitutional right of secession?" Is this lack of specificity a bug or a feature? That is, *should* the Constitution have explicitly addressed the potential tension between the aspiration to create a "more perfect Union" consisting of both sovereign states and a national government, on the one hand, and the empirical possibility, on the other, that the national government would not honor the rights reserved to the states? Cass Sunstein argues that a well-drafted federal constitution should *never* legitimize secession; one assumes that he would endorse the explicit prohibition of secession, even if, perchance, this makes it marginally less likely that the parties will agree to a constitution in the first place.[17] Legitimate secession, by definition, allows what economist Albert Hirschman famously labeled the option of exit from a trying political situation, as against remaining and exercising voice instead.[18] One reason to contemplate exit, however, whether from a marriage or from a state, is because one feels totally ignored; even if one is allowed, as a formal matter, to speak, no one genuinely listens or, even more to the point, responds adequately to one's complaints.

On February 11, 1861, while travelling from Springfield, Illinois, to his inauguration, Lincoln spoke to an audience in Indianapolis and derided the secessionist argument in the following way: "In their view, the Union, as a family relation, would not be anything like a regular marriage at all, but only as a sort of free-love arrangement [laughter] to be maintained on what that sect calls passionate attraction [continued laughter]."[19] Let me suggest, though, that this is no laughing matter or perhaps is best described as gallows humor. After all, how many of us, in the twenty-first century, have a view of 'regular marriage' that precludes divorce, particularly if 'passionate attraction' has disappeared, replaced by what an aggrieved spouse views as exploitation or worse? It is undoubtedly better if both sides agree to what is sometimes referred to as an amicable divorce. But what if one of them does not, whether because still hopelessly attached to the marriage or out of sheer malice? At that point, would we support what might be termed 'unilateral secession' from the marriage, based on the logic of individual consent and the illegitimacy of the state's forcing a continuing relationship upon someone who might even view such forced continuation as akin to involuntary servitude or slavery?

A different argument was presented in the concluding paragraph of James Buchanan's final State of the Union message to Congress in December 1860. The hapless Buchanan agreed with Lincoln that secession was illegal, but he believed as well that the national government was without practical power to prevent it, beyond pleading with the states in question not to do it:

> The fact is that our Union rests upon public opinion, and can never be cemented by the blood of its citizens shed in civil war. If it can not live in the affections of the people, it must one day perish. Congress possesses many means of preserving it by conciliation, but the sword was not placed in their hand to preserve it by force.[20]

March 4, 1861, at long last brought Abraham Lincoln to the White House. Much of the speech was conciliatory, at least by his lights. Devoted to maintaining the Union, he emphasized his willingness to address Southern concerns by supporting the so-called Corwin Amendment, strongly supported by outgoing President Buchanan and, in the Senate, by New York Senator William Seward (who would become Lincoln's Secretary of State). The Corwin Amendment was in fact passed by the Congress and sent to the states for ratification. It stated, "No amendment shall ever be made to the Constitution which will authorize or give to Congress power to abolish or interfere, within any State, with the domestic institutions thereof."[21] If ratified, ironically, it would have become the 13th Amendment. Lincoln could endorse it precisely because it protected slavery in *already existing* states, whose legitimacy he never challenged. Southern states found it inadequate because it protected *only* slavery in existing states and said nothing about what both sides deemed the truly important issue: the extension of slavery into the territories. Ohio, Maryland, and Illinois ratified the Corwin Amendment, but it was obviously made moot by subsequent developments.

The rest of the speech was less conciliatory, for it rejected any theory that would countenance secession:

> I hold, that in contemplation of universal law, and of the Constitution, the Union of these States is perpetual. Perpetuity is implied, if not expressed, in the fundamental law of all national governments. It is safe to assert that no government proper, ever had a provision in its organic law for its own termination. . . .
>
> [W]e find the proposition that, in legal contemplation, the Union is perpetual, confirmed by the history of the Union itself. The Union is much older than the Constitution. It was formed in fact, by the Articles of Association in 1774. It was matured and continued by the Declaration of Independence in 1776. It was further matured and the faith of all the then thirteen States expressly plighted and engaged that it should be perpetual, by the Articles of Confederation in 1778. And finally, in 1787, one of the declared objects for ordaining and establishing the Constitution, was "to form a more perfect union." But if destruction of the Union, by one, or by a part only, of the States, be lawfully possible, the Union is less perfect than before the Constitution, having lost the vital element of perpetuity. . . .
>
> I therefore consider that, in view of the Constitution and the laws, the Union is unbroken; and, to the extent of my ability, I shall take care, as the Constitution itself expressly enjoins upon me, that the laws of the Union be faithfully executed in all the States.[22]

"And," as he noted in his *Second Inaugural*, "the war came."

Laurence Tribe, in his monumental, albeit uncompleted, treatise on American constitutional law, supported Lincoln: The *First Inaugural*, wrote Tribe, is "the 'definitive articulation' of the principle that 'the Constitution forbids secession from the Union by any state.'"[23] It is with some trepidation that I disagree with Professor Tribe—and, therefore, with Lincoln himself. It is not that I think that Lincoln is wrong; rather, in place of a convincing argument, I see a series of question-begging and more than a bit tendentious arguments that ultimately persuade only those who wish to be persuaded in the first place. The same is true, incidentally, with regard to those arguments proffered by Judah Benjamin, Jefferson Davis, and other proponents of secession. The point is precisely that the

Constitution does not speak with sufficient clarity that one can express complete confidence as to the one true meaning of the Constitution. Professional techniques of constitutional interpretation simply do not generate a Dworkinian right answer to this most primal controversy about the nature of the American Union. Part of the reason for my skepticism is that it is not clear what constitutes placing the Constitution in its 'most attractive light,' as required by Dworkinian method. There is much to be said for perpetual union as a normative ideal—it is, after all, the promise made in every traditional marriage ceremony—but there is also at least as much to be said for recognizing the right to self-determination of constituent units that no longer wish to be affiliated with that union, as reflected in the social fact that we allow the dissolution of marriages that do not live up to even one party's expectations.

This book is being published during the commemoration of the sesquicentennial of the war that began in 1861 and killed, according to most recent estimates, 750,000 Americans in the next four years. Lincoln obviously did not start the war, but his decision to respond to the attack on Fort Sumter was a cause-in-fact of the conflagration. Was it worth it? If so, is it justified by the simple preservation of the Union against the desire of eleven states to go their own way, as had the then-British colonies in 1776, or must one emphasize the importance of eradicating slavery? If it is the latter that justifies the war and its costs, though, then what does that suggest about accepting the particular form of American federalism that was proposed and ratified in 1787? Were antislavery Anti-Federalists, who counseled rejection of the Constitution, correct after all (not to mention William Lloyd Garrison, who advocated secession under the slogan "No Union with Slaveholders")?

III. CONCLUSION

Federalism is an unusually complex concept; there is no universally accepted definition of the term. Moreover, and perhaps more importantly, there is no easy way to determine the relationship between federalism, however defined, and political values. The German political scientist Franz Neumann wrote in 1955 a notable article on the relationship between federalism and freedom, in which he ultimately concluded 'it all depends.' Thus, he wrote, it "seems impossible to attribute to federalism, as such, a value; or to assert that the federal state—as contrasted to the unitary state—enhances political and civil freedom by dividing power among autonomous territorial subdivisions. . . . There are no values that inhere in federalism as such, and federalism cannot be defended successfully on the grounds that the inevitable tendency of a unitary state is toward political repression."[24] Perhaps the key word is 'inevitable.' Neumann certainly does not denounce federalism and proclaim that it has its own inevitable tendencies, whether fortunate or unfortunate. In some countries, among them the United States, federalism, at least historically, is impossible to disengage from slavery and racism. Thus, William Riker, an eminent political scientist, once declared that "if in the United States one disapproves of racism, one should disapprove of federalism."[25] On the other hand, those who analogize discrimination against gays and lesbians to racism can point to the lead taken by a number of states, including New York, in legalizing same-sex marriage.

Perhaps one can say the same thing about secession—that its appeal or consequences are indeterminate and contingent on particular facts. It is easy enough to presume that all readers of this book opposed Southern secessionists who wanted to create an independent Confederate States of America based on the legitimacy of a thoroughly racialized conception of chattel slavery. But I also presume that everyone supports the secessionists of 1776 who rejected their loyalties to King George and the British Empire in the name of national independence. Moving forward to the present, one can compare and contrast secessionist episodes in, among others, the former countries of Yugoslavia or Czechoslovakia or the now smaller countries of Pakistan or Sudan.

Even within the United States, notice was taken of Texas Governor Rick Perry's suggestion in 2010 that Texas, now the second-largest state (in population) in the Union, might be advised to think of secession should the national government continue, from Perry's perspective, to engage in oppressive overreach. So the concluding thought experiment for those readers who are Americans is to consider your own reaction should Texas in fact pass a contemporary ordinance of secession. Would you demand that the President call out the troops and arrest the traitors—and shoot to kill any members of the Texas militia who might attempt to defend the revived Lone Star Republic—or instead demand only that negotiations be entered into on what might constitute fair terms of dissolution, given, for example, the extensive bases of the U.S. armed forces that dot the Texas landscape? Is Texas necessarily worth fighting for simply because it chose to enter the Union in 1845, even if the state, through some process—say, a statewide referendum—declared that it wished to return to its former juridical condition? And, finally, is your decision based on abstractions about the nature of perpetual Union or, rather, on what you might actually think about Texas and the degree to which it contributes to achieving what you regard as the great purposes of the Union?

NOTES

1. Sanford V. Levinson, *Is Secession the Achilles Heel of "'Strong'" Federalism?, in* Patterns of Regionalism and Federalism 207–28 (Jorg Fedtke & Basil Markesinis eds., 2006).

2. Alfred Stepan, *Federalism and Democracy: Beyond the U.S. Model, in* Theories of Federalism 255, 257–58 (Dimitrios Karmis & Wayne Norman eds., 2005).

3. The standard citation for this notion is John Marshall's opinion in McCulloch v. Maryland, 17 U.S. 316, 405 (1819): "The Government is acknowledged by all to be one of enumerated powers." See also Chief Justice Rehnquist's opinion for the Court in U.S. v. Lopez, 514 U.S. 549, 562 (1995): "We start with first principles. The Constitution creates a Federal Government of enumerated powers. See U. S. Const., Art. I, §8. As James Madison wrote, '[t]he powers delegated by the proposed Constitution to the federal government are few and defined.' The Federalist No. 45, pp. 292–293 (C. Rossiter ed. 1961)." Chief Justice Roberts recently cited what he calls Marshall's "acknowledgment" in National Federation of Independent Business v. Sibelius (2012) (slip opinion, p. 2).

4. Mikhail Filippov, Peter C. Ordeshook & Olga Shvetsova, Designing Federalism 125–26 (2004).

5. Calvin Johnson, Righteous Anger at the Wicked States 1 (2005).

6. The Federalist No. 15 (Alexander Hamilton).

7. Jenna Bednar, The Robust Federation 64 (2009).

8. The Federalist No. 48 (James Madison).

9. *See, e.g.,* T. H. Breen, American Insurgents, American Patriots (2010).

10. William Freeling, *The Louisiana Purchase and the Coming of the Civil War, in* The Louisiana Purchase and American Expansion, 1803–1898, at 69 (Sanford Levinson & Bartholemew Sparrow, eds., 2004).

11. *See, especially,* Mark A. Graber, *Dred Scott* and the Problem of Constitutional Evil (2006).

12. See, e.g., http://www.ushistory.org/gop/convention_1856republicanplatform.htm.

13. See (James Madison) Virginia Resolution of 1799, *available at* http://www.constitution.org/rf/vr_1799.htm.

14. The Federalist No. 46 (James Madison).

15. Anjeanette Damon & David McGrath Schwartz, *Nev. Senate Hopeful Sharron Angle Talks of Armed Revolt,* Las Vegas Sun, June 17, 2010, *available at* http://www.scrippsnews.com/content/nev-senate-hopeful-sharron-angle-talks-armed-revolt.

16. A July 2011 Gallup poll indicated that only 16 percent of their sample was satisfied with "the way things were going in the United States." Stephanie Samuel, *Americans' Satisfaction with Country's Direction at 2-Year Low,* July 14, 2011, *available at* http://www.christianpost.com/news/americans-satisfaction-with-countrys-direction-at-2-year-low-52316/.

17. Cass Sunstein, *What Should Constitutions Say? Secession and Beyond, in* Designing Democracy 95 (2001).

18. Albert Hirschman, Exit, Voice, and Loyalty (1970).

19. 4 Collected Works of Abraham Lincoln 195, *available at* http://quod.lib.umich.edu/l/lincoln/lincoln4/1:313.1?rgn=div2;view=fulltext.

20. James Buchanan, Message to Congress, December 3, 1860, *available at* http://www.infoplease.com/t/hist/state-of-the-union/72.html.

21. See Peter Suber, The Paradox of Self-Amendment, appendix one, *available at* http://www.earlham.edu/~peters/writing/psa/app1.htm. See also Mark Brandon, Free in the World 171 (1998).

22. Abraham Lincoln, First Inaugural Address, *available at* http://avalon.law.yale.edu/19th_century/lincoln1.asp.

23. Laurence Tribe, American Constitutional Law 32 (3rd ed. 2000).

24. Franz L. Neumann, "*Federalism and Freedom: A Critique,*" *in* Karmis and Norman, *supra* note 2, at 212, 217.

25. William Riker, Federalism: Origin, Operation, Significance 4 (1964), quoted in Daniel Halberstam, *Federalism: A Critical Guide Daniel Halberstam* (U of Michigan Public Law Working Paper No. 251), *available at* http://papers.ssrn.com/sol3/papers.cfm?abstract_id=1924939.

11 Remembering Our Second Revolution

Sesquicentennial Reflections on Civil War Historiography

Norman W. Spaulding, Stanford University Law School

"We do not repeat because we repress, we repress because we repeat."
—Gilles Deluze, Difference and Repetition

I. THE SESQUICENTENNIAL AT FORT SUMTER NATIONAL MONUMENT

Slavery and secession rest in uneasy union at the Fort Sumter National Monument. This remains true even after an elaborate 'interpretive' renovation by the National Park Service (NPS) in preparation for the sesquicentennial commemoration of the Civil War in 2011. The alterations were made to meet Congress's demand that Civil War battlefields "recognize and include in all of their public displays and multimedia educational presentations the unique role that the institution of slavery played in causing the Civil War."[1] The explicit inclusion of slavery represented a substantial deviation from past practice. When the NPS published its first master plan for Fort Sumter before the centennial of the war, "the fort's interpretive program was based on the 1860 election of President Abraham Lincoln, the secession of South Carolina, and the subsequent movement of Major Robert Anderson from Fort Moultrie to Fort Sumter. The major focus was on the initial Confederate attack of 1861 and the federal bombardments of 1863 and 1864, known as the siege of Charleston."[2] The relationship between slavery, secession, and the war appeared nowhere until 1995 when a "small exhibit" was installed inside the fort.[3]

The absence of attention to slavery at Fort Sumter and other Civil War battlefields had been quite intentional up to that point. As the NPS's chief historian describes:

> [T]he NPS recognized early the sensitivity among southerners of a federal agency interpreting the Civil War in the South. In the 1930s, the National Park Service created an outside review process so that all interpretive scripts for Civil War battlefields in Virginia were reviewed by Virginia's state historian, H. J. Eckenrode, and Douglas Southall Freeman, Robert E. Lee's reverential biographer. . . . NPS managers wanted to ensure that the causes of the war, especially issues related to slavery, remained outside battlefield interpretive programs. . . . Between 1933, when Franklin D. Roosevelt transferred the Civil War battlefields from the War Department to the Department of the Interior, and the late 1990s, the NPS avoided all mention of the causes of the war in its exhibits, films, and publications. Eighty years after the 50th reunion at Gettysburg in 1913, the agency still adhered to Governor William Mann's admonition that "we came here, I say, not to discuss what caused the war of 1861–1865, but to talk over the events of the battle here as man to man."[4]

The effect of this approach to interpretive programs, Michael Kammen has observed, was "to extract a mythic Confederate moral victory from the facts of defeat, with histrionics and warped history as minor costs."[5]

Attachment to the use of battlefield memorials to prompt both nostalgia for Southern resistance and what Nina Silber has called "patriotic reflection" on the war as a sentimental foundation for the "romance of reunion," still runs deep.[6] As late as 2000, news of the interpretive renovations provoked "incendiary" accusations that the NPS planned to "'demoniz[e] and slander[]' the South with its 'new' interpretation of the war."[7] The NPS nevertheless transitioned from a "slice of time commemorative experience" showcasing martial valor to a "holistic interpretation" that made slavery a part of the "compelling story" of each memorial.[8]

But as a visit to Fort Sumter today makes painfully clear, attempting to draw slavery into a 'holistic' narrative of secession and war has proved nearly as vexing as past efforts to leave it out. The bronze marker at the entrance to Liberty Square—the new garden and visitor education center erected at the dock for the ferry from Charleston to Fort Sumter—rather ambiguously reassures visitors that "'We are not accountable for decisions made by those who came before.'"[9]

The marker gives no indication whether it is the decisions of Abraham Lincoln, Charles Sumner, Jefferson Davis, John Calhoun, or Charles Pinckney for which we are not accountable. But if we are not accountable for any of their decisions, what is there to commemorate at Fort Sumter? Like all national memorials, the site is a drawing to account before the bar of collective memory. National Parks tend to seduce more than menace visitors with the past,[10] but sites marking the conjunction of slavery in democratic society and fratricidal violence on the scale of the Civil War can scarcely avoid either effect.

Perhaps park historians wanted visitors to be at liberty to identify for themselves the decisions and decision makers for whom they refuse to feel accountable as they enter the place where the war began. Hence the name Liberty Square. Additional bronze markers in the gardens of the square leading to the visitor education center offer inspiring quotations from people who have made "significant contributions to expanding the cause of liberty" (including Benjamin Franklin, Sojourner Truth, Harriet Tubman, W. E. B. Du Bois, Pearl S. Buck, and Albert Einstein). "Each marker," we are instructed, "invites the visitor to reflect on the meanings of liberty."[11] And each, in its own way, testifies rather seductively to the eventual success of what the introductory marker states is the "great experiment" upon which "this nation embarked . . . based on the self-evident truth that 'all men are created equal.'"[12]

But the markers and the reflections of none too few visitors are surely shadowed by the obviously missing defenders of alternative ideas of liberty that flourished in South Carolina—figures such as Robert Barnwell Rhett (owner of the *Charleston Mercury*, lawyer, United States Senator, and "incessant drum major[] of secession"[13] who helped split the Democratic party along sectional lines and draft the Constitution of the Confederate States of America), Edmund Ruffin (a farmer, slaveholder, and notorious Virginia Fire-Eater who aided the initial attack on Fort Sumter and committed suicide when the South lost the war),[14] Christopher Memminger (the wealthy Charleston lawyer, slaveholder, drafter of the "Declaration of the Immediate Causes Which Induce and Justify the Secession of South Carolina from the Federal Union," and delegate to the provisional congress that formed the Confederate States of America),[15] and Wade Hampton (the South Carolina plantation owner, Lieutenant General in the Confederate cavalry, and 'Redeemer' who became governor of the state after the war and helped bring an end to Reconstruction).[16]

Inside the visitor education center, an exhibit traces the causes of the Civil War in six panels entitled "Colonial Roots of the Conflict," "Ambiguities of the

Constitution," "Antebellum United States," "Charleston in 1860," "South Carolina Declares its Independence," and "Fort Sumter: Countdown to Conflict."[17] The history of slavery begins to emerge here, and with it the decisions for which visitors are apparently not to be held accountable. As the introductory text of the exhibit portentously states:

> When the Civil War finally exploded in Charleston Harbor, it was the result of a half century of growing sectionalism. Escalating crises over property rights, human rights, states' rights and constitutional rights divided the country as it expanded westward. Underlying all the economic, social and political rhetoric was the volatile question of slavery. Because its economic life had long depended on enslaved labor, South Carolina was the first state to secede when this way of life was threatened.[18]

The proposition that South Carolina's 'way of life' was actually threatened by Lincoln's election is, of course, contested. Compare, for instance, Henry Adams's characterization of the events leading to secession in late 1860: "After a long and bitter contest the slave power was for the first time defeated, and deprived, not of its legitimate power, not of its privileges as originally granted in the Constitution, but of its control of the Government; and suddenly in the fury of its unbridled license, it raised its hand to destroy that Government."[19] The exhibit text recognizes none of this interpretive dissonance regarding causation and accountability. Yet the causes of the war and the rather persistent 'volatility' of the question of slavery—well beyond emancipation and Appomattox—lie precisely in the shadows of doubt Adams's account casts over the 'threat' disunionists perceived.

The challenges of interpretive equanimity diminish significantly once visitors disembark from the ferry at Fort Sumter. The exhibits there concentrate almost exclusively on political events in the North and South leading up to secession and details of the military clashes in Charleston Harbor during the war. Visitors are immersed in the minutiae of military tactics, from the initial assault upon and surrender of the fort to Confederate forces in the spring of 1861 to the series of Union bombardments that reduced the fort to ruins three years later.

Accounts of heroic Confederate efforts to hold the fort set against accounts of equally heroic Union attempts to retake it play up the sentimental and symbolic importance of the fort as a site of mutually exchanged sacrifice and valiant Southern resistance. One section entitled "The Siege Becomes a Stalemate" includes an oil painting by Conrad Wise Chapman of the Confederate flag flying in a stiff breeze over the ruins of Fort Sumter captioned by a defiant statement of the beloved Confederate General P. G. T. Beauregard in the midst of a sustained Union bombardment in the late summer of 1863: "Sumter is now a noble mass of ruins, over which still float our colors. . . . Two hundred infantry garrison the ruins to defend them to [the] last extremity."[20] The official video of the sesquicentennial commemoration on April 12, 2011, opens with the sound of a cannon and then cuts to black and white teenage boys being organized into military ranks by a park ranger who enlists them in a miniature reenactment. The boys are quite literally drawn to account: they are handed toy rifles, informed that they are now in "the Army of 1860" where "a lot of things are going down . . . political issues, social strife throughout the country," and instructed: "You are going to have to make a decision . . . about what side you are going to fight for."[21]

Lavishing attention on tactics, the consequences of technological advances in weaponry, martial valor, and the personal experience of war neutralizes, even as it draws into sanguinary relief, the depth and complexity of the social, economic, and legal conflict suggested by the exhibit at the visitor education center. Visitors are swept into a "personal journey of historical inquiry"[22] in the subject position of soldiers at the fort—dead soldiers, to be precise—for whom the drama, urgency, and terror of the experience of siege reduce history to chronicles of survival, chance, courage, tactical brilliance, folly, and disappointment. It is the historical consciousness of emergency, of transubstantiation, and of martyrdom in which past and present fuse in crescendos of real and imagined violence. Causation and just cause become simultaneously overwhelming and utterly irrelevant.

If the city prevails in locating a memorial to Martin Luther King, Jr., in Liberty Square, where the ferry returns visitors to Charleston, the transition to holistic interpretation will be complete.[23] Confrontation with slavery will occur on terms that carefully circumscribe both history and memory of the institution—entrance to the visitor education center's panels on slavery via Liberty Square, a ferry ride to the celebration of martial valor at the fort, and an exit past a synecdoche for the ostensible success of the second Reconstruction. The difficulty with this brand of holism is not simply that the historical representation of slavery as a cause of the Civil War renders it a mere "*preface* to . . . the military interpretation of the battlefields."[24] That is, after all, precisely how the Park Service ultimately decided to meet its new congressional mandate.[25] Nor is the difficulty merely that the celebration of martial valor "extracts a mythic Confederate moral victory from the fact of defeat."[26]

The victory is more than moral, and as much national as Confederate. In the organization of space at the monument, slavery and secession are drawn together on terms that provide for their ultimate dissociation. Slavery is historically fixed at the visitor education center, archived as a cause of the war in a past for which no one is accountable. And it is surrounded—indeed, antiseptically quarantined—by assurances of the inexorable progress of freedom in Liberty Square. Secession, the audacity of it, its politics and the terrible grandeur of its martial consequences, by contrast, are reproduced in the fort as innocent (indeed, noble) objects of collective memory that only briefly interrupted, if they did not in fact elevate, the trajectory of the 'great experiment' launched by the nation in 1776. Real and imagined sesquicentennial reenactments at Fort Sumter and other battlefields thus provide a picturesque, sentimental veneer for secession, one that deflects interrogation of the darker elements of its antebellum and postbellum histories even as an elaborate display is made of the moment of secession itself. And once slavery is dissociated from secession in this way, it can be dissociated from the practices of terrorism and white supremacy that followed secession and war in the form of resistance to Reconstruction, as well as from the principles of federalism in which the antebellum doctrine of states' rights now functions to circumscribe the Reconstruction Amendments. Slavery appears a merely inconvenient integument of the doctrine of states' rights, which needs only to be shed for "loyal[ty] to the ideals and dreams of Our Federalism" to be acquitted and to flourish.[27]

Fundamentally, holism errs by assuming that drawing the history of slavery into Civil War battlefields underscores rather than effaces the relationship of slavery to secession and war. But propinquity can confirm difference as well as identity. If prior interpretive approaches suppressed the contradictions and democratic paradoxes presented by slavery and secession, the conceit of holism is that it is possible to resolve these contradictions and paradoxes—that the events, their antecedents, and their implications can be framed in a new set of narratives that recognize the fact of slavery without drawing the trajectory of our 'great experiment' into doubt. The error and conceit belong not just to the Park Service, nor to other public institutions engaged in 'official' memory work, such as the Supreme Court (where an antebellum federalism revival is currently in full swing on terms that mirror the interpretive renovations at Fort Sumter[28]), but to even the most searching professional histories of secession.

II. REVISIONISM, POSTREVISIONISM, AND REALISM IN CIVIL WAR HISTORIOGRAPHY

It is no accident that history is implicated with law and collective memory in this way. To begin with, the Park Service drew on the work of professional historians in planning its interpretive renovations in much the same way as law draws upon history. It sought to capitalize upon ostensibly detached expertise not merely for insight but for the imprimatur expert authority can provide against charges of improvisation and interpretive bias. But law, history, and memory are intertwined at an even more elemental level. "Only in a State cognizant of laws," wrote Hegel in his *Lectures on the Philosophy of History*, "can distinct transactions take place, accompanied by such a clear consciousness of them as supplies the ability and suggests the necessity of an enduring record. . . . [I]t is the State which first presents subject-matter that is not only adapted to the prose of History, but involves the production of history in the very progress of its own being."[29] There is, as I have elsewhere argued, "[n]o history without law."[30]

"Before the Civil War," Robert Penn Warren reminds us, "we had no history in the deepest and most inward sense. . . . [T]he Revolution did not create a nation except on paper; and too often in the following years the vision of the Founding Fathers . . . became merely a daydream of easy and automatic victories. . . . There was little awareness of the cost of having a history."[31] That cost "became a reality, and we became a nation, only with the Civil War."[32] Thus, more than any other period of American history—including the Founding—the Civil War draws the legal and allegorical attributes of the production of history into relief and makes them objects of contestation. The perceived need to conceal the production of history in official narratives (both legal and commemorative) that rely upon history for authority is correspondingly acute.[33]

But even in professional histories of the Civil War period, tolerance for interpretive dissonance is low. The first Civil War histories were heavily influenced in the South by what David Potter called the "compulsive memories of the Lost Cause"[34] and in the North by the myth of Lincoln as "no mere mortal, but rather an instrument of God's will and Justice."[35] One school insisted upon the legality of secession, condemned Reconstruction, and denied or ignored the role of slavery; the other insisted upon the perfidy of secession, identified slavery as *the* cause of the war, and denied or ignored Northern racism and the compromises on slavery entertained and promoted by Republicans who sought to avoid war. The extraordinary martial valor of those who fought and died in the war provided a critical and yet fragile point of consensus for the two historiographic camps.

Attempts to disentangle history from the memory work entailed by sectional reconciliation and the retreat from Reconstruction began in the middle of the twentieth century with revisionists such as Avery Craven in *The Coming of the Civil War* (1942) and James G. Randall in *The Civil War and Reconstruction*

(1937). Both scholars lamented the country's failure to avoid what they argued was a "'needless war.'"[36] Although no avowed apologist for the South, Craven's pacifism and "post World War I disillusionment" nevertheless appeared to ratify Southern sentiment. He suggested that the war resulted from unjustifiable Northern "'injustice, insult and domination,'" and he rather pointedly questioned whether, notwithstanding the emancipation of four million enslaved black Americans, the war was worth what it cost the nation.[37]

> The cost was more than five billion dollars and more than a half a million human lives. When the struggle was over few vital problems other than those dealing with nationalism and slavery had been solved, and others equally vexing had been created. Later historians would talk about "a blundering generation."[38]

Randall, for his part, blamed a failure of statesmanship on both sides but found the brinksmanship of abolitionists most condemnable.[39] The revisionist thesis provoked strident defenses by Alan Nevins, Kenneth Stampp, and Arthur Schlesinger, Jr., of the inevitability of the Civil War, the imperative of preserving the Union, and the morality of ending slavery.[40] Aspects of Lost Cause ideology and the myth of Lincoln thus resurfaced in the very effort of historians "to come as near to the truth as possible regardless of personal and sectional interests."[41]

Seeing an embarrassment of the discipline in this oscillation between variations of Lost Cause ideology and the myth of Lincoln, David Potter famously called for interpretive renovation in the name of dispassionate historical "realism."[42] Daniel Crofts summarizes Potter's position: "The myth of the Lost Cause required an unquestioning defense of secession and the doomed quest for southern independence. 'No Southerner could apparently write history without rehearsing again the legalistic defense of the constitutional right of secession.' . . . [And] Northern myths made it hard to understand what really happened in late 1860 and 1861," including Lincoln's desire to avoid war and his "'reluctan[ce] to become an Emancipator.'"[43] Potter worried that even revisionists and their critics had fallen into the same trap as their predecessors. They, too, had become more concerned about "justification than explanation" and allowed present events and perspectives to shape analysis of the past.[44] The legal and allegorical attributes of the production of history remained, in his view, altogether too prominent.

But even Potter could not escape the historiographic dilemma he had so astutely identified. As the Second Reconstruction invited renewed attention to slavery and race, and as it brought greater diversity to some history departments, Potter warned of yet another threat to realism:

> [He] remarked ruefully in 1968 that "a widespread sense of guilt about American racial attitudes had reached such a degree of intensity that many people, both inside and outside of the historical profession, had lost all interest in the complexities of the relationship between the slavery issue and the war, and had come to regard emancipation and equality for the Negro as the only meaningful aspects of the conflict."[45]

Coming from the most zealous and sincere twentieth-century advocate of realism in Civil War historiography, Potter's expression of frustration about the way historians belatedly turned to slavery and race is striking. Crofts rather gently suggests that Potter's otherwise laudable "quest for objective truth came to appear naively out of date" by the 1960s.[46] But that ignores, as Potter did, the many respects in which guilt and the avoidance of guilt had *suppressed* attention to the complexities of slavery since the retreat from Reconstruction, indeed, arguably since Emancipation.

It also downplays just how partial Potter's 'realism' had always been, how distinctive a style of attention to "the complexities of the relationship between the slavery issue and the war" it demanded. Political sources, events, and actors took center stage in Potter's analysis—especially political actors who, prior to the outbreak of war, were committed to compromise. The decisions of people willing to trade concessions regarding slavery to preserve the Union thus became the most salient, and as his treatment of William Seward reveals, the most rational and laudable.[47] The effect was not only to relegate abolitionists, Fire-Eaters, and, it must be said, the fate of enslaved people, to the fringes but to subtly endorse the revisionist thesis that the most important question about the outbreak of the Civil War was how it might have been avoided. That interpretive approach, while not indifferent to slavery, nevertheless quarantined its complexities and lingering consequences just as effectively as the oscillation between variations on Lost Cause ideology and the myth of Lincoln.

Indeed, Potter's remark about the distortions of guilt about slavery is perhaps best read less as a statement of the merits of realism than as an expression of methodological nostalgia for a time when Civil War historians could examine causation, martial valor, and statesmanship without slavery overwhelming the analysis and provoking recriminations. As Avery Craven's preface to the 1966 edition of *The Coming of the Civil War* makes clear, Potter was not alone in the sentiment:

> Thirty years ago the Civil War story was written almost exclusively as a Northern story and with slavery as the sole cause of the conflict. The effort in this

> work was to balance the picture, not to present a Southern point of view or to defend slavery. . . . It is not possible, however, even now, to say that slavery was basically a labor system and should be equated with labor in Northern factories. Even one who is a Quaker with five generations of antislavery Quakers behind him, and who attended school from kindergarten through college in Iowa, is called "a defender of Slavery" for doing so. He is even charged with being "educated in the South."[48]

Nor has this sentiment faded in certain circles. Among the most pointed expressions is a speech by Charles P. Roland entitled *Why the War Came,* given at the Deep Delta Civil War Symposium in the late 1990s after Roland learned about the Park Service's plan to incorporate discussion of slavery at Civil War battlefield sites.[49] Roland, author of *An American Iliad: The Story of the Civil War* (1991), several other military histories of the war,[50] and himself a Park Service historian in the 1940s,[51] began with a tirade about the distortions of political correctness: "I hope the decision by the Park Service is not a product of the 'political correctness' lobby—an effort . . . to ensure favorable treatment and comfort to all the minorities within the population, and to present the findings of history . . . in a manner that is congenial to liberal revisionist ideas about the past."[52] Liberal revisionism, he continued, teaches that the war was "caused exclusively or primarily by slavery,"[53] but the doctrine of states' rights—which "had a long and honorable history apart from slavery"[54]—was clearly the "fundamental cause."[55] "Slavery did not itself cause the Civil War," Roland insisted.[56] "After all, Americans had lived with slavery for over two hundred years without resort to arms. The crisis of the times was precipitated by the Northern change of attitude toward the institution and toward the relationship between the nation and the states. The rhetoric and announced positions of the Republican Party, an exclusively Northern party, appeared to southerners to repudiate the rights and guarantees of the Constitution."[57]

The dissociative impulse in Roland's analysis is breathtakingly explicit. But, as I have argued above, a rather different kind of revisionism quite congenial to Roland's theory of causation and his acquittal of states' rights emerged from the Park Service's interpretive renovation at the Fort Sumter National Monument, even as slavery received new emphasis. So he may have had less to worry about than he thought; or perhaps historians who shared his concern influenced the new holistic interpretation. In any case, neither Potter nor Roland succeeded in arresting deeper interrogation of the role of slavery by professional historians,[58] nor has that deeper interrogation arrested the oscillation between variations of Lost Cause ideology[59] and the now massive body of work supporting the myth of Lincoln in one way or another.[60] The historiographic status quo thus appears rather similar to General P. G. T. Beauregard's report in the midst of withering Union bombardment of Fort Sumter in 1863. As at the site of Southern resistance after it had been reduced to "a noble mass of ruins," defenders of Lost Cause ideology "still float [their] colors," prepared to defend the ruins "to the last extremity."[61]

All histories are, of course, frustrated by incomplete evidence, by questions of plurality and priority in causation, and by the omissions and divisions necessary to represent the past as past. As Michel de Certeau has observed, omissions and divisions are part of the process by which "historiography separates its present time from a past."[62] Repetition of "the initial act of division" establishes the periods "between which, in every instance, is traced the *decision* to become different or no longer such as one had been up to that time."[63] It is a process of "breakage."[64] "The labor designated by this breakage," de Certeau reminds us,

> promotes a selection between what can be *understood* and what must be *forgotten* in order to obtain the representation of a present intelligibility. But whatever this new understanding of the past holds to be irrelevant—shards created by the selection of materials, remainders left aside by an explication—comes back, despite everything, on the edges of discourse or in its rifts and crannies: "resistances," "survivals," or delays discreetly perturb the pretty order of a line of "progress" or a system of interpretation.[65]

That Civil War histories are not immune from the process of breakage in the production of history is hardly surprising. But if de Certeau's observation should have made historians of the period more tolerant of certain kinds of interpretive dissonance, it has not. Indeed, as late as the sesquicentennial, the intensity of disagreement over the 'fundamental cause' of the Civil War and the legality of secession is remarkable. Equally remarkable is the conviction that there must be a fundamental cause, that the riddle of the legality of secession (much like the constitutional riddles posed during the war and Reconstruction) *must* be solved, and that opponents have not simply committed interpretive errors but betrayed their craft. Complexity of explanation is both a shibboleth and casualty of this internecine rivalry. Perhaps the time has come to interrogate the source of our desire to solve these riddles.

III. THE INTERPRETIVE INSTABILITY OF REVOLUTIONS

It is not now fashionable, nor for much of our history has it been fashionable, to identify anything but relatively superficial commonalities between the French and American revolutions. The two events supposedly provide sharply contrasting examples of social versus constitutional revolution. Americans fought to vindicate rights already guaranteed in the English constitution and then created a stable constitutional republic of their own; French revolutionaries, on the other hand, fought to create an entirely new order and caused paroxysms of mass violence, hysteria, and disorder. There is thus an air of self-congratulation in the conviction that the American Revolution was accompanied by no Terror, no sustained counterrevolution. Even historians of the French Revolution have joined in "invidious comparison of the French and American Revolutions, favoring the latter over the former."[66] However, Arno Mayer's description of the interpretive dissonance that accompanied the bicentennial of the French Revolution suggests deeper commonalities between the two archetypical beginnings of modern democracy, particularly if the American revolutionary period is not treated as closed by the ratification of a constitution in 1789. Mayer begins *The Furies: Violence and Terror in the French and Russian Revolutions* (2000) with the following observations:

> I spent much time in France in 1987–90, the years of the rites of the bicentennial of the French Revolution, in which historians were prominent officiants. There was nothing exceptional about French historians, particularly the public intellectuals among them, playing their assigned roles. They had been doing so practically ever since 1789, taking three distinct positions: abjure and excoriate the Revolution, root and branch; redeem the "revolution without a revolution" over against the radical revolution of the Terror; exalt and justify the Revolution, *en bloc*. There is something archetypical about these three positions: since 1917 they have defined the debates about the Russian Revolution, except that the third position eventually split in two over the question of the continuity or break between Lenin and Stalin.... For the bicentennial, French historians reenacted the tried and true battle between the prosecutors who blame one or more ideologically driven political leaders for the spiraling Furies, including the Terror, and the defenders who attribute them to the force of circumstance. Indeed, it seemed as if old polemical wine was being poured into new historiographic bottles.[67]

The disintegration of a state into revolution (by secession, civil war, popular revolt, military coup, totalitarian purge, genocide, guerilla campaign, and even nonviolent resistance) creates radical legal, social, and cultural displacements and attendant crises of authority.[68] As Mayer puts it, "A reign of upward spiraling chaos and violence provides the enabling context for a radically new beginning not only in political regime, but also in society, law, church, and culture."[69]

These new beginnings, and "what Edmund Burke decried as 'the enormous evils of dreadful innovation'" they invite,[70] at once heighten the desire and anxiety to produce stable histories even as they destroy the determinacy of legal and allegorical representations from which the appearance of stability derives. Thus along with "new language[s]" expressing "new ideas and principles,"[71] shards, remainders, resistances, survivals, and delays are pervasive, circulating kaleidoscopically about attempted narrative orderings. As Mayer explains, "There can be no revolution without counterrevolution; both as phenomenon and process they are inseparable, like truth and falsehood."[72]

Interpretive instability and counterrevolutionary interventions are most acute when victor and vanquished, perpetrator and victim, remain in the same state—and in liberal democratic regimes when profoundly illiberal acts are committed to establish or maintain a 'new' political order. The French Revolution and America's "second revolution," to embrace James McPherson's provocative term for the Civil War, share these features.[73] As in the French Revolution, albeit on a longer epicycle, the Civil War featured fratricidal violence on an unprecedented scale (deaths rivaling all other American military engagements combined)[74] and violent counterrevolutionary reactions (most prominently the terrorism and white supremacy that brought the Black Codes, helped end Reconstruction, and insulated Jim Crow segregation for a century after the war).[75]

The interpretive problem for historians of the Civil War is thus not so much a failure to uphold Potter's standards of realism—though some works are obviously more tendentious than others along the lines Potter sketched.[76] It is rather a failure, in some cases outright refusal, to recognize that slavery, secession, and the Civil War ruptured the legal and allegorical frameworks of national identity upon which the production of history depends. As with the French Revolution, the historiographic temptation, if not imperative, to write over these ruptures and resolve the contradictions presented by events has proved irresistible.

Notice, from this perspective, how normatively freighted the ostensibly neutral term 'Civil War' is. Neither side used that term at the time. For Southerners, it was the 'War for Southern Independence' (later, the 'War between the States' and sometimes the 'War of Northern Aggression'), while for Northerners, it was often the 'War of the Rebellion,' emphasizing that secession was an extralegal act.[77] Each side also accused the other of being the section committed to revolution while claiming to be the rightful heir of the spirit of 1776 and protector of the Constitution of 1789, and each, on occasion, steadfastly denied the revolutionary ambitions and implications of its own position.[78] The almost universal conclusion that the war preserved the Union is equally freighted—submerging the revolutionary implications of what people fought for, what was required in the exertion of national authority over the states to win the war, and what was lost (particularly for black Americans) in the reassuring illusion that continuity with the Founding was maintained.[79] Even historians such as James McPherson, who have documented the contemporaneous understanding of the war as a revolution, have tended to emphasize the progressive rather more than the regressive and contradictory elements of events during the period.[80]

The point is not that historians of slavery, secession, and the war should become paralyzed by these contradictions, much less make any pretense of agnosticism. President James Buchanan's infamous reaction to secession (that Southern states had no power to secede and the federal government no power to prevent secession) is every bit as limp a historiographic principle as it was a political position. Nor is the point to suspend judgment. Frederick Douglass justifiably insisted that "[t]here was a right side and a wrong side in the late war, which no sentiment ought to cause us to forget."[81] But neither can the contradictions be ignored or treated as ordinary objects of interpretation and resolution. What makes a revolutionary moment revolutionary is *precisely* its violent compression of the contradictions and paradoxes of democracy we have the luxury of ignoring or mediating at much lower cost during periods of stability.[82]

Foremost among these is the assumption that self-government and majoritarian politics are mutually reinforcing. As Bonnie Honig has argued,

> Every day, established citizens mistake, depart from, or simply differ about their visions of democracy's future and the commitments of democratic citizenship. Every day the traces of the traumas of the founding generation are discernable in the actions of their heirs. Every day, democracies resocialize, recapture, or reinterpellate citizens into their political institutions and culture in ways those citizens do not freely will, *nor could they*. Every day, in sum, new citizens are received by established regimes, and every day established citizens are reinterpellated into the laws, norms, and expectations of their regimes such that the paradox of politics is replayed rather than overcome in time.[83]

The perceived authority of various mediating practices and institutions (including the production of history, public commemorations, and the legal process) may induce us to forget or shrug at the extent to which ordinary democratic politics is not consensual. But in revolutionary moments, the problems of consent, political ventriloquism, and duress become inescapable. Months before the Civil War began, for instance, the least democratically representative state

(South Carolina was one of only two states in which a majority of the population was enslaved) seceded from the Union after the election of Abraham Lincoln, who led a party that neither campaigned nor distributed ballots in the South. "Republicans did not even have a ticket in ten southern states, where their speakers would have been greeted with a coat of tar and feathers—or worse—if they had dared to appear. In the remaining five slave states—all in the upper South—Lincoln received 4 percent of the popular votes, mostly from antislavery Germans in St. Louis and vicinity."[84]

Paradoxes of consent only multiplied as the secession winter wore on. Following the failure of the Crittendon Compromise, which contained a wide range of concessions tailored to draw the Deep South back into the Union, both houses of Congress passed a constitutional amendment by the necessary two-thirds vote that would have immunized slavery from federal interference. The so-called Corwin Amendment is significant not only because it came closer to ratification than other compromise measures (the outbreak of war interrupted state ratification), but because it would have prevented *any future reversal by amendment*. The proposed amendment provided: "No amendment shall be made to the Constitution which will authorize or give to Congress the power to abolish or interfere, within any State, with the domestic institutions thereof, including that of persons held to labor or service by the laws of said State."[85] However reluctant Lincoln was to compromise with the South on the question of expanding slavery, he had long conceded the right of slavery where it existed. And he offered the following endorsement of the Corwin Amendment in his *First Inaugural*: "[H]olding such a provision to now be implied constitutional law, I have no objection to its being made express and irrevocable."[86] A month earlier, he had written to William Seward regarding various compromises that "as to fugitive slaves, [slavery in the] District of Columbia, slave trade among the slave states, and whatever springs of necessity from the fact that the institution is amongst us, I care but little."[87]

The Corwin Amendment receives only glancing attention in histories of the period. McPherson, for instance, short circuits any serious interrogation of the amendment and its implications by drawing a straight line to the amendment ratified in 1865. Before the process of ratification "got anywhere," he concludes in a single paragraph on the proposed amendment, "other matters intervened to produce four years later a Thirteenth Amendment that abolished slavery."[88] Thus even in the hands of a historian acutely sensitive to the significance of slavery to secession and the war, the paradox of an unamendable amendment protecting the least democratic attribute of the Constitution is quarantined, chronologically and normatively, by the eventual abolition of slavery. He is not alone. William Freehling, who concedes that "three fourths of the states would have doubtless affirmed this widely popular attempt at peacemaking, if war had not intervened," nevertheless frames the significance of the amendment in exclusively counterfactual terms: "Another intriguing 'what if' question here arises," regarding how long slavery might have endured under such an amendment.[89] But even that query is briskly dismissed as inviting "Monday morning quarterbacking."[90] And in subsequent work, Freehling pivots to McPherson's position, celebrating Lincoln's (and by implication, the North's) "growth" away from the errors in judgment early in his presidency.[91]

In either narrative frame, the moment in which this paradox was lived, the desire and ambivalence surrounding it in March of 1861, and of course the occasion it presents to consider what kind of federalism could possibly have survived the war, are lost. Much the same can be said about historical analysis of the Emancipation Proclamation and the extraordinarily paradoxical circumstances of the ratification of the Reconstruction Amendments.[92] Amendments that had the most immediate implications for life in the South, most especially newly emancipated black Americans, were "ratified" on terms that strain, if they do not flatly contradict, any definition of consent.[93] Every Southern state other than Tennessee refused to ratify the Fourteenth Amendment in 1866.[94] Only after Congress broke up existing state governments, divided the South into military districts supervised by federal officers, disenfranchised certain "unreconstructed" Southerners, and made federal recognition of new state governments contingent upon ratification, was it possible to achieve the necessary "consent" of three-fourths of the states to ratify the new Amendment.[95] To characterize this process of constitutional amendment as "democratic in goals while military in means," as very capable historians have,[96] is not simply an understatement. It obscures what should be the central object of historical inquiry—the extent to which liberal democratic reforms have depended upon strikingly illiberal acts.

Honig contends that if we take the paradox of democratic politics seriously,

> the first thing to go... is our confidence in linear time, its normativity and its form of causality... orderly connections between what comes before and what comes after (Decline and Rise), such that one thing *leads* to another.... *All* these elements—linearity, its normativity, causality—are thrown off balance by the paradox of politics in which what is presupposed as coming before (virtue, the people, the law) invariably comes after (if at all), and what comes after invariably replays the paradox of politics that time was supposed to surmount.[97]

Many aspects of the relationship between slavery, secession, and the Civil War have precisely this unstable temporal character. Formal assurances of authority or the absence of authority arrive well after contested actions were taken (if at all), and the assurances given are hollowed out over time. As in all revolutionary moments, law lags embarrassingly behind.[98]

The 13th Amendment trailed after emancipation by executive proclamation during the war. And the amendment's more "elastic, organic, dynamic understandings . . . about positive duties on the nation and states to secure [individual] rights, and about limitations on states in the federal Union" were all too quickly obscured by the conviction that the war, emancipation, and ratification of the amendment had already absolved the nation of responsibility for slavery.[99] The 14th and 15th Amendments arrived only after the resuscitation of Southern resistance by President Andrew Johnson's policies of pardon and conciliation and the subsequent emergence of Black Codes. Within decades, they, too, were reconfigured to permit the very discrimination they were enacted to eliminate.[100] The Supreme Court strained to declare secession unconstitutional fully nine years after the war broke out and did so without meeting the core arguments that had been made by Confederates in support of the right.[101] And the Court withheld decision on the use of trial by military commission for civilians where regular courts were open until well after Appomattox.[102]

The legal status of secessionists arrested in the North—particularly the applicability of the treason clause of the Constitution—remained uncertain until at least 1863, when the Supreme Court decided the *Prize Cases*.[103] The constitutionality of Lincoln's unilateral suspension of habeas corpus to help suppress popular dissent in the North was even more doubtful.[104] Indeed, the administration worked to "keep off the Court's docket other litigation involving habeas corpus, treason, martial law, conscription, emancipation, or the novel wartime income tax. Any of these, decided adversely to the national government, might seriously, even fatally affect its capacity to carry on the war."[105]

More recently, each new claim that the enforcement authority contained in the Reconstruction Amendments is necessary to address state or national failure to provide equal treatment and due process to minorities (rights that are supposed to precede and thereby secure the legitimacy of majoritarian democratic politics) has become a further source of embarrassment. The Supreme Court has dissociated even further any asserted relationship between slavery and illiberal features of the status quo. Standing to sue under the 14th Amendment is denied to minorities but expanded for whites claiming discrimination,[106] the burden of proof necessary to establish that present injuries flow from past discrimination is set at a threshold few victims of discrimination can meet,[107] and remedies for the rare litigant who meets this threshold are limited by the very antebellum federalism doctrines against which the Reconstruction Amendments were written.[108] In this way, slavery is rendered legally irrelevant to its own devastating legacy.[109]

The dissociation of slavery from its legacy is a problem not only in judicial interpretation and in interpretive programming at Civil War battlefields but in historical interpretation, as well. Roland's separation of slavery and states' rights in the search for a 'fundamental cause' of secession is the obvious example. But the problem of dissociation persists even among scholars committed to more sensitive and rigorous examination of the relationship between slavery and secession. The very act of drawing the singularity, abjection, and democratic contradictions of slavery into relief as a cause of secession and war can make it difficult to represent the transition from enslavement to what followed as something other than progress, however halting, flawed, and delayed that progress has been. Narrating a rise, rather than a decline or a persistent cycle of repetition, offers irresistible relief from the paradoxes and unstable temporal character of American slavery and white supremacy.

Even Freehling's detailed exploration of the relationship of slavery to secession in *The Road to Disunion*, for instance, frames the arrival of war as the result of a struggle between democracy, on the one hand, and the despotism of slaveholding, on the other.[110] As with the denial of tardiness and embarrassing contradiction in legal interpretation, emancipation serves as a radical temporal and normative break, an event that postdates but nevertheless reassuringly prefaces engagement with the intersection of slavery and secession. We are thus invited to take for granted that slavery is over, that nothing in a liberal democratic state could be as bad as slavery, and as the introductory marker at the entrance to Fort Sumter admonishes, that "we are not accountable for decisions made by those who came before." Thanks to what he alluringly calls the "antislavery antidote," Freehling's account assures us, there is no despotism *in* democracy to worry about.[111]

The 'unknown immensity' of our second revolution still awaits us. Fascinating contradictions in the experience of revolutionary moments (the strange imbrications of surprise and inevitability, fear and temerity, deliberation and fanaticism, calculation and mad passion, reluctance and zeal for violence, as well as forbearance and excess)[112] have too long been ignored or explained away by assignment along sectional or partisan lines. Even in quite sophisticated historical studies of the Civil War, desire for resolution has obscured the very crises of authority from which revolutions emerge and in which their deeper implications lie. Not only the variety of revolutionary and counterrevolutionary discourse but the cultural media through which revolutionary sentiment is created, sustained, and (in counterrevolutionary moments) subverted have also remained largely obscure. Political, military, editorial, and epistolary texts have been privileged over visual, oral, and popular representations.

Deeper inquiry into these aspects of the Civil War will make confrontation with democratic paradox inevitable and dissociation of slavery from secession, the war, and the Constitution impossible. If revolutions bring the blessings of liberty and elicit our most promising capacities as modern liberal subjects, they do so via appallingly illiberal, indeed, quite often barbaric means. And we know all too well that the blessings of liberty have been mixed. As late as the sesquicentennial we should be capable of meeting these paradoxes even if doing so may draw the trajectory of our great experiment into doubt.

NOTES

1. John Tucker, *Interpreting Slavery and Civil Rights at Fort Sumter National Monument*, 19 George Wright Forum 15, 22 (2002).
2. *Id.* at 16.
3. Dwight T. Pitcaithley, *Public Education and the National Park Service: Interpreting the Civil War*, Perspectives, Nov. 2007, at 44.
4. *Id.*
5. Michael Kammen, Mystic Chords of Memory 603 (1991).
6. Nina Silber, The Romance of Reunion 1–12 (1997).
7. Pitcaithley, *supra* note 3.
8. Tucker, *supra* note 1, at 15, 18, 21, 24.
9. *Id.* at 26.
10. Michel de Certeau, The Writing of History 3 (1988).
11. *Id.* at 25–26.
12. *Id.* at 26.
13. Shearer Davis Bowman, At the Precipice 76 (2010).
14. Avery Craven, Edmund Ruffin, Southerner (1932).

15. 2 William W. Freehling, The Road to Disunion 50 (1990); National Park Service, The Swedish House Historic Structure Report 5–6 (2005).

16. Rod Andrew, Wade Hampton: Confederate Warrior to Southern Redeemer (2008); Walter Brian Cisco, Wade Hampton: Confederate Warrior, Conservative Statesman (2006); Edward G. Longacre, Gentleman and Soldier (2009). Memminger and Rhett make brief appearances within the confines of panels on display inside the visitor education center.

17. Tucker, *supra* note 1, at 27.

18. Fort Sumter National Monument, Visitor Education Center, Exhibit Text 2 (2002), *available at* http://www.nps.gov/fosu/historyculture/upload/ls_exhibit_text.pdf.

19. Henry Adams, The Great Secession Winter of 1860–61 and Other Essays 30 (George Hochfield ed., 1958).

20. Fort Sumter National Monument, Fort Sumter Museum, Exhibit Copy 27 (1993), *available at* http://www.nps.gov/fosu/historyculture/upload/fosu_exhibit_text.pdf.

21. National Park Service, Sesquicentennial Commemoration at Fort Sumter National Monument, YouTube (Oct. 14, 2011), *available at* http://www.youtube.com/watch?v=M7SmQikhYpk.

22. Tucker, *supra* note 1, at 21. For parallel effects in historical analysis of the capture of Fort Sumter, *see* Robert Hendrickson, Sumter (1990).

23. Schuyler Kropf, *Charleston's Martin Luther King Monument Facing Long Steps*, Post & Courier, June 21, 2012.

24. Pitcaithley, *supra* note 3.

25. *Id.*

26. Kammen, *supra* note 5.

27. Younger v. Harris, 401 U.S. 37, 44 (1971).

28. Norman W. Spaulding, *Constitution as Countermonument: Federalism, Reconstruction and the Problem of Collective Memory*, 103 Colum. L. Rev. 1992 (2003). *See also* National Fed. of Indep. Bus. v. Sebelius, 132 S.Ct. 2566 (2012). For these reasons I obviously disagree with James G. Randall's conclusion that "constitutionally and otherwise, secession has been a dead issue since the Civil War." Constitutional Problems Under Lincoln 522 (1926).

29. Georg Wilhelm Friedrich Hegel, The Philosophy of History 61 (J. Sibree trans., 1956) (1837).

30. Norman W. Spaulding, *The Historical Consciousness of the Resistant Subject*, 1 Irvine L. Rev. 677, 684 (2011); *see also* Hayden White, The Content of the Form 12–14 (1987).

31. Robert Penn Warren, The Legacy of the Civil War 3 (1961). *Cf.* Elizabeth R. Varon, Disunion! The Coming of the American Civil War, 1789–1859, at 4–5 (2008).

32. *Id.* at 4.

33. *See* Charles B. Dew, Apostles of Disunion 10 (2001) ("Historians seem no more able to agree on the causes of the war than the public at large. Indeed the slavery versus states' rights argument is only the tip of a very large scholarly iceberg."); David Goldfield, Still Fighting the Civil War 2–3 (2002) ("The intersection of history and memory creates traditions, and traditions are central to a people's identity. . . . Traditions banish time, connect-

ing the past to the present until they are indiscernible."); W. Stuart Towns, Enduring Legacy (2012). *See also* Cynthia Nicoletti, *The American Civil War as a Trial by Battle*, 28 Law & Hist. Rev. 71 (2010).

34. Much of what follows in this section draws on Daniel W. Crofts' fine survey of twentieth-century Civil War historiography in his introductory essay to the 1995 edition of David M. Potter's Lincoln and His Party in the Secession Crisis. Daniel W. Crofts, *Introduction* to David M. Potter, Lincoln and His Party in the Secession Crisis, at vii (1995). A slightly different classification is offered by Edward Ayers in What Caused the Civil War: Reflections on the South and Southern History (2005). *See also* Michael F. Holt, Political Parties and American Political Development from the Age of Jackson to the Age of Lincoln 313–23(1992); Edwin C. Rozwenc, Slavery as a Cause of the Civil War, at vi–vii (1949).

35. Crofts, *supra* note 34, at ix.

36. *Id.* at xi; *see also* Avery Craven, The Coming of the Civil War 2 (1957) (describing the "process by which a repressible conflict was being made into an irrepressible one").

37. Craven, *supra* note 36, at 2.

38. *Id.* at 3. For a more recent restatement of the revisionist thesis emphasizing the triumph of irrationality, emotion, and political extremism, *see* James L. Abrahamson, The Men of Secession and Civil War, 1859–1861, at 168 (2000).

39. James G. Randall, The Civil War and Reconstruction (1937). *See also* James G. Randall, Constitutional Problems Under Lincoln (1926).

40. Crofts, *supra* note 34, at xi–xii. Stampp may also be classified with modern revisionists such as David Potter. *See* Kenneth Stampp, And the War Came (1950).

41. Craven, *supra* note 36, at viii.

42. Crofts, *supra* note 34, at vii.

43. *Id.* at vii–x.

44. *Id.* at ix, xii.

45. *Id.* at xv.

46. *Id.* at xiii.

47. David M. Potter, Lincoln and His Party in the Secession Crisis 25–26 (1995). Others have followed suit. *See* Lawrence M. Denton, William Henry Seward and the Secession Crisis 9 (2009) ("[T]here was one man on the scene in 1860 with the vision and political experience necessary to avert war—William Henry Seward . . . the nation's leading Republican and the man who was driven to saving the nation without war.").

48. Craven, *supra* note 36, at vii–viii.

49. Charles P. Roland, History Teaches Us to Hope 41, 93 (John David Smith ed., 2007).

50. Charles P. Roland, Albert Sidney Johnston (1964); Charles P. Roland, The Confederacy (1962); Charles P. Roland, Reflections on Lee (1995); *see also* Charles P. Roland, Louisiana Sugar Plantations during the Civil War (1957). Even for historians who *insist* upon the importance of slavery to the Civil War, an element of methodological nostalgia can be seen in their insistence upon retaining the grand narrative style of writing "mainstream political history." Freehling, *supra* note 15, at xiii ("Where many academic historians dismiss epic stories as old-fashioned fluff, I believe that classic tales of headline events, when retold from fresh angles, help sort out the culture's underlying forces.").

51. 2 Who's Who in America, 1982–1983, at 2844 (1982).

52. Roland, *supra* note 49, at 93.

53. *Id.* at 94.

54. *Id.* at 103.

55. *Id.* at 99.

56. *Id.* at 105.

57. *Id.*

58. The early scholarship is gathered at Crofts, *supra* note 34, at xvi; *see also* John Ashworth, Slavery, Capitalism, and Politics in the Antebellum Republic (1995); Edward Ayers, In the Presence of Mine Enemies (2003); Ayers, *supra* note 34; Bowman, *supra* note 13, at 18, 38–76; Bruce Chadwick, 1858: Abraham Lincoln, Jefferson Davis, Robert E. Lee, Ulysses S. Grant and the War They Failed to See 26–27, 177–207 (2008); Charles B. Dew, Apostles of Disunion (2001); William Freehling, The Reintegration of American History (1994); Freehling, *supra* note 15; Kenneth Greenberg, Honor & Slavery (1996); Kenneth Greenberg, Masters and Statesmen (1985); Harold Holzer, Lincoln 54–55 (2008); William A. Link, Roots of Secession (2003); Russell McClintock, Lincoln and the Decision for War 24 (2008); James Oakes, The Ruling Race (1982); James Oakes, Slavery and Freedom (1990); W. Scott Poole, South Carolina's Civil War 3, 19 (2005); Anne Sarah Rubin, A Shattered Nation 1, 100 (2005); Brian Schoen, The Fragile Fabric of Union (2009); Philip J. Schwartz, Twice Condemned (1988); Manisha Sinha, The Counterrevolution of Slavery (2000); Mitchell Snay, Gospel of Disuinion 53–109 (1993); Frank Towers, The Urban South and the Coming of the Civil War (2004); Towns, *supra* note 33, at 40–61; Varon, *supra* note 31, at 16; Andrew J. Torget, *Unions of Slavery: Slavery, Politics, and Secession in the Valley of Virginia*, *in* Crucible of the Civil War 9, 25 (Edward L. Ayers, Gary W. Gallagher & Andrew L. Torget eds., 2006). For a prominent alternative approach emphasizing party politics, *see* Michael F. Holt, The Political Crisis of the 1850s, at 258–59 (1978) ("The sectional conflict over slavery had been crucial in causing the Civil War, but the basic issue had less to do with the institution of black slavery than has been thought. . . . [Clashes between Northern and Southern politicians over slavery] in the national political arena . . . increasingly caused the constituents of those politicians to view people in the other section as enemies of their rights, and as they worried about their own rights they shifted their focus away from the institution of black slavery itself."); *see also* Daniel Crofts, Reluctant Confederates (1989).

59. For evidence of the persistence of Lost Cause ideology in histories of secession and the war, *see* Charles Adams, When in the Course of Human Events (2000); Frank Conner, The South Under Seige, 1830–2000 (2002); Thomas J. DiLorenzo, The Real Lincoln (2002); John J. Dwyer, The War between the States (2007); Marshall L. DeRosa, The Politics of Dissolution, at i–ix (1998); Kevin R. C. Gutzman, The Politically Incorrect Guide to the Constitution 122 (2007); James Kennedy & Walter Kennedy, The South Was Right! (1993); Thomas E. Woods, Jr., The Politically Incorrect Guide to American History (2004); Joe Sobran, *The Imaginary Abe: A Reply to Harry Jaffa's In Re Jack Kemp v. Joe Sobran*, Sobran's: The Real News of the Month (Aug. 2001), *available at* www.sobran.com/replyJaffa.shtml. The seminal early text is Jubal A. Early, Narrative of the War Between the States (1912); *see also* John S. Tilley, Facts the Historians Leave Out (1952).
For analysis, *see* Terry A. Barnhart, Albert Taylor Bledsoe (2011); Dew, *supra* note 33, at 74; Gary W. Gallagher, The Myth of the Lost Cause and Civil War History (2000); Goldfield, *supra* note 33, at 6; James W. Loewen & Edward H. Sebesta, The Confederate and Neo-

Confederate Reader (2010); Charles S. Watson, From Nationalism to Secession 139 (1993); Charles Reagan Wilson, Baptized in Blood (2009); David Byron Davis, *Free at Last: The Enduring Legacy of the South's Civil War Victory*, N.Y. Times (Aug. 26, 2001).

60. Among the works most obviously committed to the myth of Lincoln are Michael Burlingame, Lincoln and the Civil War (2011); Harold Holzer, Lincoln President-Elect (2008); William Osborn Stoddard, Abraham Lincoln (1884). Conservative scholars have been among the most enthusiastic proponents of the myth of Lincoln. *See, e.g.*, David Herbert Donald, Lincoln (1996); Harry V. Jaffa, A New Birth of Freedom (2000); Thomas L. Krannawitter, Vindicating Lincoln, Defending the Politics of Our Greatest President (2008). On 'Lincolnography' generally, *see* Merrill D. Peterson, Lincoln in American Memory 374 (1994); David W. Blight, *The Theft of Lincoln Scholarship, Politics, and Public Memory, in* Our Lincoln 269, 274 (Eric Foner ed., 2008). *See also* Michael S. Green, Freedom, Union, and Power (2004); Allen Guelzo, Lincoln's Emancipation Proclamation (2006); Maury Klein, Days of Defiance, at xii (1997); James M. McPherson, Abraham Lincoln and the Second American Revolution (1990). For recent work favorably reviewing Lincoln's constitutional decisions, *see* David P. Currie, The Constitution in Congress 225–56 (2005); Daniel Farber, Lincoln's Constitution (2003); Mark E. Neely, Jr., Lincoln and the Triumph of the Nation (2011); Stephen C. Neff, Justice in Blue and Gray (2010); Herman Belz, *Lincoln, Secession, and Revolution: The Civil War Challenge to the Founding, in* Challenges to the American Founding 81 (Pestrito & West eds., 2005). *Cf.* Arthur T. Downey, Civil War Lawyers (2010).

61. Kammen, *supra* note 5.

62. de Certeau, *supra* note 10, at 3.

63. *Id.* at 3–4.

64. *Id.* at 4.

65. *Id.*

66. Lynn Hunt, *The Experience of Revolution*, 32 French Hist. Stud. 671, 672 (2009); *see also* Arno Mayer, The Furies 26–27 (2000); Alexis de Tocqueville, The Old Regime and the French Revolution (1955); Alexis de Tocqueville, Democracy in America 18, 21, 87 (2007). On differential treatment of the American and French Revolutions in political thought, *see* Hannah Arendt, On Revolution (1965).

67. Mayer, *supra* note 66, at xiii. As Francois Furet put it, "Historians engaged in the study of the Merovingian Kings or the Hundred Years War are not asked at every turn to present their research permits. So long as they can give proof of having learned the techniques of the trade, society and the profession assume that they possess the virtues of patience and objectivity. . . . The historian of the French Revolution, on the other hand, must produce more than proof of competence. He must show his colours." Francois Furet, Interpreting the French Revolution 1 (1997). *See also* Steven Laurence Kaplan, Farewell Revolution (1995).

68. *See* Samuel P. Huntington, Political Order in Changing Societies 264 (2006) ("A revolution is a rapid, fundamental, and violent domestic change in the dominant values and myths of a society, in its political institutions, social structure, leadership, and government activity and policies."); *see also* Jack A. Goldstone, Revolution and Rebellion in the Early Modern World 8–11 (1991); Lynn Hunt, Politics, Culture, and Class in the French Revolution 15 (1984); Mayer, *supra* note 66, at 31; Steven Pincus, 1688: The First Modern Revolution 11–12 (2009); Vijay Prashad, Arab Spring, Libyan Winter (2012); Richard Stites, Revolutionary Dreams

(1989); Dan Edelstein, Remarks at a Harvard Colloquium for the Center for European Studies, *The Myth of Revolution: Reflections on Political Authorities* (Feb. 7, 2012).

69. Mayer, *supra* note 66, at 31.

70. *Id.*

71. *Id.*

72. *Id.* at 45.

73. McPherson, *supra* note 60. Other historians have seen revolutionary attributes in the intersection of slavery, secession, and the war. Eric Foner has identified Reconstruction as the central, albeit failed, revolutionary moment of the period. *See* Eric Foner, Reconstruction (1988). Manisha Sinha contends that secession was a counterrevolution by slaveholders: "Like European conservatives who bemoaned the spread of democracy and the alleged excesses of the age of revolution, they sought to safeguard racial slavery from the onset of forces that defined modernity." Manisha Sinha, The Counterrevolution of Slavery 7 (2000); *see also id.* at 255. And she provocatively positions "the slaves of the New World," not Northerners or Southerners, as "the true inheritors of the revolutionary fervor" of the founding. *Id.*

74. Drew Gilpin Faust, This Republic of Suffering, at xi (2008).

75. *See* Douglas A. Blackmon, Slavery by Another Name (2009); Foner, *supra* note 73; William Gillette, Retreat from Reconstruction, 1869–1879 (1979); Harold Hyman & William M. Wiecek, Equal Justice under Law 319 (1982). The discriminatory application of criminal law to black Americans continues; *see* Michelle Alexander, The New Jim Crow (2012).

76. The effort to retool the myth of Lincoln for conservative political purposes comes to mind. *See, e.g.*, Krannawitter, *supra* note 60.

77. *See* Early, *supra* note 59; James M. McPherson, Battle Cry of Freedom 310 (1988) (hereinafter McPherson, Battle Cry); Alexander H. Stephens, A Constitutional View of the Late War between the States (1870); James M. McPherson, *The War of Southern Aggression*, N.Y. Rev. of Books, Jan. 19, 1989 (hereinafter McPherson, Southern Aggression).

78. Don Fehrenbacher, The Slaveholding Republic 295 (2001) ("At the heart of the matter was Southern perception of the Republican party not as a mere political opposition, but as a hostile, revolutionary force bent on total destruction of the slaveholding system."); McPherson, Battle Cry, *supra* note 77, at 202–75.

79. Klein, *supra* note 60, at xii ("It has long been the conventional wisdom that the great achievements of the Civil War were the preservation of the Union and the abolition of slavery."); Russell McClintock, Lincoln and the Decision for War 276 (2008) ("The common goal of virtually all Northerners was to preserve the Constitution and the Union. However, through most of the crisis Republicans and anti-Republicans disagreed fundamentally over just how to do that.").

80. *See* 2 Bruce Ackerman, We the People: Transformations (2000); Freehling, *supra* note 15, at 19; Klein, *supra* note 60, at 430; McPherson, *supra* note 60; *cf.* Mark E. Brandon, Free in the World (1998); Sinha, *supra* note 73.

81. Frederick Douglass, *There Was a Right Side in the Late War, Speech Delivered at Union Square New York City, on Decoration Day, May 30, 1878, in* Frederick Douglass: Selected Speeches and Writings 632 (Philip Foner ed., 1999).

82. Douglass was, of course, keenly aware of these contradictions. Speaking on Memorial Day in 1878—the year Reconstruction ended following the compromise necessary to secure Rutherford B. Hayes's election—Douglass admonished his audience that the proper objects of commemoration and "marvel" were not the "bravery," "steady valor," martial "skill," and "fiery ardor," of those who died in the war. *Id.* The real "marvel" was that "after the rebellion was suppressed, and treason put down by the loss of nearly half a million men . . . the Government has so soon been virtually captured by the party which sought its destruction." *Id.*

83. Bonnie Honig, Emergency Politics 15 (2011) (emphasis added).

84. McPherson, Battle Cry, *supra* note 77, at 223.

85. J. Res. 13, 36th Cong., 12 Stat. 251 (1861).

86. Hyman & Wiecek, *supra* note 75, at 218–19; Abraham Lincoln, *First Inaugural Address*, March 4, 1861.

87. *Id.*

88. McPherson, Battle Cry, *supra* note 77, at 256.

89. Freehling, *supra* note 15, at 470.

90. *Id.* at 471.

91. *Id.* at 470 n.12; William W. Freehling, *Address at the Abraham Lincoln Institute's Thirteenth Annual Symposium* (Mar. 20, 2010); *see also* Hyman & Wiecek, *supra* note 75, at 222–23; Krannawitter, *supra* note 60, at 277.

92. On the legality of the Emancipation Proclamation, *see* Allen C. Guelzo, Lincoln's Emancipation Proclamation (2004); Neff, *supra* note 60, at 141.

93. Spaulding, *supra* note 28. *Cf.* John Harrison, *The Lawfulness of the Reconstruction Amendments*, 68 U. Chi. L. Rev. 375 (2001).

94. Hyman & Wiecek, *supra* note 75, at 423.

95. *Id.* at 441–47.

96. *Id.* at 444.

97. Honig, *supra* note 83, at 15.

98. In some instances, delay was extended for strategic purposes. *See* Jeffrey L. Amestoy, *The Supreme Court Argument that Saved the Union: Richard Henry Dana, Jr. and the* Prize Cases, 35 J. Sup. Ct. Hist. 1, 10 (2010).

99. Hyman & Wiecek, *supra* note 75, at 276–77, 464; *see also* Ira Berlin, Barbara J. Fields, Steven F. Miller, Joseph P. Reidy & Leslie S. Rowland, Slaves No More (1992).

100. Hyman & Wiecek, *supra* note 75, at 439–515; *cf.* Pamela Brandwein, Rethinking the Judicial Settlement of Reconstruction (2011).

101. Texas v. White, 74 U.S. 700 (1869).

102. Ex Parte Milligan, 71 U.S. 2 (1866). The case had significance for military reconstruction. *See* Hyman & Wiecek, *supra* note 75.

103. Hyman & Wiecek, *supra* note 75, at 240.

104. Ex Parte Merryman, 17 F. Cas. 144 (C.C.D. Md. 1861); Mark E. Neely, The Fate of Liberty (1992).

105. Hyman & Wiecek, *supra* note 75, at 241.

106. *Compare* Allen v. Wright, 468 U.S. 737 (1984), *and* City of Los Angeles v. Lyons, 461 U.S. 95 (1983), *with* Ne. Fla. Chapter of Associated Gen. Contractors v. City of Jacksonville, 508 U.S. 656 (1993). *See also* Girardeau A. Spann, *Color-Coded Standing*, 80 Cornell L. Rev. 1422 (1995).

107. Parents Involved in Cmty. Schs. v. Seattle Sch. Dist., 551 U.S. 701 (2007) ("remedying past societal discrimination does not justify race-conscious government action"); McClesky v. Kemp, 481 U.S. 279 (1987); Washington v. Davis, 426 U.S. 229 (1976); Milliken v. Bradley, 418 U.S. 717 (1974); *see also* Mario L. Barnes & Erwin Chemerinsky, *The Once and Future Equal Protection Doctrine*, 43 Conn. L. Rev. 1059 (2011).

108. *See Milliken*, 433 U.S. at 280.

109. A similarly dangerous social and political disaggregation of race and racism is identified by Barbara Fields in *Of Rogues and Geldings*, 108 Am. Hist. Rev. 1397 (2003).

110. Freehling, *supra* note 15, at 9–10, 532–33.

111. Freehling, *supra* note 15, at 534.

112. I have in mind here what Friedrich Nietzsche, writing about the French Revolution in *Human, All Too Human*, called "the semi-insanity, histrionicism, bestial cruelty, voluptuousness, and especially sentimentality and self-intoxication, which taken together constitutes the actual *substance of the Revolution*." The revolution, he observed, had become the "violent and impulsive companion" of the Enlightenment, indeed, so much so that "the Enlightenment has thereby become violent . . . impulsive . . . perilous[]." Nietzsche, *Human, All Too Human* 367 (1996).

Index

B

C

G

H

V

W

Y

Z